Migration Stigma

Understanding Prejudice, Discrimination, and Exclusion

Strüngmann Forum Reports

Julia R. Lupp, series editor

The Ernst Strüngmann Forum is made possible through
the generous support of the Ernst Strüngmann Foundation,
inaugurated by Dr. Andreas and Dr. Thomas Strüngmann.

This Forum was supported by the
Deutsche Forschungsgemeinschaft

Migration Stigma

Understanding Prejudice, Discrimination, and Exclusion

Edited by

Lawrence H. Yang, Maureen A. Eger, and Bruce G. Link

Program Advisory Committee:

Maureen A. Eger, Irena Kogan, Christian Albrekt Larsen, Bruce G. Link, Julia R. Lupp, and Lawrence H. Yang

The MIT Press

Cambridge, Massachusetts
London, England

Series Editor: J. R. Lupp
Editorial Assistance: A. Gessner, C. Stephen
Lektorat: BerlinScienceWorks

The book was set in TimesNewRoman and Arial.
Printed and bound in the United States of America.

Library of Congress Cataloging-in-Publication Data

Names: Yang, Lawrence H., editor. | Eger, Maureen A., editor. | Link, Bruce G., editor.
Title: Migration stigma : understanding prejudice, discrimination, and exclusion / edited by Lawrence H. Yang, Maureen A. Eger and Bruce G. Link.
Description: Cambridge, Massachusetts : The MIT Press, [2023]. | Series: Strüngmann Forum reports | Includes bibliographical references and index.
Identifiers: LCCN 2023050276 (print) | LCCN 2023050277 (ebook) | ISBN 9780262548120 (paperback) | ISBN 9780262378826 (epub) | ISBN 9780262378833 (pdf)
Subjects: LCSH: Emigration and immigration--Social aspects. | Immigrants--Social conditions. | Immigrants--Cultural assimilation. | Stigma (Social psychology) | Social integration. | Discrimination.
Classification: LCC JV6225 .M5685 2023 (print) | LCC JV6225 (ebook) | DDC
325--dc23/eng/20231214
LC record available at https://lccn.loc.gov/2023050276
LC ebook record available at https://lccn.loc.gov/2023050277

10 9 8 7 6 5 4 3 2 1

Contents

List of Contributors

Adem, Muna Dept. of Sociology, University of Maryland, College Park, MD 20742, U.S.A.

Blasco, Drew Dept. of Social and Behavioral Health, School of Public Health, University of Nevada, Las Vegas, Las Vegas, NV 89119, U.S.A.

Bohman, Andrea Dept. of Sociology, Umeå University, 90187 Umeå, Sweden

Castañeda, Heide Dept. of Anthropology, University of South Florida, Tampa, FL 33620, U.S.A.

Czymara, Christian S. Dept. of Sociology and Anthropology, Tel Aviv University, Tel Aviv 6997801, Israel; Dept. of Sociology, Goethe University Frankfurt, 60323 Frankfurt am Main, Germany

Dollmann, Jörg Mannheim Centre for European Social Research (MZES), University of Mannheim, 68131 Mannheim, Germany; German Centre for Integration and Migration Research (DeZIM), 10117 Berlin, Germany

Eger, Maureen A. Dept. of Sociology, Umeå University, 90187 Umeå, Sweden

Forman, Tyrone A. Depts. of Black Studies and Sociology, University of Illinois Chicago, Chicago, IL 60607-7112, U.S.A.

Gabrielsson, Daniel Dept. of Sociology, Umeå University, 90187 Umeå, Sweden

García, San Juanita Chicana and Chicano Studies, University of California, Santa Barbara, Santa Barbara, CA 93105, U.S.A.

Gorodzeisky, Anastasia Dept. of Sociology and Anthropology, Tel Aviv University, Tel Aviv 6997801, Israel

Hatzenbuehler, Mark L. Dept. of Psychology, Harvard University, Cambridge, MA 02138, U.S.A.

Helbling, Marc Mannheim Centre for European Social Research (MZES), University of Mannheim, 68131 Mannheim, Germany

Hjerm, Mikael Dept. of Sociology, Umeå University, 90187 Umeå, Sweden

Holmes, Seth M. Dept. of Environment, Science, Policy, Management and Program in Medical Anthropology, University of California, Berkeley, Berkeley CA, 94720, U.S.A.; Dept. of Social Anthropology, University of Barcelona, 08001 Barcelona, and Catalan Institution for Research and Advanced Study, 08010 Barcelona, Spain

Ivarsflaten, Elisabeth Dept. of Government, University of Bergen, 5020 Bergen, Norway

Jiménez, Tomás R. Dept. of Sociology, Stanford University, Stanford, CA 94305, U.S.A.

Kogan, Irena Dept. of Sociology, University of Mannheim, 68131 Mannheim, Germany

Larsen, Christian Albrekt Dept. of Political Science and Society, Aalborg University, 9220 Aalborg Ø, Denmark

Link, Bruce G. School of Public Policy and Dept. of Sociology, University of California, Riverside, Riverside, CA 92521, U.S.A.

Maxwell, Rahsaan Dept. of Politics, New York University, New York, NY 10012, U.S.A.

Misra, Supriya Dept. of Public Health, San Francisco State University, San Francisco, CA 94132, U.S.A.

Okamoto, Dina Dept. of Sociology, Indiana University Bloomington, Bloomington, IN 47405-7000, U.S.A.

Pachankis, John E. School of Public Health, Yale University, New Haven, CT 06510, U.S.A.

Rüsch, Nicolas Section of Public Mental Health, Dept. of Psychiatry II, Ulm University and BKH Günzburg, 89073 Ulm, Germany

Schomerus, Georg Klinik und Poliklinik für Psychiatrie und Psychotherapie, Universitätsklinikum Leipzig, 04103 Leipzig, Germany

Simon, Patrick International Migrations and Minorities Unit, INED, and Institute on Migration (ICM), 93322 Aubervilliers, France

Vassenden, Anders Dept. of Media and Social Sciences, University of Stavanger, Stavanger, 4036 Norway

Velásquez, Paolo Dept of Sociology, Umeå University, 90187 Umeå, Sweden

Wang, Katie School of Public Health, Yale University, New Haven, CT 06510, U.S.A.

Weißmann, Markus Mannheim Centre for European Social Research (MZES), University of Mannheim, 68131 Mannheim, Germany

Wilkes, Rima Dept. of Sociology, University of British Columbia, Vancouver BC V6T 1Z1, Canada

Yang, Lawrence H. Dept. of Social and Behavioral Sciences, New York University, New York, NY 10003, U.S.A.; Dept. of Epidemiology, Columbia University, New York, NY 10032, U.S.A.

Zhou, Min Dept. of Sociology, University of California, Los Angeles, CA 90095-1551, U.S.A.

Preface

Science is a highly specialized enterprise—one that enables areas of inquiry to be minutely pursued, establishes working paradigms and normative standards in disciplinary fields, and supports rigor in experimental research. Yet all too often, "problems" are encountered in research that fall outside the scope of any one discipline, and to get past the intellectual "dead ends" that result, external input is needed.

The Ernst Strüngmann Forum was established in 2006 to address such issues. The topics that we select transcend classic disciplinary boundaries and center on problems encountered in ongoing research: issues that require scrutiny from multiple vantage points and the requisite expertise to do so, where conceptualization has stagnated, and the way forward is anything but certain. Our approach promotes interdisciplinary collaboration among international researchers, facilitates the expansion of knowledge, and generates potential trajectories for future research to pursue.

Approach

The Ernst Strüngmann Forum is guided by an independent Scientific Advisory Board that is responsible for identifying topics to develop and for reviewing submitted proposals. These topics emerge from a need in basic science, address a problem of high-priority interest to the scientific disciplines involved, are interdisciplinary by nature, take an unbiased approach to the defined problem, involve active researchers from the respective fields, and aim to delineate ways for future research to consider and pursue.

Topics are developed in partnership with active research scientists. Given the relevance of a theme to multiple disciplines, each topic benefits from being proposed by senior representatives of the primary research areas involved. Once accepted, the following stages define further development:

Program Advisory Committee

To bring the issues outlined by the proposal into a scientific framework that will support the focal meeting, or Forum, we convene a Program Advisory Committee. Open, unbiased discourse at a Forum requires a diversity of perspectives and viewpoints. Thus, as it selects Forum participants, the committee aims for balanced representation from the various disciplinary areas involved.

The Forum

Best imagined as an intellectual retreat or week-long think tank, formal presentations do not take place at a Forum. Instead, participants engage in an evolving dialogue designed to maximize intellectual outcomes. To prepare for this, invited "background papers" introduce key topics and unresolved problem areas which will be addressed at the Forum. These papers are circulated in advance, so that by the time everyone arrives in Frankfurt, a basis for discussion has been established.

The central theme is approached by four working groups, comprised of researchers from various scientific disciplines. Each participant plays an active role in the discussion. Groups work autonomously, guided by a moderator, yet interact over the course of the week. To ensure that emerging insights do not get lost, each group generates a draft report. Attention is given to areas where agreement could not be reached as well as ideas for future research. On the final day of the Forum, the plenum evaluates collective progress and identifies remaining work. This feedback guides the finalization of the group reports.

Strüngmann Forum Reports

For research to benefit from the ideas generated at each Forum, results are made available through the Strüngmann Forum Reports, a monograph series published in partnership with The MIT Press. Each volume offers up-to-date information on the topics discussed at a Forum and highlights proposed research directions. A two-tier peer review process guides the editing. Each volume is available in book form as well as online via MIT Press Direct and the Ernst Strüngmann Forum website.

The 32nd Ernst Strüngmann Forum: Stigma Processes in the Context of Migration-Generated Diversity

The impetus for this Forum began at a meeting of our Scientific Advisory Board in February 2018. Initiated by Amber Wutich, the topic of stigma emerged as a focal point requiring future attention; specifically, the need to expand understanding on the origins and processes inherent to stigma as well as its cross-cultural manifestations and potential approaches to destigmatize. To pursue this theme, I met with Lawrence Yang in November 2018 to discuss the state of research into the processes of stigmatization. Having just attended a Forum on youth mental health in July 2018 (Uhlhaas and Wood 2019), I was interested to learn what types of problems were being experienced, and whether the Forum's approach could be of assistance. A series of discussions followed and ultimately led Lawrence Yang, Bruce Link, and Maureen Eger to submit a proposal entitled "Stigma, Prejudice and the Immigration Experience: Understanding and Addressing the Consequences of Migration Stigma." A thorough review process resulted in further development, and in September 2019, the Scientific Advisory Board approved the proposal.

From February 27–29, 2020, the Program Advisory Committee was invited to Frankfurt, Germany, to fine-tune the proposal. Joining us on the committee were Irena Kogan and Christian Albrekt Larsen. Together, we worked to refine overarching goals, delineate discussion topics, and select participants.

The Forum was originally scheduled to take place on June 6–11, 2021, but like so many other gatherings, it needed to be rescheduled due to conditions imposed by the COVID pandemic. A year later, conditions improved and we were able to convene an in-person Forum in Frankfurt (a) to scrutinize the relationships between stigma and migration-generated diversity and (b) to explore the linkages that underpin stigma in the context of migration-generated diversity at multiple levels and from diverse perspectives. The ensuing discussion was constructed around four general themes:

1. How are stigma processes related to different aspects of migration-generated diversity?
2. How do differences in the daily lived experiences of minority and majority social groups contribute to stigma and, alternatively, processes of resilience and social cohesion?
3. How are stigma processes reflected in (social, public, and private) policies? How do policies mitigate and/or amplify stigma processes?
4. Stigmatization and destigmatization: Emergence, persistence, and dissipation.

This volume, structured around these topical areas, contains the background papers that initiated the discussion. Each paper has been finalized to reflect the current state of knowledge on the topic. In addition, summary reports of each discussion group are provided (see Chapters 2, 5, 8, and 10). They provide a synthesis of a vibrant discussion and seek to highlight areas that require further consideration and research.

As one might imagine, a Forum is not a linear process. The initial framework put into place triggered lively debate and created unique group dynamics (see Yang et al., this volume). I wish to thank each person who participated in this Forum for their time, efforts, and positive attitudes, which greatly helped offset conditions brought about by COVID restrictions. A special word of thanks goes to the Program Advisory Committee as well as to the authors and reviewers of the background papers. In addition, the work of the discussion groups' moderators—Bruce Link, Tomás Jiménez, Christian Albrekt Larsen, and Maureen Eger—and rapporteurs—Drew Blasco, San Juanita García, Supriya Misra, and Paolo Velásquez—deserves special recognition. To support lively debate and transform this into a coherent, multiauthor report is no simple matter. Finally, I extend my appreciation to Lawrence Yang, Bruce Link, and Maureen Eger, whose expertise and commitment accompanied the entire project.

The Ernst Strüngmann Forum is able to conduct its work in the service of science and society due to the generous backing of the Ernst Strüngmann Foundation, established by Dr. Andreas and Dr. Thomas Strüngmann in honor of their father. I also wish to acknowledge the support received from our

Scientific Advisory Board as well as the Deutsche Forschungsgemeinschaft, which provided supplemental financial support for this project.

Expanding the boundaries to knowledge is never simple and can be easily compromised by long-held views, which are difficult to put aside. Yet once such limitations are recognized, the act of formulating strategies to get past these points can be a most invigorating activity. On behalf of everyone involved, I hope this volume will expand understanding of the multilevel and temporal processes that contribute to migration stigma and equip societies to address its harmful consequences.

Julia R. Lupp, Director, Ernst Strüngmann Forum
Frankfurt Institute for Advanced Studies
Ruth-Moufang-Str. 1, 60438 Frankfurt am Main, Germany
https://esforum.de/

1

Migration Stigma

An Introduction

Lawrence H. Yang, Maureen A. Eger, and Bruce G. Link

International migration and societal reactions to it constitute some of the most important issues of the contemporary era. This does not mean that migration itself is a recent phenomenon. Throughout history, humans have crossed geographic and political boundaries for economic, social, and political reasons. In the modern era, international migrants are defined as individuals who reside outside of their country of birth. Myriad factors motivate individuals to migrate: economic opportunity, family reunification, war, or persecution as well as instability brought on by climate change, economic recession, political turmoil, and pandemics. Although the reasons why people migrate vary considerably, growing skepticism toward immigration is evident worldwide. Indeed, nationalist rhetoric and the politicization of immigration have increased in recent decades, spurring political unrest, racial and ethnic conflict, and the scapegoating and inhumane treatment of immigrants. Persistent global trends, such as climate change, suggest that immigration and its consequences will continue if not increase in coming years. Thus, it is imperative to understand the interplay of societal reactions to immigration and the patterns of exclusion or inclusion among immigrants and their descendants.

This volume is a concerted effort to improve the analysis of international migration and its consequences for individuals and societies. It is the result of converging ideas and efforts. From one perspective, in the wake of crises at the southern European and United States borders, Lawrence Yang began to question whether current research approaches were up to the task of understanding contemporary challenges let alone solving them. His field is the scientific study of stigma, which has been defined as the co-occurrence of labeling, stereotyping, separation, status loss, and discrimination in the context of power differentials (Link and Phelan 2001). Yang's work utilizes a culturally grounded lens to examine stigma as a circumstance that naturally drew him to the issue of stigma experienced by migrants (Yang et al. 2007, 2014). Given how crises in Europe and the United States have played out, it seemed obvious to Yang that immigrants and their descendants were being subjected to a full array of stigma processes. Yet researchers from the field of stigma had not fully taken up the phenomenon of international migration—which involves macro-social forces, such as colonialism, that span countries and generations, intergroup and interpersonal interactions across various domains within countries as well as the psychological experiences of individuals—as a focus of study. Moreover, it seemed to Yang that absent from scholarship on the causes, trends, and consequences of international migration was any critical engagement with the concept of stigma.

Simultaneously, as described in the Preface, the Ernst Strüngmann Forum assessed a pressing need in research to develop a Forum that addressed stigma: its origins, how it manifests cross-culturally as well as potential processes of destigmatization. Thus, in November 2018, Julia Lupp, director of the Ernst Strüngmann Forum, approached Lawrence Yang to begin a discussion that ultimately led to the convening of this Forum, intended to advance a potentially transformative new application of the concept of stigma in the analysis of immigration-related processes. Their discussion quickly grew to include Bruce Link, a renowned stigma expert (Link and Phelan 2001), who helped formulate an initial proposal, which identified that while much more was understood about the impact of stigma on health, very little was known about the processes of stigma in relation to immigration. In the critique of this initial proposal, the lack of a migration perspective became evident; a nuanced understanding of international migration would be required to illuminate what benefits a "collision" between these two fields (i.e., migration and stigma research) might yield. Thus, Yang and Link recruited immigration expert Maureen Eger to join in the preparation of the proposal.

Over the next few months, a series of virtual meetings helped us develop a cogent proposal. In the beginning, we provided overviews of our respective fields, even assigning each other background homework. Given migration scholars' long-standing attention to research questions related to prejudice, discrimination, and exclusion, the initial questions that immediately emerged were: Isn't there already a field that addresses these issues? What, if anything, could be useful about incorporating the stigma framework with migration research? We quickly realized that despite some overlap in our fields of research (e.g., the analysis of prejudice and discrimination), there was little critical or comparative engagement between the fields, primarily due to the use of different concepts and theories. For example, one of the seminal accounts of prejudice consistently used by migration scholars is group threat theory (Blumer 1958), whereas stigma scholars regularly employ Link and Phelan's conceptual work on stigma (Link and Phelan 2001). We wondered if the analytical challenges facing our respective fields might be overcome with increased engagement between them. We pondered what we might learn from each other if we kept talking. So, we did. Ultimately, our discussions yielded three observations that underscored the need for a Forum:

1. Stigma associated with international migration exists, though arguably varies within and between societies.
2. Conceptual and analytical frameworks are lacking to guide research on "migration stigma."
3. Without a greater understanding of the phenomenon, our ability as societies to confront the multitude of challenges that arise from it is severely limited.

Based on these discussions, we outlined key areas of inquiry, proposed additional migration experts, Irena Kogan and Christian Albrekt Larsen, as members of the Program Advisory Committee, and submitted a proposal to the Ernst Strüngmann Forum. The Program Advisory Committee met in Frankfurt, Germany (February 27–29, 2020), where it became clear that although the stigmatization of (some) international migrants has long been recognized to occur, comprehensive conceptual and analytical frameworks to guide research was lacking. Thus, the Forum offered an invaluable opportunity to explore commonalities, understand differences, and develop an integrated framework capable of supporting future cross-disciplinary research between the fields of stigma and international migration. We also hoped that the creation of a new field, migration stigma, might produce novel knowledge that would better inform pragmatic economic, educational, health, and other social policy responses to alleviate the stigma faced by immigrant groups and to help facilitate their full participation and inclusion into societies worldwide.

Following delays brought on by the COVID-19 pandemic, the 32nd Ernst Strüngmann Forum, entitled "Stigma Processes in the Context of Migration-Generated Diversity," took place from June 5–10, 2022, in Frankfurt, Germany. The Forum brought together researchers from the (im)migration and stigma fields to scrutinize the relationships between stigma and international migration and to explore the linkages that underpin stigma in the context of immigration-generated diversity at multiple levels (e.g., interpersonal, intrapersonal, structural) and through multiple perspectives (e.g., social, cultural, economic, historical, political).

To advance these goals, scholars were assigned to one of four working groups which reflected the areas of inquiry previously identified as essential for unpacking and advancing understanding of migration stigma (detailed below). This book synthesizes the intense conversations among scholars from two different fields and introduces the concept of migration stigma to help generate new understandings of the complex challenges facing immigrants, their descendants, and contemporary societies. Forum participants worked together to identify gaps in knowledge and interrogate taken-for-granted assumptions in their fields. They listened, debated, and engaged across disciplinary, theoretical, and methodological boundaries. They put forth novel ideas and digested critical feedback on the fly. The resulting discussions were both intellectually exhausting and exhilarating. The emergent insights and new ideas and analytical tools developed through these discussions are captured in the resulting group reports (see Chapters 2, 5, 8, and 10). We are excited to share these new ideas and analytical tools and hope they will inspire future empirical research to expand our collective knowledge.

Overview of Chapters

It is important to note that at the Forum, the working groups used the term "migrant" in different ways. Group 1 highlighted the role of movement in its understanding of the term, while Group 3 used the language of existing social policies. Group 2 showed that "migrant" may be an objective or subjective category or identity, while Group 4 concluded that the term "migrant" can be a stigmatizing label. In different chapters, the term "migrant" is used objectively to describe individuals who have crossed international borders as well as to refer to the children of immigrants. Sometimes it is used in multiple ways. These inconsistencies reflect the actual discussions and provide starting points for future study, theorizing, and empirical research.

As stigma is the co-occurrence of labeling, stereotyping, separation, status loss, and discrimination in the context of power differentials (Link and Phelan 2001), we define "migration stigma" as *the co-occurrence of these phenomena in relation to a racial or ethnic group with a history of international migration.* Contributions in this volume (a) contemplate how migration stigma, so defined, affects areas such as health, financial well-being, and social cohesion; (b) identify the multilevel and temporal processes underlying migration stigma; and (c) propose social, economic, and policy frameworks to address its harmful consequences. Below, we provide an overview of the four focal areas of inquiry and the chapters that contributed to intensive discussions of them.

Group 1: How Are Stigma Processes Related to Different Aspects of Migration-Generated Diversity?

The core ambition of Group 1, moderated by Bruce Link, was to achieve a conceptual mapping of the terms prejudice and stigma as they are used in the research literature focused on migration and on stigma. The group sought to identify overlap, detect differences, but most importantly to find points of insight that might emerge from considering the two fields together. The product that emerged (Blasco et al., Chapter 2, this volume) serves to inform readers regarding concepts, theories, and frameworks that might be useful to scholars working at the intersection of these two fields.

To inform stigma researchers of core terminology in the migration field, Blasco et al. review distinctions among immigration, emigration, and migration. Pushing somewhat deeper, they identify the centrality of movement, noting that both the movement of people across borders as well as the movement of borders around stationary people create circumstances of relevance for the new field of migration-related stigma to address.

In considering differences between concepts of prejudice and stigma, Blasco et al. drew on the background paper by Bohman et al. (Chapter 3, this volume), which compared Link and Phelan's (2001) conceptualization of stigma to Blumer's (1958) threat theory. Bohman et al. noted overlap but also key differences between theories. For example, the stigma framework includes a broad set of interrelated concepts (including labeling, stereotyping, othering, devaluing, and discriminating in a circumstance of power differentiations), and group threat theory focuses on a majority group's defense of their position in a country's social hierarchy resulting in prejudice and other forms of exclusion.

Noting that stigma researchers had developed multiple concepts and measures to assess circumstances that are subject to stigmatization, Blasco et al. engaged in the task of developing a "stigma tool kit" that investigators seeking to understand migration-related stigma more deeply might use in future research. In their report, Blasco et al. (Chapter 2, this volume) provide definitions of each concept along with references that identify the origin of each measure. To facilitate the use of the identified "tools," Blasco et al. also offer suggestions about how the measures might be used to study migration-related stigma and note that for stigma measures to be used effectively, they need to be adapted to multiple cultural contexts. In keeping with this reality, the group invoked the conceptual framework developed by Yang et al. (2007), which instructs investigators to identify "what matters most" to actors in local contexts to identify the content of any measures they might use. The advice is to identify what is crucial in any local context for being regarded as a whole person worthy of full participation in social activities and to then focus the content of any stigma measures on whatever that is.

While the tool kit was conceptualized as something the stigma field might bring to the migration literature, the group was also quick to recognize that whether and to what extent stigma might matter depended heavily on the nature and circumstances of the human movement that the migration entailed: Who was moving, from where to where, and how much, if any, threat would the majority group in the destination country perceive in any movement that occurred? This kind of specification is obviously important for understanding the particulars of any migration experience, but the insights provided also delivered a critical lesson to stigma researchers in terms of the need to specify the conditions under which stigma is likely to arise in any circumstance.

Two background papers contributed to the group's discussion and deeply underscored some of its general conclusions. As mentioned above, in their comparison of "group threat theory" (Blumer 1958) and "conceptualizing stigma" (Link and Phelan 2001), Bohman et al. (Chapter 3, this volume) explore the possibility and value of comparing core works from the two research traditions. In addition, they provide a strong example of how work in each research tradition might be advanced when issues are considered through the lens of the other research tradition. Further, Bohman et al. emphasize the critical importance of the threat experienced by the destination country's majority population, in keeping with the group's goal of specifying the conditions under which prejudice and discrimination are operative.

Pachankis and Wang (Chapter 4, this volume) examine the issue of "intersectionality," underscoring the need to understand multiple status configurations to capture the full stigma experience of migrants. An ostensibly similar migration from one place to another could be substantially different for groups such as different LGBQT populations, social classes, or people with different race and ethnic identities. Pachankis and Wang equipped the group with a language to understand some of these complexities and emphasized the need to specify the conditions under which migration stigma is likely affect the lives of people who migrate.

Group 2: Migration, Stigma, and Lived Experiences: A Conceptual Framework for Centering Lived Experiences

The overarching aim of this discussion group, led by Tomás Jiménez, was to examine the daily lived experiences that occur among migrant groups and communities in a destination country. Group 2 was distinct from other groups in that it focused on how differences in "everyday lived experiences" between groups contribute to stigma as well as processes of resilience and social cohesion. The "lived experience" of groups refers to the everyday engagements that take place in a local world where one's standing as a "respected person" is continuously defined, sought, or lost. From the outset, the group identified that the lived experience of being in a migrant group had yet to be fully conceptualized while considering processes of stigma as well as migration. The group thus sought to center the intersection of lived experiences of migrants in the context of macro-social forces that powerfully shape the everyday experience of migrants—both at the macro (i.e., institutions and policies) and meso levels (i.e., interactions with more proximal institutional actors). The purpose of this focus was to highlight stigma processes confronted by migrant groups and the response mechanisms that are evoked to counteract stigma.

In a first orienting framework, García et al. (Chapter 5, this volume) articulate how lived experiences of stigma among "migrant groups" are shaped in interaction with two large-scale societal forces:

1. Institutional mechanisms comprised of economic, immigration, education, and welfare systems determine access to resources (e.g., work opportunities) and shape migrant groups' experiences of stigma in the structural realm.
2. Salient categories or statuses (e.g., ethnicity, religion, and language) associated with migrant groups interface with the destination country's

> preexisting social class and racial hierarchies; this interface then shapes the extent to which the immigrant group is welcomed (or not).

García et al. relate these two macro-social forces to the migrant groups' subjective perception of their group identity as "migrants," thus situating the lived experience of stigma as being influenced by, as well as reciprocally influencing, these macro-social forces.

García et al. consider how meso-level institutions (e.g., officials in school or housing agencies) are experienced in the everyday life of migrants. These meso-level institutions and actors can be of the type that are more desired by people in their lives (e.g., those that enable educational and work opportunities) or can take the form of institutions where contact is undesired and coercive power and stigma is brought to bear on migrants (e.g., contact with immigration control and the associated stigma of being "undocumented"). The circumstances by which individuals from migrant groups encounter these institutions are shaped by institutions' recognition (or labeling) of individuals as belonging to a migrant group. Here, García et al. view the very act of being identified as belonging to the migrant social group as shaping and constraining the lived experience.

In their contribution, Kogan et al. (Chapter 6, this volume) illuminate these dynamics by examining short-term consequences of migrants' discriminatory experiences in German public schools (i.e., a meso-level institution), with a focus on how self-reported discrimination is associated with different trajectories in the German education and training system. Importantly, as identified by this working group, some meso-level institutions that exist on behalf of migrant groups (e.g., ethnicity-based rights groups) could also buffer the lived experience of stigma at the level of organizations.

Finally, García et al. formulate a typology of the lived experience of stigma among migrants and their response to it, expanding on how stigma operates to include within-individual (i.e., when an individual internalizes negative views about their own migrant group) as well as between-individual experiences (i.e., when discrimination is expressed between receiving group and migrant group members). Migrants are not merely passive recipients of stigma; they actively respond to it. One major contribution from the group was an expansive classification of the potential range of responses to stigma: this can include internalizing the stigma of being identified as a migrant group member, "doing nothing" by giving up efforts in accordance with a stereotyped characteristic, or resisting stigma (e.g., by taking denigrating labels and embracing them to create new and positive meanings).

In addition to analyzing how stigma occurs, Castañeda and Holmes (Chapter 7, this volume) helped the group focus on "responses" to stigma by illustrating immigrant youths' active responses to stigma by embracing, renegotiating, or navigating its narratives. Concepts in their chapter contributed to the working group report itself, which identified the effects that these strategies have on the stigma itself, in that responses to stigma at the individual and group levels can shape the salience of the stigma itself across multiple life domains. The lived experience of stigma, therefore, impacts important life outcomes such as health, access to educational, housing, and employment opportunities.

Group 3: How Are Stigma Processes Reflected in Policies That Impact Migrants? How Do Policies That Impact Migrants Amplify and/or Mitigate Stigma Processes?

The overarching goal of Group 3, moderated by Christian Albrekt Larsen, was to theorize about relationships among stigma processes and social policies. Focus was thus both on the potential impact of stigma on macro-level structures as well as how institutions and policies affect the stigmatization of immigrants. A background paper by Hatzenbuehler (Chapter 9, this volume) laid the foundation for discussion by synthesizing recent research from the stigma field on what he calls "structural stigma," or "societal-level conditions, cultural norms, and institutional policies that constrain the opportunities, resources, and well-being of the stigmatized" (Hatzenbuehler and Link 2014:2). The key insight is that policies have the capacity (a) to mitigate stigma and improve outcomes for individuals or (b) to amplify stigma and generate worse outcomes for the stigmatized. Sometimes policies that are aimed at stigma reduction may have harmful, unintended consequences, thus suggesting that the interplay between macro-level structures and individual outcomes is not always straightforward.

In the report of the group's discussions, Misra et al. (Chapter 8, this volume) relied on comparative analytical tools and applied abstract typologies from the field of comparative social policy to understand stigma in the context of immigration-generated diversity. The result is sweeping in scope. To consider how stigma processes are embedded in policies affecting immigrants, Misra et al. theorized about the ways in which national policy narratives and frames shape types of policies. For instance, they considered how ideal typical approaches to the incorporation of immigrants (assimilationist, integrationist, and multiculturalist regimes) strengthen or weaken the social and economic boundaries between native-born and foreign-born. Further, they considered the stigmatizing potential of specific policy types (targeted, universal, mainstream, and antidiscrimination) and their theoretical impact on immigrants' rights, opportunities, and outcomes. Misra et al. point out that the relationship between policies and outcomes are dynamic, affecting immigrants and natives alike. Indeed, policy feedback effects may reinforce existing policies that are stigmatizing, may generate demands for change and policy reform, or contribute to backlash and polarization.

A clear tension raised by Misra et al. is the unresolved issue of whether policies that draw attention to inequalities due to minority status are necessary for the reduction of inequality or whether such policies only reinforce boundaries between majority and minority groups. They explain the potential trade-offs of these approaches in the stigmatization of immigrants and their descendants but concede that this remains an open question, requiring future empirical inquiry. Results from analyses that test these propositions would contribute much to our knowledge of stigma and would also speak to ongoing debates in many countries about how best to combat inequality stemming from the differential treatment, whether historic or contemporary, of racial and ethnic minority groups.

Group 4: Processes and Pathways of Stigmatization and Destigmatization over Time

Led by Maureen Eger, this discussion group aspired to incorporate insights gleaned from other groups' discussions of key concepts and micro- and macro-level processes and to apply a longer-term temporal lens to the analysis of migration stigma. The group began with the observation that the experiences of immigrant groups vary both between and within societies. Through a discussion of historical and contemporary examples, they identified key commonalities and differences related to group outcomes and trajectories over time.

In looking for conceptual overlap between the fields of international migration and stigma they sought to clarify what stigmatization and destigmatization means in the context of immigration-generated diversity over prolonged periods of time. The group determined that the absence of stigma is conceptually more similar to "inclusion" than "integration." Some groups may be well integrated into society (i.e., high employment rates, speak the national language) but still face stigma, whereas other groups may never be stigmatized regardless of levels of economic and cultural integration.

In their discussions, Velásquez et al. (Chapter 10, this volume) focused on abstract processes and mechanisms capable of accounting for the trajectories of groups over longer periods of time (i.e., multiple generations). Here, the contribution by Okamoto and Adem (Chapter 12, this volume) was especially helpful. Focusing on destigmatization, which involves changing the cultural constructions of what it means to be a stigmatized group, Okamoto and Adem provide a sociological account of how patterns of interactions within specific societal domains may reduce the stigma that immigrants and their descendants face over time.

Three important insights emerged (see Velásquez et al., Chapter 10, this volume):

1. The labeling of some groups as "migrants" but not others does not always follow from actual histories of immigration, and without this label, a group is not stigmatized.
2. Understanding processes of stigmatization and destigmatization requires that we adopt a longer time horizon than stigma researchers typically do.

3. To analyze stigma over significantly longer periods of time (i.e., decades and centuries), we must think about the stigmatization of groups rather than individuals.

To expand, first, some groups of immigrants, who reside in a country where they were not born, are never truly regarded as migrants, whereas others who were born and raised in a country but whose ancestors immigrated are still considered migrants, sometimes for generations (i.e., second- and third-generation immigrants). Thus, the label "migrant" is the first constitutive component of stigmatization and has further implications for stereotyping, separation, status loss, and discrimination. Without this label, by definition, a group is not stigmatized. Second, adopting a longer-term view allows us to understand better the experiences of immigrants as well as their descendants, who are sometimes still erroneously referred to as migrants, despite no personal history of immigration. A longer time horizon puts us in a position to analyze stigma over time, specifically processes of stigmatization and destigmatization, which may unfold over generations. Velásquez et al. argue that this approach makes the identification of specific causes underlying the different trajectories of stigma that immigrant groups face more likely. Third, expanding the time span of analysis necessitates an explicit focus on experiences of racial and ethnic minority groups rather than individuals. This focus on groups does not negate the experiences of individuals (within groups) and individual-level processes in the short term. Instead, Velásquez et al. contend that the personal experiences of individuals at any one point in time depend to a large extent on levels of stigma faced by immigrant groups and their descendants.

Based on these three insights, Velásquez et al. developed two analytical models. They provide a framework for understanding why particular immigrant groups are labeled migrants while others are not. They argue that existing social hierarchies in a destination country trigger a sorting process which influences the extent to which immigrants and their descendants are subject to separation, stereotyping, status loss, and discrimination. Over time various societal domains, exogenous events, and feedback loops affect the levels of stigma experienced by the minority group. In addition, they identify five ideal-type pathways that immigrants and their descendants may experience over time: non-emergence, status reversal, stigma increase, stigma reduction, and stigma reinforcement.

Taken together, Velásquez et al. provide an abstract framework for understanding migration stigma over time. They conclude that a stigma lens will enhance the analysis of reactions to immigration and the experiences of immigrants and their descendants. Moreover, they see benefits of adopting this analytical framework for stigma research more generally. Previous research on stigma has focused mainly on experiences within the life course, but a longer-term perspective that treats stigma as a group-level feature has the potential to elucidate the causes of stigmatization and destigmatization, shedding light on the status of groups over time. Accordingly, empirical tests of the models developed by Velásquez et al. could change theoretical understanding of stigma and its application to other stigmatized groups and conditions.

From Phenomenon to Concept to Field of Inquiry

Through the invited papers and in-depth discussions within and between working groups at this Forum, a new concept emerged—migration stigma—that holds the potential of integrating research from two fields to create a new area of inquiry. As detailed above, the chapters in this volume make theoretical and analytical contributions that provide a roadmap for future empirical research. Taken together, four key contributions stand out.

Insights Can Be Gained by Integrating Stigma and Migration Research Traditions

By integrating these two fields, we have constructed new ways of conceptualizing and analyzing the phenomenon of migration stigma. Specifically, we bring new analytic power via a multicomponent stigma framework to the multilevel phenomenon of migration, creating a greatly deepened perspective that researchers can use to broaden understanding of migration stigma. Analysis of how stigma processes are manifest in the macro- and meso-level causes of and responses to migration—and how these factors shape the micro level, lived experience of stigma—offers new insights into this phenomenon.

While the discussions in each group advance this endeavour, Blasco et al. (Chapter 2, this volume) provide a way to map prejudice and stigma concepts, drawn from both fields, which will enhance the lens by which future questions about migration stigma may be pursued. By advancing thinking around the role of macro-level forces and societal-level domains in the stigmatization of some immigrant groups and their descendants over decades and even centuries, Velásquez et al. (Chapter 10, this volume) provide a way to account for the emergence, persistence, and dissipation of stigma over a prolonged time span.

Concepts from the Migration Field Help Specify Whether and to What Extent Stigma Is Experienced

While the conceptualization of stigma carries some significant value for understanding the experience of immigrants and their descendants, the conditions of migration, as explicated by migration researchers, reveal when and how strongly stigma may be expressed and experienced. Extant concepts from the stigma field are suggestive with respect to the intensity of stigmatization (e.g., how sticky the labels are, how strong the stereotypes are, how powerful the distinctions between "us" and "them" are). Although these concepts bring to light some aspects of the severity of the stigma experience, migration-related issues strongly underscore the need for greater clarity. To understand stigma, we need to know who is moving, what caused them to move, what conditions are present where they move, and the nature of any (perceived) threat experienced by citizens and residents in destination countries. All this is obviously important for understanding migration stigma, but a more generic contribution is there for stigma researchers to absorb. It is critical, in any situation, to conceptualize and identify the circumstances that turn stigma on and off.

This insight emerged in multiple groups. The construction of a stigma tool kit by Blasco et al. (Chapter 2, this volume) stimulated discussion as to when concepts would be applicable and when they would not. García et al. (Chapter 5, this volume) conceptualized the capacity to resist stigma, thereby specifying circumstances that might turn off stigma processes. Misra et al. (Chapter 8, this volume) identified types of policies that would amplify stigma or reduce its impact. By adopting a longer time horizon that focuses on groups' trajectories over time, the analytical framework in Velásquez et al. (Chapter 10, this volume) identifies that some immigrant groups and their native-born descendants are labeled "migrants" and subject to further stigmatization whereas other immigrant groups are not.

Reciprocal Connections between Macro-Level Structures and Lived Experience Can Be Identified

A multilevel, comparative, and temporal approach to examining migration stigma helps elucidate how macro-level forces affect individuals' experiences of stigma and, reciprocally, how the lived experience of migrants can, over time, shape macro-level forces. For example, policy frameworks and related policy types reflect a country's ideological and bureaucratic approach to immigration. They also affect the roles, rights, and opportunities of immigrants and their family members who (do and do not) live there. Over time, these lived experiences (in particular, organized efforts, such as individual and group advocacy) may contribute to feedback processes for policies governing immigration and the inclusion of immigrants and their families in national institutions, such as the welfare state (e.g., Eger et al. 2020). In other words, the very macro-level forces that affect the lives of immigrants may, in some cases, be self-reinforcing or, in other circumstances, altered by immigrants' and others' actions over time.

While each discussion group addressed these points, Misra et al. (Chapter 8, this volume) gave particular attention to how social policies reflect stigma processes and how policies, in turn, contribute to the amplification or reduction of stigma facing immigrants and their descendants. In addition, García et al. (Chapter 5, this volume) center the complex interplay of the lived experiences of immigrants in the context of macro-level and meso-level institutions and explain how individual-level experiences and responses reciprocally shape community- and country-level policies, institutions, and settings.

Promising Approaches to Mitigate Stigma through Policy and Intervention

Our conceptualization of migration stigma and the accompanying analytical models presented in this volume provide new and enhanced opportunities to measure, explain, and understand stigma associated with international migration across societies and over time. This is an essential first step in the path to developing pragmatic social, educational, health, and economic policies as well as other interventions to reduce migration stigma experienced by immigrant groups and their descendants.

Conclusion

This Forum facilitated dialogue among scholars from two distinct fields: immigration and stigma. Although both examine the causes and consequences of prejudice, discrimination, and exclusion, prior to the Forum, engagement between these fields was virtually nonexistent. A common reason why scholars in different fields do not engage with each other is because those fields do not cross disciplinary boundaries. However, that was not the case in this situation. Indeed, both fields are multidisciplinary, with contributions from across the social sciences. Therefore, and especially given these two fields' overlapping concern with prejudice, discrimination, and exclusion, it may seem surprising that it required a Forum to initiate this dialogue. However, the vast majority of previous research investigating phenomena related to immigration did not adopt the lens of stigma, and previous scholarship using a stigma framework tended not to focus on immigration. Further, migration researchers typically examine phenomena related to immigration separately and thus employ a variety of theoretical frameworks to explain distinct reactions to immigration and specific experiences of immigrants. In contrast, stigma researchers use a theoretical lens that sees prejudice, discrimination, and exclusion as elements of one multifaceted phenomenon.

Over the course of a week, we introduced our respective fields to each other, comparing concepts, theories, research practices, insights, and conclusions. In doing so, our respective strengths came to light as did the myriad ways that our distinct fields contribute important knowledge about the world. However, this process also forced us to grapple with limitations in our fields and acknowledge that despite our best efforts, we still lack understanding. These intensive conversations ultimately led us to introduce and develop the concept of migration stigma as well as new analytical tools, which we believe will improve the examination and understanding of the challenges which face immigrants, their descendants, and contemporary multiethnic and multiracial societies.

To be clear, this volume does not merely apply the concept of stigma to a new group, immigrants, nor does it repackage immigration research as stigma research. It is a novel, rigorous attempt to push the boundaries of *both* fields so that they intersect in ways that will overcome limitations in scientific knowledge about *both* stigma and immigration. While we claim to have taken a substantial step forward, we remain humbled by what is left to be done:

- Many new ideas require further development.
- Theoretical propositions regarding when, why, and how migration stigma emerges need to be tested with empirical research.
- Enacted polices must be evaluated with respect to consequences for migration stigma.
- Strategies for managing or resisting stigmatization require further consideration.
- Identifying the reasons why levels of migration stigma change or do not change over long periods of time (i.e., generations, decades, even centuries) requires investing in both long-term data collection and innovative use of historical data sources.

In summary, we hope to have provided a new concept and analytical tools that can be deployed to advance knowledge in the new and wide-open field of migration stigma. We are excited by the possibility that this new field of inquiry will one day be in a position to propose evidence-based social, economic, health, educational, and other policy solutions to address the harmful consequences of migration stigma.

Acknowledgments

We wish to thank all who participated in the Ernst Strüngmann Forum and coauthored this volume, as well as the Forum's staff, who through their significant contributions made this volume a reality. We are also indebted to the Dr. Ernst Strüngmann Foundation for its generous support of our experience at the Forum, which led to the development of this book and launched a new field of research. Thank you.

2

How Are Stigma Processes Related to Different Aspects of Migration-Generated Diversity?

Drew Blasco, Bruce G. Link, Andrea Bohman, Tyrone A. Forman, Anastasia Gorodzeisky, John E. Pachankis, Georg Schomerus, and Lawrence H. Yang

Abstract

Research in the fields of migration and stigma have much to offer each other yet to date, collaboration has been lacking. When migration occurs, diversity is generated. Inherent in this "migration-generated diversity" is the key role that the "movement" of people or the political boundaries around them plays in outcomes such as prejudice, stigma, and discrimination. Under certain conditions, migration-generated diversity may result in prejudice (a concept historically used more often by the migration field), stigma, or a combination of prejudice and stigma (or neither). To advance dialogue between these fields, this chapter presents a "conceptual mapping tool," developed to assist researchers as they formulate questions to be addressed by the migration field for which stigma frameworks and perspectives may better inform results. In addition, three theoretical perspectives—group threat theory, intersectionality, and "what matters most," some of which were selected from the conceptual mapping tool are discussed, presenting key examples to elucidate the implications of migration-generated diversity and stigma. Future research should (a) explore additional ways to conceptualize the relationship between stigma concepts and migration-generated diversity, (b) evaluate the tool's utility in relation to migration-related phenomena, and (c) develop more precise ways to measure relevant concepts with the aim of generating more informed and tailored interventions to reduce the impacts of prejudice, discrimination, and stigma.

Introduction

How the stigma and migration research fields can inform one another is an important question yet these two fields have rarely been in conversation to date. Understanding how these research fields may inform one another is crucial to better contextualize the lived experience of migrants given that the movement of people and boundaries has been one of the defining characteristics of humans across time. Throughout our discussions, we sought to set the stage regarding concepts, theories, and frameworks that might be useful to scholars working at the intersection of these two fields, yet who may be unfamiliar with such important concepts for their research agendas. A better understanding of the key concepts, theories, and frameworks from both the stigma and migration fields is crucial to inform research seeking to understand the impacts of "migration-generated diversity." In this chapter, we present several topics from the migration and stigma fields that we determined were particularly important for the integration of these two fields.

We begin by pointing to the overarching importance of "movement" for the scholarship that we hope will result from the intersection of these two fields. To achieve a merging of fields, it is critically important to create a shared understanding of how to think about ways in which prejudice and stigma may, under a certain set of conditions in a specific time and place, emerge from the movement of people through migration. To inform each field about the core concepts and theories that an emerging focus on "migration-related stigma" might have, we created a conceptual mapping tool (see pp. 23–26). In addition to creating a conceptual mapping tool, we selected three theoretical perspectives, some from this tool, to further engage: group threat theory, intersectionality, and "what matters most." We selected these theoretical perspectives because they provide generative lenses through which migration-related stigma can be considered and may help to further elucidate how stigma processes may change over time. We conclude by providing suggestions aimed at moving research at the intersection of stigma and migration forward.

Setting the Stage: Defining Key Concepts to Understand Migration-Generated Diversity

The Role of Movement

What is the role of movement in migration-generated diversity and its relationship to stigma? To preface this section, we briefly introduce several basic migration-related terms (migrants, immigrants, emigrants, international migrants, and internal migrants) critical for understanding differences in experiences of prejudice, discrimination, and stigma, including their specific nuances to ensure a shared understanding of these terms for the following discussion of the role of movement in the framework of migration-related prejudice and stigma. The general term *migrant* is used here to refer to individuals who changed their country of residence at least for a certain period of time. This allows issues to be discussed from both the point of view of the country of origin and the country of destination. Comparatively, *immigrant* is used mostly from a point of view of a country of destination, or what is often termed the receiving country. *Immigrants* are classified as individuals who arrived in such receiving countries, wherein a part of the local population may hold anti-immigrant attitudes. In addition, the term *immigrants* is more often used to describe permanent immigrants (i.e., individuals who arrived with the intention to settle permanently in the country of destination), as compared to *temporal migrants* (e.g., labor migrants, student migrants). *Emigrant* is a concept used from a point of view of the country of origin: people who leave their country of origin are emigrants in the eyes of those who stayed behind. To further elucidate this, *immigration* is arriving in a country of destination and *emigration* is leaving a country of origin. Migration, thus, is a relatively flexible and general concept that allows for discussion of diverse patterns of migration (including multiple migration, circular migration, return migration, temporal migration[1]) as well as different points of view.

An additional distinction between *international migrants* and *internal migrants* is important to the discussion of movement and migration-related stigma. *International migrants* are typically defined as individuals who migrated or moved from one sovereign state (i.e., their country of birth or country of origin) to another sovereign state (i.e., their current country of residence or country of destination). When conceptualizing the change of one's place of residence within a sovereign state, the term *internal migrant* is used (e.g., when a person does not cross national borders at the time of migration).

In the research literature on prejudice and stigma, there is often an overlap in how the terms international migrant and ethnic/racial minorities are used. Yet not all ethnic/racial minorities are international migrants, and not all international migrants are ethnic/racial minorities. Thus, we sought to first focus on what we argue is key to understanding migration-related stigma; namely, movement. *Does movement invoke essential features of stigma?* We argue that movement from one country to another is an essential feature of how migration-related stigma may develop and therefore discuss three types of movement as routes through which migration and migration-related stigma may occur: (a) movement of people across national borders, (b) movement of borders around people, and (c) movement and racial/ethnic minorities. Further, we directly address the issue of whether there is a useful distinction between

1 Yet, some scholars also questioned the term migration (Urry 2007) because it implies permanent or long-term migration from one sovereign state to another, in other words, patterns of migration, such as labor migration and settlement migration, that mostly characterized the nineteenth and twentieth centuries (Castles 2016). Defining the twenty-first century as an era of technological and communication advances, transnationalism, fluidity and openness, these scholars have used "mobility" as a theoretical concept that better fits the description of diverse large-scale and small-scale movements of people in the twenty-first century (Sheller and Urry 2006; Urry 2007). Here we use the term "migration" to describe the diverse patterns and pathways of people movements from one country to another and adopt Castles's (2016) view of migration as a regular part of social relations and "a part of complex and varied processes of societal change" (Castles 2016:22).

migrant groups and ethnic/racial minority groups within the study of majority population attitudes (prejudice, stigma) toward them.

Movement of People across National Borders

We refer to the *movement of people across national borders* as a movement from a country of origin to a country of destination with the intention to reside at least for a certain period in the latter. This type of movement, however, can happen for different purposes. Migration can be forced or voluntary and for diverse reasons. People may, for instance, seek asylum, better employment possibilities, or educational or professional advancement. They may strive for a better lifestyle or improved living conditions (e.g., retirement migration) or pursue personal reasons (e.g., marriage, family reunification, return migration, co-ethnic repatriation).

In our conceptualization of the prejudice and stigma generated by this type of movement, we suggest that prejudice toward migrants be viewed from the point of view of a country of destination (stigmatization of immigration) as well as from the perspective of a country of origin (stigmatization of emigration). Not only immigration, but also emigration from a country is perceived as a problem in the country that is being left (Kustov 2022). Emigrants may be stigmatized or suffer from prejudice in their country of origin even though they may belong to an ethnic majority in that country. In this case, the act of migration itself, as a movement across national borders, may evoke prejudice. From the perspective of the country of origin, emigration can be stigmatized to achieve norm enforcement: people should stay in a place where they are born and contribute to that place (Phelan et al. 2008).

Goodhart's (2017) conceptualization of British citizens as "anywheres" or "somewheres," which he put forth in his analysis of why Britain voted to leave the European Union, may be helpful when thinking about prejudice toward migrants as people who moved across national borders regardless of their ethnicity. "Anywheres" are cosmopolitans who are ready to live in different countries, embrace pluralism, respect diversity, and are open to change (Goodhart 2017). By contrast, "somewheres" resist change and cherish their national identity and cultural homogeneity of their society and place of birth (Goodhart 2017). These people prefer to stay in the community, are less open to cultural complexity, and are concerned about their collective borders (Goodhart 2017). Following Goodhart's (2017) argument, for "somewheres," migration (i.e., movement of people across borders of sovereign states or even across regions within national states) can be disturbing, regardless of the migrants' ethnicity. Thus, "somewheres" will often hold prejudicial views and may stigmatize migrants to keep them away, thereby controlling the borders of their own collective. They may hold prejudice against both immigrants and emigrants. "Anywheres," however, tend to view migration and its consequences as valuable rather than threatening (Goodhart 2017). In other words, some people ("anywheres") view the movement of people across borders, regardless of migrants' ethnicity, as beneficial, whereas others ("somewheres") perceive it to be intimidating (Goodhart 2017).

Movement of Borders around People

We refer here to the movement of borders as geopolitical changes and state formation. Although the political reality of the Global North is composed of autonomous nation units with borders that have remained relatively stable since the end of World War II, this does not apply for other parts of the world over the last several decades. For example, following the dissolution of former communist/socialist federations at the end of the twentieth century, 24 independent states were (re)established along new territorial borders. In addition, consider the ethnic enclave exchange between India and Bangladesh in 2015 in which Indian ethnic enclaves in Bangladesh were swapped for Bangladeshi enclaves in India.

What consequences exist when borders, but not people, move? In Europe, for example, the category of standardized international migrant includes a large number of people who did not actually cross international borders at the time of their migration. These people were born in one of the three federations (USSR, Czechoslovakia, Yugoslavia) and migrated from one republic of a federation to another republic of the same federation during the period when the republics were part of the same federal sovereign state. Later, these individuals were named international migrants according to OECD, Word Bank Indicators, and Eurostat data sets, not because they moved from one sovereign state to another, but because the international borders moved around them as new post-socialist nation-states were (re)established. In other words, the category of international migrant, defined as a person born abroad according to present-day borders, may now also include people who migrated internally within the borders of one sovereign state (Gorodzeisky and Leykin 2022). Individuals who did not cross international borders are referred to as international migrants, and under certain conditions they may suffer as a group from prejudice and discrimination. Such a label may be used to legitimize exclusionary citizenship policies toward them, such as happened to Russian-speaking residents in Estonia and Latvia (Gorodzeisky and Leykin 2022). Furthermore, movement of borders may make a certain population group extremely vulnerable to stigma and discrimination, due to the loss of legal status following the movement of borders, as the case of "erased" residents in Slovenia demonstrates (Pistotnik and Brown 2018). The negative consequences of stigma for people who did not migrate internationally but were labeled as international migrants may be particularly severe since these individuals are denied agency: they did not intend to migrate internationally or to cross international borders yet are still labeled as international migrants and may be treated as such after the borders changed.

Movement and Racial/Ethnic Minorities

In the conceptualization of movement and its relationship to migration-related stigma, it is important to consider whether it is solely movement that results in stigma. Does prejudice exist toward migrants as outsiders, as foreigners, as people who moved from a country of birth to live in another country, or are migrants only stigmatized if they belong to an ethnic/racial minority? Is there a useful distinction between migrant groups and ethnic minority groups when we study prejudice or stigma? Our group discussion provided different responses for different social contexts.

In the context of the United States, the distinction between migrant groups and racialized groups may not be quite as useful in the study of stigmatization in certain contexts. In the United States, nowadays, Black and White people are commonly perceived as nonimmigrants, whereas Asian and Latino/a people are frequently perceived as immigrants, even in the third generation (Fussell 2014; Zhou 2004). Comparatively, in the contemporary European context, the situation is different. There is a distinction between being a migrant and being a member of an ethnic or racialized minority in the framework of public attitudes toward these groups. Race can be a signifier of migration background, but it is only one signifier (e.g., language may be another one). There are many European-origin migrants in different European countries who may be stigmatized as migrants but not as a racialized minority.

Another example of migrant groups, which are distinct from ethnic minorities but still experience prejudice, are ethnic German repatriates to Germany or ethnic Greek repatriates to Greece. These immigrants belong to the same ethnic groups as the majority population, but the majority population in Germany and Greece still hold prejudice against these migrant groups (e.g., Matejskova and Leitner 2011 for Germany; Pratsinakis 2014 for Greece). In European contexts as well as in Israel, there is an important distinction in the study of prejudice between ethnic minority groups and migrant groups.

While these examples provide evidence for our argument that there is something unique about the contribution of movement to migration-related stigma, we acknowledge that just because movement may generate stigma, the thrust of the stigma faced by migrants also involves racial/ethnic stigma as well as other markers of difference.

Stigma versus Prejudice

The concepts of stigma versus prejudice have been examined in prior literature, with Phelan et al. (2008) concluding that there are many similarities between these two conceptualizations. Similarly, although scholars from the fields of migration studies and stigma lack a shared understanding of terminology, they share the essence of the types of experiences these separate fields utilize to explain the phenomenon which occurs following migration-generated diversity. In other words, the concepts of stigma and prejudice, clearly overlap but have developed in the context of different literatures: stigma is more likely to be applied in the context of illness (mental illness, HIV, leprosy) or "deviant" behaviors (LGBTQ, sex work), whereas prejudice is more likely to be used in race relations (White racism) or religious animus (anti-Semitism) (Phelan et al. 2008). Despite this difference, Phelan et al. (2008) concluded that the issue of whether "stigma and prejudice: one animal or two" could be answered, for the most part, as "one animal" (Phelan et al. 2008:358). Their review led to the conclusion that concepts and theories could generally be translated from one framework to another with little loss of meaning. In our group's discussions, exchanges between migration researchers (who generally used the concept of prejudice) and stigma researchers led to several observations about the correspondences and differences. Bohman et al. (this volume) discusses this by comparing Blumer's (1958) threat theory to Link and Phelan's (2001) conceptualization of stigma. Drawing from Bohman et al.'s arguments and our conceptual analysis, we conclude that consistent with Link and Phelan (2001), stigma is a broad umbrella concept that constitutes multiple components; stigma is considered to be present when components of labeling, stereotyping, setting apart, status loss, and discrimination occur together. Further, to accomplish consequential discrimination, stigma requires power to affix labels, confer stereotypes, implement separation, achieve the diminution of status, and exert control over access to jobs, housing, education, and medical care. This concept of stigma (Link and Phelan 2001) differs from the way prejudice is used in the migration literature in its broader bundling of associated concepts, as further developed below. In the stigma definition, an additional difference lies in the centrality of power. It takes power to stigmatize and consequently, powerful groups are often exempted from full-blown stigma. Therefore, even if they may be recipients of labels and stereotypes, powerful groups do not often experience extensive separation, status loss, or discrimination and are thus not subject to stigma (Link and Phelan 2001). In addition to the bundling of concepts and the focus on power, stigma researchers were more likely to investigate the consequences of stigmatization for the targets of such stigmatization.

Given the importance of the concept of prejudice in the migration studies field, let us review the ways in which it has been defined. As previously noted, the migration studies field has often utilized concepts of threat and prejudice to examine the reactions and consequences generated due to migration. Historically, prejudice has been conceived by social scientists as an individual-level phenomenon (see Allport 1954). Conceptualizing it at the individual level suggests that "the individual is a unit separable from 'society' " (Williams 1988:345). A common criticism of this view of prejudice is that it ignores the larger social structure and power dynamics (see Blumer 1958; Bobo 1999; Bobo and Tuan 2006; Jackman 1994). Blumer (1958) provides a useful framework for thinking about prejudice as a normal human action rooted in an individual's defense of his or her group position. This perspective locates the study of prejudice at both individual and group levels. Conceptualizing prejudice in this way provides important leverage for the study of stigma and migration. It also allows scholars to understand the deep and dynamic connection between micro-level psychological processes and meso- and macro-level social structural dynamics. Prejudice, we suggest, not only involves views held by one individual against another: it reflects the social structural relations between groups.

To conclude, differences between the concepts of prejudice and stigma have been examined extensively (e.g., Link and Phelan 2001; Phelan et al. 2008). If taken together, stigma is a broad conceptual scheme or framework that covers an entire process, starting with labeling differences and resulting in devaluation and discrimination. Prejudice, which is closely related to stereotyping and negative emotional reactions in the stigma literature, covers these central aspects of stigma, but does not, as a concept, generally include consequences like discrimination. It is important to note that discrimination has been extensively examined in the migration literature, as a separate construct from prejudice. Considering the overlap and distinctions between the terminology that is utilized by these two fields, we pulled together the most useful concepts and constructs from both fields and developed a conceptual mapping tool to enable scholars to contextualize future research questions and to respond to urgent issues related to stigma associated with migration diversity. This conceptual mapping tool (Table 2.1) is meant to provide researchers a broad tool that may aid them in selecting the most useful and appropriate concepts relevant to their particular area of research. It is not meant to be exhaustive and researchers utilizing it should decide what "dimensions" are most relevant for their particular research questions. It is meant to provide a collection of potentially useful concepts from the stigma and migration literature. Every situation involving migration stigma is likely to be different and as a result readers should use the conceptual mapping tool to identify concepts that might possibly be useful. In the future it is possible that integrated models for particular forms of migration stigma might emerge but currently the best use of our conceptual mapping tool is to suggest possibilities that users of this tool can creatively deploy.

The Conceptual Mapping Tool

Table 2.1 captures the core "dimensions" of relevant concepts from the stigma and migration fields. In it you will find the concept's name (Column 1), a brief description of the concept and citation(s) to consult for further information (Column 2), and, when relevant, suggested measures to operationalize the concept (Column 3). The dimensions or groupings of concepts are organized to address specific aspects of stigma/prejudice. We briefly describe the overall dimensions of relevant concepts below but encourage researchers to consider Columns 2 and 3 to gain an in-depth understanding of these concepts.

Table 2.1 This conceptual mapping tool provides a way to understand migration-generated diversity. Integral concepts, which need to be considered within their historical and social contexts, are listed, followed by brief descriptions and suggestions for further reading. Measures by which to evaluate each component are given where available.

Concept	Description; Further Reading	Suggested Measures
	Components of Stigma	
Othering ("Us" vs. "Them")	Separation into distinct and unequal groups; Link and Phelan (2001), Tajfel and Turner (1979), and for alternative terminology Allport (1954)	Continuum measures (Peter et al. 2021)
Prejudice	A negative attitude directed toward a group or an individual belonging to the group; Allport (1954)	Subtle and blatant prejudice scale (Pettigrew and Meertens 1995)
Emotional reactions	Anger, fear, disgust; Link et al. (2004)	Emotional Reactions to Mental Illness Scale, ERMIS (Angermeyer et al. 2010)
Status Loss	Downward placement in social hierarchies; Link and Phelan (2001)	
Stereotype	Generalization of (negative) characteristics, sometimes conceived of as the cognitive component of prejudice; Link and Phelan (2001)	Attribution Questionnaire (Corrigan et al. 2014)
Labeling	Designation or tag selected for social salience; Link and Phelan (2001)	Responses to open-ended questions about mental illness or a described mental illness are coded to create measures (e.g., Angermeyer and Matschinger 2003)
Power	Stigma cannot be exercised in the absence of power; Link and Phelan (2001)	
	Levels of Stigma	
Intrapersonal	Impacts thoughts, emotions, behavioral reactions of those stigmatized, e.g., due to anticipated stigma or self-stigma; Major and O'Brien (2005)	For separate measures of anticipated and internalized stigma (Link et al. 2015)
Self-Stigma	Driven by the attitudes of the stigmatized individual, internalizing and application of prevalent negative stereotypes leads to a decrease in self-esteem and self-efficacy, shame, and embarrassment; Corrigan et al. (2011), Meyer (1995)	Self-Stigma of Mental Illness Scale (Corrigan et al. 2011) Internalized Homophobia (Meyer 1995) Internalized Stigma Scale (Ritsher et al. 2003) Internalized Stigma of Mental Illness (Link et al. 2015)
Interpersonal	Discriminatory behavior by individuals toward individuals based on one's membership in a socially disadvantaged group, also referred to as public stigma; Link et al. (2004)	Social distance scale (Link et al. 1987) Measure of discrimination (Meyer 1995) Scale of Daily Indignities (Link and Phelan 2014)
Structural	Manifested through laws, policies, and allocation of rights and resources; Hatzenbuehler (2016)	Measure of preferences for forms of strucural discrimination (e.g., Schomerus et al. 2022)

Table 2.1 (continued)

Concept	Description; Further Reading	Suggested Measures
	Subject of Stigma Assessment	
The stigmatizer	General public, members of the majority, members of the in-group	
The person stigmatized	Migrants	
Associations	People connected to the stigmatized person (e.g., relatives, helpers); courtesy stigma; Goffman (1963)	Affiliate Stigma Scale (Mak and Cheung 2008)
	Types of Stigma Experiences	
Enacted	Discrimination as an outcome of public or structural stigma; Earnshaw and Chaudoir (2009)	
Anticipated	Anticipated stigma, irrespective of whether it will actually happen or not; Link (1987), Pinel (1999)	Stigma-consciousness questionnaire (Pinel 1999; Link and Phelan 2014) Rejection sensitivity questionnaire (Downey and Feldman 1996)
Avoided	Putting yourself at a disadvantage by avoiding situations where stigmatization could occur, label avoidance; Earnshaw and Chaudoir (2009), Link et al. (1989)	Modified HIV stigma scale (Saine et al. 2020; Wanjala et al. 2021) Withdrawal scale (Link et al. 1989)
	Causes/Functions of Stigma	
1. Threat		
Levels:	To individual interests; Bobo (1983) To group interests of an individual; Scheepers et al. (2002)	Individual level (economic) (Raijman and Semyonov 2004)
Dimensions (economic, political, cultural)	What Matters Most; Yang et al. (2007). In-group; and Citrin (2007) General anxiety, unspecific fear related to discomfort, lack of predictability, control; Raijman and Semyonov (2004)	Individual and group level (economic) (Gorodzeisky 2013) Group level (economic and cultural) (Heath et al. 2020)
2. Function		
To dominate and exploit	Defense against a perceived threat to securing or expanding power, status, wealth of the dominant group; Phelan et al. (2008)	Measures relevant to these concepts are included in other boxes. For example, a measure of discrimination captures the function of domination and exploitation. Rejection or social distance measures capture punishment of norm violating behavior as well as keeping people away.
To enforce norms	Penalizing deviant behavior, signaling the boundaries of acceptable behavior; Phelan et al. (2008). What does it take, e.g., to be Swedish? To what extent do immigrants need to know the language?	
To exclude	Avoidance of danger, increasing perceived security, avoidance of disease; Phelan et al. (2008). Opposition to immigration, desire for social distance; Heath et al. (2020)	

Table 2.1 (continued)

Concept	Description; Further Reading	Suggested Measures
	Difference between Stigmatized Circumstances	
Peril	Perceived dangerousness; Angermeyer and Matschinger (1996), Link et al. (1999), Jones et al. (1984), Pachankis et al. (2018)	Link and Cullen (1986) multi-item scale
Disruptiveness	Awkwardness in social interactions by virtue of non-smooth traits or attributes; Hebl et al. (2000), Jones et al. (1984), Pachankis et al. (2018)	Social distance scale (Link et al. 1987)
Origin	Blaming people for their stigmatized condition; onset and offset responsibility can be distinguished; Weiner (1995), Corrigan (2000), Jones et al. (1984), Pachankis et al. (2018)	Attribution questionnaire (Corrigan et al. 2014)
Aesthetics	Invoking disgust through visible marks; Crandall and Moriarty (1995), Jones et al. (1984), Pachankis et al. (2018)	Social distance scale (Link et al. 1987)
Course	Presence of stigma at birth; emergence and persistence later in life; Levy and Pilver (2012), Jones et al. (1984); Pachankis et al. (2018)	
Concealment	Obscurement under specific situations; Pachankis (2007), Jones et al. (1984), Pachankis et al. (2018)	Modified HIV stigma scale (Saine et al. 2020; Wanjala et al. 2021)
	Consequences of Stigma	
Discrimination	Unjust or prejudicial treatment of a person or group based on a label or designation affixed to them; Williams et al. (1997)	Everyday Discrimination Scale (Williams et al. 1997)
Devaluation	Downward placement as a person of worth or value; Goffman (1963), Link et al. (2004), Yang et al. (2007)	Perceived Discrimination and Devaluation Scale (Link 1987)
Exclusion	Blocking people from access or participation in desired circumstances; Priebe et al. (2008)	SIX (objective social outcome index) (Priebe et al. 2008)
Life chances	Probability that certain circumstances (housing, jobs, schooling) can be achieved; Savage (2015)	
Physical/ mental health		Symptom checklists like SCL-90 (Derogatis 1994)
	Stigma Reduction	
Covering	Hiding a (concealable) stigmatized condition or identity; Yoshino (2006)	Secrecy measure (Link et al. 1989)
Coping	Using personal resources and strategies to be able to cope with stigma and its consequences; Miller and Kaiser (2001)	Coping with discrimination scales (modified from other stigmatized groups, e.g., LGBTQ)
Resistance	Efforts by stigmatized individuals to counter the effects of their stigmatization by denying the labels and stereotypes applied to them or by challenging claims of those who would stigmatize them; Thoits (2011)	Subscale Stigma Resistance of the Internalized Stigma of Mental Illness scale (Ritsher et al. 2003). Stigma resistance scales (Thoits and Link 2016; Thoits 2016)
Contact	Contact needs to be established in a targeted, credible, local, and continuous manner; Allport (1954), Corrigan (2011)	Familiarity scale (Corrigan et al. 2001). Contact with persons with mental illness scale (Link and Cullen 1986)

Table 2.1 (continued)

Concept	Description; Further Reading	Suggested Measures
	What Matters Most	
Local worlds	The embeddedness of individuals in networks that constitute a context of shared meaning and understanding; Yang et al. (2007)	Cultural Factors Shape Stigma (CFSS) and Cultural Capabilities Protect against Stigma scales (CCPS) (Yang et al. 2021)
Core personhood	That which is essential for an individual to be a full participating member of a local world; Yang et al. (2007)	CFSS and CCPS scales (Yang et al. 2021)

The first dimension, "components of stigma," seeks to specify what must be present for an investigator to indicate that a circumstance is "stigmatized" or that "prejudice" exists. For stigma, these components are labeling, stereotyping, setting apart, emotional reactions, status loss, and discrimination, in the context of power and wherein these components exist at least to some degree (Link and Phelan 2001; Link et al. 2004). Prejudice is defined as antipathy focused on an individual or a group that is based on an overgeneralization (Allport 1954). The utility of this set of concepts in any stigma domain, including migration, would be to provide a type of checklist for a researcher to apply:

- Are there pejorative labels? Attendant stereotypes? Accompanying emotions?
- Is there an in-group/out-group or us versus them separation?
- Do the recipients experience status loss and are they discriminated against?

Attending to these concepts can help sensitize the researcher to what may be important to investigate.

The second dimension, "levels of stigma," points to various levels at which stigma may occur. Its aim is to alert investigators to the possibility that stigma, for both perpetrators and recipients, can be expressed or experienced at multiple levels. Stigma-related processes can operate within a person (intrapersonally), between people (interpersonally), or at the structural level (structural stigma). A special component that has been emphasized in the stigma field is "self-stigma," in which a person internalizes stereotypes and risks experiencing a self-esteem decrement as a result (Corrigan et al. 2011).

The third dimension, "subject of stigma assessment," indicates that the study of stigma and of migration-related stigma can be focused on groups that differ in their relationship to the stigmatized circumstance being examined. Thus, it can involve potential stigmatizers, or what the stigma field sometimes refers to as "public" stigma. Alternatively, it can involve the recipients of stigma. Finally, people connected to the stigmatized person may experience "courtesy" stigma (Goffman 1963)—in the stigma literature, this is commonly referred to as "associative stigma" or "vicarious" in the migration literature.

The fourth dimension, "types of experiences of stigma," can help sensitize investigators to the possibility that stigma may be experienced in multiple ways, as people can experience the enactment of stigma by others, the anticipation of stigma that may or may not ultimately occur, and avoidance stigma that results when a person cuts off potentially beneficial outcomes for fear of encountering enacted stigma. This can help investigators better understand that stigma, in general, or migration-level stigma can be experienced in multiple ways and thus may result in multiple unexpected consequences.

In the fifth dimension, "causes/functions of stigma," we identify sources of stigma/prejudice. The concept of threat, as it has been applied in the migration field, can be conceptualized as applying individual or collective interests and includes threat to multiple dimensions, including economic, political, cultural, and security aspects (Bobo 1983; Scheepers et al. 2002). The threat component is clearly highly relevant to migration, as it was developed as a theoretical explanation for prejudice and discrimination directed to migrant groups. The stigma literature has also developed potentially relevant concepts related to desired ends that stigma can bring to those who stigmatize. These include domination/exploitation, norm enforcement or control of others, and exclusions or what is called, "keeping people down" (exploitation/domination), "keeping people in" (norm enforcement), or "keeping people away" (exclusion) (Phelan et al. 2008:362). In this framework, stigma functions to get the dominant group things they want; because of this, it creates and sustains the enactment of stigma in all its forms and at all levels. These concepts are potentially useful for migration stigma as they point to circumstances in which efforts are in place to keep people in (e.g., burkas) or keep people down to exploit them (e.g., migrant workers).

The next dimension of concepts, "difference between stigmatized circumstances," addresses the fact that circumstances that are stigmatized are often very different from one another—the term stigma is applied to everything from racial stigma to irritable bowel syndrome to prostitution. Although these different circumstances have stigmatization in common, it is also clear that they are very different. Here Jones et al. (1984) and Pachankis et al. (2018) point out that stigmatized circumstances differ in terms of whether they can be concealed (racial differences vs. mental illness), involve peril (incarceration history vs. blindness), are disruptive in taken-for-granted interactions (facial disfigurement vs. sexual minority status), and involve aesthetic qualities (leprosy vs. abortion recipient) or whether the origin of the circumstance is controlled by the person (substance use vs. Down syndrome) or the course of the stigmatizing circumstance can be altered (cleft lip vs. having dwarfism).

The experience of stigma differs radically according to these dimensions. For the field of migration stigma, these concepts are potentially useful for reasoning about how different migration circumstances may differ. For example, different situations involving migration may or may not involve peril, disruptiveness of taken-for-granted interaction, or aesthetics. In some circumstances, migrants might be able to conceal their origins, in others not. Similarly, the issue of origin may be important in terms of whether the migrating person chose to migrate and may also be useful to consider regarding when, over the life course, migration occurred.

The next dimension contains potential "consequences of stigmatization" which in the stigma field have included the broad scope of life chances from jobs, housing, health care, educational opportunities, social relationship, self-esteem, and physical and mental health. To understand the experience of the migrant, these domains may represent useful possible outcomes for the migration field to consider.

The next dimension, "stigma reduction," involves efforts to mitigate or resist the impact of stigmatization. In the stigma field, individual-level coping efforts involve covering/concealment, educating others about one's situation, avoiding/withdrawing to reduce exposure to anticipated/enacted stigma, distancing oneself from others who are stigmatized ("I am not like them"), and effortful coping aimed at countering stereotypes (working twice as hard) (Miller and Kaiser 2001; Yoshino 2006; Link et al. 1989). Resistance strategies can involve individual strategies, such as deflecting (stereotypes exist but "that is not me") or challenging others when they enact stigma, as well as social strategies, such as joining social movements (for further discussion on these coping strategies, see Misra et al., this volume). All these coping and resistance strategies are potentially useful in migration studies, especially if attention is turned to the consequences for people who have migrated.

The final dimension is the "what matters most theory/conceptual scheme." In the stigma literature, its value lies in the conceptualization of cultural circumstances and in the idea that stigma is most impactful when it challenges the lived engagements that are "most at stake" (or "what matters most") to people in their local worlds (Yang et al. 2007). We expand on this approach below, as it holds the potential to integrate the stigma and migration fields, where life activities that "matter most" in the migrant group may cohere or lie in opposition to what is most valued by dominant groups in the receiving society.

This brief overview of the conceptual mapping tool (Table 2.1) points to its potential usefulness for the migration and stigma fields. Still, we acknowledge the complexity and scale of the conceptual mapping tool. We encourage scholars in these fields to take what is most applicable to their specific research questions to better conceptualize migration-related stigma. To better facilitate the use of this conceptual mapping tool, Table 2.2 provides an example of how a researcher might utilize particular concepts from it.

Sample Application of the Conceptual Mapping Tool

Due to its comprehensive approach, the conceptual mapping tool offers a way to study the migrant experience and social positions for a specific group of migrants (e.g., by country of origin, legal status). Applying the conceptual

Table 2.2 An overview of levels of stigma and types of stigma experiences in migration-related stigma.

Type	Public Level	Structural Level	Self-Stigma
Enacted	Individual discrimination	Disadvantaged by law Discriminatory migration policies Unequal access to health care	Shame Self-devaluation Why-try effect
Anticipated	Stress and its sequelae	Stress and its sequelae	Stress and its sequelae
Avoided	Conceal migration status Social withdrawal Choose to change name to resemble the in-group Avoid speaking in mother tongue in public	Select destination country with low structural stigma Conceal immigration status Avoid complaining if treated unfairly Tolerate unfair labor or housing conditions Avoid seeking health care Avoid calling the police when victimized by crime	Avoid speaking in mother tongue in public Deny one's cultural heritage Choose to change name to resemble the in-group Avoid immigrant communities

mapping tool, we can examine structural, interpersonal, and intrapersonal manifestations of stigma in the case of a specific migrant group. Having such a multilevel examination would enhance our understanding of the integration outcomes for a specific migrant group and enable us to examine migration laws and policies that target this specific group (structural manifestation), discriminatory behavior toward this group (interpersonal manifestation), as well as the impact that stigma has on self-evaluation, emotions, and behavioral reactions of those who belong to this specific group. Moreover, this kind of application of a stigma perspective may help to identify causes for the differences in integration outcomes of several groups of migrants in a certain country, or differences in integration of the same group of migrants (in terms of country of origin) in different countries of destination. To apply the conceptual mapping tool, one should use the most fine-grained definition of the migrant group, not only in terms of country of origin but also in terms of time of arrival.

In Table 2.2, we selected three levels of stigma (public or interpersonal, structural, and self-stigma as a form of intrapersonal stigma) from Table 2.1 and integrated them with three types of stigma experiences (enacted, anticipated, and avoided stigma, see Table 2.1 for definitions). We then hypothesized how each combination might affect people who are identified or self-identify as migrants. Notably, not only enacted, but also anticipated and avoided stigma can have detrimental effects on the life chances of migrants. Combined, all levels and types of stigma experiences result in diminished life chances, social exclusion, and adverse physical and mental health outcomes.

Conditions That May Result in Prejudice and/or Stigma or Neither

While there is something about movement (e.g., migration) that can lead to prejudice and/or stigma, it is critically important to understand the conditions under which prejudice and stigma occur to a greater or lesser extent. Below we highlight three possible outcomes that might result when a group migrates into a new context: (a) prejudice and stigma, (b) prejudice but no stigma, and (c) no prejudice and no stigma. Figure 2.1 illustrates how migration-generated diversity may or may not be met by instances of prejudice and/or stigma. We make the key distinction as stigma scholars have previously noted that for stigma to occur, unequal power between groups is essential (Link and Phelan 2001); however, prejudice may occur with or without a power differential.

Prejudice and Stigma

Migration-generated diversity may lead to differential outcomes when a migrant moves to a new context and experiences prejudice that ultimately results in stigmatization. A key aspect of this process is the nature of the power dynamics between migrants and citizens of the receiving country (see Blumer 1958).

Power is essential for successful stigmatization. Link and Phelan (2001) maintain that there needs to be a power gradient so that stigmatization can occur. People in groups with little power may label and form stereotypes of people with more power (Link and Phelan 2001). For instance, an individual who experiences homelessness may generate labels for the police that control them and link those labels to stereotypes of brutality, indifference, and rage. In addition, large segments of the public may generate labels and stereotypes about politicians and Wall Street bankers (Link and Phelan 2001). Does this make the police, politicians, and Wall Street bankers victims of stigma, relative to people experiencing homelessness or the general population, respectively?

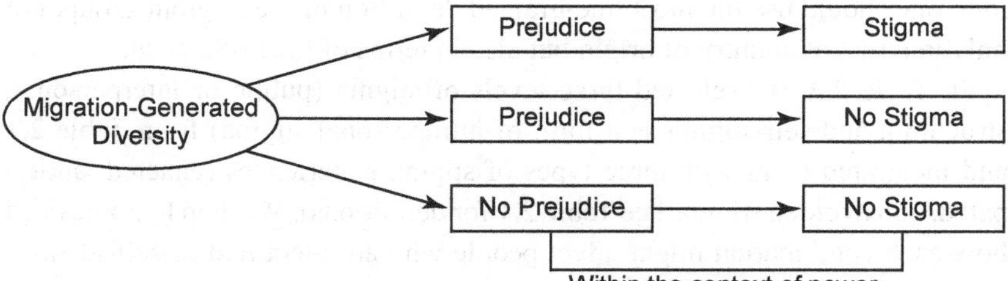

Figure 2.1 An illustration of three pathways in which migration-generated diversity may or may not be met by instances of prejudice and/or stigma.

Answering yes to such a question would render stigma an overly broad concept, with little muscle for analytic purposes (Link and Phelan 2001).

To allow for more specific analytic utility around the framework of stigma, the concept of power must be considered (Link and Phelan 2001):

- Do people who might stigmatize have the power to ensure that the human difference they recognize and label is broadly identified in the culture?
- Do the people who might confer stigma have the power to ensure that the culture recognizes and deeply accepts the stereotypes they connect to the labeled differences?
- Do the people who might stigmatize have the power to separate "us" from "them" and make it stick?
- Do those who might stigmatize control access to major life domains (e.g., educational institutions, jobs, housing, and health care) have the ability to enforce the distinctions they draw?

If the answer is yes, we can expect stigma to result. If the answer is no, some of the cognitive components of stigma might be present but full-blown stigma would not exist.

Prejudice but Not Stigma

As previously mentioned, stigma occurs when there is a difference in power between groups (Link and Phelan 2001). From this perspective, prejudice may exist, but without the context of power there cannot be stigma. This has been demonstrated when a migrant group has power over the receiving society. For example, after Reunification in Germany, most leadership positions in the East were assumed by people born and trained in the West. This conscious decision was made for two reasons: First, leaders in the former German Democratic Republic (East Germany) were suspected of having collaborated with the communist regime, and there was a consensus in the Federal Republic of Germany (West Germany) that their power should not be perpetuated. Second, in almost all branches of society (e.g., education, economy, politics), governance followed the system that had been in place in the Federal Republic of Germany. People who had been trained in West Germany knew how to act within this system: how to achieve goals and enact an agenda. This knowledge was crucial to getting work done in the former East German areas. Thus, top leadership positions (e.g., professorships, CEO positions, political appointments) went almost exclusively to individuals from former West Germany. Effectively, this resulted in increased career opportunities for an entire generation of West Germans. At the same time, it crippled opportunities for potential leaders in the East. In addition, since World War II, individuals from West Germany had amassed far greater financial resources than their counterparts in communist

East Germany. Accordingly, companies and estates that went up for sale after Reunification were purchased primarily by individuals from the West.

These two conditions—knowledge of the system and financial resources—gave people who migrated from the West to the East an enormous advantage over their East German peers. This led to massive resentment with the receiving population. Labeled *Besserwessis*—a pejorative term derived from *Besserwisser* (know-it-all) and *Wessi* (West German)—these West German migrants were not subjected to overt discrimination, because their professional status gave them the power and opportunities to maneuver successfully within the system. Not surprisingly, people in the East soon detested the overconfident *Besserwessis*. This resentment would only be understood as stigma under conditions where the East Germans had more power (e.g., social acceptance); however, this was not the case and therefore did not amount to stigma.

Similar examples can be found in colonial activities; that is, when a minority group entered a country and exerted power over the receiving society. The labeling of the receiving country's citizens as "primitives" and subsequent application of racial stereotypes, the othering as well as the exploitation and domination mechanisms that were enacted demonstrate how a powerful minority can stigmatize a powerless majority, rather than vice versa. It also makes clear that stigma is more than negative attitudes toward a group.

Neither Prejudice nor Stigma

When migrants move into a new context and are welcomed by the receiving society, neither prejudice nor stigma may occur. An example of this is when a migrant possesses a skill or talent that fills an important void in the destination society (e.g., H-1B Visas in the United States, Mexican guest workers, White retirees to Mexico, Ukrainian refugees). In Europe, for instance, positive attitudes have been extended toward Ukrainian refugees from the ongoing war compared with much stricter attitudes toward Syrian refugees a decade ago. Underlying racial prejudice may play a role, as well as the age and gender composition of the refugee groups. In addition, there may be a higher level of familiarity and previous contact with Ukrainians. Most important to the acceptance of Ukraine refugees is the perception of a common enemy: Russia, which threatens not only Ukraine but residents of European countries as well.

Prejudice and stigma necessitate an "us" versus "them" distinction (Link and Phelan 2001). Thus, because Ukrainian refugees are perceived as "us" by Europeans, there is no prejudice or stigma in this case. Other examples include student migration or the migration of individuals in creative professions that rely on international mobility. An example of the latter is the migration of classical musicians from different parts of the world to Berlin to play in its many classical orchestras. Rarely do these migrants suffer from prejudice or stigma.

Additional Perspectives: A Consideration of Threat, Intersectionality, and What Matters Most

In our discussion, we selected three topics, some of which were included in our conceptual mapping tool, for further consideration: threat, intersectionality, and "what matters most." Although these concepts/theories have not always been utilized in both fields, they are important in further highlighting phenomena that reside at the intersection of stigma and migration-generated diversity. This may also include a better understanding of differences in the "degree of stigmatization" that may occur under certain conditions (Link and Phelan 2001). These perspectives are also useful in illuminating more complex dynamics regarding evolving stigma processes to elucidate differing stigmatizing circumstances over time.

Threat

The concept of "threat" has been a central theoretical orientation in migration research, and much theorizing in sociology and social psychology points to feelings of threat as an important trigger of prejudicial attitudes (e.g., Blalock 1967; Sherif 1967; Stephan and Stephan 2000). Over the years, a wealth of empirical studies has lent support to these predictions (e.g., Bobo 1983; Quillian 1995; Scheepers et al. 2002; Semyonov et al. 2006). One of the most prominent theories, which has been widely applied to explain anti-migrant attitudes, is group threat theory (Blumer 1958). This theory conceptualizes prejudice as a matter of intergroup relations that arise when members of the dominant group perceive a threat to their privileged position (Blumer 1958). In the original formulation of the theory, Blumer (1958) specifies four feelings always present in prejudicial attitudes and identifies threat as the key feeling. This implies that you may have a feeling that the other is inferior, fundamentally different and alien, and that you and your fellow group members, based on your group belonging, have the right to certain resources and privileges; however, critical to group threat theory is that if you do not have a perception that the other group threatens your position, it is not prejudice (Blumer 1958). Meanwhile, we argue that in line with how Allport's (1954) conditions for intergroup contact to reduce prejudice have been reformulated as "facilitating" rather than "essential" (Pettigrew 1998), it may be useful to think about Blumer's (1958) four feelings in a similar way. Further, while group threat theory originally emphasized group threats, empirical studies have demonstrated that threat may also operate on the individual level (Hjerm and Nagayoshi 2011; Scheepers et al. 2002). In other words, migrants can be perceived both as a threat to the individual (e.g., competition for work and earning a living) and as a threat toward the group that the individual identifies with, meaning that although the individual in question does not fear losing his or her job, migrants are considered a threat to the economic position of the group as a whole.

Dimensions of Threat

The threat literature further distinguishes between different dimensions or "types" of threat, the main dimensions being *economic, cultural, political, and security* threat (Blalock 1967; Hellwig and Sinno 2017; Scheepers et al. 2002). While threat may vary among different contexts and across time, anti-migrant attitudes seem to stem primarily from perceptions that migrants are undermining strongly held values, national symbols, or cultural traits (Sides and Citrin 2007). Such perceptions are often grouped under the label cultural or symbolic threat and are also discussed in terror management theory (Solomon et al. 1991), which is part of the stigma framework (Pachankis and Wang, this volume). In terror management theory, the need to defend cultural value systems from an outside threat is tied to human beings' awareness of their own mortality, and to the key role of cultural systems in providing meaning and a promise of immortality (Greenberg et al. 1986). In addition to economic, cultural, political, and security threat, perceived threats may also be more unspecific and related to a general sense of unease or lack of control (Harell et al. 2017). The presence of migrants may disturb needs of predictability and control among the native-born population, which in turn may increase anxiety and general unease and therefore raise, for example, susceptibility to anti-migrant political rhetoric.

The different dimensions of threat can be useful to understand differences in the degree of prejudice faced by migrant groups (Hellwig and Sinno 2017), as well as attitudinal differences among the native-born population (Hjerm and Nagayoshi 2011). The dimensions may also be useful to understand prejudice between groups more equal in status; that is, groups that both are positioned in a subordinate position in relation to the dominant group. Many prejudice theories, including group threat theory, assume a dichotomous relationship (dominant–subordinate, majority–minority, native-born–immigrants), but reality is of course more complex. For example, the category "native-born" is far from homogeneous, in terms of race and ethnicity, and in terms of a family history of migration. Indeed, many born in the country, but with migrant parents or grandparents, are labeled as "migrants" or "immigrants" by the majority population. Thus, their level of prejudice is likely to diverge from that of the part of the native-born population that also belongs to the majority population. From empirical research we know that so-called second-generation immigrants and ethnic\racial minorities generally are more tolerant toward migrants (Sarrasin et al. 2018). One of the explanations for this is provided by cultural marginalization theory (Fetzer 2000), which suggests that those who were socialized as being disadvantaged or discriminated against develop solidarity and empathy toward other vulnerable groups. Still, prejudice between distinct minority groups, including between different groups labeled as "migrants," exists. Acknowledging that the hierarchical relationship (and thus, who poses a threat to whom) between different groups may vary depending on such dimensions may possibly be a way forward in understanding prejudice between different subordinate groups.

How "Threat" and "Stigma Functions" Can Be Conceptualized as Comparable

While the concept of threat primarily has been applied in the migration literature as a tool to explain variations in anti-migrant attitudes, we note that the three functions of stigma (see Table 2.1 for definitions) largely can be reformulated in terms of threat (Phelan et al. 2008). The function of exploitation and domination, to keep "them" down, can be reformulated as the others threatening "our" (e.g., the dominant group's) privileges and resources; the function to uphold norms, to keep people in, as the others threatening "our" values and symbols; and the function of avoiding diseases, to keep people away, as the "others" (e.g., the migrant group) bring diseases and threaten "our" health and survival (Phelan et al. 2008). Taken together, this suggests that the concept of threat is present also in a stigma framework, although the concept per se is rarely used. The parallel to Blumer is also clear as he explicitly writes that the different feelings that constitute prejudice as a group position places the subordinate group below (feeling of superiority) and beyond (feeling of alienation) (Blumer 1958). The feeling of proprietary claim excludes them from resources and privileges, but the actual threat, according to Blumer (1958), is more of an emotional response, an emotional "recoil" or defensive reaction. It functions, he says, (although rarely long term) to preserve the integrity and position of the dominant group.

The overlap is clear, but there is also a difference in the emphasis on domination and exploitation in the stigma framework and the emphasis on threat in group threat theory. This difference implies a tension between the two literatures in how the threat perspective posits that prejudice is primarily grounded in a perceived discrepancy between how it should be but no longer is (or is about to become), while the dominance function in stigma implicates actual and retained power. Stigma, in this sense, is a way to exploit and dominate, whereas prejudice is primarily a reaction to (perceived) status loss. While our purpose here is not to solve this tension, we still note that it may be alleviated if the two (dominance vs. threat) are conceived of as operating on different levels. For example, studies in the threat literature show that often individuals in more precarious positions hold the most prejudiced attitudes, including in working class occupations or those with less education (e.g., Scheve and Slaughter 2001; Velásquez and Eger 2022). This is generally explained by a greater perceived (and sometimes actual) individual threat on behalf of these individuals. Thus, although the function of "dominance and exploitation" may be the reason that prejudice exists (i.e., on a more basic level), threat may still be more useful to explain such in-group variations.

Thinking about the power dynamics of the stigma process together with group threat theory, a kind of paradox emerges: a stigmatized group of migrants is powerless in the first place. When the group gains access to resources, increases in numbers, or even in perceived power, the stigma process seems not to be lessened, but rather amplified. This is because the perceived threat that this group poses to the native-born population increases. So, the function of stigma, to reduce the threat posed by the migrant group to the native-born population's norms, security, and wealth and status, becomes more salient when the migrant group is perceived as more powerful and threatening, increasing the stigma of this group. This continues to be effective if there still is a power gradient—it is only when migrants become powerful, secure, settled, and influential enough, such that they cannot be devalued and discriminated against, that stigma stops.

Intersectionality

Intersectionality refers to the multiple interlocking systems of oppression that operate to disadvantage individuals whose social positions lie across multiple axes of marginalization. Emerging from Black American feminist scholarship (Collins and Bilge 2016; Combahee River Collective 1983; Crenshaw 1991; Hooks 1984), the construct of intersectionality has historically been applied to understanding the disadvantage experienced by Black women. When applied to legal contexts, an intersectional approach highlights how discrimination affecting Black women can remain unseen when analyzed only through the separate lens of either racism or gender bias. As a solution to such problems, an intersectional approach highlights the unique forms of discrimination directed toward Black women that are inseparable from either identity alone.

Given its solution to the problem of unseen interlocking forms of oppression toward other multiply stigmatized populations, intersectionality can theoretically expand understanding of stigma as it affects migrants who possess one or more additional marginalized statuses beyond their migrant status. Examples might include migrants who also possess a mental illness, migrants who are also LGBTQ, migrants who also possess a racialized identity, migrants with undocumented status, migrants with a minority religious identity, and migrants who are women. For these individuals, whose social positions incorporate at least one other stigmatized status in addition to being a migrant, their experience of stigma and migration is arguably distinct from those individuals who possess no other stigmatized status beyond their migrant position. For instance, from a structural level, possessing a mental illness might preclude migrants from certain opportunities (e.g., for employment, for health care, for citizenship status) that would not be denied to nonmigrants with the same mental illness. At a more personal level, a migrant's mental illness might be seen or interpreted (e.g., as more unpredictable, as more dangerous) by others as a function of their migrant status whereas this same mental illness would not be interpreted in the same light when seen by others. In these cases, intersectional influences and experiences could be understood as being a function of the multiple stigmatizing structures that are directed toward each of the component statuses but in such a way that the impact of each form of structural stigma (e.g., toward migrants) is enhanced or at least made distinct in the context of the others (e.g., toward people with mental illness). An intersectionality lens could also be fruitfully used to understand experiences at the personal level, for instance when unique forms of oppression affecting multiply marginalized individuals muddies the ability of these individuals to easily attribute their experiences of discrimination to any one stigmatized characteristic.

Numerous aspects of the migrant experience could be considered through an intersectionality framework, including features of both the sending and the receiving context. Factors of the sending context that might influence the migrant experience in an intersectional manner include an individual's reasons for migrating—for instance, whether those reasons are voluntary or forced. Influential factors of receiving contexts might include whether one's reasons for migrating are deemed as deserving of protection in the receiving country. In this way, the experience of any one migrant might differ from the experience of another, at least in part because of the distinct intersections of these migration-related factors in addition to any other stigmatizing social status they might distinctly possess. At the same time, questions remain about whether other features of the migration experience can also be considered through an intersectional lens.

As both a theoretical and analytic tool, intersectionality poses opportunities and challenges for future research. Like with stigma concepts more generally, whether and how migration is racialized will inform whether race can be meaningfully analyzed in interaction with other aspects of migration-generated diversity to capture stigma not directed toward migration alone. For instance, does an intersectionality lens further aid in the explanation of the distinct forms of treatment experienced by Ukrainian versus Syrian refugees to Europe not explained through simply migration stigma or racism alone? Similarly, can the distinct stigma experience of Ukrainian residents not born in Ukraine—for example, students from African countries studying in Ukraine—offer another opportunity for intersectional analysis? Although intersectionality might be most frequently considered through the lens of binary, or at least group-based, categories (e.g., Black vs. White X man vs. woman), this approach might not best capture reality, for instance, in the case of race analyzed along a continuum of skin color or gender analyzed as a continuous function of masculinity and femininity. Finally, multiplicative interaction terms capturing an individual's multiple social positions represent one approach to studying intersectional influences. At the sample time, analytic approaches to intersectionality should not lose sight of the original impetus and value of an intersectionality framework in being able to capture the existence and influences of the structurally stigmatizing forces directed toward those whose identities lie at the statistical intersection. That is, ideal future analytic approaches will stay true to intersectionality theory by not only parsing stigmatized individuals into discrete units of analysis but also bringing to light the stigmatizing structures that make this necessary in the first place.

What Matters Most

Another observable dynamic that could elucidate a more complex understanding of migration-related stigma processes within migrant groups are the "core everyday engagements," or "what matters most" (below), within migrant groups. Systematically assessing these daily lived experiences could aid in capturing stigma processes related to dearly held, everyday cultural practices, in addition to assessing other (mostly) observable statuses related to migration (e.g., race, ethnicity, religion). Simultaneously, these, and oftentimes distinct, core everyday activities are being lived out by local community groups (including those most proximal to the migrant group) in the receiving society as well as across the broader receiving society itself. As described below, these core daily activities that are lived out in everyday interactions may overlap, diverge, or come into conflict with one another, and may transform as the groups interact and exert influence upon one another over time (below), with implications for migration stigma. This perspective, by understanding, and operationalizing "matches" and "mismatches" between the daily cultural activities that "matter most" between migrant and receiving groups (below), can expand upon more traditional measures of structural or economic integration (see Okamoto and Adem, this volume) by assessing key "cultural components" of integration.

What is "most valued" by a local community can be defined, and observed as "the felt flow of engagements in a local world" (Kleinman 1999:358). In the context of migration, a local world refers to a somewhat circumscribed domain within which the everyday life activities of the migrant group take place (also, other, parallel local worlds exist within local communities in the receiving society). A local world is most observable in a tightly knit social network or neighborhood/community by which migrants arrive to the receiving society where members of the local world share social connections (i.e., may know, or know of, one another or one's families or neighbors, or share a common locale); however, for migrants who come from large urban areas and who are not socially connected, the concept of the local world may not be as applicable. What defines all local worlds, including the one in which migrants and those from the local receiving groups reside in, is the fact that something is deeply at stake (Kleinman 1999). Daily life matters and is upheld via everyday lived participation by actors within local worlds. If local group members find that what is held to be "most at stake" may be seriously menaced or even entirely lost, these threats may lead them to respond to the perceived threat by discriminating against and marginalizing others (Yang et al. 2007). Deepening the above understandings of threat-based processes that migrants are seen to threaten strongly held values, national symbols, or cultural traits, people with local worlds have something observable to gain or lose, such as: status, money, life chances, health, good fortune, a job, or relationships. This feature of daily life, called "moral experience" by Kleinman (1999), refers to that register of everyday life that defines "what matters most" or "what is most at stake" for ordinary men and women (Kleinman 1999, 2006; Kleinman et al. 1997). What is key is that "what matters most" is observable, and discoverable, typically through robust ethnographic and qualitative methods.

Participation in what matters most demarcates individuals as full participants in social life or delegitimates others as not quite integrated. For example, among a sample of primarily undocumented Chinese immigrants with psychosis from Fujian Province, China, perpetuating the lineage (and engaging in employment as a strategy to achieve this) reflected actualization of "what matters most" (or "personhood") in this cultural group (Yang et al. 2014). That is, if a Chinese immigrant with psychosis was able to consistently work and to accrue sufficient material resources to attract a spouse and have children, they were seen as a full-fledged "person" within their local world. Everyday lived activities centered around perpetuating one's immortal lineage are seen to reflect what is "most at stake" across many Chinese communities and was discovered as being continuously enacted within this particular immigrant group via qualitative methods (i.e., semi-structured qualitative interviews); in a similar fashion, qualitative methods can be used to identify what is most valued within particular migrant groups and comparing and contrasting this to what is "most valued" by local receiving communities.

Implications of adopting this framework for migration research include the following. First, recognition of fulfilling the cultural roles that affirm personhood within the local migrant group could act to buffer prejudice, stigma, or discrimination enacted by the larger receiving society. To build upon the prior example, if an undocumented Chinese immigrant with psychosis engaged in the activities of being a "respected person" by fulfilling obligations to lineage (i.e., by working and accruing material resources) and is recognized as such by their local world, this could act to buffer against prejudice, stigma, or discrimination from the receiving society. Conceptions of "personhood" can further extend to social networks in sending contexts. For example, for Chinese immigrants, lineage obligations also extend to sending remittances to family members from the sending country; the amount of these remittances are recognized (and publicly recorded) by the migrant's social network in the sending country, thus enhancing the family's status (and that of the contributing migrant within their local network). The "what matters most" framework enables discovery of the capabilities that are core to personhood for migrant groups (Yang et al. 2014); enactment of these core cultural capabilities could be an important source of self-esteem, continued integration into the local migrant world, and other positive psychosocial outcomes, and could potentially buffer from prejudicial or stigmatizing experiences from the receiving society.

Second, the "what matters most" framework could be used to examine core everyday activities that are lived out in daily interactions that may overlap, diverge, or come into conflict with one another as the migrant group contacts local receiving groups, and may transform as the groups interact. For migrant groups that are encouraged to integrate to the receiving society's dominant norms and values, loss of "what matters most" to the migrant group and adoption of core lived values of the receiving society can be both a threat and an opportunity. For example, as migrant group members begin to adopt the lived engagements that "matter most" to receiving group members, this may be perceived as greatly threatening by members of the migrant network (e.g., older family members, who may be invested in preserving the activities and traditions that "matter most" to them). On the other hand, this route may lead to increased opportunities via adaptation to the receiving society (e.g., increased opportunities via education and work opportunities; although this strategy may have limits—see the "integration paradox," Okamoto and Adem, this volume). Alternatively, if migrant group members choose to preserve their participation in the core lived values of the migrant social group, this could preserve "personhood" within their social networks (per above) but may also lead to corresponding loss of higher status educational and vocational opportunities in the receiving society. Further, highly visible markers of continued participation in "what matters most" to the migrant local world, especially if seen to be foreign or alien to receiving society members, may also be perceived as a significant source of societal threat (below).

Identifying and classifying "what matters most" within the migrant and receiving group local worlds, and potential "mismatch" between these, could be empirically evaluated for their significance in migration processes (e.g., perceived threat by the receiving group). That is, rather than assessing whether a migrant group poses a threat to the receiving society's "national identity" as broadly constructed, identifying the specific core lived values in the receiving group (e.g., human rights, including gender equality), and how those of the migrant group could threaten these values (e.g., ostensibly patriarchal values leading to visible subordination of women), could be empirically evaluated. Questions could then be identified and evaluated after operationalizing to what extent the activities that "matter most" converge, overlap, and/or conflict between the two groups. For example, would receiving groups be more likely to stigmatize and feel strongly threatened by migrant groups whose core lived activities directly conflict with that of the receiving community? For example, if a migrant group's conceptions of what it means to be a "respected woman" in their community meant holding a (visibly) subordinate role that conflicted with a receiving society's norms of gender equality, would this be perceived as more threatening by the receiving group? An initial hypothesis is that a greater (visible) degree of mismatch would be associated with greater endorsed threat by the receiving group. Alternatively, circumstances could exist whereby opportunities for the migrant group to directly participate in "what matters most" for receiving society groups could mitigate migration stigma. For example, migrants who can immediately participate in economic activities to bolster withering local economies may earn acceptance as being part of the receiving community (see Okamoto and Adem, this volume). This leads to a broader question: If migrant groups over time and the course of integration are able to participate in daily lived activities that "matter most" to receiving groups, might this lead to fuller acceptance and integration with receiving societies? Further exploration of whether a migrant group participates in the receiving groups' daily lived activities, and in what spheres of life (e.g., economic, social, religious), and whether this could lead to reduced migrant stigma, could yield additional insights.

Two further key considerations are noted. First, actual mismatch between "what matters most" between the migrant and the receiving group may not be most salient in determining endorsed threat; instead, the mismatch elicited by what is *perceived* by receiving group members as "mattering most" to migrant group members may be most influential. Second, "what matters most" for the receiving society should be considered at distinct levels: (a) per above, at the group level for the most proximal local receiving group, as cultural matches and conflicts between groups may be experienced in daily intergroup interactions; (b) "what matters most" (e.g., what is promoted in terms of protected rights and privileges, such as gender equality, and who is eligible for these) as represented at the macro policy/institutional levels. Nonetheless, bringing in the "lived experience" of daily cultural activities in the ways outlined above can enhance our understanding of migration stigma.

Conclusion

To conclude, we distill down what this chapter aimed to contribute to this emerging field (i.e., what we know) in addition to what we have identified as key future directions for the emerging intersection of migration and stigma (i.e., migration-related stigma).

What Do We Know about Migration-Generated Diversity?

How migration and stigma scholars might conceptualize the processes that may follow migration-generated diversity (e.g., negative attitudes and emotional reactions, occurrences of exclusion, and discrimination or "overall stigma") have been written about differently in the migration and stigma fields, yet these fields have much to offer one another. There are many concepts, theories, and frameworks utilized in these fields that could aid in future research at the intersection of migration-related stigma. Therefore, to better inform each field of relevant and important concepts to be used by researchers, we created a conceptual mapping tool (and an example of how to utilize this conceptual mapping tool) which we hope is useful for scholars at this intersection in their formulation of new research agendas.

We further discussed the core aspect of movement inherent in migration and its relation to prejudice and stigma. While we believe that movement is an essential core of migration-generated stigma, we also recognize that it is not the only piece and other statuses, such as one's race/ethnicity, may matter above and beyond this. Further, the intersection of multiple disadvantaged statuses may explain more differences in the "strength" (or the degree) of migration-related stigma that groups may experience (Link and Phelan 2001). To reiterate an important claim, all migrants are outsiders but the strength (including the absence of) stigma often varies. Other key concepts such as group threat theory (Blumer 1958) and "what matters most" (Yang et al. 2014) may further elucidate functions of stigma and/or threat leading to more refined understandings of why people stigmatize and relatedly why people are stigmatized, further leading to creation and/or refinement of stigma-reduction methods related to migration stigma. Further, we concluded that prejudice can take place without stigma necessarily occurring—specifically that for occurrences of stigma to truly happen there must be a power differential (Link and Phelan 2001). In the absence of this, migrants may (or may not) experience prejudice but cannot experience stigma.

What are key future directions for these now intersecting fields? Numerous questions remain unanswered and will be important for future scholars to consider. To begin, let us consider the following areas:

1. Although we have defined key concepts, theories, and frameworks from both the migration and stigma fields in this chapter (see Table 2.1), further refinement may be necessary, especially for key concepts, theories, and frameworks which remain under- or undefined in the context of migration-generated stigma.
2. We have discussed some examples of measures that may aid researchers in developing new research agendas in the field of migration-related stigma, but also recognize that to date most of these measures lie in the stigma area and that it may be methodologically difficult to implement these concepts, theories, and frameworks in new studies that are seeking to understand migration-generated diversity and whether and to what degree this is met by prejudice and/or stigma. In relation to new studies on migration-generated stigma, greater specificity in how best to define, utilize, and measure these relevant concepts, theories, and frameworks will allow for the creation of better informed and tailored interventions aimed at reducing prejudice and/or stigma due to migration-generated diversity.

Conceptions

Future research should seek to construct better models designed to analyze and more deeply understand under what conditions migration-related stigma is strongest when conceptualizing stigma as gradient or a "matter of degree" (Link and Phelan 2001). Key to reduction of migration-related stigma is to conceptualize what moderates the strength of stigma including how to think about what constructs are most useful in this endeavor. Some specific constructs/theories to further consider and elucidate include "what matters most" (also in relation to the stigmatizer), the intersection of race/migration, documented/undocumented status, and "deservingness" of the migrant group.

Measurement

Overall, researchers should think about how we can further operationalize concepts so that they better translate to both (and at the intersection of) the migration and stigma literatures. One specific way in which this might be accomplished is to think about how stigma scholars can better integrate Blumer's (1958) group threat theory into their stigma research (more broadly and specifically in relation to migration-generated diversity). Additionally, scholars should seek to better construct, or if necessary, reexamine how our existing methods of measuring the relationships between migration-generated diversity and stigma can be better conceptualized to incorporate key theories and concepts such as "what matters most" and intersectionality that might be especially relevant in the context of migration and conceptualizing changes in migration stigma over time. Finally, it is important to address how we can incorporate these into current measurements that look at the perspective of the stigmatizer. For instance, can the core theories that we elucidated in this chapter be applied in the context of examining the stigmatizer?

Stigma-Reduction Interventions

Better elucidating the concepts from the migration and stigma fields, the potential relationships between them, and how best to measure them is crucial to inform more effective stigma-reduction methods when migration-related diversity is met by prejudice, stigma, and/or discrimination. Some of the questions that future research may wish to explore further include:

- How does the intersection of these concepts from the migration and stigma fields better inform interventions to reduce prejudice, stigma, and discrimination prompted by migration-generated diversity?
- What do experiences of threat and prejudice do for the stigmatizer, and how are such insights useful in developing strategies to alleviate threat and reduce prejudice/stigma?

- Are there other ways to alleviate threat, such as by addressing perceived vulnerability or realistically apprising potential threats that migrant groups pose to achieving "what matters most" in receiving groups?

Acknowledgments

Drew Blasco was supported in part by funds from US National Institutes of Health grant T32 HG010030 (University of Michigan ELSI Research Training Program). The content is solely the responsibility of the author and does not necessarily represent the official views of The National Institutes of Health.

3

Revisiting Group Threat Theory Using Insights from Stigma Research

Andrea Bohman, Maureen A. Eger,
Daniel Gabrielsson, and Paolo Velásquez

Abstract

This chapter focuses on group threat theory (Blumer 1958), one of the main sociological approaches used to explain prejudice toward minority groups. It examines the utility of the theory when applied to prejudice in the context of migration-generated diversity and analyzes how its original formulation by Blumer compares with the conceptualization of stigma by Link and Phelan (2001). Similarities and differences are drawn between Blumer's "four feelings" in prejudice and Link and Phelan's "four components" constitutive of stigma. Despite overlapping, complementary, and at time divergent arguments, using these two approaches in tandem may overcome the limitations of group threat theory and, in the process, advance research into anti-immigrant sentiment. In turn, it is posited that scholarship on stigma may gain from incorporating the concept of threat into its framework.

Group Threat Theory

Group threat theory is an explanation of a dominant group's prejudice toward subordinate groups in society. The theory is based on the work of Blumer (1958), who in his seminal article, "Racial Prejudice as a Function of Group Position," discussed the role of threat in regard to social relations between the White majority and Black minority in the United States. Since then, group threat theory has been used to explain other instances of racial and ethnic prejudice and anti-immigrant sentiment. Beginning with Quillan's (1995) application of group threat theory to study European attitudes toward immigrants, thousands of studies related to immigration (according to Google Scholar almost 12,000) have cited Blumer's theory. In sociology and political science, group threat theory and related competition theories (Olzak 1992; Scheve and

Slaughter 2001) are the most often tested accounts of prejudice in empirical studies of anti-immigrant sentiment, opposition to immigration, and support for political parties with explicitly anti-immigrant stances.

Fundamentally sociological, group threat theory (Blumer 1958) understands prejudice as a social phenomenon, dependent on the nature of social relations between racial groups. Specifically, when members of the racial majority group perceive a threat to their collective dominant social position, feelings of fear and anger manifest as prejudice toward a racial minority group. Prior to this theoretical proposition, prejudice was largely understood as something originating from innate dispositions, personality types, and/or individual experiences (e.g., Adorno et al. 1950; Allport 1954). By contrast, Blumer (1958) argued that prejudice arises from a real or perceived threat by a minority racial group to the majority racial group's dominant position. This "sense of social position" requires social categorization: identification with a racial in-group vis-à-vis a racial out-group. According to Blumer (1958:5):

> [A perceived threat] may be in the form of an affront to feelings of group superiority; it may be in the form of attempts at familiarity or transgressing the boundary line of group exclusiveness; it may be in the form of encroachment at countless points of proprietary claim; it may be a challenge to power and privilege; it may take the form of economic competition. Race prejudice is a defensive reaction to such challenging of the sense of group position. It consists of the disturbed feelings, usually of marked hostility, that are thereby aroused. As such, race prejudice is a protective device. It functions, however shortsightedly, to preserve the integrity and the position of the dominant group.

Limitations

Although research on racial attitudes lend empirical support for group threat theory (e.g., Bobo 1983; Dixon 2006; Quillian 1995), the application of it in explanations of native-born responses to immigration has yielded mixed results, leading some to question the theory's explanatory power (e.g., Eger et al. 2022; Hjerm 2007). We see this as stemming both from issues with its application in the field as well as limitations of the theory itself.

First, most of the previous research has tested a specific version of the theory. This version, sometimes referred to as realistic group conflict theory (Bobo 1983; Sherif and Sherif 1953), sees a direct relationship between immigration and anti-immigrant prejudice. Thus, in empirical studies, the relative size of the minority population has been the most consistent measure of group threat (Blalock 1967; Quillian 2006). In studies of anti-immigrant sentiment, threat is operationalized as the percentage of the population in a country or subnational region that is foreign born (Quillian 1995). However, recent meta-analysis studies cast doubt on the theory's explanatory power when threat is measured this way. Across 55 studies, Pottie-Sherman and Wilkes (2017) find both positive and negative relationships between out-group size and attitudes toward immigrants, and most are insignificant. Focusing on differences in the size of geographic units across 171 post-1995 studies, Kaufmann and Goodwin (2018) find some support for the theory: in the smallest and largest geographic units, the relative size of the out-group population corresponds to individual-level threat perceptions, but not when group size is measured in midrange units like neighborhoods. Most recently, a meta-analysis of 48 studies published between 1990 and 2017 (Amengay and Stockemer 2019) demonstrated that neither levels nor increases in objective immigration have consistent effects on radical right voting in Europe.

Taken together, these results indicate that the empirical relationship between objective immigration and out-group prejudice is not straightforward. Although population innumeracy likely contributes to the weak relationship between objective group size and natives' attitudes (Herda 2010), variation in how "immigrant" is actually measured (i.e., who counts as an immigrant) also plays a role (Pottie-Sherman and Wilkes 2017). For example, some scholars contend that the category "percent foreign born" is too broad and that the size of specific immigrant groups, such as non-Western (Schneider 2008) or non-White (Hjerm 2009), are more appropriate tests of the theory. This suggests, however, that anti-immigrant prejudice may not stem from being foreign born per se but from other characteristics, such as race or religion. Indeed, particular immigrant groups—including their native-born descendants—tend to be primary targets of hostilities (Dancygier et al. 2022) and discrimination (Bursell 2014, 2021). This has led some scholars to operationalize threat with the relative size of a more specific subpopulation, such as the share of a European country's non-European racial and ethnic minorities (Gorodzeisky and Semyonov 2016) rather than the relative size of the entire foreign-born population.

Further, most empirical studies also privilege indicators of economic competition. Examples at the individual level include natives' employment status, occupational skill level, and income (Haubert and Fussell 2006; Scheve and Slaughter 2001); at the contextual level, unemployment rates and other labor market conditions (Quillian 1995). This is, however, only one of many forms of threat, as Blumer points out in the above quote. According to Blumer (1958:5), perceived challenges to the dominant group's position may also include "an affront to feelings of group superiority," which also implicates the dominant group's subjective experiences: perceptions, fears, and concerns that are not necessarily consistent with either objective out-group size or zero-sum economic conditions. Indeed, elite political rhetoric (Bohman 2011), media attention (Czymara and Dochow 2018; Erhard et al. 2021; Van Klingeren et al. 2015), and even violence against immigrants (Eger and Olzak 2023) may increase the salience of immigration, activating threat and making anti-immigrant prejudice more likely. Thus, scholars increasingly acknowledge that perceptions of immigrants may ultimately matter more than objective immigration numbers (Gorodzeisky and Semyonov 2020; Pottie-Sherman and Wilkes 2017).

Second, we emphasize that group threat theory was originally developed to explain anti-Black prejudice among White Americans, which calls into question whether it is also appropriate for explanations of anti-immigrant sentiment. Although the theory's scope conditions were never made explicit, the time and place of its formulation may limit its ability to explain a phenomenon that differs from social relations between a majority population and a historic, national minority, also understood as two racial groups. Consequently, applying the theory to other contexts may require considerations of differences in characteristics both of the dominant "perpetrator" group and the target group. Indeed, not all immigrant groups encounter the same degree of anti-immigrant prejudice (Ford 2011), which is related, at least partially, to their visibility in society and overt features such as skin color or religious practices (Schalk-Soekar et al. 2004).

While race is central to Blumer (1958), the original focus on a dyadic relationship between two racial groups implies that differences between subordinate groups, and how this feeds into prejudice, remains undertheorized. Applying the theory to attitudes toward a foreign-born population not only means overlooking important aspects of Blumer's theory regarding race but also obscures how anti-immigrant prejudice targets some groups of immigrants to greater degrees and in different ways than others. Further, while group threat requires collective identities, the theory does not address how the content of such identities play into feelings of threat and anti-immigrant prejudice. This may be important as studies show that native-born groups whose national identity is based on nonvoluntary features (e.g., ancestry, race, and cultural practices learned through early socialization) display higher levels of prejudice—at least toward certain groups of immigrants—compared to native-born groups that emphasize voluntary features (e.g., citizenship, language, and respect for laws and institutions) (Kosterman and Feshbach 1989). Hence, expanding group threat theory to account for heterogeneity, both in relation to immigrants as the target of prejudice and the collective identity of national majorities as the perpetrators, would be helpful to the study of anti-immigrant sentiment.

Third, it remains unclear what happens to prejudice when the perceived "threat," whatever it is, dissipates or decreases. Despite the key role assigned to "threat" in the account, group threat theory says little about what happens if important resources cease to be scarce or the out-group decreases in size or salience. For example, although operationalizing threat through mere numbers has yielded mixed results, the approach has been useful in relation to a sudden increase in the immigrant population. During the migration crisis of 2015, the political salience of immigration significantly increased throughout Europe (Eger et al. 2020) and increases in asylum seeking were met with a spike in anti-immigrant sentiment (Heath and Richards 2019; Messing and Ságvári 2019). Still, group threat theory provides no clues as to what should theoretically happen to prejudice once the migration crisis ended. In terms of empirical observations, some research suggests that anti-immigrant sentiment did not return to precrisis levels (Czymara 2020a; Velásquez and Eger 2022), which highlights the importance of adding a dynamic perspective to group threat theory.

Furthermore, recent research has revealed an integration paradox; that is, increased structural integration among immigrants does not equate to more positive attitudes toward the native-born population and host society (de Vroome et al. 2014; Steinmann 2019; Tolsma et al. 2012; Verkuyten 2016). From a group threat perspective, the theoretical expectations regarding structural integration are twofold: the immigrants best adapted to the host society should be less of a threat (at least culturally), and therefore face less prejudice, however, their stronger economic and political position may elicit other feelings of threat and thus more prejudice. While it is unclear what determines which of these scenarios is realized, research indicates that immigrants who are structurally better integrated, who theoretically should be less of a threat since they adopt the host society's "ways," often experience more alienation and feel less like they belong than those immigrants who are less structurally integrated. Subsequently, if one focuses solely on socioeconomic indicators, the most integrated immigrants articulate less positive attitudes toward the native population than one would expect (Geurts et al. 2021). Although there are several explanations for this pattern (e.g., van Doorn et al. 2013; van Maaren and van de Rijt 2020; Verkuyten 2016), this indicates at the very least, that native-born prejudice does not always disappear as structural integration increases.

To summarize, there are three main limitations to how group threat theory has been used in previous research to explain anti-immigrant prejudice:

1. A narrow focus on out-group size and economic indicators in empirical tests.
2. A limited ability to account for heterogeneity both within the target and the perpetrator group.
3. Vague or contradictory predictions in regard to decreasing threat.

The first point addresses how the theory has been applied but not necessarily the theory itself, whereas the second and third points implicate the theory itself. When applied to anti-immigrant prejudice, it becomes clear that certain aspects of the theory are undertheorized. Next, we look closer at the theoretical foundations, by comparing Blumer's original formulation of group threat theory to the conceptualization of stigma, as developed by Link and Phelan (2001).

Conceptual Comparison: Four Feelings versus Four Components

In his seminal piece, Blumer (1958) specified four feelings that are always present in racial prejudice. More than forty years later, Link and Phelan (2001) argued that stigma is rooted in the convergence of four interrelated components; interestingly, these components align partially with Blumer's four constitutive feelings. Table 3.1 illustrates how group threat theory relates to the conceptualization of stigma, identifying where these models overlap and where they differ. To achieve an effective comparison, Table 3.1 includes assumptions that underlie the different components, drawn from a larger theoretical discussion within each approach. To distinguish the constitutive components from these assumptions, the components are numbered and highlighted in gray. Although some sort of chronology is implied by the table, in the sense that "consequences" are listed last, the numbers do not specify a particular order of events, nor do they indicate the importance of the individual components to the process leading to prejudice/stigma. To be clear, Link and

Table 3.1 Conceptual comparison of group threat theory (Blumer 1958) and stigma (Link and Phelan 2001).

	Group Threat Theory: "Four Feelings"	Stigma: "Four Components"
Identification	Racial prejudice is a matter (a) of the racial identification made of oneself and of others.	1. *People distinguish and label human differences.* 2. *Labeled persons are placed in distinct categories to accomplish a degree of separation of "us" from "them."*
Hierarchy	Racial prejudice is a matter (b) of the way in which the identified groups are conceived in relation to each other, i.e., "sense of group position." 1. *A feeling of superiority.*	Stigmatization is entirely contingent on access to social, economic, and political power.
Stereotyping and alienation	Disparaging qualities are imputed to the subordinate racial group. 2. *A feeling that the subordinate race is intrinsically different and alien.*	3. *Dominant cultural beliefs link labeled persons to undesirable characteristics—to negative stereotypes.*
Resources	3. *A feeling of proprietary claim to certain areas of privilege and advantage.*	
Threat	4. *A fear and suspicion that the subordinate race harbors designs on the prerogatives of the dominant race.*	
Consequences		4. *Labeled persons experience status loss and discrimination that lead to unequal outcomes.*

Phelan explicitly state that stigma exists when the four interrelated components converge, and Blumer emphasizes that prejudice exists only when all four components are in place.

Identification

Blumer as well as Link and Phelan stress the primacy of identification and social categorization in the process leading to prejudice/stigma. For Blumer, racial identification lies at the heart of racial prejudice in the sense that holding such attitudes is contingent on group identification. As prejudice is essentially about relationships between groups, prejudiced individuals must, by definition, consider themselves members of a specific collective. Thus, from Blumer's perspective, "a scheme of racial identification is necessary as a framework for racial prejudice." Not accounting for this or for how the identified groups conceive of their position in relation to each other is "to miss what is logically and actually basic" (Blumer 1958:3). In the case of stigma, one of the basic components involves the distinction and labeling of human difference. Stigma presupposes that individuals distinguish and assign social significance to certain differences, albeit not to all. This process converges with a separation of an "unlabeled" us from a "labeled" them, in ways that increase social saliency and set the conditions for social interaction.

The labeling and sorting of individuals into social categories and groups, distinct from the ones assigning the labels, is a second constitutive component of stigma. As for the active principle of differentiation, or the characteristics that become the object for stigma, it may either sort individuals into larger collectives, based on skin color, origin, religion, and so forth, or function to single out specific individuals from a larger collective based on nonnormative behavior or illness. In this sense, stigma may be based on both group and individual characteristics: that is, both on features that are transferred across generations and hence, shared by family members, as well as on characteristics with greater within-family variation, which are not necessarily passed on from one generation to the next (see Phelan et al. 2008). The groups in Blumer's original formulation of group threat theory are distinguished on the basis of race, a "group characteristic," in that it is transferred across generations and thus often shared by members of the same family. In later applications to explain anti-immigrant prejudice, groups are often differentiated based on national origin (born inside or outside the country). As one's status as an immigrant, based on place of birth, rarely is transferred across generations, this departs from the principle of differentiation underlying the original theory. Still, at least for some ethnic and racial minority groups in societies, "immigrant status" does not seem to reflect objective individual experiences with migration. Native-born children and grandchildren of immigrants may be categorized by the majority group as "immigrants" (i.e., "second-" or "third-generation immigrants") and thus become targets of prejudice based on this status.

While both perspectives emphasize that prejudice/stigma is contingent on social identification and categorization, it remains unclear why certain differences become salient but not others. Indeed, while Blumer places analytical primacy on groups, the focus lies on understanding how a sense of group position relates to prejudice once the groups are established. He does note, however, that the racial identification underlying racial prejudice "is not spontaneous or inevitable but a result of experience" (Blumer 1958:3) and assigns particular importance to collective and historical processes. Both identification per se and the central "sense of group position" are conceived of as historical products: as shaped and reshaped in a "complex human social and interpretative process" (Bobo 1999), a process in which abstract images, big events, political actors, and public discussions are more consequential than individual experiences and direct contact with other people (Blumer 1958). Still, why certain distinctions are assigned social meaning, while others are not, is not developed as a part of group threat theory.

Like Blumer, Link and Phelan stress the socially constructed nature of the categorizations underlying stigma. To underscore its basis in social processes, they use the word "label" instead of "attribute." Using "attribute," they argue, may signal that stigma is tied to a particular aspect of human difference. Using "label," on the other hand, suggests a less rigid and more socially negotiated basis, while simultaneously directing focus to the labeling, rather than the one labeled by others. Similar to group threat theory, to our knowledge, the stigma literature provides no further clues regarding why certain identities, attachments, and distinctions become socially relevant whereas others remain unimportant. Indeed, Link and Phelan (2001:368) end their discussion on distinguishing and labeling by saying:

> the critical sociological issue is to determine how culturally created categories arise and how they are sustained. Why are some human differences singled out and deemed salient by human groups and others ignored? What are the social, economic, and cultural forces that maintain the focus on a particular human difference?

Hierarchy, Stereotyping, and Alienation

A second aspect highlighted by both Blumer and Link and Phelan is the hierarchical ordering of various categories. The very starting point for Blumer is that prejudice should be understood as "a sense of group position." Besides tification, this also includes conceptions of how the groups are, and should be, positioned in relation to each other. Further, for prejudice to arise, this sense of intergroup ordering cannot be "about the same." Indeed, one of Blumer's four constitutive feelings is a self-assured sense "*of being naturally superior or better*" (Blumer 1958:4). Link and Phelan are also clear about stigma being contingent on unequal power relations. Although subordinate groups may be spiteful toward more powerful groups, the latter can never become "stigmatized." As long as they have the upper hand, in terms of political, social, and economic power, such processes will have limited bearing on their life chances. In this sense, all listed components of stigma must be exercised from higher up in the social hierarchy. This applies, for example, to the component of stigma which involves associating human differences with negative attributes, where the key is that "*dominant* cultural beliefs link labeled persons to undesirable characteristics—to negative stereotypes" (Link and Phelan 2001:367) [italics ours].

Further, both group threat theory (in Blumer's original formulation) and stigma (as specified by Link and Phelan) point to alienation and stereotyping as constitutive features. According to Blumer, the dominant group's feeling of superiority is often expressed in how members impute denouncing and degrading qualities to the subordinate group, including "laziness, dishonesty, greediness, unreliability, stupidity, deceit and immorality" (Blumer 1958:4). He also emphasizes that assigning qualities to another group conversely, or "by opposition," implies defining their own group, suggesting that stereotyping also plays into the second constitutive feeling; namely, that the subordinate group is different and alien. While Link and Phelan put greater emphasis on social cognition when discussing stereotyping, they also highlight how such images relate to the distancing of the labeled "them" from an unlabeled "us." Stereotyping facilitates alienation, since "they" clearly represents a different type, but stereotypes also become more likely to resonate if "they" already are perceived as intrinsically different.

Taken together, we note significant overlap in how both group threat theory and stigma emphasize stereotyping, alienation as well as a power imbalance between the perpetrator/target, and the stigmatizer/stigmatized. Interestingly, however, Link and Phelan strongly push power as the one thing that cannot be taken out from the equation. Stigma, in their words, "*is entirely dependent on social, economic and political power—it takes power to stigmatize*" (Link and Phelan 2001:375). Blumer, by contrast, claims that although feelings of superiority and distinctiveness can lead to negative feelings toward the subordinate group, they do not in themselves engender prejudice. For prejudice to arise, he argues, feelings of superiority and distinctiveness on behalf of the dominant group must be supplemented by a feeling of proprietary claim and a fear of encroachment. As evident in Table 3.1, the rows "resources" and "threat" are empty in the stigma column.

Resources and Threat

The stigma and group threat accounts differ as to the role played by resources and threat. According to Blumer, a third feeling that is always present in prejudice as a sense of group position is a feeling of entitlement; this means that the dominant group feels it has the exclusive or principal right to certain resources and areas of privilege. This may concern everything from rights to employment and land, the usage of cultural symbols, access to schools, or positions of power. As long as the claims are solidified and institutionalized in the sense that they are accepted and seen as "natural" by most members in society, they do not explain prejudice, not even in combination with feelings of distinctiveness and superiority. Instead, prejudice arises only when "a fear or apprehension that the subordinate racial group is threatening, or will threaten, the position of the dominant group" (Blumer 1958:4) is added to the other three feelings. Such a felt challenge to the dominant groups' sense of group position sets off an emotional reaction, or "recoil" in Blumer's words, which according to group threat theory is essential to prejudice.

While threat is key to prejudice as a sense of group position, it is not included in Link and Phelan's four constitutive elements of stigma.[1] As for the feeling of proprietary claim, the emphasis on unequal power relations implies that resources and privilege are central to stigma. However, within the framework of stigma, a power differential implies an objectively unequal distribution not only in resources but in the ability to act. This differs from access to resources, as Blumer describes it, as an "imperative" or feeling of "what ought to be" (Blumer 1958:5). It also ties in with a broader discussion on the very source of prejudice/stigma, to which we return in the final discussion.

Consequences

The remaining part of Table 3.1 describes what the different perspectives posit regarding the consequences of prejudice/stigma. As group threat theory (in Blumer's original formulation) is a theory that explains prejudice, no description of consequences has been listed. Like most theories of prejudice, Blumer's focus lies exclusively on the perpetrator (i.e., the people who hold prejudiced attitudes), with the goal of identifying the source of their antipathies. By contrast, stigma takes a broader view in that it focuses on the entire process. This makes it an overarching theoretical framework that encompasses the stigmatizer, stigmatization, and the stigmatized. Thus, Link and Phelan stress consequences as one of the four constitutive components of stigma. Specifically, they argue that stigma exists first when the labeling, differentiation, and stereotyping generate unequal outcomes: "People are stigmatized when the fact that they are labeled, set apart, and linked to undesirable characteristics leads them to experience status loss and discrimination" (Link and Phelan 2001:371).

1 This does not mean that threat is not central in specific stigma theories, e.g., in terror management theory (Solomon et al. 1991) or theory of identity threat (Steele 1997). Still, in Link and Phelan's definition, threat is not considered a constitutive element of stigma, which is a clear departure from the fundamental role it plays in prejudice according to group threat theory.

Discussion

In this chapter we have critically discussed the explanatory power of group threat theory in accounting for prejudice in the context of migration-generated diversity. We have also conceptually compared the constitutive features of prejudice, in Blumer's original group threat model, to stigma, as defined in Link and Phelan (2001). While certainly not exhaustive, this undertaking has begun to shed light on the extent to which the concept of stigma may be helpful in overcoming limitations associated with the application of group threat theory in studies of anti-immigrant prejudice. In this concluding section, we identify three areas where we see potential for advancement.

The first criticism addressed how most studies have tested a specific version of group threat theory, analytically equating "threat" with out-group size. The explanatory power of these models is limited, and they also imply a significant loss of nuance compared to Blumer's original writing. Thus, we believe that much is to be gained from pursuing group threat as an explanation of anti-immigrant attitudes with more sensitivity to the perceived nature as well as collective and historical roots of such feelings, as originally emphasized in Blumer (1958). These factors have attracted some interest in more recent studies (Bohman 2011; Strabac 2011), and we encourage future tests of group threat theory to follow suit. Our comparison reveals great similarities between Blumer's understanding of racial prejudice and stigma, as defined by Link and Phelan (2001), in terms of how both accounts emphasize the socially constructed nature of identities and categories ("labels"); thus, we consider the two perspectives to be *overlapping* rather than complementary in this regard. However, we also note that both group threat theory and stigma remain vague about why certain distinctions are assigned social meaning and not others.

In our second criticism, we argued that because group threat theory originally was developed to understand the relationship between two racial groups—a majority population and a historic national minority—applying the theory to understand anti-immigrant prejudice requires us to consider the heterogeneity of both the target and perpetrator groups. A group threat explanation of why some immigrant groups face more prejudice posits that they constitute a greater threat to the national majority. Meanwhile, if greater threat leads to more prejudice, by consequence, the largest, most powerful immigrant group should also face the most prejudice. This prediction is rarely confirmed in research that compares opposition toward specific immigrant or minority groups (Ford 2011; Spruyt and Elchardus 2012). While the nature of the threat may vary, in the sense that a group with limited economic or political power may still be considered a welfare or a cultural threat, group threat theory does not specify what determines when a given threat becomes activated. In fact, for many immigrant groups, this seems to be a matter of shifting goal posts, in the sense that there is always something threatening about their presence. This, in turn, suggests to us that their vulnerable position may have additional roots beyond threat, and may stem from, for instance, a stigmatized position. Thus, we identify this as one area where we believe the concept of stigma could be useful, *complementing* a group threat approach by shedding light on the stickiness of certain prejudices.

Relatedly, our third criticism points to a lack of theorizing in situations where threat is objectively diminishing; for instance, when immigration is halted due to the closure of national border, reversed at the local level due to the closure of a refugee center, or the result of structural integration. As an example of the latter, we referred to research on the integration paradox, which indicates that reduced (cultural) threat at least does not cancel out immigrants' experiences of being targets of prejudice. This relates to our discussion earlier on how some immigrant groups continuously appear to constitute a threat in the eyes of the native population, but it also raises a broader question about the role of threat. This question is by no means new (see Bobo 1983) but was made evident through our comparison (Table 3.1). Threat is the core component of group threat theory but has not been included in Link and Phelan's stigma model. According to Blumer, prejudice is first and foremost "a protective device" (Blumer 1958:5) that the dominant group adopts to preserve supremacy in the wake of a perceived challenge to their group position. As for the main motives behind stigma, Phelan et al. (2008) discuss three distinct functions, where the first is exploitation and domination. Stigma, in this sense, prevails because it serves the interests of more powerful groups by legitimizing and preserving the existing order (i.e., by keeping the stigmatized down). This, however, cannot be equated with threat, because the main driver on behalf of the dominant group is not a fear of losing one's privilege but rather a desire to maintain privilege and power. The difference compared to any threat model, in the words of Phelan et al. (2008:363), lies in "what is at stake for the perpetrators." In the case of perceived threat, a group feels vulnerable to a loss of power, whereas in the case of stigma the clear imbalance in power is what makes the act of stigmatizing even possible. It can also be understood in terms of a difference in emphasis between prejudice, as defined by Blumer (1958), and stigma, as understood by Link and Phelan (2001) and Phelan et al. (2008), concerning the extent to which prejudice/stigma (from the perspective of the perpetrator) is used primarily as a tool for the powerful or for the threatened. Here, we find that group threat and stigma imply *diverging* or even *conflicting* perspectives.

Our comparison has generated insights that should advance scholarship in both fields. Specifically, we believe that stigma may be useful in understanding how prejudice is related to other phenomena such as labeling, which in turn may provide important clues about the stickiness of such biases. This includes the idea that stigma may reinforce prejudice in ways that do not involve threat; for instance, through institutionalized bias and the persistence of stigma's other constitutive components (e.g., labeling, stereotyping, and alienation). In addition, we believe that group threat theory can be useful to stigma research; for instance, it may shed light on why levels of stigma vary due to the degree and type of threat that stigmatizers perceive. We encourage scholars who utilize a stigma framework to explore the ways in which group threat theory may further enhance their research.

4

The Conceptualizations, Causes, and Consequences of Stigma

Background for a Model of Migration-Generated Stigma

John E. Pachankis and Katie Wang

Abstract

To provide a foundation for understanding migration-generated stigma, existing theoretical and research accounts of general stigma processes are reviewed. Existing frameworks of stigma are discussed, including those that have organized stigma according to its social functions, evolutionary functions, and associated stereotype contents, and structural, interpersonal, and intrapersonal manifestations of stigma are reviewed. These manifestations impact numerous health outcomes through replaceable intervening mechanisms and make stigma a fundamental cause of poor health. Postulated causes and dimensional features of stigma are considered that highlight similarities and distinctions across diverse stigmatized characteristics. The application of existing theory and research is explored for the specific case of migration-generated stigma and several future research directions highlighted. By providing a broad overview of several decades' worth of theory and research into stigma, this chapter positions the field of migration-generated stigma to understand the nature and function of this particular form of stigma and pursue the most promising paths toward its reduction.

Organizational and Functional Frameworks of Stigma

As a sociopsychological process, stigma refers to the negative stereotyping, discrimination, and social, emotional, and physical separation that is directed toward individuals who possess a socially devalued mark (Crocker et al. 1998). Goffman, who initiated the formal study of stigma, noted that the stigmatized individual "is reduced in our minds from a whole and usual person to a tainted, discounted one" (Goffman 1963:3). Yet, lest the concept become overly encompassing of any trait deemed disagreeable or distasteful by any individual in any context, the sociological definition of stigma also requires that such stereotyping, labeling, and separation occur in societal systems of unequal power in which individuals possessing the devalued trait are deemed less worthy of, and given less access to, power than individuals who do not possess the trait. As a result of this power inequity between the stigmatized and nonstigmatized, stigma necessarily elicits material disadvantage, including lower access to the resources necessary for equal health, well-being, and life chances available to the nonstigmatized (Hatzenbuehler et al. 2013). When defined as such, it can be argued that stigma affects numerous populations, if not most individuals, at some point in the life course. Reflecting this possibility, Goffman (1963:129) noted: "The issue becomes not whether a person has experience with a stigma of his own, because he has, but rather how many varieties he has had his own experience with." Indeed, stigma encompasses numerous highly prevalent attributes, impactful identities, and health conditions, such as old age, obesity, mental illness, and migration status (Pachankis et al. 2018).

Given the magnitude and complexity of stigma's influence on societies and populations, various frameworks have been utilized to characterize and organize the forms and functions of stigma. For instance, Goffman (1963) organized manifestations of stigma into three categories: moral failings (e.g., mental illness), tribal blemishes (e.g., immigrant status), and body abominations (e.g., physical disabilities). He categorized stigma more broadly according to whether it can be considered to be automatically discredited in daily life (because it is visible) or discreditable (because it is concealable and would only become discredited if known). As reviewed below, later empirical research has validated the utility of these general categorizations for highlighting distinct social and evolutionary functions of various stigmas and distinct impacts on psychosocial well-being.

Various types of stigma have also been categorized in terms of their social functions (Phelan et al. 2008). For instance, some stigmas serve the social function of allowing the powerful to exploit and dominate a socially subordinated group for material gain. Stigma directed to race and ethnicity represents a clear example. Other stigmas serve the social function of allowing the dominant, power group to enforce the social norms that reflect and preserve their social positions and culture. Stigmas such as sexual and gender minority identities, polyamory, and nonmainstream political beliefs serve as examples. Still other stigmas serve to motivate avoidance of the threat of perceived disease. Research finds that this avoidance can be relatively nonspecific and even extend to nontransmissible conditions, including physical disabilities and overweight status. These three social function categories highlight what is at stake for the perpetrators of stigma; namely, loss of power, purpose, and health, respectively (Phelan et al. 2008).

The categorizations of stigma reviewed above overlap somewhat with the evolutionary functions that have been argued to underlie stigma (Kurzban and

Leary 2001; Schaller and Neuberg 2012). Specifically, the evolutionary argument suggests that stigma evolved to help us avoid high-risk social investments that could end with a high probability of being cheated out of resources, to strengthen the fitness of one's own group through the exploitation of other groups, and to avoid parasitic infection. These evolutionary functions correspond to Goffman's categorization of moral failings, tribal blemishes, and body abominations, respectively. According to the evolutionary view, these stigmas evolved to solve problems inherent to humans' sociality and operate through cognitive processes that facilitate social decision making.

Finally, the stereotype content model (Cuddy et al. 2007; Fiske et al. 2002) categorizes stereotypes—a key component of stigma—according to dimensions of warmth and competence. These dimensions stem from perceptions of a group's status and competitiveness; namely, perceptions of whether the group's goals pose harm or benefit and whether the group can achieve those goals. These combined perceptions predict distinct emotional and behavioral reactions toward the target group. For instance, groups perceived as warm and competent (e.g., the in-group, a society's reference group) elicit admiration and helping tendencies. Groups perceived as cold and incompetent (e.g., the homeless) elicit contempt and harm tendencies. Groups perceived as cold and competent (e.g., Asian Americans) elicit envy, passive helping (e.g., tolerance) tendencies, as well as active harm (e.g., exclusion) tendencies. Finally, groups perceived as warm and incompetent (e.g., the elderly) elicit pity, active helping tendencies (e.g., inclusion), and passive harm tendencies (e.g., neglect). These two dimensions—warmth and competence—are also likely functional in that the ability to discern these traits has been argued to facilitate social success and even survival (Major and O'Brien 2005). While various stigmatized populations can be categorized according to these two dimensions, with predictable emotional and behavioral reactions among the stigmatizers, all the above categorization systems can also predict the characteristic psychosocial experiences of individuals within various categories of stigma, as reviewed later in this chapter.

Structural, Interpersonal, and Intrapersonal Manifestations of Stigma

A common framework used to understand the nature and impact of stigma on the health and well-being of the stigmatized organizes stigma in terms of the socioecological levels in which it manifests. Here we summarize the socioecological model of stigma by focusing on three such levels: the structural, interpersonal, and intrapersonal.

Given that stigma ultimately relies on power inequities (Link and Phelan 2001), stigma can be argued to manifest most broadly in the form of laws, policies, and other levers of a society's allocation of rights and resources. This broadest form of stigma is known as structural stigma (Hatzenbuehler 2016). Taking advantage of geographic variability in laws, policies, and other indicators of structural inequality, researchers have sought to quantify the impact of that variability on the health and well-being of the stigmatized who live in those geographic areas. For instance, greater country-level structural stigma, in the form of aggregated anti-immigrant attitudes in one's current country of residence, is associated with lower access to health services among sexual minority male migrants who had moved to one of 38 European countries (Pachankis et al. 2017b). Among sexual minority individuals in general, greater structural stigma, in the form of country-level anti-sexual-minority laws, policies, and national attitudes across 44 countries, is associated with higher odds of depression and suicidality (Pachankis et al. 2021). Additional research establishing an association between structural stigma and health and well-being has relied on natural experiments showing that changes in structural stigma are associated with hypothesized changes in health and that this effect is specific to the target stigmatized group and operates through hypothesized mechanisms, such as social isolation, internalized stigma, and identity concealment (Hatzenbuehler 2016). Together, this research establishes the validity of the nature and impact of structural stigma.

On the interpersonal level, stigma is enacted through discriminatory behaviors indicative of unfair treatment based on one's membership in a socially disadvantaged group. In some contexts, these discriminatory behaviors manifest as blatant acts of hostility, such as police violence that disproportionately impacts African Americans (Hetey and Eberhardt 2018) and elevated levels of bullying and peer victimization facing sexual minority youths (Clark et al. 2020). In other contexts, discrimination manifests in more subtle forms, such as sitting farther away from the stigmatized person, making less eye contact, and terminating interactions prematurely (Hebl et al. 2002; Trawalter et al. 2009). Notably, interpersonal forms of stigma can also be perpetuated through seemingly positive behaviors, such as unsolicited, excessive offers of assistance often directed toward members of stigmatized groups stereotyped as warm and incompetent (e.g., people with physical disabilities; Wang et al. 2015) and compliments based on racial stereotypes (e.g., Blacks are good athletes; Czopp 2008). According to two meta-analyses encompassing individuals with a wide range of stigmatized identities, interpersonal forms of stigma have been linked to myriad physical and mental health outcomes, including a number of chronic health conditions (e.g., obesity, hypertension), depression, anxiety, sleep disturbance, and overall health-related quality of life (Pascoe and Smart Richman 2009; Schmitt et al. 2014).

Stigma also affects health and well-being via intrapersonal mechanisms such as the impact that stigma has on the thoughts (e.g., self-evaluation), emotions (e.g., anxiety), and behavioral reactions (e.g., avoidance) of the stigmatized. For instance, through social learning, a stigmatized person comes to predict how they will be treated in any given situation because of their stigmatized identity. Of course, various characteristics of the stigma (e.g., its concealability or visibility) determine this treatment and the resulting intrapersonal consequences (e.g., Smart and Wegner 1999). These expectancies shape the stigmatized individual's thoughts, emotions, and behaviors in any given social interaction and can lead the stigmatized individual to confirm these expectancies through nonconscious self-fulfilling mechanisms. For instance, experimental research into stereotype threat (Steele 1997) demonstrates that activation of common societal stereotypes can undermine the performance of stigmatized individuals in ways that confirm negative stereotypes about their group (Shih et al. 2002). Possessing a stigma can also undermine self-esteem or lead an individual to disengage their self-esteem from domains in which their group is expected to underperform (e.g., academic success; Crocker and Wolfe 2001). Another way in which stigma can undermine health and well-being is through yielding chronic, anxious expectations of stigma-based rejection (e.g., Mendoza-Denton et al. 2002). For instance, sexual minority individuals who experience parental and peer rejection report more expectations of future rejection toward their stigmatized identities (Pachankis et al. 2008). Ultimately, possessing a stigma can lead the individual to perceive that the threat in their environments outweighs their resources for coping with this threat, thereby generating excess stress and poorer health and well-being (Meyer 2003). As a result, stigma-related stress compounds the effects of general life stress to jeopardize disproportionately the health and well-being of the stigmatized compared to the nonstigmatized. In this way, stigma serves as a fundamental cause of poor health.

Stigma as a Fundamental Cause of Health Inequities

As we have illustrated thus far, stigma represents a major source of stress for a wide range of marginalized populations and disadvantages them through structural-, interpersonal-, and intrapersonal-level processes. To this end, it is not surprising that stigma has been increasingly recognized as a key driver of physical and mental health inequities along with other known social determinants of health (e.g., socioeconomic status). Drawing upon the fundamental cause theory (Link and Phelan 1995), Hatzenbuehler et al. (2013) posited stigma as a social factor that is persistently associated with multiple disease outcomes over time and across geographic locations, even though the intervening mechanisms underlying these associations might vary across contexts. Below, we highlight several pathways that link stigma to myriad adverse physical, mental, and behavioral health outcomes.

By definition, stigma undermines health via status loss and discrimination, thus hindering access to opportunities in important life domains. Specifically, substantial disparities in employment, housing, and health-care access have been documented among members from various stigmatized groups, including racial/ethnic minorities (Williams and Collins 2001), sexual and gender minorities (Downing and Rosenthal 2020), people with mental illnesses (Corrigan et al. 2012), and people with disabilities (Krahn et al. 2015). Ample evidence suggests that stigmatized individuals, especially those with disabilities and chronic physical/mental illnesses, are disproportionately impacted by social isolation (Chou and Chronister 2011; Tough et al. 2017). Taken together, these inequalities restrict stigmatized individuals' access to flexible resources (i.e., knowledge, money, power, prestige, and beneficial social connections) that can be deployed to avoid health threats and maximize health benefits. For instance, poverty and residential segregation may limit stigmatized individuals' access to healthy food, preventative care, and transportation and put them at greater risk to develop chronic medical conditions, such as cardiovascular disease, cancer, and diabetes (Dovidio et al. 2018) as well as infectious diseases, such as HIV and COVID-19 (Pareek et al. 2020).

In addition to thwarting access to flexible resources, stigma also compromises health by exposing individuals to elevated levels of stress. Both minority stress theory (Meyer 2003) and identity threat models of stigma (Steele et al. 2002) posit that possessing a stigmatized identity increases exposure to stressful situations, including external events (i.e., experiences of discrimination) and internal events (e.g., fear of being stereotyped or rejected). Experimental studies have shown that the stress associated with experiencing enacted and anticipated stigma can trigger a host of cognitive, affective, and physiological responses, including hypervigilance, negative emotions (e.g., anger, anxiety), and increases in blood pressure and cortisol (Guyll et al. 2001; Townsend et al. 2011). When chronically activated, these stress responses can undermine both physical and mental health, exacerbating cardiovascular disease risk and driving symptoms of depression and anxiety (Major et al. 2013).

Given the myriad challenges associated with stigma, it is not surprising that the act of contending with stigma-related experiences can also compromise health by hindering adaptive psychological responses to stress, such as self-regulation. As noted by Inzlicht et al. (2006), stigmatized individuals use and deplete executive resources to manage their socially devalued identities, leaving them less able than their nonstigmatized counterparts to monitor and regulate their emotions effectively. A daily diary study, for example, showed that both sexual and racial/ethnic minority participants were more inclined to engage in maladaptive emotion regulation strategies, such as rumination (i.e., passively and repetitively focusing on one's problems and their causes) and suppression (i.e., inhibiting emotion-expressive behaviors), on those days when they experienced stigma-related stressors (Hatzenbuehler et al. 2009b). In other studies, encompassing individuals with a wide range of stigmatized identities, chronic exposure to stigma has been linked to deficits in emotion regulation abilities (e.g., ability to understand and accept one's emotions), which were in turn associated with adverse mental and behavioral health outcomes such as depression, anxiety, and substance use (Burton et al. 2018; Pachankis et al. 2015; Rendina et al. 2017; Wang et al. 2018).

In sum, a straightforward evidence base supports the role of stigma as a fundamental cause of health inequities. Specifically, stigma has been shown to influence multiple physical and mental health outcomes by disrupting access to flexible resources, increasing stress exposure, and hindering adaptive coping responses such as self-regulation. This theoretical framework highlights the pervasive impact of stigma on population health. To capture the full impact of a given stigmatized identity, such as migration, on health, it is important to consider the impact of migration-related stigma across multiple mechanisms and outcomes, as well as how other intersecting identities (e.g., race/ethnicity, sexual orientation) might shape the experience of migration stigma. Since stigma, by definition, entails power differentials between socially dominant versus marginalized groups, the reduction of health inequities can be particularly challenging, given that stigma operates through varying intervening mechanisms and outcomes that are seemingly designed to evade progress toward health equity. As such, the theoretical framework summarized here underscores the importance of attending to stigma, along with other social determinants of health, in the development and implementation of effective public health interventions.

Causes of Stigma

While the nature of stigma can be discerned through its multilevel manifestations and impacts, it can also be understood by examining its underlying causes. Although stigma is ultimately a social process, the search for the causes of stigma tends to focus on processes within the individual, including personality traits, cognitive processing, fears of one's own mortality, evolutionary adaptive threat detection, or psychological preferences to maintain a predictable social order. Thus, the question, "Why do humans stigmatize?" has been answered in several ways:

1. Some humans possess a prejudiced personality (Adorno et al. 1950; Altemeyer 1981; Sidanius and Pratto 1999).
2. Stigma facilitates cognitive efficiency (Macrae et al. 1994).
3. Stigma helps stave off the specter of human mortality (Rosenblatt et al. 1989).
4. Stigma represents an evolved functional means to avoid disease (Schaller and Neuberg 2012).
5. Stigma is motivated by desire to maintain beliefs in a just, predictable world (Jost and Banaji 1994).

Below we review the theory and evidence for each of these possibilities.

Perhaps the earliest of the proposed causes of why people stigmatize each other—the prejudiced personality—was pursued in the postwar environment by European social scientists and intellectuals from the Frankfurt School who were motivated to explain anti-Semitism and fascism. Relying on psychoanalytic understandings of human development, Theodor Adorno and colleagues (1950) hypothesized the "authoritarian personality," posited to reflect deference toward authority figures resulting from overly punitive parental punishment and the subsequent displaced anger toward one's parents and suppressed homosexuality. Adorno developed a multi-item scale to capture the nine traits proposed to underlie authoritarian leanings, such as submission to authority and perception of the world as dangerous. Reflecting the popularity of personality-driven conceptualizations of stigma, Gordon Allport (1954) noted in his classic text on prejudice: "prejudice is basically a trait of personality" (Altemeyer 1981:73). Yet around the same time, the validity of Adorno's scale was found to be psychometrically lacking and was further called into question by its biased participant sampling and item wording. Nevertheless, this early work inspired subsequent studies that examined two of the traits proposed by Adorno—right-wing authoritarianism (Altemeyer 1981) and social dominance orientation (Sidanius and Pratto 1999)—measured with psychometrically reliable instruments predictive of a range of intergroup phenomena (as reviewed in Sibley and Duckitt 2008). More recent research, however, has suggested that because these factors are not strongly predictive of behavior, they represent something closer to social attitudes rather than personality traits and are themselves predicted by personality traits and socialization experiences (Sibley and Duckitt 2008).

The next purported cause of stigma is its functional role in cognitive processing. Specifically, research shows that stereotypes operate as mental "energy-saving" devices by freeing up cognitive resources for optimal navigation of complex, information-heavy worlds (Macrae et al. 1994). Indeed, perceiving others by attending to their specific, individuating attributes requires more mental energy and time than relying on their simple category membership (Fiske and Neuberg 1990; Fiske and Pavelchak 1986). Research suggests that stereotypes are more accessible under mentally demanding conditions and that people become more efficient at completing a cognitive task (e.g., reading) when presented with stereotypic information during a simultaneous impression formation task (Macrae et al. 1994). Notably, this type of reliance on stereotyping is unintentional and occurs subconsciously (Bargh 1989). However, reliance on stereotypes is not a universal, or even necessarily automatic, process. Indeed, a person's motivation, goals, values, and social accountability pressures can steer them toward engaging in more resource-intensive attentional processes, such as attribute-based impression formation instead of simple reliance on category membership (e.g., Neuberg and Fiske 1987).

A third hypothesized cause of stigma is offered by terror management theory (Ernest 1973; Solomon et al. 1991). Terror management theory relies on the proposition that humans are unique in being cognizant of their own mortality, of the fact that they are nothing more than "an ambulatory assemblage of blood, tissue, and guts, inherently no more significant or enduring than a barnacle, a beetle, or a bell pepper" (Solomon et al. 2000:200). As a result of this terrifying awareness, humans rely on cultural systems to provide collective meaning and purpose and ultimately the promise of immortality. Religious institutions often communicate a promise of immortality directly. At the same time, terror management theory argues that all culturally imbued practices, including formal (e.g., the arts) and daily (e.g., work) enactments of culture, serve to keep humans removed from the specter of their mortality. Humans collectively and personally defend their specific cultural systems from attack, especially from distinct systems that might call into question the validity of one's own culture. These defenses can manifest in war and other forms of extreme collective sacrifice, argued to match the extremeness of the psychological threat to one's immortality. Evidence supporting terror management theory comes from experiments in which mortality primes greater liking for people who possess similar worldviews as oneself and threat and hostility toward people who possess alternate worldviews (e.g., Greenberg et al. 1997; McGregor et al. 1998).

Stigma has also been argued to have evolutionary origins (Schaller and Neuberg 2012). Evolutionary arguments specifically suggest that distinct prejudices and their associated affective (e.g., fear, disgust) and behavioral (e.g., avoidance, poor treatment) action tendencies have a genetic basis that emerged from ancestral environments in which such tendencies were adaptive. These tendencies are argued to have increased reproductive fitness in the ancestral environment even if today they might often lead to more social harm than good. Perhaps the clearest evidence for the evolutionary cause of stigma comes from studies which show that distinct types of threats give rise to distinct types of prejudicial responses (e.g., Cottrell and Neuberg 2005) and the existence of discrimination-like behavior among nonhuman primates (e.g., Goodall 1986). Ancestral threats mostly involved interpersonal hostility, infectious disease, and being cheated out of resources. Therefore, natural selection produced psychological mechanisms that allow for quick detection and avoidance of these threats that thereby confer evolutionary advantage (Neuberg et al. 2011). These threat-detection mechanisms persist today and, depending on the environment, can err on the side of caution and produce overgeneralized threat perceptions and associated responses. For instance, the "behavioral immune system," argued to have originally evolved to help humans avoid infectious disease, often yields overgeneralized false positives, including extension to avoidance of immigrants and people who are overweight (Schaller and Park 2011). The evolutionary argument for stigma extends and refines the personality argument by suggesting that, although associations exist between personality traits such as social dominance orientation (a general type of threat tendency associated with preference for traditional hierarchies) and prejudice, this association can be better explained by the association between more specific types of threat (e.g., possible infection) that give rise to distinct types of prejudice (e.g., avoidance of certain physical traits).

The final hypothesized cause of stigma is guided by system justification theory (Jost and Banaji 1994; Jost et al. 2004), which posits that people's need for predictable social order often supersedes their own and their group's self-interest. Support for system justification theory comes from numerous experimental and observational studies finding that people do, in fact, seek to uphold the existing social order, even if that order actively disadvantages or oppresses one's own stigmatized group (e.g., Jost et al. 2003; Newman 2002). This desire is reflected most strongly in implicit, compared to explicit, attitudes, which among the stigmatized manifests as implicit internalized stigma such as implicit favoritism of heterosexuals among sexual minorities or Whites among African Americans (Nosek et al. 2002). Paradoxically, justification of the status quo is often stronger among those who are most oppressed by it; namely, the stigmatized (Jost et al. 2004). In this way, rather than explaining stigma solely as a matter of a dominant group imposing its will on subordinated stigmatized group, system justification theory highlights the role of the stigmatized in maintaining the social order. Indeed, it has been argued that across human history, individuals and societies have sought to maintain the status quo more than they have sought to revolt and rise up even in the face of extreme oppression (Zinn 1968). At the same time, system justification theory proposes that individuals will advocate for social change when their needs for self- and group esteem override their needs to maintain the existing social order. Given the strength of needs for self- and group esteem, such advocacy is argued to be relatively rare.

Variations among Stigmatized Attributes

In addition to the overarching antecedents and consequences of stigma across various socially devalued groups discussed above, it is important to acknowledge that each stigmatized attribute is associated with a distinct set of perceptions and experiences. Indeed, since the field's inception, stigma researchers have been developing systematic frameworks to organize myriad stigmatized identities, conditions, and attributes along shared dimensions. Such dimensional conceptualizations of stigma serve two important goals. First, they help elucidate the diverse social and health implications of stigma across different stigmatized groups by identifying the most relevant dimensional correlates with negative interpersonal and health outcomes. Second, they allow researchers to determine the generalizability of findings from one stigma to another based on their similarities and differences in dimensional ratings, thereby maximizing scarce research resources and facilitating information exchange among stigma researchers. In this section, we highlight one of the most prominent dimensional taxonomies in the stigma literature and describe its utility in quantifying the variations among stigmatized attributes.

In their pioneering book, *Social Stigma: The Psychology of Marked Relationships*, Jones et al. (1984) outlined six dimensions along which all stigmas are expected to vary:

1. Concealability (the extent to which a stigma is visible to others),
2. Course (the extent to which a stigma persists over time),
3. Disruptiveness (the extent to which a stigma interferes with smooth social interactions),
4. Aesthetics (the potential for a stigma to evoke a disgust reaction),
5. Origin (the extent to which the onset of a stigma is believed to be controllable), and
6. Peril (the extent to which a stigma poses a personal threat or potential for contagion).

Using this theoretical framework, previous research has examined how each of these six dimensions relates to the perceptions and experiences of stigmatized individuals, with concealability and origin having received the most empirical attention.

Regarding concealability, individuals with concealable stigmas have been shown to utilize less social support to cope with stigma-related stressors, feel greater social isolation, and experience more adverse psychological outcomes, such as greater negative affect and lower self-esteem (for a review, see Chaudoir et al. 2013; Frable et al. 1998; Hatzenbuehler et al. 2009b). At the same time, however, concealability can be beneficial as it may enable individuals to pass as "normal," thus avoiding prejudice and discrimination in less supportive environments. Among HIV-positive individuals, for example, those with visible symptoms reported more stigmatizing experiences and greater psychological distress than those without visible symptoms (Stutterheim et al. 2011). Relatedly, children with congenital heart disease were better adjusted than children with facial scars, even though the former group actually experienced greater functional limitations than the latter (Goldberg 1974).

Regarding origin, stigmas perceived to be uncontrollable at onset (e.g., physical disabilities, cancer) tend to elicit pity and helping behaviors, whereas stigmas perceived to be controllable (e.g., obesity, HIV) tend to elicit hostility and behavioral avoidance (Weiner et al. 1988). Onset controllability was also identified as a key dimension in predicting social rejection toward individuals with various physical and mental illnesses (e.g., Crandall and Moriarty 1995; Feldman and Crandall 2007; Hebl and Kleck 2002). Recent research on mental illness stigma, however, has demonstrated that attributing mental illnesses to biological causes, such as neurochemical imbalances and genetic abnormalities, can be problematic. Specifically, although these explanations might reduce personal blame, they can exacerbate other aspects of stigma by enhancing the public perceptions of mental illnesses as severe and persistent (Phelan

2005) and contributing to pessimism about one's prognosis among individuals affected by mental illnesses (Lebowitz 2014).

Integrating prior research, Pachankis et al. (2018) developed and validated a taxonomy that organized 93 stigmatized attributes along all six dimensions, with the goal of better understanding the individual and joint impact of stigma dimensions on social perceptions and health. Among both stigma experts and members of the general public, greater desired social distance was associated with those stigmas that were perceived to be more disruptive, perilous, aesthetically unappealing, and onset controllable. Relatedly, among individuals who endorsed a wide range of stigmas, disruptiveness was most strongly associated with poor mental health and overall well-being. Pachankis et al. proposed that each stigmatized attribute can be located within one of five clusters characterized by a unique dimensional fingerprint with distinct relationships to social perceptions and health. Notably, stigmas that are highly visible, highly disruptive, and persistent in course (e.g., physical disabilities; the "awkward" cluster), as well as stigmas that are highly perilous, onset controllable, and aesthetically unappealing (i.e., HIV, substance use; the "threatening" cluster), were associated with more frequent experiences of discrimination and higher levels of health impairment compared with other stigmatized attributes.

Taken together, the research reviewed here provides compelling evidence for the utility of applying a dimensional framework to the study of migration-generated stigma. Given that migrants represent diverse racial/ethnic groups, nations of origin, and cultural backgrounds, a dimensional framework would help quantify these heterogeneous experiences and elucidate health discrepancies across different migrant groups. Additionally, noting that migration often intersects with other marginalized identities (e.g., membership in racial/ethnic minority groups, low socioeconomic status), a dimensional framework can advance the understanding of these intersectional experiences, both by enabling researchers to compare the health-compromising effects of individual stigmas with one another and by fostering innovative quantitative solutions for capturing intersectionality when predicting health (e.g., aggregating dimensional ratings across all stigmas endorsed by an individual, weighting more heavily those stigmas that are considered to be more personally impactful).

Application of Stigma Concepts to Migration-Generated Stigma

The conceptual models and categorical frameworks reviewed above can be usefully applied to increase our understanding of stigma directed toward migrants, including its nature, function, and impact on the health of migrant populations. Indeed, in applying predictions of these models and frameworks to migration-generated stigma, existing research has identified theoretically derived predictors of migration-generated stigma and located migration-generated stigma across socioecological levels. It also suggests that migration-generated stigma fundamentally causes adverse health for migrants, serves specific social and perhaps evolutionary functions, and locates this stigma within dimensional classifications.

In the framework by Goffman (1963), stigma toward migrants would be classified as a tribal blemish, given that migrant status is commonly attached to a particular race, ethnicity, religion, and/or ideology. According to the evolutionary framework, research finds that stigma toward migrants is related to fears of infectious disease threat and the behavioral immune system (Faulkner et al. 2004). However, when considering the social function of migration-related stigma, it is possible that stigma toward migrants emanates not only from a hyperactive disease avoidance mechanism but also serves to reinforce in-group dominance, exploiting and enforcing its cultural norms onto migrants.

Research that applies the stereotype content model to stigma suggests that the type of stigma directed toward migrants might depend on the perceived traits of particular migrant groups. This research recognizes that not all migrant groups are stigmatized equally. For instance, migrant groups perceived as high competence and low warmth elicit envy whereas those perceived as low competence and high warmth elicit pity (Caprariello et al. 2009). Of course, how migrants are perceived and categorized in these frameworks is ultimately a function of the social structures to which they arrive.

Stigma toward migrants has been shown to manifest across structural, interpersonal, and intrapersonal levels. For instance, the implementation of anti-immigrant laws and policies have been shown to influence health outcomes such as missed primary care appointments and increased emergency department visits (e.g., Samuels et al. 2021) as well as anxiety (Frost 2020). Further, experiences of interpersonal discrimination have been linked to poorer self-rated physical health, psychological well-being, and health risk behaviors, such as substance use (Chen 2013; Jasinskaja-Lahti et al. 2006; Lin et al. 2011). Although less research has directly examined the intrapersonal manifestations of migration-related stigma, perceived pressure to assimilate into the culture of one's destination country, which can be conceptualized as one facet of anticipated stigma, was negatively associated with life satisfaction among migrants who valued conformity (Roccas et al. 2000). Consistent with the fundamental cause theory discussed above, stigma toward migrants has been shown to influence a wide range of physical and mental health outcomes by disrupting access to flexible resources (e.g., social capital; Chen et al. 2011), thereby making migration-generated stigma a fundamental cause of health inequities facing this population.

Research has found support for the applicability of various causal models of stigma to stigma toward migrants specifically. For instance, drawing upon the notion of the prejudiced personality, research has found that various personality traits (e.g., narcissism, psychopathy, low openness) predict right-wing authoritarianisms and social dominance orientation, which in turn predict anti-immigrant stigma (Hodson et al. 2009). Some of the predictions of terror management theory, as applied to migrant-generated stigma, also find empirical support. For instance, mortality salience has been shown to generate more negative evaluations of immigrants among people high in right-wing authoritarianism, but more positive evaluations for people low in right-wing authoritarianism (Weise et al. 2012). Further, mortality salience has been shown to affect evaluations of undocumented immigrants depending on whether the immigrant is from a culturally familiar versus less familiar country (Bassett and Connelly 2011). In support of disease avoidance mechanisms being generally applied to migrants, research has found that perceived vulnerability to disease predicts negative reactions only to subjectively "foreign" people, but not subjectively to familiar people (Faulkner et al. 2004). In further support of this notion, COVID-19 pandemic threat exposure in 105 European regions was shown to be associated with more negative attitudes toward immigrants (Freitag and Hofstetter 2022).

Finally, in terms of locating migrant-generated stigma along the various dimensional features of stigma, research has shown that how migrants are perceived varies depending on the specific group to which they belong. For instance, in the United States, people who are Latinx, South Asian, and Middle Eastern are perceived to possess a highly visible status with a persistent course but low disruptiveness, peril, and onset controllability. By contrast, Muslims are perceived to possess a relatively perilous, concealed, and onset-controllable status (Pachankis et al. 2018). Similarly, research applying the stereotype content model to migrant-generated stigma finds variation across migrant groups: Arabic populations in the United States are perceived as low in competence and warmth; British, Jewish, and Asian populations are perceived as being high in competence but low in warmth; and Irish people are perceived as being high in competence and warmth (e.g., Cuddy et al. 2007).

Conclusion

The study of migration-related stigma can be enhanced by applying several decades' worth of theory and research into stigma, including its conceptual frameworks, multilevel manifestations, mechanisms, causes, and variations. To the extent that future scholarship draws upon this existing foundation, remaining questions about the specific form and function of migration-related stigma can be formulated and informed solutions posed to speed its reduction. To this end, the following topics are highlighted for future study:

- Determine the societal and personal characteristics, and their interactions that predict migration-related stigma.
- Establish the temporal and spatial conditions under which migration-related stigma is strongest.

- Ascertain the extent to which migration-related stigma is similar to or distinct from other stigmatized conditions in terms of its multilevel determinants.
- Identify variations within and across migrant populations, including along established dimensional features of stigma, that predict different manifestations of migration-related stigma.
- Determine the specific causes of migration-related stigma that can be addressed through mechanistically informed interventions.

The existing body of stigma theory and research reviewed here, even if not always specifically referencing migration-related stigma, lays a solid foundation for scholars to advance understandings and solutions of stigma as it directly affects migrant populations.

Acknowledgments

The authors would like to acknowledge Jared Selby's support with manuscript preparation.

5

Migration, Stigma, and Lived Experiences

A Conceptual Framework for Centering Lived Experiences

San Juanita García, Tomás R. Jiménez, Seth M. Holmes, Irena Kogan, Anders Vassenden, Lawrence H. Yang, and Min Zhou

Abstract

This chapter explores the lived experiences of immigrants, the stigma processes they confront, and the response mechanisms that they use to counteract and challenge stigma. It introduces a multilevel conceptual framework to further understanding of the lived experience of and resistance to stigma among immigrant groups. Drawing heavily on migration studies, which often highlight lived experiences of stigma without referencing the concept by name, it is argued that the stigma concept can enrich our understanding of immigrants' lived experiences. The stigma literature provides abundant examples of how members of diverse and minoritized groups experience stigmatization and the consequences this creates for people's life chances (e.g., mental health, physical health, education, employment, housing segregation). A typology is created to highlight how immigrants become aware of, respond to, and affect stigmatization. This typology is then incorporated into macro and meso frameworks to emphasize the multiple forces that act upon stigma among immigrant groups. Focusing on immigrants' lived experiences enables us to understand how immigrants confront and challenge stigma.

> The understanding [*Verstehen*] of other persons and their expressions of life is based upon both the lived experience [*Erlebens*] and understanding of oneself, and their continual interaction. —Wilhelm Dilthey (1927:123)

Introduction

To cultivate *Verstehen,* or an understanding of others, requires us to focus on actual lived experiences; only then can we make sense of how people understand themselves and their social universe. To put oneself in the shoes of others, to gain an understanding from others' perspectives, is what Wilhelm Dilthey (1927) argued is the foundation needed to advance the "human sciences." Dilthey advocated for experiencing the lives of others and interpreting the meaning of how people make sense of their lived experiences. Applying that lens to the lived experience of immigrants helps us to appreciate not only their humanity but the value which they bring to receiving countries (Haney-López 2018; Johnson 2004). Centering immigrants' lived experiences highlights the multifaceted reasons for emigrating, how immigrants make sense of their lives in new contexts, and how immigrants share with others what they have learned from their own triumphs and struggles at all phases of their immigration and integration journeys. Learning from immigrants' lived experiences also shows how the receiving society, including dominant groups, government policies, and social institutions, sometimes stigmatize immigrant and minoritized communities. Centering immigrants' lived experiences brings into relief the stigma processes that they confront. Asking which immigrants are welcomed, which are deported and excluded, provides a few emblematic examples of who is deemed "deserving" to join the receiving society.

A key aspect of the lived experience concerns stigma, or the "the co-occurrence of labeling, stereotyping, separation, status loss, and discrimination" (Link and Phelan 2001:363). Drawing upon our own research and reading of the literatures on migration and stigma, which often speak past each other, we develop a multilevel conceptual framework and create a typology of the lived experience of stigma and resistance to stigma among immigrant groups. Further, we explore how strategies of resistance may act on stigma itself. The frameworks that we develop make explicit the processes to which migration scholars allude to, but seldom articulate. By delineating these processes, we hope to provide a set of conceptual and theoretical tools for social scientists to better understand the lived experience of immigrants.

Stigma and the Lived Experience

The "lived experience" of immigrants, or any group for that matter, can be thought of as "the felt flow of engagements in a local world" (Yang et al. 2007:1528). Local worlds are the realms of human experience where dominant and subordinate groups interact and where moral standing is sought or lost (Kleinman and Hall-Clifford 2009). In the context of migration, a local world refers to a circumscribed domain within which the everyday life activities of immigrants take place. This could be a tight knit social network or neighborhood community by which immigrants arrive to the receiving society. Daily life matters and is deeply held by participants of local worlds. What defines all local worlds, including those of immigrants, is the fact that something is gained or lost, such as status, money, health, good fortune, a job, or relationships. This feature of daily life (what Kleinman calls "moral experience") refers to how people assign meaning and value to "what matters most" or "what is most at stake" (Kleinman 1999, 2006; Kleinman et al. 1997). For example, among a sample of primarily undocumented Chinese immigrants with psychosis, engaging in employment as a strategy to perpetuate the lineage reflected achievement of "what matters most" in this cultural group (Yang et al. 2014). These everyday lived experiences can be used to identify what is most valued within particular immigrant groups. We argue that the importance of lived experience within local moral worlds is of primary concern for understanding the process of stigmatization and its diverse experiences among immigrant groups—both of stigmatizing and of being stigmatized.

Stigma is central to local moral worlds. Goffman's (1963) classic formulation of stigma as "an attribute that is deeply discrediting" (p. 3) emphasizes that stigma is a concept "between an attribute and a stereotype" (p. 4). To understand immigrants' lived experiences of stigma, we view stigma beyond a "mark," "stain," or "blemish" on an individual's character, as Goffman (1963) originally conceptualized. Instead, we understand stigma as a social process involving "the co-occurrence of labeling, stereotyping, separation, status loss, and discrimination" (Link and Phelan 2001:363). Link and Phelan (2001) conceptualize stigma as an "umbrella concept" that encapsulates interrelated processes within contexts of power.[1] Exerting power, or "the capacity to keep people down, in and/or away," through stigma-related processes (Link and Phelan 2014:30) exposes those with power as having an ability to stigmatize others. By power, Link and Phelan (2014) refer to people's ability to exercise their will, regardless of any resistance they may encounter. The role power plays in stigma shifts attention from individual attributes toward critically asking how stigma is produced, by whom, and for what purposes (Tyler and Slater 2018).

As we focus on immigrants' lived experiences, we recognize the role stigma power plays in keeping immigrants down, in, and away as they navigate life in new host countries. The stigma domains identified by Link and Phelan can also be seen to relate to "what matters most," or the core daily engagements that are most at stake for a particular immigrant group. Yet to our knowledge, the complex interrelationships between differing components of stigma, immigration processes, and the lived experience of being in an immigrant group have yet to be fully elucidated. We argue that spotlighting power in the exertion of stigma processes is an opportunity to center immigrants' lived experiences beyond micro-level (individual/interactional) stigma processes. This moves us toward connecting immigrants' lived experiences to the role that institutional

1 Goffman conceptualized three main stigmas: (a) physical disfigurements, (b) "blemishes of individual character," and (c) "tribal stigma of race, nation, and religion, these [3] being stigmas that can be transmitted through lineages and equally contaminate all members of a family" (Goffman 1963:14).

and discursive frameworks play in shaping immigrants' lived experiences of stigma and their responses to stigma.

Migration and the Lived Experiences of Stigma: A Conceptual Framework

Notwithstanding that many authors have used Goffman's stigma theory in studies in migration contexts (e.g., Handulle and Vassenden 2021; Harris and Karimshah 2019), stigma, as a concept, has been applied more widely to psychology, and to stigmatized conditions generally, than to the study of international migration (Schuster and Majidi 2015). In the initial stages of stigma research, this literature often emphasized micro-level interactions among groups or individuals. In fact, this literature was commonly criticized as being too individually focused and as overlooking structural processes undergirding the links between stigma, stereotyping, prejudice, and discrimination, which have since been addressed in subsequent conceptualizations of stigma (Link and Phelan 2001).

In migration studies, the host society in a migrant receiving country is largely defined by the "context of reception" (Portes and Zhou 1993), which shapes processes of integration. The context of reception is made up of multilayered policies, institutions, and public attitudes toward newcomers in host societies and intersects with individual characteristics to influence immigrants' everyday lived experiences. The context of reception affects how immigrants fare culturally and socioeconomically as well as how they respond to, resist, and overcome adversity associated with immigrant disadvantages (Zhou 1997).

Contemporary stigma research takes a complementary perspective in examining the structural processes that impinge upon the individual's experience and life chances. Stigma encompasses not only perceptions and attitudes but also how laws, policies, and practices may lead to systematic disadvantage for groups (Hatzenbuehler 2016). Insights from both the migration and stigma literatures deepen our understanding of the lived experiences of immigrants. Drawing on these, we construct macro- and meso-level frameworks that form the basis of a typology of the lived experience of immigrants and their responses to stigma.

Macro-Level Processes

Figure 5.1 lays out our proposed conceptual framework of the lived experiences of stigma among immigrant groups and individual members within the structure of the host society (Figure 5.1, bottom). This structure is embedded in the receiving country's social class and racial hierarchies that define the contexts of reception, or multilevel institutions and cultural milieus (Portes and Rumbaut 2014). At the macro level are the economy (the labor market) and

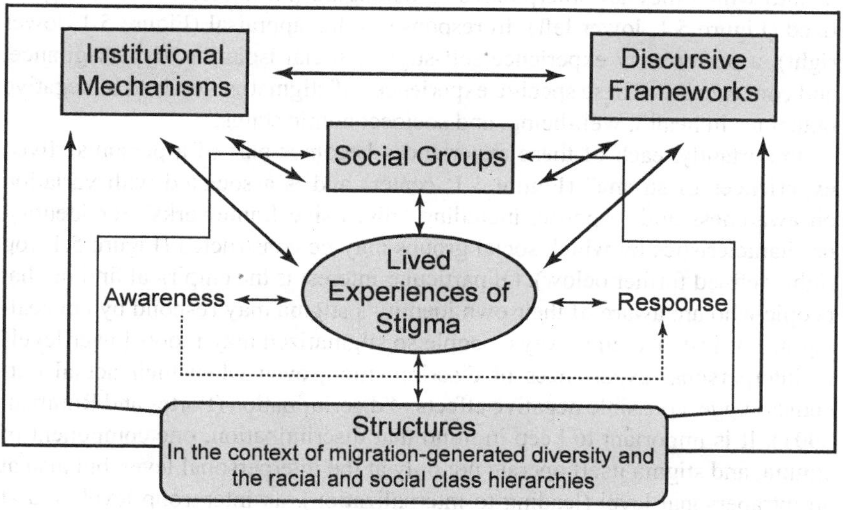

Figure 5.1 The lived experiences of stigma in context.

the state (immigration and integration policies, education, welfare, health care, and criminal justice systems). At the meso level are civil society institutions and established existing ethnic communities. At the micro level are expressions of prejudice toward immigrants and patterns of intergroup interactions. The context of reception is unique to an immigrant group and shared by all members of the group, regardless of their individual socioeconomic characteristics, leading to varied modes of incorporation and divergent socioeconomic outcomes of different immigrant groups.

Group-based stereotypes affect the "lived experiences" of immigrant group members differently. Hatzenbuehler's (2016) formulation of structural stigma describes the ways that stigmatization is produced or inflected by broader institutional mechanisms (Figure 5.1, top left), or institutions and structures. Hatzenbuehler (2016:742) defines structural stigma as "societal-level conditions, cultural norms, and institutional policies that constrain the opportunities, resources, and well-being of the stigmatized." For Hatzenbuehler there are two primary types of mechanisms through which structural stigma affects outcomes in health, well-being, and socioeconomic status. The first set of mechanisms are resource focused and may relate to education, labor market position, and access to specific resources (e.g., health care). Each mechanism, in turn, affects the daily lived experience of stigmatized individuals regarding their options for "making a livable life," supporting their family, improving the conditions in which they live and work, and their ability to engage in everyday life activities (i.e., "what matters most"). The second set of mechanisms relates to appraisal; that is, how aware someone is that the group to which they belong or into which they are interpolated as belonging (Althusser 1971) is stigmatized (Figure 5.1, lower left). In response to this appraisal (Figure 5.1, lower right), a person may experience self-stigma, social isolation, hypervigilance, and concealment. These specific experiences of stigmatization lead to negative outcomes in health, well-being, and socioeconomic status.

Importantly, each of these experiences becomes part of a person's "lived experiences of stigma" (Figure 5.1, center) and is associated with variation on awareness and response, including "discursive frameworks" for identity, or characteristics by which social groups may be constructed (Figure 5.1, top right, defined further below). Of particular interest is the empirical finding that people who are aware of their own identity's stigma may respond by concealing it. For instance, in surveys, people so stigmatized may report lower levels of interpersonal experiences of discrimination, even when their actual outcomes suggest possible negative effects of discrimination (Portes and Rumbaut 2001). It is important to keep in mind that discrimination, one component of stigma, and stigma itself operate not only at the interpersonal level, but also at an intrapersonal level (leading to internalization), an intergroup level, and at structural and institutional levels.

Meso-Level Processes

In our proposed framework, social groups are at the center of meso-level processes (Figure 5.2, center). Defined as networks of people who interact and rely on each other, social groups enact "what matters most" in their everyday lives and interactions (Yang et al. 2014). Social groups may or may not form around identity categories or statuses (e.g., ethnicity, religion, race, nationhood, culture), which we refer to as "discursive frameworks of identity" (Figure 5.2, far right). How people view themselves in regard to these statuses influences their local social worlds, although often not in ways that outsiders might anticipate. How groups are defined by others also draws from the same discursive frameworks of identity. Prejudice and stereotypes of specific groups, which may be positive or negative in value and lend themselves to stigmatization, draw from a collective "pool" of discursive ideas about statuses. Here, concealability factors are profound. In various situations, immigrants may be able to avoid classification, whereas others will not. Examples of dimensions that determine concealability include race, (visible) religious characteristics, language, and names.

Discursive frameworks of identity differ cross-nationally. In the United States, against a backdrop of distinct racial hierarchies, race is the primary classificatory scheme through which newcomers and established social groups will be defined by others (and come to see themselves). In Europe, race is a dominant factor, but religion constitutes a more important boundary than in the United States. Identifications and classifications form in a discursive landscape

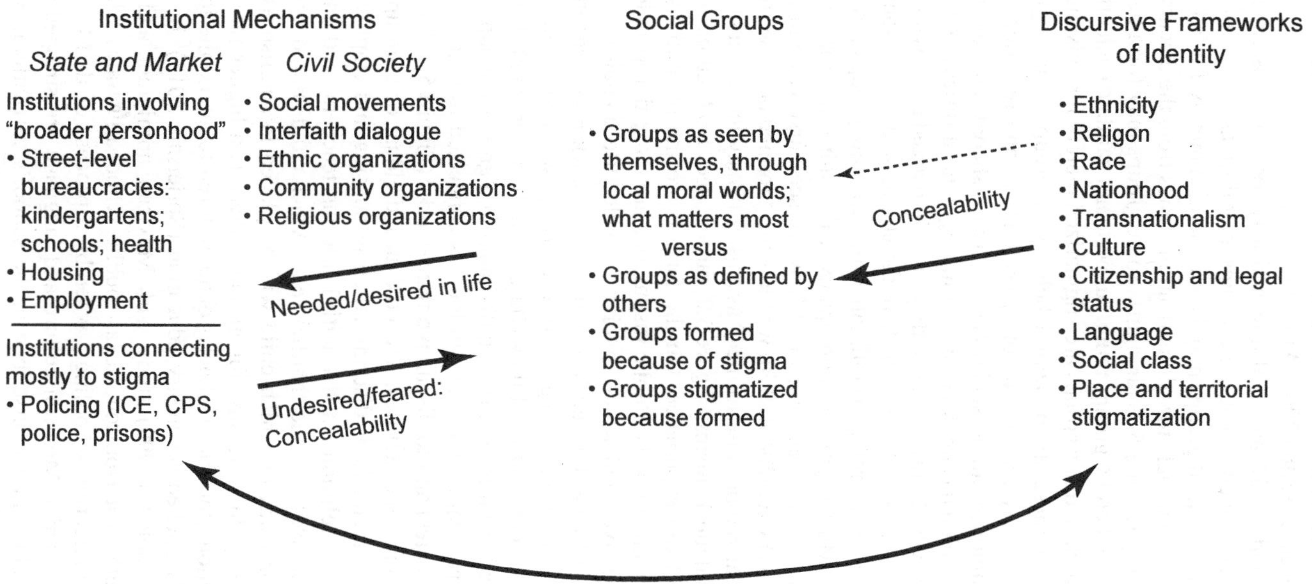

Figure 5.2 Meso-level framework for migration and the lived experiences of stigma. From discursive frameworks of identity to social groups, the dotted arrow indicates indirect influence between how social groups define themselves and how others define groups, and the solid arrow indicates direct influence between how groups define themselves and how others define groups.

where secular mainstream is pitted against Muslim "others" (for a discusion on these differences, see Alba 2005; Alba and Foner 2015).

To understand the dynamics of how and why social groups emerge and reproduce, we acknowledge that some groups may form as a response to stigmatization and other social groups may be stigmatized merely for belonging to a group. The "raw material" for stigmatization comes from the discursive frameworks of identity (Figure 5.2, far right). Some groups may form because they are stigmatized whereby groups unite, support, and validate each others' experiences. Meanwhile other groups are stigmatized merely for existing, whereby those in power impose stigmatizing labels on the group. As immigrants strive to adapt, and if they are victims of discrimination and rejection, some may engage in "minority ethnic social capital" (e.g., shared language). Minority ethnic social capital has implications for immigrants' abilities to cope (Anthias 2007). Groups which form because they are stigmatized align with Goffman's category of "the own:" those who share the stigma and with whom a stigmatized person can seek refuge (Goffman 1963:32). Few groups rarely fall into a single type. Most stigmatized groups exist through some form of two-way identification (cf. the social mirror of how we see ourselves and how others see us; Suárez-Orozco 2000). Still, we view the "formed because stigmatized" versus "stigmatized because formed" as a useful analytical distinction.

Institutional mechanisms (Figure 5.2, far left; see also Figure 5.1, top right) surround the lived experience. On the far left are the institutions of public sector and private markets. Public institutions are those that people need and desire in their lives and which involve "broader life domains" (e.g., health care, schools, housing for families, and employment). Public institutions also include those with varying degrees of coercive power that connect mostly to stigmas (e.g., police, courts, child welfare institutions, prisons). They are typically undesired, even feared. How individuals and groups encounter, and their treatment in navigating these institutions, is connected to both social groups (Figure 5.2, center) and to discursive frameworks (Figure 5.2, far right). The latter frameworks and statuses, and how an individual or a group is defined with respect to them, fuels discrimination in housing and employment (e.g., class, language, religion), and (tacitly) informs teachers' and caseworkers' decisions about children and families (e.g., which child should pursue a specific education track or which child will be placed in English as a Second Language class). In Germany, for instance, there is a higher rate of teacher recommendations for Turkish-background children to attend the lowest track in Germany's tracked secondary education (Sprietsma 2013). In the United States, Valenzuela's (1999) study with Mexican immigrant and U.S.-born Mexican youth in a Houston, Texas, public school illustrates what she describes as "subtractive schooling," whereby a process of de-Mexicanization takes place in which Mexican culture and language are stripped away. One example of subtraction is inscribed in the school's curriculum, which feeds students into two dominant tracks: the "regular" English-only track and the

English as a Second Language (ESL) track. Labeling ESL youth as "limited English proficient" instead of as "Spanish dominant" classifies Spanish as a barrier and not an asset.[2]

As these examples suggest, when immigrants encounter the institutions of their receiving societies, it is primarily through interactions with street-level bureaucrats, rather than distant state agencies. Coined by Lipsky (1980), street-level bureaucrats are frontline professionals charged with implementing policy, while also holding varying degrees of discretion in casework and professional practice. Typical examples are teachers and social workers. As with employers and lessors in private markets, the work of these street-level bureaucrats will be informed by the discursive frameworks of identity.

The other type of institution that produces stigma and impacts immigrants' lived experiences are branches of the state, which exerts coercive power over the decisions of professionals (street-level bureaucrats or higher-level) and impact people's lives directly, arguably in more immediate and consequential ways than other institutions. Two examples are Child Protective Services (CPS) and state agencies charged with immigration control and deportation. Although these agencies differ in nature, with child welfare operating with a dual role of support and discipline, they provide two contrasting heuristic tools to understand different institutional mechanisms. Moreover, a concept like "mass deportability" (Asad 2020; De Genova 2002) may apply more specifically to the United States than many other parts of the Global North. Regardless, both types of agencies generate fear within certain immigrant and minority groups that lead to the cultivation of skills to manage stigma. In the case of CPS, some parents will relate with hesitancy toward adjacent or connected agencies where professionals are mandated reporters (like schools). The fear of having children removed from the home has been shown by U.S. researchers to generate both systems avoidance and "selective visibility" vis-à-vis public institutions (e.g., schools, the health system) by immigrant, ethnic minority, and poor parents, in an effort to avoid CPS referrals (Fong 2019). The latter has also been shown in Norwegian studies of immigrant parents (Handulle and Vassenden 2021). In this sense, the coercive power of some institutions can lead immigrants to cultivate the portrayal of identities that conform with majority norms vis-à-vis adjacent or connected institutions like schools to avoid exposure to the feared institutions (Handulle and Vassenden 2021). Alternatively, they may take measures to avoid system contact altogether, such as refraining from

2 Another example is when Black teachers in the United States promote White students to higher tracks because of anticipatory insights from structural factors (including aggregated norms) with concern that White parents might be more likely to complain and to be taken more seriously by the administration if they complain (Lewis and Diamond 2015). This also means that Black students and other students are not promoted to higher tracks. Therefore, the White and Black students have different experiences of schooling as well as different educational, labor market, social class, and health outcomes.

seeking medical assistance (Fong 2019). The same has been shown regarding fears of deportation (Asad 2020; García 2018).

Another vital role that institutions play in stigmatization relates to the stigma concept of labeling (Link and Phelan 2001). Formal institutions such as the state (including federal, state, regional, provincial, and municipal governments), schools, and social services are particularly powerful in labeling immigrants. The state, for example, classifies immigrants' legal status, which then dictates their access to rights, resources, and institutions. These legal labels, however, also become the premise for social identities that inform stereotypes and lead to interpersonal and institutional discrimination (i.e., structurally based stigma). In addition, schools attach formal labels to immigrant children. These labels come in the formal academic tracks and linguistic designations applied to immigrant children (Valenzuela 1999), in the legal categories that form the basis for stigmatization, as well as in destigmatizing social categories (Abrego 2008).

Civil society organizations mediate between stigmatized groups and individuals and state and market institutions (Figure 5.2, left). Social movements and ethnic and immigrant organizations may, for instance, channel grassroot organizing and social activism in response to the state and state agencies' treatment of groups and individuals. Ethnic and community organizations may also provide guidance, advice, and a sense of solidarity to individuals and families sharing insights on how to engage schools, housing, employment, as well as the police. Civil society and ethnic institutions may thus be important moderators (or "buffers") of the lived experiences of stigmatization. These are meso-level institutions, including neighborhood-based organizations, nonprofit social service providers, immigrant rights groups, and ethnic-based community organizations. These institutions may alleviate some of the negative effects of structurally based stigmatization but may also increase stigmatization inadvertently. For example, some ethnic-based organizations in immigrant communities support educational achievement of their children through an ethnic system of supplementary education (Zhou and Li 2003). The resulting school success among immigrant children leads teachers to believe that these immigrant children, as opposed to others, are high achievers and worthy students. This contributes to the racialized formation of "stereotype promise," or the process of being understood through the lens of positive stereotypes which, in turn, leads individuals to behave in ways that conform to the positive stereotype (Lee and Zhou 2015). Such stereotype promise may become part of the enactment of a mechanism of stigmatization, allowing schools and teachers to promote certain groups of students but not others based on the racialized categories to which they belong as opposed to their capacities. Civil society organizations and social movements may also serve as collective platforms for responding to stigma, including possibilities of renegotiation, re-representation, rejection, distancing, and overcompensating (discussed below).

The Lived Experiences of Stigma: A Typology

To illustrate the relationship between migration and stigma in the lived experiences of immigrants, it is important to outline responses to stigma and their potential effect (Figure 5.3). The precursor to the response and effect is an awareness of stigma that operates at the intrapersonal, interpersonal, and collective levels. This typology brings us into conversation with the chapter by Castañeda and Holmes (this volume), in which they center lived experiences of Latinx undocumented youth. Castañeda and Holmes illustrate how Latinx undocumented youth resist stigma by creating and embracing counternarratives that empower them and directly challenge stigmatized narratives surrounding undocumented youth. Collectively, Figures 5.1, 5.2, and 5.3 illustrate our interest in centering lived experiences, beyond individual and micro-level stigma processes, toward connecting immigrants' lived experiences within structural contexts that can be highly racialized, classed, and nativist. Our goal is to make explicit contributions to both migration and stigma research by bridging these two rich literatures to profile how structural conditions shape the lived experiences of immigrants and their responses and effects on stigma.

Types of Stigma

With its focus on immigrants' lived experiences and stigmatization processes, Figure 5.2 elucidates three mechanisms that shape immigrants' lived experiences of stigma: (a) how and where stigma is produced, (b) who the stigmatizers are, and (c) how stigma processes shape the lived experiences of those with family or social ties to immigrant communities. These mechanisms are not mutually exclusive and illustrate a relational approach to the study of stigma. They are shaped by a social context in which immigrants are embedded and which varies across their life course.

Immigrants are often stigmatized and are thus on the receiving end of stigma, but not all immigrants are treated equally. In the United States, for instance, White European undocumented migrants are not perceived to be undocumented and thus experience their undocumented status in ways that are different to undocumented Latinx immigrants. Mexican immigrants and Mexican Americans born in the United States, regardless of citizenship or generation status, often continue to be racialized and treated as undocumented migrants (García 2017). Even among undocumented Latinx immigrants, those with lighter skin can "legally pass" and may confront less discrimination (García 2019). We recognize that individuals who are stigmatized may also shift into a stigmatizing role, despite being stigmatized themselves. For example, a male undocumented Mexican immigrant who experiences stigma in his workplace (e.g., by being ostracized, ridiculed, or overworked without compensation) may engage in stigmatizing his Black and Indigenous coworkers. Put simply, the same person who is stigmatized may actively engage in stigmatizing others. A final

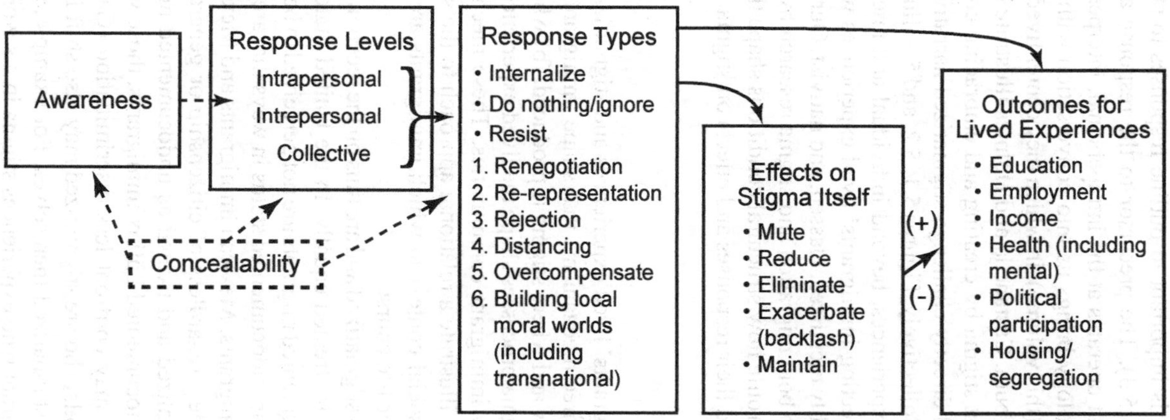

Figure 5.3 Lived experiences of stigma: a typology.

way in which stigma manifests itself is through vicarious stigma; that is, when stigma processes spillover impacting the lives of family, friends, or those in the circle of caring of the stigmatized. An example of vicarious stigma can be seen within mixed-status families (or families composed of different citizenship and legal statuses) whereby family members with legal statuses continue to bear the brunt of stigmatizing processes meant to target their undocumented family members (Castañeda 2019). Vicarious stigma closely relates to courtesy stigma, or stigma by association, whereby the stigma is also felt by those closely associated with the stigmatized (Goffman 1963).

Potential concealability of one's immigrant status is an important moderating factor in the lived experience of stigma. For instance, the degree to which one's immigrant status is concealable shapes the potential repertoire of an individual's responses to stigma (Figure 5.3, step 3). Choosing to conceal one's immigrant status can avert direct person-to-person discrimination, but it can also lead to higher concern about one's status being discovered and associated mental health consequences, such as elevated stress (Valentín-Cortés et al. 2020). Potential concealability may also modify consequences of being aware (or unaware) of stigma or affect an individual's experience of stigma, which in turn would modify response at intrapersonal, interpersonal, and collective levels (Figure 5.3, steps 1 and 2).

Awareness

There are some contexts in which stigmatization occurs because the structural factors of oppression and exploitation are not visible or appraised (i.e., an immigrant remains "unaware" of the source of structural stigma). For example, Fanon writes about the context of Algeria under French colonization (Fanon 2003). An Algerian who experiences hunger does not necessarily associate French colonization with the cause of their hunger. Instead, they are more likely to label the French shop owner (who sells but does not share food products) as selfish or cruel. Inversely, the shop owner does not view French colonization as the cause of hunger but instead labels the Algerian who attempts to steal bread from their shop as selfish, cruel, or lazy. As another example, consider Korean shop owners in the United States who are situated in Black neighborhoods, where those neighborhoods may experience something similar (Lee 2006). Each group is unlikely to be aware of the context of exploitation enacted by racial capitalism that affects them both. Instead, each group tends to focus on the nearest out-group. The Black community may label and stigmatize the Korean shop owners not only as selfish but also as noncitizen outsiders, while the Korean shop owner may label and stigmatize members of the Black community as poor, lazy, or unsuccessful (Min 1996).

Awareness of the stigma that affects an individual or their group has implications for potential responses. Some responses (e.g., forms of active resistance) may require some level of awareness. Others may be possible with or without awareness of stigmatization. Power—the ability to exercise one's will, regardless of any resistance that one may encounter from another (Link and Phelan 2014)—is critical here. Stigma functions as a form of power by explicitly turning attention to how stigma is produced, by whom, and for what purposes (Tyler and Slater 2018). Returning to the Algerian and Korean shop owner examples, each group is unaware of the structural forces that shape their everyday life experiences. The power at work in these examples shifts attention to larger structural forces (e.g., French colonization, racial capitalism) and shapes social relations between the respective groups. Indeed, stigma is a form of power. Yet regardless of how aware an individual is of stigmatizing processes, the precursor to the response and effect is an awareness of stigma that operates on three levels: intrapersonal (i.e., or within an individual or groups, such as self-stigma), interpersonal (i.e., across or between individuals and groups), and collective (i.e., individuals or groups that share a collective social identity).

Response Levels

Intrapersonal stigma occurs within an individual and shapes their attitudes, thoughts, beliefs, emotions, or ideologies. In response, individuals enact cognitive, affective, and behavioral processes. Intrapersonal responses may manifest as concealment, internalized stigma, self-stigma (i.e., where individuals internalize negative and devalued views about one's group), or stigma consciousness (i.e., the extent to which people expect to be stereotyped) (Pinel 1999). For example, undocumented immigrants often navigate when and to whom they will conceal or reveal their undocumented status.

Interpersonal stigma refers to the prejudice and discrimination that is expressed between groups (i.e., the stigmatized and the stigmatizer). At an interpersonal level, stigma can unfold whereby negative feelings and biases toward stigmatized groups are prevalent and lead to discrimination and unfair treatment. Interpersonal stigma includes intergroup processes, which can help inform interpersonal interactions and lead to stigmatization of certain groups or individuals on the basis of class, race and ethnicity, citizenship status, gender, and sexuality, among other types of classifications. Interpersonal stigma can occur through overt actions, such as hate crimes targeting immigrants, or covert actions, such as treating and perceiving immigrants (regardless of citizenship and legal status) as undocumented based on stereotypes conflating race, legal status, and national origin.

Collective stigma underscores the relational nature of stigma, as it captures the far-reaching effects that stigma has beyond individuals (e.g., targets of stigma) into social groups (e.g., stigma by association) (Aranda et al. 2023). Collective stigma refers to stigma applied to a category of people who share a stigmatizing "mark" (Crocker et al. 1998). This mark and the associated stigmatization become a collective social identity (Dovidio et al. 2000). Similar to Figure 5.2, collective stigma may push social groups to form because of their shared and collective stigmatized experiences (i.e., "formed because stigmatized"). Others may be "stigmatized because formed," like individuals that experience vicarious stigma as these people may experience stigma by association with a stigmatized group. Collective stigma helps illustrate how stigma transfers across linkages and social connections between the targets of stigma, those associated with them, and the relationships that occur between them (Aranda et al. 2023).

Types of Responses

As immigrants navigate stigmatizing processes, they respond to stigma at intrapersonal, interpersonal, and collective levels. As a first potential response, immigrants may internalize notions of what it means to be labeled with a "stigmatized" status, in this case being identified as belonging to a particular immigrant group. Consider a model of internalized stigma (see Link et al. 1989), originally formulated for use with mental illness, which identifies how "labeled" individuals become at risk for negative consequences. We adapt this model to illustrate how stigma processes related to labeling and awareness of societal conceptions toward immigrants apply to immigrant groups. First, how a society may come to think about a particular immigrant group is constructed by socialization with family, school, community, media, and social media. Globalization, social media, and transnationalism facilitate an awareness of societal conceptions toward immigrants and impact socialization processes for immigrants across borders. Second, labeling occurs through being identified as a member of a particular immigrant group by members of the receiving society; this which can occur via intermediary structural processes, such as schools, articulated earlier (e.g., Figure 5.2). At this point, beliefs about how the community will treat a person of a particular immigrant group become personally relevant. Shaping the likelihood of being labeled as coming from an immigrant group, certain immigrant statuses may not be as readily concealable (due to phenotypes such as darker skin complexion or distinctive garb associated with a religious affiliation), whereas other statuses may be better concealed (e.g., undocumented status).

A crucial aspect of internalization takes place when labeled individuals anticipate treatment based on how a society thinks about their particular immigrant group; for example, undocumented individuals being treated as "undeserving" or as "unfairly benefiting from society's resources" (Holmes et al. 2021). Because beliefs about a particular immigrant group become personally relevant, individuals may thus anticipate (and actually experience) unfair treatment after they are identified as belonging to an immigrant group. Fear of being labeled shapes the decision of undocumented immigrants to conceal their status, thus protecting as well as empowering them to participate in society without bringing attention to themselves. In the case of a potentially concealable immigrant status (e.g., undocumented status), the individual anticipates negative responses from others, following disclosure of their immigrant status (Patler 2018b), and adopts strategies to conceal this status. If individuals from a particular immigrant group anticipate unfair treatment from others, they may pursue a strategy of secrecy by concealing their immigrant status from friends, families, dating partners, prospective employers, and colleagues. Another potential coping strategy includes withdrawal or restricting social contact to people who accept one's status. Other potential strategies include denying or ignoring one's immigrant identity when relating with others.

While potentially protecting the immigrant from negative person-to-person discrimination, these coping strategies can also elicit negative outcomes. In the United States, for instance, undocumented youth in educational settings must decide whether to conceal or reveal their legal status when they interact with teachers, counselors, and administrators (Patler 2018b). The political and social contexts surrounding undocumented youth as well as the perceived support from their co-ethnic social networks play a role in these decisions. First-person accounts among people who have concealed their undocumented status in the United States reveal how shame leads to reduced social connections. Furthermore, loss of relationships (e.g., being broken up with by a romantic partner) have been reported following actual disclosure of being undocumented (see Castañeda and Holmes, this volume). In additional, teasing and harassment at school has also been commonly reported by undocumented Mexican youth in the United States (see Castañeda and Holmes, this volume).

A related process of internalization of stigma or "self-stigma" may occur when an immigrant becomes aware of and believes in a social stereotype (e.g., immigrants are not hard workers). Internalization of the stereotype leads to negative consequences (Figure 5.3) and may be exacerbated by the absence of stigmatized group members in high-status social, political, and economic roles. The absence of a relevant role model may cause group members to conclude that "I am not a leader," "I'm not good enough to attend college," or "people will not view me as a leader or college material, so I should choose a different path" (Debrosse et al. 2020). Self-stigma necessitates buying into the stereotypes and is coupled with a lack of representation from people that share similar characteristics in important social roles, leading to negative consequences.

Do Nothing

When individuals become aware of negative stereotypes associated with their immigrant group, they may choose a coping response to "do nothing" (see Figure 5.3). In one version of "do nothing," an immigrant may give up efforts in accordance with a stereotyped characteristic (e.g., stops trying to succeed academically in line with societal perceptions of one's group possessing poor scholastic ability). This "why try" effect has been applied to mental illness stereotypes (Corrigan et al. 2009). It delineates relationships between negative stereotypes of a group (i.e., how the general public conceives of and reacts to members of an immigrant group), which may lead to internalized stigma and result in a loss of self-esteem, self-efficacy, and empowerment. Impacts on these psychosocial outcomes can lead to maladaptive behaviors, such as no longer participating in important life goals and activities.

In a second version of "do nothing," immigrant groups may feel obligated to isolate and disengage from society to avoid bringing attention to themselves. Others may disengage or "do nothing" for their own self-preservation, as a form of self-protection from the harmful and damaging effects associated with stigmatizing processes. For example, undocumented immigrants may decide not to engage in activism to avoid bringing attention to themselves. Another version of this is to demonstrate one's subscription with the mainstream, majority culture, as has been shown in "strategies of normalization" taken by young Australian Muslims (Harris and Karimshah 2019:624), which include performing ordinary Australianness or acting like what Goffman (1963:37) described as "heroes of adjustment" (Harris and Karimshah 2019:627). As a form of self-preservation, undocumented immigrants may consciously decide not to engage (i.e., do nothing) to counter stigmatizing views of their group because they understand the negative and injurious consequences that stigma induces. These forms of disengagement have negative consequences for the stigmatized, as they may become even more isolated, preventing them from forming strong social bonds and social connections with other stigmatized immigrants. Yet, disengaging or to "do nothing" as a form of self-preservation may circumvent the negative and injurious consequences that stigma induces because individuals may choose not to engage and thus do not ruminate on negative stigmatizing views of immigrants, despite a level of awareness of stigmatizing views. Others may "do nothing" as a form of self-preservation, but constantly ruminate on the negative stigmatizing views of immigrants, and thus are negatively impacted by the injurious consequences that stigma produces. To "do nothing" is a decision one makes that disadvantages stigmatized groups and incurs an advantage for the stigmatizers because stereotypes remain alive and not challenged. In other words, the status quo remains, ultimately privileging the stigmatizers.

Resist

By confronting stigma head-on immigrants may follow a strategy to resist stigma discursively. Below we describe six strategies that can be understood through Gramsci's conceptualization of the "war of position": different groups fight over meanings and representations to reach goals, pursue interests, and vie for power. As evinced by the following examples, the efficacy of a strategy depends on both historical context and the power the stigmatized group holds.

The first strategy responds to labels through renegotiation, which involves taking labels applied to them in a denigrating way and embracing them to create new meanings. In the United States, this may involve slogans such as "Undocumented and Unafraid." Examples of allyship across stigmatized groups include the slogan "Coming Out Undocumented," in which LGBTQ+ groups and immigrant groups share metaphors in relation to one another (De Genova and Peutz 2010; Terriquez 2015).

The second strategy that involves labels is known as re-representation: novel words, phrases, or actions are used to construct and enforce counter-narratives. In the United States, examples include the terms "Dreamers" and "DACAmented." These terms create new understandings of a group that runs counter to the stigmatizing tropes. Some produce new forms of belonging, such as "Oaxacalifornia," a term utilized by Oaxacan people in California to denote their identity as both Oaxacan and Californian and their belonging in a place that is culturally hybrid. Policy changes can also provide new labels that immigrants adopt to resist stigma. Such labels may stem from more inclusive policies, such as the California Assembly Bill 540 (AB 540), which allows any high school student who has attended three years of high school in California to pay in-state tuition at the state's public colleges and universities (Abrego 2008). Undocumented students used the title of the law AB540 as the basis for a positive label ("AB 540 students") to counter the stigmatizing label ("illegal") created by the federal government. A similar phenomenon happened with Deferred Action for Childhood Arrivals, an executive order signed by President Obama in 2012 that gave some undocumented immigrant young adults reprieve from deportation (U.S. Citizenship and Immigration Services 2022). Here, the same institution that labeled some immigrants as "illegal" offered select immigrants a new legal label ("DACAmented") that has more positive valence.

The third sociolinguistic strategy involves rejection or the annulment of a label as opposed to proposing another. This strategy, seen in many languages and sociodemographic locations around the world, may best be exemplified by the slogan "No Human Being is Illegal." Other groups may collectively engage in rejecting a host society's stigma by separating themselves from the stigma through co-ethnic community building or even ethnic exclusion. Rejection is likely most effective when undertaken collectively.

The fourth strategy is distancing. Here, immigrants' distance themselves from the meaning of a label attached to their group, by avoiding contact (spatially or socially) with their group or dressing and speaking differently from its members. In Scandinavia, for instance, refugees from the Middle East may perform counternarratives that demonstrate "Scandinavian-ness" or show that they do not fit the labels they are given (Bygnes 2022). In the United States, lighter-skinned Mexican immigrants may distance themselves from the stigmatization that affects darker-skinned or Indigenous Mexican immigrants; they may even engage in stigmatizing groups to avoid being stigmatized themselves (Holmes 2013).

The fifth strategy involves overcompensation. An immigrant may work deliberately to achieve a specific goal that runs counter to a specific label or stereotype that deems them unlikely to achieve that goal. For example, Asian Americans face blocked opportunities (a "bamboo ceiling") in leadership positions because of negative stereotypes about their abilities as leaders. In response, some might double their efforts to get into leadership positions as a means of pushing back against the stereotype (Lee and Zhou 2015). Inversely, an immigrant may work extra hard to achieve a specific goal because a label indicates that they should strive to achieve this goal. In this way, stigmatization can lead to overcompensation in everyday life. Borrowing again from the example of Asian Americans, stereotypes related to their abilities in math and science might drive individuals inclined to follow other career paths to nonetheless pursue a career in math and science because the stereotype prescribes it (Lee and Zhou 2015).

The sixth strategy involves building local moral worlds of resistance. This strategy may be enacted through local community building, such as through ethnic-focused organizations, institutions, or social ties. Participation in these local communities or networks (i.e., "local worlds") can provide a sense of acceptance and worth (or locally recognized, full-fledged "personhood"), which can be used to ward off stigma from outside societal structures. In addition, this strategy may be complemented through "transnational compensation," in which an immigrant group may focus on "what matters most" in a transnational context (e.g., sending back remittances to families abroad, thus achieving recognition within one's local network or community) to avoid the negative effects of outside stigmatization in one specific society, community, or region.

Effect of These Strategies on Stigma

Do these strategies have an effect on stigma? Individual and collective responses to stigma can shape the severity or salience of the stigma. We conceptualize intrapersonal, interpersonal, and collective responses to stigma by migrants as having five nonmutually exclusive effects on stigma—mute, reduce, eliminate, exacerbate, and maintain (Figure 5.3, step 4)—which extend the responses to stigma described above.

The first response is to *mute* the stigma, thereby temporarily reducing or making it irrelevant. Muting does not eliminate the stigma; it situates individuals or groups in insulating situations. For example, in interpersonal interactions, individuals can conceal characteristics associated with the stigmatized category (discussed above). Examples include later-generation Mexican Americans overcompensating by initiating casual conversations with White Americans to mute associations between Mexican ancestry and foreignness (Jiménez 2009). This does not conceal an individual's association with the stigmatized category (Goffman 1963) but rather mitigates parts of the stigmatized characteristic while the individual remains associated with the stigmatized category. Likewise, undocumented immigrants may distance themselves from the stigmatized category by adjusting their style of dress to signal a class standing not normally associated with undocumented immigrants (García 2019). Collective forms of responses to stigma can likewise mute stigma. Organizations on college campuses in the United States create communities of support with other undocumented students, thus allowing undocumented individuals to temporarily mute the stigma associated with legal status and even invert the valence of the status so that it becomes a positive source of identity (Abrego 2008). Importantly, in all these examples, stigma remains outside of the muting situation.

Responses to stigma can also *reduce* the severity and salience of the stigma in multiple realms of life. Though short of eliminating the stigma, reduction is wider in scope and less fleeting than muting. Stigma reduction is more likely to result from group-level processes, including collective action aimed at the stigma itself or processes that incidentally affect stigma. An example of the former is ethnic civic organizations in Canada that promote the political and social advancement of a particular ethnic group, increasing the likelihood that group members participate in civil society more broadly and mitigating any impacts of structural stigma toward this ethnic group (Bloemraad 2006). An example of the latter is the upward mobility of Muslims in the United States. Here, upward mobility likely stems from the relatively high socioeconomic status of Muslim immigrants and the pursuit of economic aspirations once in the United States. Upward mobility leads to greater contact with non-Muslims, and a resulting reduction in stigma.

Responding to stigma may also *eliminate* it altogether. This most likely occurs due to collective and larger societal processes that transpire over extended periods, perhaps even generations whereby stigmatized categories become subsumed into the larger societal mainstream. For example, in the mid-1800s in the United States, Irish immigrants (and later, Southern and Eastern European immigrants) were stigmatized because they were Catholic. Fears regarding potential papal influence receded as immigrants and their subsequent generations integrated socially, politically, and economically, and today, Catholicism is no longer a stigmatized category in the United States. The elimination of Catholicism as a stigmatized category was the result of deliberate collective action as well as group-level changes in socioeconomic status (Alba and Nee 2003).

Responding to stigma does not always act on the stigma in ways that might be beneficial to the stigmatized group. Collective responses may *exacerbate* stigma, making it more salient and thus consequential in multiple areas of life. Examples abound of immigrants advocating for rights, resources, and access to institutions that often heightens stigma. For instance, in the early 2000s in the United States, immigrants participated in nationwide demonstrations against restrictive federal immigration policies and in favor of immigrant rights. The southern United States, an area with a more recent history of immigrant settlement, saw widespread protests that caused a social and political backlash and made Latino immigrants a more identifiable and stigmatized category in the eyes of long-residing Southerners (Jones 2019).

Finally, resistance may do little to alter stigma, which may *maintain* its relevance despite a group's actions. Stigma maintenance is more likely to result from internalization and do-nothing responses on the part of immigrants. It can, however, also result from power differentials between immigrants and established communities or institutional arrangements. Resistance does not immediately change the status quo.

Outcomes for Lived Experiences of Stigma

Immigrants experience stigma in their lives differently: some are impacted directly by stigma, others shift into the role of stigmatizing, still others experience stigma indirectly. These diverse lived experiences are relational and context dependent. They are interspersed at individual, meso-institutional, and macrosystemic levels, yielding divergent and cumulative effects on the individual immigrant and/or the immigrant group being stigmatized. How one responds to stigmatizing processes shapes the direction, magnitude, and impact that stigma has on immigrants lived experiences (Figure 5.3, step 5). Many outcomes have been highlighted in existing research to demonstrate that anti-immigration stigma, racial discrimination, and stereotyping bear directly on disparate outcomes in physical and mental health, access to educational, housing, labor market opportunities, and socioeconomic attainment. People who report, for example, discrimination on the basis of race are more likely than others to have high blood pressure, hypertension, as well as chronic cardiovascular, respiratory, and pain-related issues (Chae et al. 2010; Gee et al. 2007; Mays et al. 2007). People who experience discrimination and hate, because they "look like" foreigners and are thus treated as outsiders, are more likely than others to suffer from anxiety, depression, and sleep disorders (Armenta et al. 2013; Lee and Waters 2021). Internalized racism by marginalized racial groups has been found to damage self-esteem and reinforce self-doubt and powerlessness of stigmatized group members (Jones 2001). Systemic racism and discriminatory policies, regulations, and practices that result include redlining, residential segregation, deportation, and detention (Massey and Denton 1993; Morey 2018).

Capturing the Lived Experience

Our framework provides a conceptual map for migration and stigma processes, but implementing the map requires a range of methodological instruments. In providing new insights into the lived experience of immigrants and stigma, we have relied on a rich set of largely qualitative studies for illustration. Advancing research on migration and stigma using ethnographic methods, according to the concepts or frameworks described here, would be a straightforward approach. However, using our model in large-scale quantitative migration research requires a substantial expansion of existing approaches. Here we present some of the main challenges to and opportunities for doing so.

Studies using such large-scale, survey approaches tend to rely on existing secondary data, which despite overall large sample sizes are hardly able to provide sufficient power to "zoom into" the lived experiences of single ethnic minority groups, particularly if these groups are relatively small in size. A second issue in quantitative survey research is that origin categories for immigrants and their descendants have to be meaningfully defined; this is a challenging task due to the diverse experiences of ethnic minority groups. Whereas for first-generation immigrants, countries of origin and/or citizenship may serve as a basis for classification, for the descendants of immigrants the task of classification becomes more challenging. This is particularly true given the growing proportion of immigrant descendants that are born into interethnic, binational, or biracial families, where one parent belongs to the charter population and another to a minority group (Kalter and Heath 2018). The categorization of mixed ancestry (i.e., children of parents who occupy distinct positions on the migration generation line or with regard to ethnic origin) can never do justice for both sides of the ancestral lineage. Pragmatically taken, classification decisions to treat a person who happens to have one parent born outside the host country as a second-generation migrant or as belonging to a certain ethnic minority group could itself lead to labeling and potentially (unintended) stigmatization.

To further complicate matters, in secondary data sources, certain origin categories are predefined and grouped based on geography in pan-geographical categories. This would probably not be an issue if the experiences of minorities within the categories concur, but this is often not the case, as we have learned from in-depth qualitative and quantitative studies. Creating overly broad categories that capture people with diverging experiences might again lead to labeling and stereotyping (and potentially stigmatization). As a result, potential disadvantages or prejudice toward a single origin group within a pan-geographical category can be transmitted to immigrants who originate in other countries also categorized as belonging to this group. Moreover, in comparative studies, the composition of the very same pan-geographic groups might differ. For example, the bulk of Eastern Europeans in Germany are from Poland and the countries of the former Soviet Union, whereas in Sweden, countries of the former Yugoslavia dominate. Still, researchers might compare the Eastern Europeans as a group, as if these were comparable. The practice of treating immigrants from the earlier existing and then disintegrated national entities (e.g., the former Yugoslavia, the former Soviet Union) as homogeneous groups might be misleading and even erroneous, as very often the successor countries (and their people) follow entirely different paths in terms of societal, economic, and cultural development and identities (e.g., Russia, Belarus, and Ukraine).

Objective classification uncertainties require a good deal of pragmatism, as data often do not leave many options for meaningful analyses. Yet quantitative migration researchers might utilize stigma research prior to collecting their own data or drafting questionnaire modules for large-scale data collections (e.g., European Social Survey). A first important issue to consider is that labeling categories are not necessarily formed around individuals' countries of origin; instead, using country of origin might conceal certain Indigenous cultural and ethnic minorities (e.g., Assyrians and Kurds in Turkey, Roma or Jews in many European countries) or long-standing subnational groups, such as Scots in the U.K., Catalans in Spain (Heath et al. 2016), or Biafrans in Nigeria. Particularly if some of these minority groups are stigmatized in some contexts but not others, migration research runs the danger of missing systematic disadvantages caused by group stigmatization. A second lesson to be learned from stigma research is to give a stronger voice to the research participants in defining their group identities. Deviations between the respondents' subjective interpretations of their identities and group boundaries set by researchers, based on a set of objectively defined criteria, might be meaningful and a topic of research in itself, as they might indicate a group's responses toward stigmatization. Finally, critically asking ourselves to grapple with our own lived experiences, coupled with the privileging of hegemonic Western ways of designing and conducting research, is desperately needed in both migration and stigma-related research. Doing so will provide us a way to place more attention to "how our culture-specific inner eyes shape and limit how we, as researchers/scholars/analysts see, name, frame and go about our research" (Lukate 2023:66).

Conclusion

Scholars and literatures analyzing stigma, those investigating migration, and those theorizing lived experience often do not overlap. This gap in the literature leads to missed opportunities, insights, and responses from all three communities. Theoretical insights, analytical clarity, and ideas for solidarity, advocacy, and policy can be gained if we consider the lived experience of stigma processes in contexts of migration. In our consideration of the nexus of these, often separate, topics and literatures, we find especially compelling the diversity of responses to stigma processes in the everyday lives of immigrant communities. These responses, both individual and collective, include resistance that takes different forms. These responses affect not only the stigma processes of these individuals and communities but also their lived experience on multiple levels. We call on scholars of stigma, migration, and lived experience to consider these responses in their research and conceptualization as well as in their more public-oriented policy and solidarity work. At this intersection lies one of the most critical issues in our world today: stigma processes that affect immigrant communities under different social, political, and geographic contexts.

6

Defying Discrimination?

Germany's Ethnic Minorities within Education and Training Systems

Irena Kogan, Markus Weißmann, and Jörg Dollmann

Abstract

To establish the impact that discrimination or unfair treatment has on ethnic minority students, this chapter explores the trajectories and outcomes of students in the German education and training system. Compared to native-born students, migrant and ethnic minority students who report discriminatory experiences are, on average, more likely to enter more educational pathways marked by larger uncertainty. However, results from the authors' study indicate that minority students who experience discrimination in school are also likely to pursue favorable educational paths, perhaps because they develop better coping strategies and resilience in light of adverse situations in school. Ultimately, students who report discrimination at school are more likely to fail in attaining any degree. Yet, the relationship between discrimination experienced in school and educational or training outcomes is largely uniform for minority and for native-born students.

Introduction

Ethnic and migration-related inequalities in the German education system has been the subject of extensive research (Beicht and Walden 2019; Dollmann 2010, 2017; Kristen et al. 2008; Mentges 2020; Tjaden 2017; Tjaden and Hunkler 2017). Scholars emphasize differences in scholastic performance and educational decision making between descendants of immigrants and native-born students without migration backgrounds (Kristen and Granato 2007). In terms of educational decision making, research has established that immigrants and their descendants generally strive for more demanding educational tracks (Dollmann 2017; Dollmann and Weißmann 2020; Kristen et al. 2008; Tjaden and Hunkler 2017). One explanation for this lies in the higher educational and occupational aspirations that immigrants usually hold (Kao and Tienda 1998; Raleigh and Kao 2010; Salikutluk 2016; Wicht 2016). Furthermore, the *expectations and anticipations of discrimination in the labor market* have also been identified as another potential driver of immigrants' ambitious educational choices (Beicht and Walden 2019; Dollmann 2010; Heath and Brinbaum 2007; Tjaden 2017). Yet little is known about whether and how *experiences of discrimination in school* relate to educational and training outcomes in minority students.

In this chapter, we address whether those who report discrimination or unfair treatment in school follow different trajectories within the German education and training system than those without such experiences. Further, we examine whether students who experience discrimination or unfair treatment are subjected to penalties, in terms of educational attainment or training qualifications. Particular attention is given to discriminatory experiences among immigrants and ethnic minority groups.

Perceptions of Discrimination by Minorities

Before we address the consequences of discrimination on educational trajectories and educational or training outcomes, it is necessary to understand the concept of perceived or self-reported discrimination. On one hand, self-reported discrimination can reveal actual instances of discrimination (Diehl et al. 2021). On the other, it reflects a subjective evaluation of often ambiguous situations (Diehl et al. 2021) and may be related to an individual attributing (or failing to attribute) negative situations to discrimination, for example, as a sort of a coping strategy (Major and O'Brien 2005).

Starting with the subjectivity behind discrimination perceptions, it is argued that members of nonstigmatized and stigmatized groups react differently to the same situation, in part because they bring different collective representations to the situation (Major and O'Brien 2005:400). In other words, members of ethnic minority groups, particularly those facing salient ethnic boundaries, are more likely to attribute negative feedback to discrimination (Branscombe et al. 1999:136; Phinney et al. 1998:938), not least as a way to protect their self-esteem (Crocker et al. 1991). Furthermore, being socialized in preparation for bias and discrimination makes minorities aware of discrimination and helps them adopt coping strategies in terms of psychological resources (Iqbal 2014). This point resonates with the notion of immigrant resilience (discussed below).

The ambiguity of the attribution process presents a challenge for utilizing self-reported discrimination to detect actual discrimination. Another challenge is that reports of discrimination reflect cases of group discrimination even in the absence of individual discrimination (Lindemann 2020). Empirically, individuals tend to perceive more group discrimination than individual discrimination, which leads to overreporting of discrimination (Taylor et al. 1990).

Underreporting is also possible, as some individuals might not be entirely aware of experiencing discrimination or undercount acts of discrimination in a type of coping strategy (Blank et al. 2004).

Assuming that reports of discrimination are accurate and reflect actual instances of individual discrimination, we might ask why ethnic minorities should be more prone to experience discrimination in a school setting. Several theoretical approaches address the existence of ethnic discrimination in schools (Diehl and Fick 2016). One possible explanation for migration-related or ethnic discrimination is *intergroup bias* (Sidanius and Pratto 1999). The key elements of intergroup bias are that individuals distinguish between in- and out-group members and evaluate the attributes of in- and out-group members differently: the attitudes toward out-groups are more negative (see also the concept of separation within the stigma framework, Link and Phelan 2001; Pachankis and Wang, this volume). One of the most prominent social–psychological theories that seeks to explain this phenomenon is *social identity theory* (Tajfel 1982; Tajfel and Turner 1986), whereby integrated or intergroup threat theory addresses the variation across ethnic groups in the extent of out-group discrimination (Stephan and Stephan 2000; Stephan et al. 2009).

Another strand in social psychology considers important underlying causes of discrimination in cognitively based stereotypes and emotionally charged prejudices (Diehl and Fick 2016; Fiske 1998). The concept of stereotyping is prominent in stigma research (Link and Phelan 2001) and refers to the ways in which immigrant or ethnic groups become represented by generalizations, which typically carry negative connotations (Castaneda and Holmes, this volume). A common stereotype in the German context would be, for example, to view immigrant descendants of Turkish origin as coming from resource-poor, rural backgrounds. Such stereotypes might create low expectations in teachers, regarding the potential scholastic achievement of students with Turkish heritage (Lorenz et al. 2016). Yet stereotypes are not always negative; "stereotype promise" is used in reference to the positive stereotypes of Asian Americans in the United States (Lee and Zhou 2014).

When an individual holds and acts on negative prejudices, actual discrimination results. For instance, Becker's (1971) theory of taste discrimination assumes the existence of stable tastes among individuals, which result in effective discrimination of unpreferred groups (Hunkler 2014; Kalter 2003). In contrast, the statistical discrimination approach assumes that due to lack of full information on individual skills (productivity), some group characteristics are assigned to individuals perceived to belong to the group in question (Aigner and Cain 1977; Arrow 1972; Phelps 1972). Statistical discrimination in the education and vocational education/training (VET) systems occurs at entry and transition points; it is less likely in daily classroom interactions due to teachers' direct access to information (Kristen 2006).

In summary, the concept of perceived discrimination reflects both actual discrimination and subjective interpretations of nonsuccess in school. Both might differ, depending on whether a student stems from a migrant or native-born background. In the following, we outline what consequences actual and perceived discrimination might have for educational and VET trajectories as well as their outcomes among minority students.

Consequences of Discrimination for Individual Educational and Training Trajectories

Discrimination by teachers can lead to negative consequences for minority students through several distinct mechanisms. First, when a teacher awards low grades or gives poor track recommendations to a student, this can result in the student being placed in a less ambitious school or training track. Yet, claims about the existence of direct teacher discrimination in the German education system are largely equivocal (Diehl and Fick 2016). Field experiments document average causal effects of ethnic discrimination against minority students in track recommendations (Sprietsma 2013) and teacher expectations (Bonefeld et al. 2020; Wenz 2020). However, experimental evidence for discrimination in grading is rather inconclusive (Sprietsma 2013; Wenz 2020). Whereas Wenz (2020) does not find any discrimination in grading of essays hypothetically written by students with Turkish sounding names, Sprietsma (2013) reveals that essays with a Turkish name receive significantly lower grades. Yet, the observed effects originate from a small group of teachers, whereas most teachers do not discriminate based on the students' origin.

Second, regarding achievement expectations, teacher bias toward minority or students from low socioeconomic backgrounds may lead to differential treatment in the classroom, as in the amount of emotional support a student receives, the quantity and quality of teachers' feedback, as well as exposure to learning materials (Alexander and Schofield 2012; Gentrup et al. 2021; Lorenz et al. 2016). This, in turn, can affect students' competency and curb scholastic advancement. Both direct and indirect teacher discrimination can potentially create a stereotype threat to students, which becomes problematic when the affected students internalize and act according to these stereotypes regarding their migration status, ethnicity, or socioeconomic background (Owens and Lynch 2012; Steele and Aronson 1995). The underlying mechanism—a self-fulfilling prophecy (i.e., the idea of expectancy confirmation processes, see Jussim et al. 2009; Merton 1948)—operates as follows: The stereotypes and related behavior by classroom teachers may lead students to develop lower self-esteem and decreased interest in school, eventually resulting in poorer scholastic performance (Alexander and Schofield 2012; Diehl and Fick 2016; see also Pachankis and Wang, this volume, for a discussion of intrapersonal stigma mechanism). Indeed, research has shown that discrimination, both actual and attributed, has serious consequences for an individual's psychological well-being (Schmitt et al. 2014) and a student's sense of belonging (Jasinskaja-Lahti et al. 2009; Skrobanek 2009). The internalization of school difficulties might lead to students' estrangement from the educational processes, not least due to the oppositional culture, particularly among the disadvantaged minorities (Ogbu 2003). As a result, perceptions of discrimination can lead to the *exclusion or diversion of minorities from more advantageous tracks.*

Negative consequences of discrimination, however, are not the only possible scenario: migrant students might be successful in defying discrimination. Indeed, ethnic minorities tend to strive for ambitious educational paths despite objective and subjective experiences of discrimination. The perception of discrimination, similar to the anticipation of discrimination, may prompt immigrants to invest strategically in further education as a means of overcoming discrimination barriers, for example, in the labor market (Heath and Brinbaum 2007; Teney et al. 2013). Earlier research has postulated that in anticipation of discrimination in their professional careers, immigrants may follow more demanding school tracks and strive to obtain higher educational qualifications, compared to their counterparts without an immigrant background once prior achievement is taken into account (Heath and Brinbaum 2007; Jackson 2012; Jonsson and Rudolphi 2011). Experiences of discrimination in school might enhance minority students' anticipation of discrimination at the labor market and potentially encourage them to choose educational and training options which increase their success in the labor market.

Another reason for minority students' persistence in the education system might be the use of effective coping strategies against minority-based discrimination. When discussing individual and family-level coping strategies under adverse conditions, psychological and sociological research has emphasized the role of resilience among discriminated groups (Gabrielli et al. 2021; see also Castaneda and Holmes, this volume, for a discussion of resistance to stigma). The term resilience has been applied to describe a trait observed among individuals or social groups who are able to defy adverse situations and become stronger through their experiences (Sandín Esteban and Sánchez-Martí 2014). Factors responsible for stronger resilience in ethnic minorities include individual attributes (e.g., self-efficacy, self-esteem, self-expectations) and social contexts, including ethnic resources, family cohesion, parental support as well as community factors in which social interactions occur, such as school settings (Marley and Mauki 2018; Motti-Stefanidi 2014). Assuming stronger resilience among minority students against challenges in school, including both actual discrimination experiences and anticipated discrimination at the labor market, one might expect minority students with discrimination experiences to be more likely *to avoid disadvantageous educational pathways* compared to the majority students.

Before the associations between perceived discrimination and educational/training outcomes can be examined, key elements of the German education and training systems must be understood. Below, we outline these as well as the major migrant groups that are currently present in German society.

Minorities in the German Education System

In the early 2010s, students in the German secondary education system who had a migrant background originated primarily from one of the following migration paths:

1. From 1950 to the 1970s, guest workers migrated from Italy, Spain, Greece, Turkey, Portugal, and the (former) Yugoslavian Republic (FYR) to fill low-skilled jobs in the industrial sector of West Germany (Olczyk et al. 2016). In East Germany, similar guest worker schemes brought migrants from "socialism-friendly" countries (Northern Vietnam, Mozambique, Angola, Cuba, North Korea, China) to work in East Germany (Bade and Oltmer 2007).
2. After World War II and particularly after the breakup of the Soviet Union (Kogan 2011), *(Spät-)Aussiedler* migrated to Germany from the (former) Soviet Union (FSU) and Central and Eastern Europe (CEE) because of their German heritage. Given the recent history of this migration wave, Eastern Europeans comprise both first- and second-generation migrants in today's education system.
3. Until the end of the 1990s, asylum seekers from Turkey, the African continent, and countries of the FYR, CEE, and FSU, including the so-called Jewish Quota Refugees (Kogan 2011), migrated to Germany. This is a rather heterogeneous group in terms of their generation (both first- and second-generation) and socioeconomic backgrounds (Olczyk et al. 2016).
4. As of the 2000s, EU-internal migration (predominantly from CEE countries) and refugee migration is reflected in the 2010 school population of mainly first-generation migrants (Olczyk et al. 2016).

In the secondary level of education, a student either enters a comprehensive school (*Gesamtschule*) or one of three separate types of schools or tracks: the *Gymnasium*, the *Hauptschule*, or the *Realschule*. The *Gymnasium* prepares students for tertiary education; successful completion opens a wide range of opportunities for high-paying jobs in the future. The *Hauptschule* and *Realschule* represent the lower and upper vocational tracks, respectively, and are designed to prepare students primarily for postsecondary, nontertiary VET. Here, successful completion leads to occupational qualifications, and hence decent jobs, or options with lower economic prospects (e.g., unqualified labor market jobs). Vocational training combines workplace-based training and schooling (a so-called dual system). To participate in dual training, students apply to companies for apprenticeship positions through a procedure that resembles a typical job search. A smaller number of students pursue their qualifications through school-based training programs, which take place primarily at vocational schools and are comparable to vocational degrees attained within the dual system of VET. In addition to these standard trajectories, students without training positions or enrollment in academic secondary tracks participate in prevocational measures—a fallback option that prepares them for certain occupations and improves their school-leaving qualifications. Finally, the education system does provide a certain level of mobility between tracks or "second chance": students on a nonacademic track are able to transition to an academic track or to a higher-level vocational track if they fulfill the necessary requirements (Schuchart and Rürup 2017).

Data and Methods

For our analyses, we relied on the data from the German section of the Children of Immigrants Longitudinal Survey in Four European Countries (CILS4EU-DE) (Kalter et al. 2016; Kalter et al. 2021). Our survey began in the school year 2010/2011 and targeted the ninth grade students who were approximately 14 years old. Students were selected through a three-stage sampling design. The first stage involved schools that had students in the targeted age groups, which were selected to enable the oversampling of schools with large shares of immigrants. The second-stage units were classes within targeted grades in sampled schools, from which two classes were randomly sampled. The third stage involved all students in the classes. As many as 144 schools with 271 school classes agreed to take part in the first wave of CILS4EU-DE, with response rates on school level of 53% before and 99% after replacements of nonresponding schools with equivalent ones (for further information, see Kalter et al. 2019).

To identify the education and training trajectories during the secondary stage of education, we relied on information from a Life History Calendar, which was administered in the survey's sixth wave and captures all episodes of education, training, work, and other activities since January 2011 (i.e., around the time of the survey's first wave). We define the time frame of secondary education as 60 months, beginning with grade 9, which in our data is September 2010 to August 2015.

The first dependent variable pertains to the patterns of educational trajectories after grade 9. Based on optimal matching analysis, a commonly used method for analyzing sequential data (see Weißmann et al. 2023), four trajectories within education and VET were identified that captured typical trajectories of the German ninth graders: the *Gymnasium*, VET, ambitious, and ambiguous paths. Whereas the first path captures education trajectories within upper secondary education (ca. 34% of the sample), the classic VET path encompasses transitions to vocational education and training directly after the lower secondary schooling option (ca. 23%). The other two pathways are nonstandard, but different in nature. The ambitious path (ca. 23% of respondents) refers to students who upgrade from nonacademic educational tracks to (vocational) academic secondary schools, with the goal of securing certification to enter tertiary education. The ambiguous path (ca. 19% of all respondents) represents a cluster of transitions within the nonacademic tracks outside of vocational training: transitions to vocational preparation courses (a fallback option), statuses outside of education or training (largely into the unqualified labor market), or transitions to nonacademic vocational schools.[1]

The second dependent variable captures the outcome of secondary education paths, measured as the educational attainment of respondents at around the age of 21 (i.e., until the time of the survey's seventh wave). These include the academic secondary certificate or *Abitur* (the prerequisite for tertiary education), vocational qualification, vocational qualification with an academic secondary school-leaving certificate, and a residual category which encompasses those who are still in education or have not obtained any vocational qualification or academic secondary degree.

Our key independent variable is reported experience of discrimination or unfair treatment in school, which was collected in wave 1. Based on the question, "How often do you feel discriminated against or treated unfairly in school?" we redivided the original four-category variable into three parts marked by the following responses: (a) "always or often," (b) "sometimes" or (c) "never." Overall, 10% of students reported frequent discrimination or unfair treatment in school: 13.2% among students with a migration background (defined below) and 8.8% among those without any migration background. Many more students reported occasional discrimination or unfair treatment in school: ca. 48.1%. Incidentally, a larger share of ethnic majority students perceived occasional discrimination (49.8%) than students in the ethnic minority (43.4%) (see Table 6.1).

Since the wording of the question does not specify the type of possible discrimination, answers may equally capture ethnic, migration-related, social, age, or gender discrimination as well as instances of being treated unfairly. It may also reflect ambiguities in student interpretations of disadvantages at school, even if these are not related to discrimination in its strict definition and just represent unfair treatment. Therefore, the reporting of discrimination or unfair treatment among native-born students should not come entirely as a surprise and may be related to feeling discriminated based on socioeconomic origin, gender or age. Furthermore, when interpreting results, one should bear

1 As many as 546 respondents did not participate in the Life History Calendar in the sixth wave and therefore did not contribute to the optimal matching analysis. We assigned these cases to one of the four trajectories using information from repeated cross-sectional interviews since the first wave. The following conditions were defined for the first wave: Students in *Gymnasium* were assigned to the *Gymnasium* path. Students not in the *Gymnasium*, who were predominantly in vocational training after lower secondary education, were assigned to the VET path. Students not in *Gymnasium*, who were predominantly in (vocational) academic secondary schools after lower secondary education, were assigned to the ambitious path. Students not in the *Gymnasium*, who were predominantly in vocational preparation courses or nonacademic vocational schools after lower secondary education, were assigned to the ambiguous path, as were those who never entered (vocational) academic secondary schools or vocational training or who were observed in both statuses equally often.

Table 6.1 Reporting discrimination by education/VET trajectory, in percent (W1 sample). Source: CILS4EU-DE v6.0.0, own calculations. Results have been design weighted.

	Overall	Trajectory				*N*
		Gymnasium	VET	Ambitious	Ambiguous	
All						
Never	41.9	44.2	39.2	43.4	39.7	781
Sometimes	48.1	47.0	50.1	47.2	48.5	831
Often/always	10.0	8.9	10.7	9.5	11.8	184
N	1796	571	339	481	405	1796
Without migration background						
Never	41.4	45.1	39.7	39.8	38.3	464
Sometimes	49.8	46.2	51.9	53.0	49.3	528
Often/always	8.8	8.6	8.4	7.1	12.4	112
N	1104	386	230	280	208	1104
With migration background						
Never	43.4	41.1	36.8	52.1	41.9	317
Sometimes	43.4	49.3	41.7	32.7	47.3	303
Often/always	13.2	9.6	21.5	15.2	10.8	72
N	692	185	109	201	197	692

in mind that perceived discrimination or unfair treatment is measured only once in school—when the students were 14—whereas the education and VET trajectories are captured between the ages of 14 and 21 years, with outcomes of secondary education paths measured at 21 years of age. Although experiences of school discrimination are captured at the latest possible time when all students are still at school, the impact of any additional perceptions of discrimination later in adolescence remain elusive in our study.

Our analyses focused on the differences between students with their own migration experience as well as students with at least one immigrant parent and German-born students with two German-born parents (natives). Overall ca. 27% of the sample were students who migrated themselves or had at least one parent who was an immigrant. In additional analyses, we defined students with migration backgrounds by their heritage, differentiating between minority students of Turkish as well as FSU/CEE origin. All other students with a migration background were classified as belonging to the "other" category. In these analyses, we were not able to differentiate students by their racial or ethnic background but could classify them by their parents' region of origin, defined broadly. Since samples sizes for the fine-graded analyses by origin groups are small, we report only robust findings to illustrate some origin group differences.

Other control variables include respondents' sex, year of birth (before 1995, 1995, or after 1995), parents' highest occupation captured by the International Socioeconomic Index of Occupational Status (ISEI) (Ganzeboom et al. 1992), and parents' highest education (intermediate secondary degree or below, academic secondary degree, university degree). As proxy measures of academic ability in wave 1, we counted a proportion of correct answers in a cognitive and a vocabulary test, instruments that are largely used in a comparable type of research in Germany (Heller and Perleth 2000; Weiß 2006). By considering whether students' background characteristics were potentially associated with discrimination experiences (e.g., discrimination based on gender, age, socioeconomic status as well as academic abilities), we were able empirically to single out the effect of ethnic or migration-related discrimination from related confounders.

To assess the role of discriminatory experiences for educational/VET trajectories as well as differences in outcomes, we applied multinomial logistic regression models. In the multivariate analyses of educational/VET trajectories, we focused on discrimination experience of students transitioning from lower secondary education to one of the following trajectories: VET, ambitious, or ambiguous trajectories. Since at this point, we are interested in the role of discrimination experiences for further educational trajectories, we excluded students who attended the *Gymnasium* from the analyses. After the lower secondary education, such students directly begin with their upper secondary studies and do not face the decision-making process regarding further education. Moreover, our measure of discriminatory experiences was administered during lower secondary education in grade 9—after students enter the *Gymnasium*. In the multivariate analyses of educational/VET outcomes, we focused on discrimination experience of students attaining one of the four outcomes: (a) the *Abitur*, (b) a vocational qualification, (c) vocational qualification with an *Abitur* or its equivalent, or (d) failure to attain any school-leaving certificate, including remaining still at school. All analyses applied design weights corrected for panel attrition until wave 6.

Discrimination within the School and VET Settings

In which educational tracks are students more likely to report discrimination experiences of various kinds, and what characteristics do these students possess? Results from Table 6.1 indicate that overall, immigrants and ethnic minorities are more likely to report frequent discrimination or unfair treatment in German schools and are less likely to report occasional discrimination. Compared to majority students, more minority students report frequent discrimination or unfair treatment both in VET and ambitious trajectories. In contrast, students without migration backgrounds, who are also in the VET and ambitious trajectories, more often report occasional discrimination or unfair treatment. Within the ambiguous pathways, we found that native-born majority students report more frequent discrimination than minority students, but the difference across the groups is negligible. Similarly, there are not many differences in the perceived discrimination among students with or without migration background in the *Gymnasium*.

Descendants of Turkish immigrants are generally more likely to experience frequent discrimination or unfair treatment. In contrast, descendants of immigrants from FSU, CEE, and other countries who report discrimination are more likely to mention occasional unfair treatment. Results pertaining to specific origin groups are not shown and should be interpreted with caution due to the small sample sizes in each group.

Next, we asked whether minority and majority students who face discrimination also differ systematically from one another on a number of characteristics relevant for school success. Our results show that students who report frequent discrimination experiences are likely to be older (born before 1995), and that this trend is particularly pronounced among students with migration background (Table 6.2). Since our data consist of a school cohort of ninth graders from the school year 2010/2011, variation in frequent discrimination experience by age may indicate that older students who have experienced grade retention perceive this to be a discriminatory action. Students who report frequent discrimination are more often male, and this pattern is similar among minority and majority students. Students with migration background who report occasional discrimination are more likely to be female compared to those without migration background who report occasional discrimination. Further, it is noteworthy that considerably fewer minority students who report frequent discrimination have tertiary-educated parents.

Students with and without discriminatory experiences differ from one another in terms of age and gender. Among minority students, parental characteristics also play a role. In addition, students with subpar academic performance often attribute their related frustrations to teacher discrimination. Therefore, we conducted multivariate analyses to predict students' pathways depending on their migration background and discrimination experiences (Model 1) and compare the effects of perceived discrimination across students with and without migration background (Model 2). Once possible confounders (e.g., age, gender, socioeconomic background) are accounted for in the model, differences in reports of experiencing discrimination or unfair treatment between students with and without migration background are no longer related to possible compositional differences between the two groups. Consequently, differences are more likely to capture the effect of perceived discrimination based solely on migration status or ethnic origin. Results are presented in Table 6.3 in the form of marginal effects; that is, differences in the predicted probabilities of an outcome between the analyzed groups. Thus, in Model 1 the marginal effect for the migration background in, for instance, the outcome "VET trajectory" represents an average difference (in percentage points) between students with migration background and those without in the probability of pursuing vocational training, when other control variables in the model are held constant.

Table 6.2 Sociodemographic characteristics of respondents with and without discrimination experiences. Source: CILS4EU-DE v6.0.0, own calculations. Results have been design weighted.

	Overall	Discrimination experience		
		Never	Sometimes	Often/always
All				
% year of birth				
before 1995	8.6	7.4	8.3	15.1
1995	47.5	48.8	46.4	47.2
after 1995	43.9	43.8	45.3	37.6
% girls	50.7	50.9	52.9	39.0
% tertiary-educated parents	26.2	25.8	27.1	23.4
Mean parental ISEI	51.2	50.8	51.8	50.4
Without migration background				
% year of birth				
before 1995	7.6	6.7	7.6	11.3
1995	47.1	48.9	45.9	45.9
after 1995	45.3	44.4	46.5	42.8
% girls	50.1	50.7	51.3	40.3
% tertiary-educated parents	28.6	28.0	28.9	30.1
Mean parental ISEI	54.7	55.1	54.2	55.1
With migration background				
% year of birth				
before 1995	11.5	9.3	10.4	22.2
1995	48.5	48.5	48.2	49.6
after 1995	40.0	42.2	41.4	28.2
% girls	52.3	51.5	57.8	36.4
% tertiary-educated parents	19.5	20.2	21.4	11.0
Mean parental ISEI	41.8	39.5	44.0	41.8

Results from Model 1, shown in Table 6.3, suggest that compared to the majority native-born students, students with migration background are less likely to be found in VET and are more likely to follow ambiguous trajectories. They are also more likely to take ambitious paths, but results are significant only at the 10% level. On average, reporting discrimination experiences at school is not associated with students' choice of education or VET trajectories. However, we observed considerable differences across students with and without migration background in the pattern of association between experiences of discrimination and their placement in education/VET trajectories. Model 2, which presents the differences between students with and without migration background in the discrimination effect, suggests that, on average, students with migration background who never experience discrimination are less likely to be found in VET, but are more likely to pursue ambitious pathways than

Table 6.3 Education/VET trajectories and self-reported discrimination (marginal effects after multinomial logistic regression models), selected results. Based on 1,225 sampling size (source: CILS4EU–DE v6.0.0, own calculations). Results have been design weighted. Control variables include sex, year of birth, parents' highest education and ISEI, vocabulary and cognitive test in Wave 1. $^{+}$ $p < 0.1$; * $p < 0.05$; ** $p < 0.01$; *** $p < 0.001$.

	VET trajectory	Ambitious trajectory	Ambiguous trajectory
Model 1			
Migration background (ref.: no)	–0.213***	0.092+	0.121*
Discriminated or treated unfairly in school (ref.: never)			
Sometimes	0.010	–0.028	0.018
Often/always	0.015	–0.034	0.018
Model 2			
Migration background (ref.: no) and discriminated or treated unfairly in school			
Never	–0.260***	0.158*	0.102
Sometimes	–0.197**	–0.009	0.207**
Often/always	–0.123	0.229+	–0.106

comparable majority students. Students with migration background who report occasional discrimination are also less likely to be in VET and are more likely to be found in ambiguous paths compared to the benchmark of the majority native-born, other things being equal. Finally, minority students who report frequent discrimination or unfair treatment are more likely to be found in ambitious trajectories (significant at the 10% level), whereas no differences across students with and without migration background is observed regarding other pathways. Although we already know that students with migration background have lower uptake of vocational training, from our analyses we learn that this is only true for minority students who do not report frequent discrimination. Our analyses further reveal that two distinct groups—minority students who never report discrimination and those who report frequent discrimination—are more likely to follow ambitious pathways. Apparently, students with migration backgrounds who experience frequent discrimination or unfair treatment do not abandon ambitious options to the same extent as majority native-born students who report the same frequency of adverse experiences at school.

A look at origin group differences suggests that avoidance of VET by immigrant students who report no or only occasional discrimination experiences is characteristic to all three origin groups. Descendants of Turkish immigrants with frequent discrimination experiences are also more likely to avoid VET. Further, these students are significantly more likely to be found in ambitious pathways once they report no or frequent discrimination.

To summarize, our results show that although students with migration backgrounds largely avoid VET, those who experience frequent discrimination are no different from the majority native-born with similar characteristics in the VET uptake.[2] In addition, minorities who experience frequent discrimination manage to enter ambitious pathways at somewhat higher odds than their majority, native-born counterparts. Although this effect is marginally significant once minorities are considered altogether, it is rather pronounced among descendants of Turkish immigrants, one of the stigmatized minorities in Germany. Finally, we observe that students with migration backgrounds who report occasional discrimination experiences are more likely to be found in ambiguous trajectories. Altogether we observe a somewhat stronger tendency on the part of minorities who experience discrimination to withstand this adversity (compared to students without migration background), which we attribute to the development of resiliency and successful coping strategies among ethnic minorities.

Discrimination Experiences and Outcomes

How do outcomes of educational and VET trajectories among immigrants and ethnic minorities differ from those of the majority native-born students? Before presenting results of our multivariate analyses, it is worthwhile to visualize the pathways and respective outcomes.

Figures 6.1 and 6.2, so-called Sankey charts, illustrate the trajectories (left) and outcomes (right) of native-born (Figure 6.1) and minority (Figure 6.2) students in the different education and VET pathways: (a) for students who never experienced discrimination; (b) for students who had occasional experiences of discrimination; (c) for students who reported frequent discrimination. For native-born students, regardless whether they experienced discrimination in school or not, educational and VET pathways are more similar than comparable trajectories among minority students. The largest difference among native-born majority students is that a higher proportion of students who report frequent discrimination end up in ambiguous pathways; a lower proportion are found in ambitious pathways. Among minorities, greater differences are observed between students who reporting occasional and frequent discrimination and those without discrimination experiences. Minority students who report frequent discrimination are less likely to progress into the *Gymnasium* and are more likely to be found in the VET trajectory. A comparison of minority students with occasional and frequent discrimination experiences reveals pronounced differences in their representation in ambitious and ambiguous pathways: students who report occasional discrimination are more often found in the ambiguous track, and less in the ambitious track.

These two figures suggest similarities in outcomes for native-born majority and minority groups without and with occasional experiences of discrimination. Greater differences are found in the outcomes of students who

2 Among students with Turkish origin, lower odds of VET participation are pronounced irrespective of discrimination experience.

reported frequent discrimination. Students without a migration background, who reported frequent discrimination in the ninth grade, are less likely to attain vocational qualification or vocational qualification with a certificate that qualifies them for tertiary education. These students are also more likely to fail to attain any qualification compared to their counterparts who did not report frequent discrimination. Among students with migration backgrounds, patterns are similar. Those who reported frequent discrimination, however, are as likely to attain their vocational qualification as the rest. This pattern is not observed among majority students. Overall, descriptive findings indicate a clear disadvantage to experiencing discrimination in school, which seems to be more pronounced among students with migration background.

Next, we examine whether these conclusions hold in a multivariate framework (see Table 6.4, constructed similarly to Table 6.3). Model 1 reports the marginal effects for migration background as well as for the experiences of discrimination or unfair treatment at school. Model 2 reports marginal effects for experiences of discrimination among students with migration backgrounds compared to students without migration backgrounds. In addition, we present coefficients for the effects of educational pathways to shed light on the path dependencies between the educational and VET trajectories and the resulting outcomes.

Table 6.4 Education/VET outcomes and self-reported discrimination (marginal effects after multinomial logistic regression models). Selected results based on 1,796 sampling size. Source: CILS4EU–DE v6.0.0, own calculations. Results have been design weighted. Control variables include sex, year of birth, parents' highest education and ISEI, vocabulary and cognitive test in Wave 1. $^{+}$ $p < 0.1$, * $p < 0.05$, ** $p < 0.01$, *** $p < 0.001$.

	Abitur	Vocational degree	Vocational degree and *Abitur*	No *Abitur*, no vocational degree
Model 1				
Migration background (ref.: no)	0.041	0.028	–0.082***	0.013
Discriminated or treated unfairly in school (ref.: never)				
Sometimes	0.002	0.046+	–0.031	–0.017
Often/always	0.040	–0.048	–0.089**	0.097*
Model 2				
Migration background (ref.: no) and discriminated or treated unfairly in school				
Never	0.062	0.009	–0.102*	0.031
Sometimes	0.040	0.032	–0.067*	–0.005
Often/always	–0.040	0.077	–0.066+	0.028
Trajectory (ref.: *Gymnasium* trajectory)				
VET trajectory	–0.740***	0.646***	0.096*	–0.002
Ambitious trajectory	–0.078*	0.003	0.007	0.068**
Ambiguous trajectory	–0.488***	0.343***	–0.025	0.171***

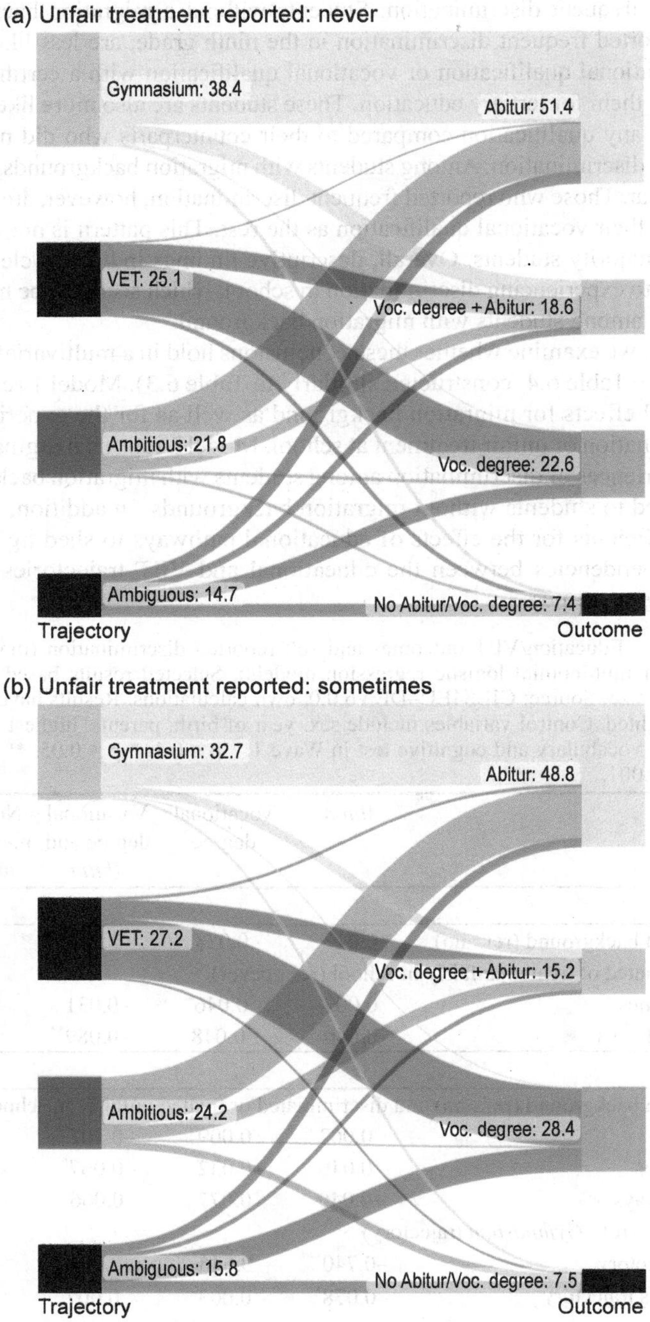
(a) Unfair treatment reported: never
Gymnasium: 38.4
VET: 25.1
Ambitious: 21.8
Ambiguous: 14.7
Abitur: 51.4
Voc. degree + Abitur: 18.6
Voc. degree: 22.6
No Abitur/Voc. degree: 7.4
Trajectory
Outcome
(b) Unfair treatment reported: sometimes
Gymnasium: 32.7
VET: 27.2
Ambitious: 24.2
Ambiguous: 15.8
Abitur: 48.8
Voc. degree + Abitur: 15.2
Voc. degree: 28.4
No Abitur/Voc. degree: 7.5
Trajectory
Outcome

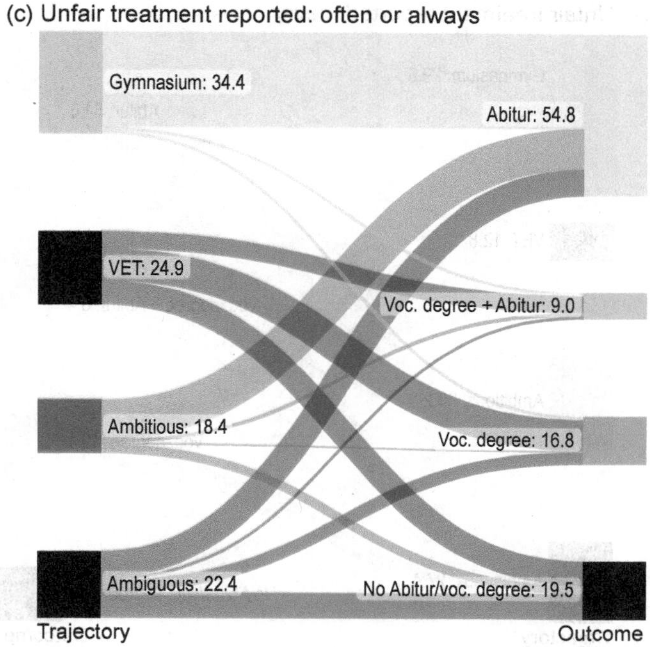

Figure 6.1 Educational and VET pathways, Sankey charts, that depict the trajectories and outcomes for native-born majority students: (a) no reports of unfair treatment, (b) occasional reports of unfair treatment, and (c) frequent reports of unfair treatment. Results are design weighted. Diagram created using SankeyMATIC. Source: CILS4EU and CILS4EU-DE, own calculations.

Results of Model 1 reveal that students with migration backgrounds are significantly less likely to attain a vocational degree and an *Abitur* than students without migration backgrounds. No other significant differences could be detected in the outcomes of education and VET transitions. Frequent discrimination and unfair treatment at school, on average, are associated with significantly lower probabilities of attaining a vocational degree and an *Abitur* and, at the same time, higher probabilities of failing to attain any degree whatsoever.

Model 2 demonstrates hardly any difference between students with and without migration background irrespective of their discrimination experiences at school. Ethnic majority and minority groups seem to differ only in the outcome "vocational degree and *Abitur*," albeit to a similar degree regardless of the extent of discrimination experiences at school.

Our results clearly demonstrate that educational and VET outcomes are very much path dependent. Students who pursue VET trajectories are more likely to attain a vocational qualification or vocational qualification with a certificate that qualifies them tertiary education and less likely to attain an academic certificate, the *Abitur*. Students in ambitious trajectories are somewhat

(a) Unfair treatment reported: never

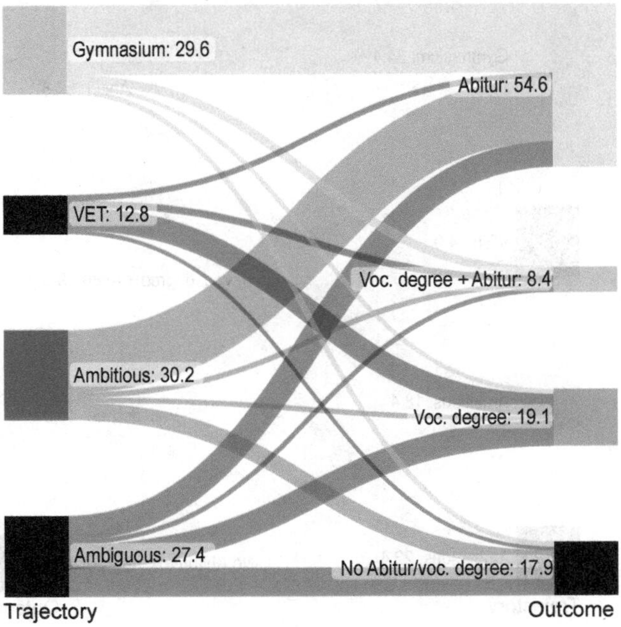

(b) Unfair treatment reported: sometimes

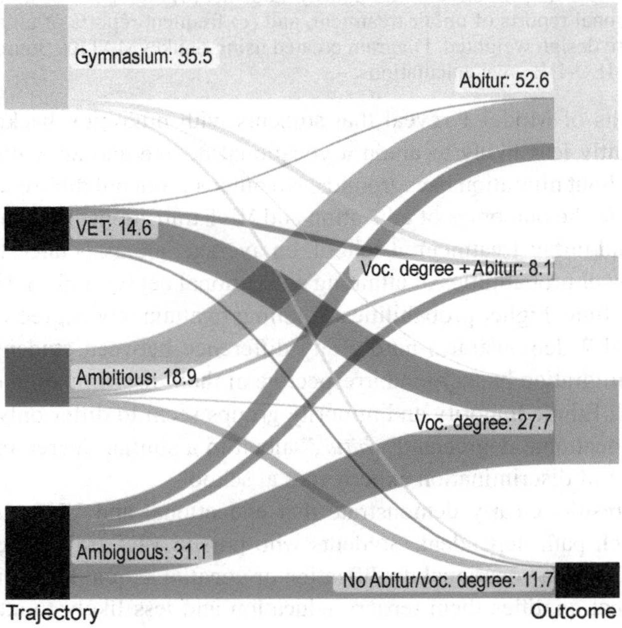

(c) Unfair treatment reported: often or always

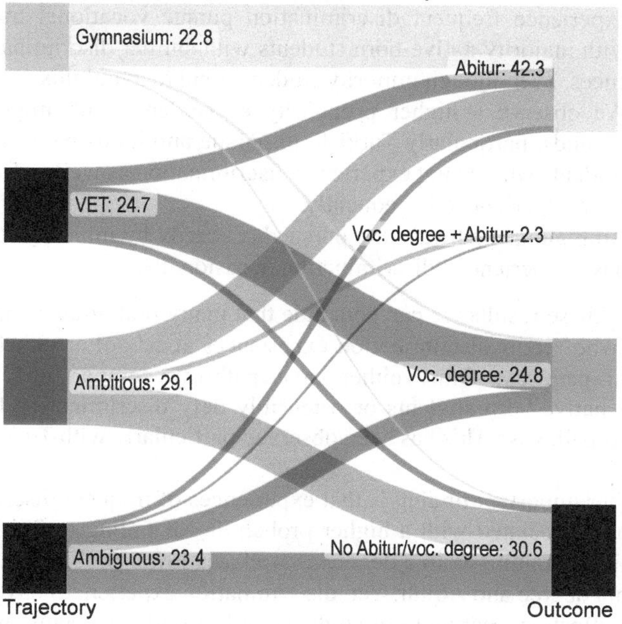

Figure 6.2 Educational and VET pathways, Sankey charts, that depict the trajectories and outcomes for minority students: (a) no reports of unfair treatment, (b) occasional reports of unfair treatment, and (c) frequent reports of unfair treatment. Results are design weighted. Diagram created using SankeyMATIC. Source: CILS4EU and CILS4EU-DE, own calculations.

more likely to obtain neither a vocational qualification nor an *Abitur* and less likely to attain the *Abitur*. Students in ambiguous tracks are considerably less likely to attain an *Abitur* but are more likely to get a vocational degree. In addition, they are more likely to end up without any qualifications, vocational or *Abitur*. It is interesting to learn that both ambitious and ambiguous trajectories carry risks, as students entering these paths are more likely to end up without appropriate certification.

Summary and Discussion

With the aim of understanding the longer-term consequences of discrimination experiences for ethnic minority students, this chapter has examined whether those who report occasional or frequent discrimination in school pursue different trajectories and attain different outcomes in the German education and training system than those without such experiences. Three important conclusions emerged from the analyses of the role of perceived discrimination in determining students' educational and vocational pathways:

1. With the exception of students of Turkish origin, minority students who experience frequent discrimination pursue vocational tracks on par with majority native-born students with similar discrimination experiences, even though minority students tend to avoid this option.
2. We observe a higher propensity of students with migration backgrounds, particularly Turkish, to pursue ambitious pathways, both for students who do not experience discrimination as well as for those who have experienced it frequently.
3. Ambiguous pathways are pursued primarily by minority students who have experienced discrimination occasionally.

Based on these results we can conclude that many immigrants and ethnic minorities who report discrimination experiences at school are likely to pursue precarious pathways. Others either pursue pathways comparable to those of the majority native-born students or ostensibly defy discrimination by pursuing ambitious pathways.This has been observed particularly with Turkish minority students.

Another important finding is that experiences of frequent discrimination in school are associated with a higher probability of failing to finish schooling or vocational training with a degree as well as a lower probability of attaining vocational degree and Abitur. Yet, discrimination experiences have practically uniform effects on native-born students and minority students, with the following exception: the attainment of a vocational degree with an *Abitur*. Here, majority students (particularly those who never report discrimination) perform better than students with migration backgrounds. Taken together, results suggest that experiences of discrimination at school in adolescence are associated with poorer education and VET outcomes in early adulthood, with little variation across majority and minority students in the discrimination effect. Education and VET outcomes are also strongly dependent on the paths chosen by students during the course of their education. The latter are also strongly determined by discrimination experiences.

Overall, discrimination and unfair treatment experienced by immigrants and minority groups at school is reflected in their overrepresentation in educational and training paths marked by a larger uncertainty. Yet minority students who report frequent discrimination, particularly Turkish students, are often found in ambitious pathways. This might indicate that these students have stronger resilience and ample coping strategies to combat adverse experiences at school. Whether such coping strategies operate at the family or community level could not be established in our study. Further, on the individual level, personality traits, such as locus of control or the big five (e.g., agreeableness and extraversion), could be associated with perceptions of discrimination (Sutin et al. 2016). This, however, remains a topic to be explored in future research.

Reports of occasional and frequent discrimination are likely to mean different things for native-born and minority students. Since our models control for a set of ascriptive characteristics (e.g., age, social origin, gender), the differences in reported discrimination between native-born and minority students are likely to capture instances of discrimination related to a student's migration background. Obviously, we cannot control for unobservable characteristics (e.g., emotional state, dyslexia, attention deficit hyperactivity disorder), which affect learning outcomes and discrimination perceptions. Still, there is no reason to suspect that such conditions are not equally distributed among students from German or non-German backgrounds. Due to the different patterns of representation between native-born and minority students who experience occasional and frequent discrimination in their educational pathways, we cautiously conclude that minority students who report discrimination experiences probably differ in their coping strategies and interpretation of the situation.

This study focused on the role that perceived discrimination in school plays in the educational success of a student, measured in terms of education and VET pathways and respective outcomes. Studying the impact of discrimination experience on anxiety, feelings of depression, and the sense of belonging to a school or the society at large (or lack thereof) among young adults would be an important extension of this research. Unfortunately, our analyses could not capture instances of objective discrimination. To what extent objective and subjective discrimination overlap, and whether discrepancies reflect cases of either underreporting (due to the ambiguity of the situation) or overreporting (based on anticipated discrimination) are questions that await further research. Indeed, the relationships among anticipated, perceived, and actual discrimination and students' educational outcomes is worthy of in-depth investigation.

7

The Lived Experience of Stigma among Immigrant Youth

Heide Castañeda and Seth M. Holmes

Abstract

The concept of stigma helps to explain the social effects of othering due to migrant status. Because stigma affects the overall distribution of life chances (e.g., health, educational success, employment opportunities, housing), it is important to consider the intersection of different stigmatized statuses and multiple outcomes. Here, five components of stigma are used to examine the stigmatization processes that affect immigrant youth: labeling, stereotyping, separation, status loss, and discrimination. Since immigrants push back against labeling as well as the accompanying exclusions and limitations that follow, the role of resistance and empowerment is explored. Different from reverse stigmatization, in which stigma reverts back to the stigmatizer, resistance, flourishing, and self-representation play major roles among the immigrant youth who experience stigmatization. This can be seen in individual and collective actions as well as in political, economic, social, and legal contexts (e.g., illegalization, undocumentation, deportability), and may inform ways to counter stigma. It is necessary to consider when stigma domains can occur independently of, and then in tandem with, the structural circumstance of migrant status, especially for those who are undocumented.

Introduction

Migration has become a defining global issue of our century, with contemporary mobilities a major aspect of public debate across the Americas, Africa, the Middle East, and Europe. Included in these mobilities are children and youth, who are migrating for multiple reasons related to war, disinvestment, global political economic inequities, legacies of colonialism and neocolonialism, and climate change. In some parts of the world, significant numbers of unaccompanied minors are moving away from danger toward alternative futures. Some are considered "first-generation immigrants," while those who are young enough to grow up primarily in a new society are often referred to as the "1.5 generation." In addition, migrants, immigrants, residents, refugees, asylum seekers, detainees, and other new members of society have families and children of their own. In many cases, people who did not migrate themselves, including the children of immigrants (often called "second generation") remain nonetheless categorized as immigrants. Despite living in a country for generations, many people, as well as their communities, are still perceived to be "foreign" (even "migrant") based on perceived notions of otherness. Children of migrants have long held a tenuous place in receiving countries and are often racialized in a way that characterizes them as perpetual foreigners, even if they are citizens (Chavez 2017; Flores-González 2017). Previous research has shown that these dynamics are heightened for immigrants who are marked visibly as different from the unmarked mainstream of a society, even after generations (Suárez-Orozco 2000). This label "migrant" follows ancestry for generations as a racialized, nationalized, and exclusionary status. At the same time, "post-migrancy" scholars and activists argue for moving beyond the category "migrant" or "immigrant" entirely due to these exclusionary outcomes (Römhild 2018, 2021). An "intersectional" (Crenshaw 2017) lens on the "interlocking systems of oppression" (Combahee River Collective 1977) allows for clear analysis of the different and conjugated forms (Bourgois 1988) of othering experienced by immigrant youth, especially in contexts in which undocumented status interacts powerfully with the status loss produced by stigmatization.

As coauthors, we each have decades of experience working with immigrant populations of many kinds, particularly in the area of health, and with a more specific, recent focus on the experiences of youth who are categorized as immigrant or migrant. As we stress elsewhere (Castañeda et al. 2015), migration itself can be considered a social determinant of health, including through the effects of racialized and exclusionary labeling. These negative health effects are visible among immigrants as well as their family members including, importantly, their children regardless of where they were born (Castañeda 2019). Exclusionary treatment and labeling of youth who are categorized as immigrant or migrant affects their education, social status, and future job prospects (Suárez-Orozco 2000). Many immigrant youth are the recipients of interim, temporary, transitional, or uncertain legal statuses that are proliferating globally (Abrego and Lakhani 2015; Smith and Castañeda 2021); this, however, only signals their incomplete inclusion. While most of our work has been conducted with immigrants in the United States and Mexico, we have also worked in Germany, Morocco, Syria, Spain, and Romania.

Drawing on our own research as well as the broader literature, discussion in this chapter focuses on the lived experiences of stigma in immigrant youth, with an emphasis on the processes of racialization that impact immigrant youth. Racialization and class, however, often overlap and are even co-constitutive in contemporary formations of racial capitalism. We explore how current public narratives and exclusionary policymaking have significantly increased discrimination, violent threats, and various forms of cruelty toward immigrants in recent years (Vaquera et al. 2021). This climate and rhetoric in the United States and other countries is driving and escalating the stigmatization of immigrants and provides an opportunity to examine the role of structural discrimination.

Stigma is one important way to understand the social effects of othering due to migrant status as it is accompanied by labeling, stereotyping, separation from others, status loss, and discrimination (Link and Phelan 2001). Stigma is a "central driver of morbidity and mortality at a population level" (Hatzenbuehler et al. 2013:813) that could be considered "a fundamental cause of health inequalities" (Hatzenbuehler et al. 2013:813). Stigma affects not only health but the overall distribution of life chances (e.g., educational success, employment opportunities, housing). This requires us to consider the intersection of different stigmatized statuses and multiple outcomes (Link and Phelan 2006:528).

In this chapter, we use the following components of stigma to structure our discussion of stigmatization affecting immigrant youth: labeling, stereotyping, separation, status loss, and discrimination (Link and Phelan 2001:363). We consider the ways in which power must be exercised for stigmatization to occur and focus on both individual and structural levels of stigma, particularly its discrimination component. It is important to note, however, that immigrants (including immigrant youth) push back against labeling along with the exclusion and limitations they imply. Therefore, we explore *resistance and empowerment as an addition to the idea of reverse stigmatization*. As Link and Phelan (2006:528) note: "There can be no stigmatization without…the exercise of power. The essential role of power is clear in situations where low power groups attempt reverse stigmatization." In addition to reverse stigmatization (in which stigma reverts onto the stigmatizer), we argue for a focus on the role of resistance, flourishing, and self-representation. We are interested in individual and collective actions against stigma (including structural stigma) as well as in how political, economic, social, and legal contexts (e.g., illegalization, lack of documentation, deportability) interact with stigma, and the possibility of counteracting this. What happens when immigrant youth actively "own," embrace, resist, and attempt to undo the effects of stigma by embracing, renegotiating, or navigating around its narratives and implications?

Here, we examine how these processes span individual and collective levels and engage structural levels of change to counteract powerful institutional sources of stigma. It is important to note, however, that the domains of stigma discussed below are deeply intertwined with the structural vulnerability (Quesada et al. 2011) of being undocumented. This structural aspect of stigma (i.e., of being undocumented) is often inseparable from other experiences of stigma. Thus, it is necessary to consider when stigma domains occur independently of, and then in tandem with, the structural circumstance of being undocumented. When the latter is present, how does stigma take on powerful and particularly oppressive forms?

Components of Stigma in the Experiences of Immigrant Youth

To understand more fully the experiences of stigma among immigrant youth, we consider the five elements of stigma in turn. Discussion centers on youth who have immigrated with their families, on their own, or with others, as well as those who grew up, and may or may not have been born, in a receiving society yet are still labeled "immigrant," "migrant," or of "immigrant background." We include the experiences of youth whose legal categorization span classifications as undocumented immigrants, legal residents, people with transitional or uncertain statuses (e.g., DACA), citizens, refugees, and asylum seekers. Although the experiences of each group differ, youth in these groups are routinely stigmatized and excluded in various and often related ways. Thus, these similarities as well as some of the distinctions are considered below.

Labeling

The first component of stigma, as laid out by Link and Phelan (2001), is labeling; that is, the attachment of a label to a person or the categorization of a group of people according to a particular label. Among immigrant youth with whom we work, labeling involves a mix of simultaneous racialization, nationalization, geographicalization, and other forms of classification. Many are routinely called "immigrant" or "migrant" even if they were born in the country in which they reside or are citizens of the country and have never left. Sometimes, these youth are "classed" in ways that are conflated with immigration status, such as being called "farmworkers" even if they have never worked on farms themselves. In the United States and other countries where we have conducted fieldwork, the category "farmworker" simultaneously and clearly connotes racialized, classed, and immigrant status (Holmes 2013). In many countries, someone who is visibly racialized as not a member of the mainstream is said to have an "immigration background" or to be a "foreigner" (Foroutan et al. 2018).

Labeling happens simultaneously on diverse levels. For example, let us consider youth who were born in the United States, whose parents are indigenous Triqui people born in the state of Oaxaca, Mexico. These youth are often called "Mexican" by their U.S. White classmates, "Oaxacan" by Mexican immigrants, Latine by U.S. citizens, and "Triqui" by people with ancestry from another indigenous group in Oaxaca. This demonstrates how one person can be simultaneously labeled in multiple and different ways by different people. Each of these labels categorizes the individual and the group through an essentialized characteristic.

Using this example, let us look further at the ramifications of labeling, based on ethnographic research and interviews among immigrant youth and their classmates at a high school in a rural region in the state of Washington (Holmes 2013). The local high school was having difficulties with a rural "gang" of self-identified White students who were harassing, bullying, and intimidating students they labeled as "Mexican." The gang, "Whites Against Mexicans (WAM)," and the students who supported the gang wrote WAM on their notebooks, phones, and in graffiti on high school property. In response, the school administration made a policy to forbid the display of WAM anywhere. At that time, a group of students who wanted to work toward intercultural understanding initiated a basketball game that played with and against the discriminatory rhetoric of WAM and called itself "Wamsketball." In interviews and conversations with members of the Wamsketball game, it became clear that the labels of "White" and "Mexican" were unstable and changing, yet powerful. One of the members of Wamsketball was a Latinx/e high school student who did not fit in the White category because of his skin color, yet he did not fit in the Mexican category because of the way he dressed. This student often served as the referee because he could not be easily labeled. He and the other students explained that to be Mexican in their school, one must not only have brown skin, but also wear a particular style of clothes and hair. Further, the label referred not only to body appearance directly but to social class (i.e., what kind of jobs they and their parents had, how much money they had) and clothing style (e.g., what they considered cool to wear). Thus, labeling reflected both social class and local culture.

This also reminds us that some immigrants are not categorized by society as immigrants, largely due to their class and unmarked racialization. In many societies, immigrant professionals are categorized as "expats" and not perceived (or labeled) as immigrants or migrants.

Stereotyping

The second aspect of stigma is, stereotyping; that is the ways by which groups of people become represented by and understood through generalizations. For stigma, these generalizations carry negative connotations. Current public narratives, including those in the media, frequently depict undocumented immigrants as outsiders, at best, and criminals, at worst. This is not new. The tone of these narratives, however, shifts over time, often aligning with the priorities of particular political moments. During the Trump presidency (2017–2021), for example, exclusionary policies increased discrimination, violent threats, and various forms of cruelty toward immigrants. This, in turn, increased the acceptance and normalization of negative media depictions of undocumented immigrants, in general, and Latinx/es, in particular (Vaquera et al. 2021).

Chavez (2008, 2017) addressed many of the negative stereotypes that have been and are still applied to Latinx/e people in the United States. To understand the ways in which Latinx/e communities are stereotyped as criminal or dangerous and as a financial drain on society, he analyzed public discourse (e.g., newspapers, television, political debate) and tracked how distinct words and categories become conflated: from "undocumented" or "unauthorized" to words that carry negative connotations which most scholars argue are incorrect representations (e.g., "illegal"). Words like "illegal," used as an adjective (e.g., an illegal alien) or noun (i.e., referring to a person as an illegal) become conflated with concepts such as "criminal," "violent criminal," or "dangerous." Thus, individuals who lack formal documentation (e.g., a residence permit) become represented by and understood through negative generalizations (e.g., dangerous, criminal) that are empirically unfounded. Abrego and Menjívar (2011) describe this kind of stereotyping as "legal violence": laws protect the rights of some but simultaneously marginalize other groups, leaving them unprotected and ultimately more vulnerable. Even though second-generation immigrant youth, who are born in the country in which they reside, have documentation, many are affected by policies that target their undocumented family members and are routinely treated as or called "undocumented" or worse.

In other writings, Chavez lays out the ways in which immigrants are represented and understood as "lazy" or a financial drain on society. These generalizations are employed regularly in political debates, the media, and public discourse, deliberately ignoring the many ways in which immigrants (including undocumented immigrants) contribute to society (including financially), far beyond what they are offered or given. As Phelan et al. (2008) argue, stigmatization can function for the mainstream group to keep the stigmatized "down, out, and away" on social, economic, political, and even physical levels. Quesada et al. (2011) show specifically how generalizations of immigrants reflect an understanding that they are in competition with an assumed, yet undefined mainstream group in the United States, which leads to negative stereotyping and amplifies separation. Quesada analyzed the language used in a voter proposition in California, which presented immigrants as financial drains on the undefined category of "Californians," and pitted the experiences of immigrants against the experiences (and so-called suffering) of the assumed and unmarked (i.e., White) mainstream in the state. Aware of the assumption that immigrants are financial drains, prominent organizations in California have more recently engaged in public media campaigns to document the multiple and specific ways that undocumented immigrants contribute to society. These competing narratives along with the changing political landscape in California are indicative of narratives about immigrants found elsewhere in the United States and the world.

Separation

Though they do not accurately represent reality, the negative stereotypes discussed above persist in many national settings and lead to the subsequent aspect of stigma under consideration here: separation. Fundamental to this component is the establishment of boundaries that separate an "in-group" from an "out-group" or "us" from "them": "they" become a threat to "us" because "they" are perceived (through labeling and stereotyping) to be criminal, immoral, lazy, predatory, and so forth as discussed above (Morone 1997). Ultimately, the intent is to keep certain groups of people out of full membership in society; effectively, it denies access to resources and may prevent people from entering a space altogether. It is crucial to note that this is not inherently an aspect of majority versus minority groups, since those categorized as immigrants or as a minority may actually constitute the majority in multiple settings. Rather, the stigma that impacts immigrant youth should be understood more clearly as a process of "minoritization" in the sense that one group is an unmarked, assumed mainstream group while the other group is a racialized, othered group.

Building on the work of Chavez (2008, 2017), Quesada et al. (2011) and Ruhs (2013), political debate and news discourse pits immigrants ("them") against an undefined, presumably White, middle-class mainstream (interpolated by the speakers and authors as "us"). Chavez and others (e.g., Holmes and Castañeda 2016) analyze the ways in which metaphors that refer to water (e.g., flood, surge, rising tide, tip of the iceberg) are utilized to instill fear in the mainstream ("us") toward the presumably dangerous immigrant ("them"). These metaphors culminate in claims that "we" are at risk of being "drowned" and must protect "ourselves." Such linguistic devices not only separate immigrants from other members of society, but also foster antagonism, fear, prejudice, and violence. This violence manifests in various forms: from young White children in Orange County, California shooting BB gun bullets at anyone presumed to be immigrants, to the torture and murder of immigrants by civilian vigilante groups in Texas and other border states, to the structural violence of racialized labor markets within a racialized and nationalized (though always transnational) capitalism. Quesada's work analyzes how the experiences of immigrants, including what some immigrants refer to as "suffering," are made invisible when lawmakers and anti-immigrant organizers publicly state that "they" (immigrants) have caused "Californians" to suffer. Negative stereotypes as well as separation led to antagonism, fear, and competition that impacts status loss, to which we now turn.

Status Loss

Status loss refers to a downward trajectory in the status hierarchy of society. The metaphors discussed above are often employed to inflict status loss, so that those affected (e.g., immigrants) are not successful in activities that otherwise would have contributed to the overall distribution of life chances (e.g., higher education, meaningful employment). For immigrant youth, status loss is mediated and reinforced through the structural mechanism of citizenship. The inability to regularize one's status or have the "right" citizenship confers a disadvantage on young adults and is the primary driver of stigma among immigrant youth. As shown in multiple contexts, these processes also lead to the experience of immigrants as second class (Castañeda 2019).

During childhood and early adolescence, the importance of one's own immigration status is largely suspended, as children may experience significant stress related to their parent's deportability (Castañeda 2019). In the United States, undocumented children navigate through the public school system in similar ways as their peers, largely because of the 1982 Supreme Court ruling that all children can assert claims to public elementary and secondary education regardless of legal status. This ruling represents a very important structural form of protection for students. During this time, children may make deliberate choices about when, why, and with whom they discuss their own or their family's legal status. In school, these decisions may begin early. Children as young as ten and eleven years old engage in decisions about whether they should disclose or disguise legal status to avoid stigmatization and status loss (Castañeda 2019). The right to education, in practice, has been interpreted as a kind of "don't ask, don't tell" policy. School districts don't ask questions about a family's immigration status and children "don't tell" as a result of socialization practices learned at home. Undocumented parents may explicitly warn their children not to provide information at school, which sometimes results in unintended consequences. Parents may not respond to school efforts to enlist their participation if correspondence includes words like "citizenship" (e.g., an invitation to attend ceremonies where "good citizenship awards" are given), as this may be perceived to imply immigration enforcement. Teachers can also create conflicts for children through assignments that generate anxiety about legal status or that inadvertently prompt disclosure (e.g., homework related to family history), which may elicit information about migration status and lead to labeling.

In the school setting, active concealment of legal status is a common way to avoid stigma among immigrant youth (Castañeda 2019). Interview research, conducted by a team that included one of the authors (HC), among mixed-status families in Texas found that parents often coach their children on how to conceal their origins (Castañeda 2019). For example, Daniela, now a 23-year-old college student who arrived from Mexico at the age of nine, was told to tell others that she was born in the United States:

> I remember when we first got here, our parents told us that if anyone asked us, we're from here. So growing up we knew that. If someone was like, "Oh, where are you from?" the answer was, "I was born here in Texas."

Samantha, another student, added:

> My dad would always say, "Don't be saying that you're not from here. If they ask you, just say you were born here."

Such strategies are embedded in the socialization of immigrants and serve as preparation for anticipated bias.

Bullying—an unmistakable expression of both separation and status loss due to stigma—is another reason for active concealment of legal status. Children may be picked on because of their own or their family's illegality. In the social sciences, illegality is not the labeling of a person or a group of people based on immigration status, but rather an analysis of the phenomenological experience of illegality, of deportability, and the possibility of policing in everyday life (Willen 2007). For example, Sarah recalled an incident at her son's school:

> There are often boys or girls who bully other kids. They will say, "Your dad is a *mojado*" [or 'wetback,' a derogatory term for Mexicans who enter the United States without official government authorization]. I was called to my son's school because he had gotten into a fight. One boy told another, "Your momma is illegal," and my son tried to defend him. He was trying to stand up for parents like me. They use "illegal" as a form of racism. I went to the school and told the principal, "I want you to respect us. We never get in trouble with anyone." And we sat down with the counselor and had a serious conversation with the boys who were bullying. My son already has his head full of ideas that I am going to leave, ever since his dad was deported when he was three. He's just scared.

This illustrates how family legal status becomes a primary site of division for children in school. As Sarah notes, the term "illegal" functions "as a form of racism."

During adolescence, individuals are particularly susceptible to social influence from their immediate social environment, especially their network of peers, which plays a key role in shaping prejudice (Hjerm et al. 2018a). Often, adolescents discover, on their own, what "illegality" means, usually through interactions with peers or at school. Most have never considered where they were born or questioned their family's legal status, yet they picked up enough clues from their social environment (through the media, in their neighborhoods, at school) to know that illegality was something that is stigmatized. This often leads to difficult conversations with parents (Castañeda 2019). Mayra, for example, was confronted by her son after an incident in school. In her account:

> They were going around the room in his freshman year, saying, "Where were you born? And where were you born?" And since he had never asked me before, he just said, "I was born here." Then he came home and asked, so I told him he was born in Mexico. He said, "So I'm from Mexico?" And then that's when he told me, "Well, up until now I was going to go to college, but I can't if I don't have a Social Security number."

This sense of surprise and disappointment on the part of youth was likewise echoed in other conversations with parents. One mother, Juana, recalled a similar story in which her son "started asking why we didn't come here to have him born as well. He says he can't have the same freedom." Like Mayra's son, Juana's son became angry after this revelation:

> Even though he studies a lot and brings home good grades, he says he can't go to college because he doesn't have a Social Security number. Or he says, why study if he can't work in the field that he gets his degree in? Now he's just always very negative.

Juana's son has even used this situation against his mother during arguments:

> If I scold him for something, he blames it on that. He says, "You don't like me because I don't have papers!" He became rebellious.

Her relationship with her son has subsequently deteriorated after the status revelation.

Status loss is reinforced via the structural mechanism of citizenship. Being undocumented or unable to obtain legal status confers massive forms of social disadvantage and interacts with and perpetuates stigma for immigrant youth.

Discrimination

The final component of the stigma process, discrimination, may occur on both individual and structural levels. Indeed, discrimination is such an important and constitutive aspect of stigma that we "cannot hold the meaning we commonly assign to it when this aspect is left out" (Link and Phelan 2005:370). While the examples described above illustrate stigma, below we examine the concept within its individual and structural levels. In addition, some examples point to the possibilities of intergroup discrimination as well as intragroup diversity and intragroup discrimination (Córdova Jr. and Cervantes 2010).

Individual Level

At the individual level, discrimination refers to the unequal treatment that arises from membership in a particular social group. In participatory visual ethnographic research conducted by one of us (SH) with indigenous Oaxacan 1.5 and second-generation youth, one of the 12-year-old participants pointed out the ways in which she has been discriminated against because of her being labeled an immigrant and a Oaxacan (Librado et al. 2021). Despite being born in the United States, she has been bullied at school because of the color of her skin and height. In one interview, she described the experiences of bullying in school and then followed this up with a sense of confident resistance, stating: "Just because we are Oaxacan, we aren't dumb" and "just because we're short, we still think, we're not dumb." This example of individual-level discrimination takes place despite the individual being a citizen. It also reminds us that the categorization of racialized "immigrant" may last for generations in many societies, as highlighted above. This example not only reveals individual-level discrimination, but also points to the role of resistance and resilience (discussed further below).

On the individual level, people may experience extortion or harassment when others use information about their immigration status. Such individual-level discrimination takes place when others prey on an individual's structural vulnerability (Quesada et al. 2011; Bourgois et al. 2017). Based on the interview research conducted in Texas, 16-year-old Selena recalled a time when a landlord sexually harassed her mother after the family fell one month behind on rent:

> He decided to take advantage of the situation and told her, "Now you have to sleep with me." My mom refused, and he threatened to deport her. I know that was really hard for her. Because of her status, he wanted to take advantage of her.

Selena's mother was too afraid to call the police and report the incident, illustrating how this type of threat effectively silences victims. There are even cases where someone's own family member has threatened to call ICE (U.S. Immigration and Customs Enforcement) out of rage or jealousy, or to extort money. Fifteen-year-old Jaime told me:

> Somebody from our own family from Reynosa, my aunt's children, threatened to call immigration on my dad. Why? They were planning to get money out of him. It's always about money. It's crazy.

Like deportability, "denounce-ability" (Horton 2016) functions as a powerful and remarkably efficient technique of governance precisely because everyone knows someone who has experienced it. There were many actual cases where people were reported to immigration authorities, and this heightens fear for everyone who is vulnerable. Michelle was in fifth grade when she, her sister, and their father were deported after an angry neighbor called immigration following a dispute. The neighbor didn't want the family to use a side yard that was part of the space they were renting, because she used to park her car there before Michelle's family moved into the rental. After months of arguments over the space, the neighbor reported the family to ICE, which led to their deportation.

Discrimination may also play out at the individual level in very intimate ways. Concealment of status and feeling like one is living a double life can strain friendships and cause shame. Eva, a 23-year-old undocumented youth, said that when it came to social situations,

> I felt sad, heartbroken. I was ashamed that I didn't have papers. I was afraid if I told one of my friends, they would make fun or just not hang out with me anymore. I'm fearful and a little ashamed.

Often, because of their status, it may take a while for people to feel comfortable with others and establish friendships. Undocumented young adults may be inhibited when they try to adhere to normative expectations of dating and courtship, especially because marriage looms large as a potential pathway to citizenship and future stability. For undocumented persons, marriage means so much more than simply a transition to adulthood: legal status (and the stigma associated with it) is a key factor at all stages of family formation, and those who are undocumented have unique concerns and experiences compared to their citizen peers. This individual-level discrimination takes place based on the structural condition of being undocumented. Most relationships are impacted to some degree by the decision to disclose one's status or not, and when. The stigma of being undocumented negatively impacts dating opportunities, as recounted by Armando:

> *Me daba mucha vergüenza.* I was so ashamed. I felt so worthless. Like, you don't deserve to go out with me, because there is no future with me. I can't be like a normal boyfriend. They have cars and take their girlfriends out everywhere. For me to have a car, I need a better job. So at the beginning of our relationship, I was so embarrassed. So ashamed of being undocumented.

Although Olivia can laugh about her experience now, the rejection endured at the time hurt deeply:

> One time I had a boyfriend, and the topic of legal status came up. He broke up with me the next day. I think he was in the same situation and wanted someone who was a citizen, so that he could fix his papers. It's like he said, "Why would I want you? You're no good to me."

Legal status can doom relationships before they even begin. Some people opt to break up rather than disclose their legal status and make themselves vulnerable. Others may doubt the sincerity of the relationship. The specter of hidden intentions can also linger, as people may worry that their partners are in the relationship only to gain legal status.

At the far end of risks associated with disclosure in intimate relationships lies the possibility of threats and intimidation, as demonstrated by Martha's account of a frightening breakup:

> My mom always says, "Be careful who you tell; they might turn you in," and there's always that fear in the back of your head. A few years ago, I had a boyfriend who wanted to do just that. He was really jealous and possessive, and when I broke up with him, he threatened to call ICE on me. For months after that I was afraid, just never knowing if they would come.

Disclosure produces vulnerability, even (and often especially) in the most intimate relationships. Like many of the participants in this study, Martha's parents taught her to disclose her legal status to as few people as possible to avoid the stigma and discrimination associated with it (Castañeda 2019).

Structural Level

Discrimination at the structural level refers to the societal conditions that constrain an individual's and a group's opportunities, resources, and well-being. This can manifest in limited job or educational opportunities, residential segregation as part of the legacy of redlining, poor health status and more importantly, as discussed above, "it takes power to stigmatize," and this power works through White supremacy; racial capitalism; citizenship; anti-immigrant prejudice, policy, and practice; and structural inequities. One of the most powerful examples of discrimination at the structural level concerns immigration enforcement raids that target Spanish-speaking or Latinx communities (Kline and Castañeda 2020; Lopez and Holmes 2020). Such raids directly impact youth because of their own or their family members' deportability and the potential this holds for the violence of family separation. The detrimental impact of deportation and detention on individual, family, and community health cannot be overstated.

It is important to recognize that it is not only youth who are immigrants themselves, but also youth who are the children of immigrants. Both are affected by structural discrimination. In research among mixed-status families in Texas discussed above, many U.S. citizen youth experienced loss of opportunities due to federal and state policies that were directed toward their undocumented parents or siblings (Castañeda 2019). Although these policies explicitly affect only undocumented individuals, the children and siblings of undocumented people also experience poor health status, fewer educational and extracurricular activities, and other forms of incomplete social inclusion. Thus, citizenship formations and the structural vulnerability caused by undocumented status, deportability, and illegalization affect undocumented people as well as those associated with them.

Perhaps the most salient area where structural forms of discrimination emerge for immigrant youth is in the realm of health disparities. Structural discrimination is a fundamental cause of health inequalities that has a bearing on distribution of life chances in such areas as earnings, housing, criminal involvement, well-being, and life itself. Hostile policy environments result in intense feelings of anxiety, fear, and depression (Gonzales et al. 2013; Kline and Castañeda 2020; Logan et al. 2021), which can exacerbate preexisting health conditions such as high blood pressure and diabetes. Experiences of racism and discrimination are in turn linked to risk factors that shape health outcomes. Undocumented immigrants and their family members experience a pervasive fear of deportation that negatively impacts their psychological, emotional, and physical health. In addition, loss of opportunity for immigrants related to social class and its inputs and components (e.g., education, home ownership, and income) are all factors that influence health status. Thus, the stigma which impacts immigrant youth affects not only the health of the youth themselves, but also their health over their life course as well as the health of their future children.

One aspect of structural discrimination important to the current and future life chances and health of immigrant youth relates to educational opportunities. Scholars have emphasized how youth labeled as immigrants, especially those who are racialized and classed, confront obstacles to educational achievement (Gonzales 2011, 2016; Suárez-Orozco 2000). Youth experiencing stigma as immigrants must contend with loss of opportunities in education: for instance, discrimination against bilingual and multilingual students/families and the inability to participate in certain extracurricular activities due to immigration status. They also experience anxiety, stress, and depression in relation to experiences of status loss and bullying. The long-term impacts of these obstacles to educational achievement cannot be underestimated, including their influence on future social standing, job opportunities, and health.

Resistance, Flourishing, and Self-Representation: Opposing Stigma

What happens when immigrant youth "own," embrace, resist, and attempt to undo the effects of stigma, as some actively do, by renegotiating or navigating around its narratives and implications? García et al. (this volume) explore processes of resilience and social cohesion and suggest that there are three general responses to stigma: it can be internalized, ignored, or resisted. Resistance, then, can be divided into a number of categories, including renegotiation, re-representation, rejection, distancing, overcompensation, and the building of local moral worlds.

Discourse is one major area in which resistance takes place as a form of re-representation. Immigrant youth in the United States have developed language to represent themselves, using terms such as "DREAMers" which was developed by and with immigrant students. Undocumented youth have formed movements to counteract the invisibilization fostered by immigration policy and stigma, including the phrase "Undocumented and Unafraid" (Abrego and Negrón-Gonzales 2020; Fiorito 2019). Indigenous Oaxacan immigrant students in California have collectively drawn attention to the discriminatory use of deprecatory terms such as "oaxaquito/a" and have successfully developed and passed policies in their school districts forbidding the use of these prejudicial terms. They have also coined novel terms to express not only their own experiences, but also their membership in society, including the term "Oaxacalifornia." Indigenous Oaxaca families and communities in the United States and Mexico have engaged in diverse forms of organizing binationally for inclusion on social, economic, educational, and political levels (Rivera-Salgado and Rabadan 2020). This speaks to the concept of the "oppositional gaze" (Hooks 1992), which marginalized groups may utilize to enact change in the face of repression, discrimination, and, especially, White supremacy.

At the same time, many youth counter forms of separation enacted against and within immigrant communities by stating that all immigrants deserve respect and social inclusion, regardless of whether they are students (and therefore "DREAMers") or not. Young immigrants deploy strategies to resist negative and dehumanizing portrayals by developing and embracing counter-narratives (Vaquera et al. 2021), or renegotiation followed by re-representation. They actively resist narratives that dehumanize them and their families by uplifting alternative representations that emphasize the diversity and dignity more reflective of their own experiences and identities. This suggests that these youth are not passively absorbing information but challenging it. Immigrant activists have long innovated to form a positive identity and challenge anti-immigrant rhetoric. Their strategies have changed over time alongside shifting political contexts, moving from close alignment with legislative efforts to increasing recognition of intersectional, marginalized, and transnational social locations (Abrego and Negrón-Gonzales 2020; Fiorito 2019). As Seif (2016:33–34) notes:

> Brave acts of speech and self-definition have allowed young immigrants to locate and support each other, organize, and advocate for assistance and rights. They allow youth during the transition to adulthood to form positive identities amidst a climate of media scapegoating and escalating deportations.

The awareness of how policies and government practices impact their daily lives gives them the courage to debunk myths and counteract discrimination.

For many young adults in the United States, "coming out" as undocumented is a critical part of their disclosure management process and autobiographical construction. This was facilitated by changes in policies and opportunities, most notably Deferred Action for Childhood Arrivals (DACA), a program that allows some undocumented young people, who came to the United States as children, to work and stay in the country. After decades of organizing by undocumented communities, this program was facilitated by the election of Barack Obama. In 2012, DACA, an Obama-era executive action, led to an estimated 1.74 million young immigrants becoming eligible for a two-year reprieve from deportation, temporary work permits, Social Security numbers, and the ability to obtain drivers' licenses. DACA changed the landscape of opportunities for many undocumented individuals, allowing beneficiaries to experience an increase in security and to develop more trusting relationships with institutions because of sanctioned educational and work opportunities. This, in turn, provided greater independence (Abrego 2018) and reassurance that they were not deportable (Gonzales 2016). Arguably, its implementation also aided immigrant youth to shed some aspects of stigma.

Indeed, these shifts in the social and political landscape have encouraged many undocumented immigrants to come "out of the shadows." As people "come out" as undocumented, they create new and complex identities and political subjectivities, which include confronting stigma head-on (Castañeda 2019). Empowered disclosure, or "strategic outness" enabled many to view their legal status as an asset, reframe its meaning, and even challenge others. From the interview research conducted in Texas described above, Camila, for example, recalled a confrontation in school. After a classmate made an anti-immigrant comment and racial slur during class discussion, she jumped in:

> I told the guy in my class, "You know what? I don't have my papers." And he's like, "Oh, you're like a *mojada*?" He didn't say it in a mean way. I couldn't blame someone that is ignorant about it. Even when people are mean about it, I don't get mad. I feel like I need to teach them. Being undocumented, to an extent, it does hurt. But at the same time, it really empowers you to make a change.

> When you're oppressed, you want to make the change. But when you're not affected by anything, it's hard to recognize you have a privilege. It's understandable. If they haven't faced it, how can they understand?

Brian, a DACA recipient, illustrated how his personal biographical construction was intimately tied to this form of strategic disclosure and stigma management and his ability to connect with others in the same social position. During college, he had become active in an immigrant rights organization and began to present in front of large crowds. As he explained:

> I started presenting, giving my story, the story of my family. It started getting to the point where it wasn't me. It was just a huge story of people who are connected to so many people around me. It was like I was telling my story, but I'm also telling your story. It got so comfortable to the point where now I can tell my story in peace without having that fear, without being nervous or scared.

Of course, while some undocumented youth are very active in challenging restrictive policy or supporting initiatives that aim for immigrant integration, this is certainly not the case for everyone. Undocumented youth carry different meanings for ascribed identity labels: some have positive connotations and denotations, while others do not. Many DACA recipients, for instance, perceive that label as having negative connotations and denotations (Cornejo and Kam 2021). To reach the many immigrant youth who are not active, there are groups dedicated to organizing and building consciousness. The Oaxacan Youth Encuentro in California, for example, is a group run by and for Oaxacan youth to build connection, community, and consciousness. Activism is often place specific. Undocumented youth who live in more politically restrictive environments or in new immigrant destinations seek collective engagement in distinct ways.

Conclusion

Various aspects of stigma affect immigrant youth differently. Although immigrant youth face forms of injustice and inequity due to individual and structural forms of stigma that unfairly affect their educational, occupational, and health chances, they also act to resist, undo, navigate, and reverse stigma in multiple creative and powerful ways. In this chapter, we have attempted to add to the concept of reverse stigmatization (Link and Phelan 2006) by focusing on simultaneous processes of resistance, flourishing, and self-representation. The examples provided demonstrate that immigrant youth do not work to stigmatize mainstream society, but rather attempt to develop and employ counternarratives that will better represent themselves, their families, and communities. At times, this leads to distinct narratives among the unmarked assumed mainstream group, for instance in some European and U.S. contexts in which immigrants are seen to contribute to society in important ways. In this chapter, we have asked: What happens when immigrant youth actively resist stigmatization and its effects by embracing, renegotiating, or navigating around its narratives and implications? In relation to their experiences, we see that an understanding of stigma and its effects, as well as an understanding of resistance to stigma and active re-representation, are extremely important.

Understanding stigma must involve a reckoning with the power of the stigmatizing group within hierarchies of power. Akin to Antonio Gramsci's understanding of hegemony as always being challenged and negotiated within a "war of position," we argue that the tactics and strategies of resistance of the stigmatized group must be considered in analyses of power and action. As we consider the experiences of stigma among immigrant youth and their actions to resist it, it is important for analysts and theorists of stigma in other contexts to attend to the diverse forms of negotiation, navigation, and resistance. Incorporating the concepts of resistance and opposition into our frameworks will increase our understanding of stigma itself.

8

How Policies That Impact Migrants Amplify or Mitigate Stigma Processes

Supriya Misra, Christian Albrekt Larsen,
Mark L. Hatzenbuehler, Marc Helbling,
Mikael Hjerm, Nicolas Rüsch, and Patrick Simon

Abstract

How are stigma processes reflected in policies that impact migrants? How might policies that impact migrants amplify and/or mitigate stigma processes for migrants? This chapter explores the role of policy narratives and frameworks (e.g., assimilation, integration, multiculturalism) in shaping specific policy types (e.g., targeted, universal, mainstream) that differentially conceptualize and affect the roles, rights, and opportunities of migrants in society. The complexity of the policy-making process is examined, including the specific policy context and political discourse, trade-offs leading to a mix of policy types, competing policies across jurisdictions (e.g., international, federal, regional), and differential implementation of policies. Throughout, policies are considered that can intentionally or unintentionally generate, amplify, and/or mitigate stigma processes. In addition, this chapter examines consequences of these policy-generated stigma experiences for both migrants and nonmigrants, the feedback processes from these stigma experiences to the demand for policy change, and strategies to improve policy making with specific consideration for stigma in the context of migration-generated diversity. Empirical gaps in the literature are noted and recommendations are made to address these knowledge gaps.

Introduction

We have come together as scholars of migration policy and stigma to understand how a stigma framework can be applied in the context of migration-generated diversity. Specifically, we consider how (a) stigma processes could be reflected in policies that impact migrants and (b) policies that impact migrants might amplify and/or mitigate stigma processes for migrants. We limit our focus to liberal democracies that aspire for equal rights and freedoms for all. We also limit our focus to the treatment of migrants *after* they have crossed a country's borders. However, we acknowledge that variation in the restrictiveness or expansiveness of policies about who is allowed to cross borders in the first place also contributes to overall stigmatization of migrants.

In this chapter, we discuss how the great narratives of equality in society shape the development, passage, and implementation of specific policies that impact migrants, at multiple levels and with multiple approaches, occurring within the context of the politics surrounding policy making. Next, we outline how these policies (and related politics) can intentionally or unintentionally generate, amplify, and/or mitigate stigma processes for migrants (Figure 8.1). We consider how to assess the consequences of policies for stigma processes, and how stigma experiences have the potential to generate feedback processes for policy change. We also consider potential strategies for policy making,

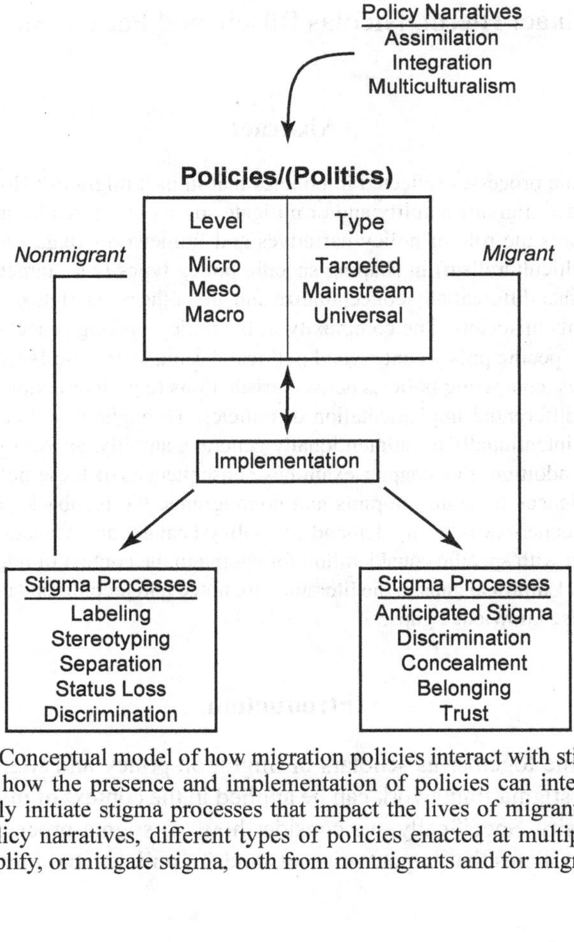

Figure 8.1 Conceptual model of how migration policies interact with stigma processes, outlining how the presence and implementation of policies can intentionally and unintentionally initiate stigma processes that impact the lives of migrants. Shaped by dominant policy narratives, different types of policies enacted at multiple levels can generate, amplify, or mitigate stigma, both from nonmigrants and for migrants.

particularly in the context of migration-related diversity, to monitor and respond to these stigma processes. Given the limited existing evidence at the intersection of these two areas of research, we highlight the many research gaps that still remain in understanding the bidirectional relationships between policies that impact migrants and stigma processes experienced by migrants across diverse contexts.

Migration as an Organizing Force and "Migrant" as a Social Category

Our definition of (international) migration and the status of being a "migrant" is embedded in the organization of the contemporary world since World War II, the era of the nation-state, wherein each country's borders are rigidly defined and enforced and individuals are assigned citizenship and/or permission for temporary or long-term residence within a country by its government. A widely applied definition of migrant is "someone who changes his or her country of usual residence, irrespective of the reason for migration or legal status. Generally, a distinction is made between short-term or temporary migration, covering movements with a duration between three and 12 months, and long-term or permanent migration, referring to a change of country of residence for a duration of one year or more."[1] Accordingly, as long as contemporary states exist, migrants will also exist.[2]

This means that migrants stand out as a social category of people at risk for stigmatization. Labeling someone as different is the first stage of the stigma process (Link and Phelan 2001). However, not every label generates stigma (e.g., labeling someone as tall is not as likely to generate stigma). Therefore, labeling is necessary but not sufficient to define stigma. It remains an empirical question whether being labeled as a "migrant" will always result in stigma. However, in any country where migrants are not entitled to the same rights as those with citizenship, such labeling will likely perpetuate stigma by designating migrants not only as different from others but also of lower status, which is most clearly demonstrated via restricted access to rights and resources.

Not all migrants are stigmatized equally. Migrants are perceived differently given the intersection with other social categorizations (particularly, class, gender, and race), and these perceptions shape policies and their consequences. In particular, certain migrant groups are more likely to be *perceived* as migrants due to visible phenotypic differences from native born groups. This is particularly true for migrant groups racialized as non-White in majority White

1 See "Definitions" at https://refugeesmigrants.un.org/definitions (accessed July 28, 2022).

2 There are scholars, however, who argue for a critical reorientation of research that shifts migration from the subject of study to the perspective of study given how use of these concepts risks reproducing their harms (e.g., Römhild 2017).

countries who continue to be perceived as outsiders regardless of their citizenship status (e.g., "Swiss by law" vs. "Swiss by culture"). In North American and Australian contexts, migrants are viewed as being distinct from indigenous populations and the descendants of enslaved people who were forcibly brought to the country. In the European context, the terms "migrant" and "ethnic minority" are used more interchangeably and there is considerable overlap. One consequence is that this terminology is also applied to the descendants of migrants (e.g., "second-generation migrant"), which may perpetuate stigma by labeling them as distinctive from other native born even when, by definition, they are not migrants.

These multiple overlapping identities exist in policy making, specifically in policies that address migration as well as, more broadly, ethnic minority groups. Given the state of these literatures, our use of "migrant" primarily focuses on first-generation migrants but includes any descendants who are still classified or perceived as "subaltern outsiders" in those countries. For simplicity, we refer to the remainder of the population without a migration background as "nonmigrants." By this, we specifically mean members of the majority or mainstream population who were born in the same country in which they now reside and are also part of the dominant racial/ethnic group(s) that possesses the power to be able to perpetuate stigma toward migrants. It is important to note, however, that use of these terms is imperfect as they legitimize the very categories that contribute to stigma and discrimination.

Policy Narratives and Frameworks

A classical question for liberal democracy is: How can a state ensure cohesion in a religiously and ethno-racially diverse landscape that is stratified according to class and gender? National narratives around social cohesion (along dimensions of homogeneity to diversity) and the resulting policy frameworks (along dimensions of race blind to race conscious) shape the construction of who "we" are, and that construction shapes and is shaped by institutions (Foner and Simon 2015). For migrants, this more specifically focuses on if and how migrants can be incorporated or integrated to feel solidarity with the national identity. In turn, these constructions create the context in which stigma processes are generated, amplified, and/or mitigated (Lamont et al. 2016). We define cohesion as sharing a set of values and norms that are deemed to be at the core of the society, such as agreements about the civic society, the rule of law and institutional procedures, a sense of connectedness and belonging, and ancestry, ethnicity, or undefined cultural commonalities.

Depending on their history of nation building and migration-related diversity, societies develop models of immigrant incorporation that differently value expressions of cultural differences and recognition of ethno-racial identifications (if not identities). Some societies have narratives and frameworks that downplay or exclude diversity (e.g., segregation). However, in societies that aspire to equality and social justice, a usual typology of narratives and frameworks for dealing with diversity distinguishes between paradigms of assimilation, integration, and multiculturalism (Alba et al. 2012; Joppke 2007). A central tension occurs between (a) monitoring different group trajectories to improve conditions for the more disadvantaged and pursue equality, and (b) ignoring group differences to achieve equality through a colorblind approach (i.e., treating everyone the same and expecting that a universal approach will improve conditions for the disadvantaged). Thus, while each of these approaches implies different policy frameworks that intend to deter stigmatization and discrimination, how successful or unsuccessful each of them are remains an open question.

Assimilation

The assimilation paradigm favors equality through invisibility of minorities and strives to design and implement colorblind policies. This paradigm can be beneficial in creating a structural function to preserve such solidarity by, for example, attempting to enable people to function equally via equal distribution of resources. Further, the strategy to downplay ethnicity and race might reduce problems of stigmatization attached to official labeling and identification by conveying these labels should not matter. However, this approach can also create a tension between social processes of racialization, which take place in interpersonal interactions and institutional settings, and the lack of positive actions against their consequences in the context of equality policies. Further, as long as the assimilation framework operates in a context where legal categorizations, such as migrants and native, or citizens and foreigners, determine differential access to civil and political resources, then neither invisibility nor equal distribution is possible.

Integration

The same can be said about the integration paradigm, which has considerable overlap with the assimilation paradigm. Despite its recognition of some dimensions of cultural differences, it promotes mostly colorblind policies to avoid reification of ethno-racial identities and fragmentation of the society along ethnic lines. Deviations from these norms are interpreted as a threat to cohesion, and thus what could have been a driver for inclusiveness can result in exclusion and stigmatization. Integration policies mostly bring outsiders (migrants and ethno-racial minorities) into the mainstream population, as this will grant full access to the social resources associated with their membership. In other words, while the existence of differences is acknowledged and recognized, the expectation is that outsiders should adopt the norms and expectations of the dominant society to achieve cohesion, rather than transform the structures and institutions of society to make them open for people to participate in society as they are. In societies that favor integration, conflicts take shape around the definition of norms and which changes, driven by participation of minority groups, are acceptable for the majority population. In this sense, the integration paradigm is more flexible to the incorporation of migration-related references into the core system than assimilation and, in an ideal scenario, might offer more avenues for stigma reduction.

Multiculturalism

Multiculturalism is usually described as a full recognition of cultural diversity that entails symbolic dimensions and forms of group-based political and social rights attributed to ethno-racial minorities (Modood 2007). This recognition might reduce the dynamics of stigmatization, even though it increases the labeling attached to identity politics. The multiculturalism paradigm is frequently associated with proactive antidiscrimination policies, in part because race-conscious policies can be adopted without raising contradictions, as in the assimilation and integration paradigms. The intention is to recognize differences without hierarchy, such as by separating identity labels from negative stereotypes of different groups, which could result in discrimination. Some argue, however, that this may result in harmful consequences; by demarcating and making the existence of certain groups salient, hierarchies between groups may be perpetuated if some groups perceive themselves as superior to others (Koopmans 2013). Hierarchies that feed into stigma could have negative consequences for individuals or groups who are perceived as not contributing positively to social cohesion by maintaining cultural differences.

Summary

In general, support for anti-migration policies is higher than anti-migrant sentiment (Margalit and Solodoch 2022). In particular, the policies and attitudes around wanting to restrict and keep people out of a country differ from those that address how to treat people once they live in the country. In our assessment, the assimilation and integration paradigms appear to be more common in countries with robust social welfare policies (e.g., Nordic and Western European countries), whereas the multicultural paradigm is more common in countries with more extensive migration histories and less regulated labor markets (e.g., Australia, Canada, United Kingdom, United States). The history of each state and the conditions needed to create change in these societies frame the context for each of these paradigms. In a time of increasing movement of people, goods, and ideas across borders, it is thus especially acute to determine how these paradigms impact stigma processes across differing contexts.

Policy Types

Based primarily within the dominant policy narratives and frameworks of each nation, three main policy types are used to address inequality and discrimination: targeted, universal, and mainstreaming. Additionally, explicit antidiscrimination policies also exist. While many of these policy types first originated to address class and gender inequality and discrimination, they have also been extended to address the conditions of migrants and ethnic minority groups. However, the effectiveness of the different policy types in deterring stigmatization and discrimination and reducing inequality remains an open question. Finally, although beyond the scope of this chapter, it is worth noting that policies that do not specifically address migrants might also be strongly impacted by the presence of migrants and thus require further consideration (e.g., housing, education, health-care access).

Targeted

Targeted policies intentionally designate resources and opportunities for groups (in this case migrants) and are most likely found in the multicultural paradigm, in countries with more extensive migration histories. One example of this type of policy would be the creation of language training programs to assist migrants in acquiring the local language. This approach explicitly recognizes that inequalities exist and that support may be needed in response. It attempts to mitigate stigma by directly addressing some of its causes (e.g., language differences) and consequences (e.g., inability to obtain a job due to language limitations). However, this approach also carries a risk, namely, it specifically labels migrant groups to receive the benefits of the policy (e.g., making language differences more salient, revealing additional resources are being invested in a subset of the population). In particular, the redistribution of resources for specific groups, rather than improving resources for everyone, could contribute to a perceived hierarchy that perpetuates stigma. Sometimes targeted policies use proxies, such as targeting deprived neighborhoods that have high concentrations of migrants without specifying the group to benefit from the policy (e.g., opening a language center in the neighborhood). Targeting neighborhoods instead of migrants is less accurate in reaching the desired population but might also mitigate stigma by not labeling the population explicitly. It remains an empirical question whether group-specific policies are possible without initiating stigma processes or by having any countervailing policies and practices in place.

Universal

Universal policies are more common in countries that have adopted assimilation and integration paradigms and are present in social democratic countries with more robust social welfare policies. According to social democratic ideology, equality is enhanced when all individuals have access to the same resources. Proponents of this approach argue that by not explicitly naming target groups, they are reducing the likelihood of stigma and discrimination. These policies were originally developed to reduce inequality based on class and gender and have now been extended to migrants and ethnic minority groups (e.g., "colorblind" policies). A central tenet here is to distribute rights and resources to individuals rather than groups. Further, by offering the same services or benefits to everyone, the intention is to improve conditions for the entire society. An example of this would be offering universal prekindergarten education that focuses on language acquisition. Such a program would benefit all children but would arguably have the greatest benefit for children who speak a different language at home. However, a critique of universal policies is that they may not address inequalities that specific groups, such as migrants, experience. For example, a similar program for adults would never exist because there is not a universal need for it. In this case, the biggest risk for stigma is through policy inaction or its dilution into generic policies that fail to reach migrants and address their specific experience of stigmatization.

Mainstream

Mainstream policies are similar to universal policies but incorporate concern for a specific target group. While universal policies intentionally do not consider any groups, mainstreaming policies acknowledge that group-specific inequalities exist and aim to reduce them through targeted policies that are implemented in a universal way (Scholten 2020). An example of this would be having school policies that require language services on campus; although any student could use these resources, they will be most beneficial to migrant students who are not native language speakers. In practice, these policies are most frequently used to combat gender inequality. However, such policies can also be used to curtail specific traditions or behaviors that fall outside of the dominant culture. For example, French laws that banned religious symbols in schools in 2004 and "full face coverings" in 2010 targeted Muslim women (e.g., wearing hijab or niqab); however, the general wording of the laws did not explicitly single out Muslims (Bowen 2010; Hennette-Vauchez 2017). Additionally, legally sanctioning some forms of stigma may enable stigma in other forms. For instance, banning "full face coverings" in schools may exacerbate how people treat Muslim women who wear such coverings in other settings, even though such behaviors are not legally condoned. The potential for mainstreaming policies to mitigate and amplify the risk of stigma overlap with both targeted and universal policies. As with targeted policies, labeling a group is required; however, as with universal policies, separation is not required. Targeted or universal policies may be the best option for specific circumstances, while mainstreaming policies may offer the best balance to manage the risk of stigma. However, comparing policy types for their influence on stigma processes remains an empirical question.

Antidiscrimination

Antidiscrimination policies create the normative framework addressing unfair treatment and disadvantages attached to protected grounds (e.g., nationality, ethnicity, race or color). These policies target not only unfair treatments or biases based explicitly on protected characteristics, but also neutral provisions and selections that entail disproportionate negative impact on individuals or groups identified by one or several protected characteristics. Detecting discrimination necessitates monitoring decision-making processes everywhere they occur and acting against these processes; their consequences require different ways to enforce equality (Fibbi et al. 2021; Fredman 2011). For institutions or individuals who intentionally or unintentionally discriminate, these policies enumerate strategies to review and respond to such incidents. Most antidiscrimination policies combine coercive actions based on sanctions and proactive actions that promote diversity. However, it is challenging to enact formal policies against discrimination in countries where data collection is lacking on race, ethnicity, or immigration status (Simon 2017). Therefore, antidiscrimination policies are implemented and enforced primarily in countries that utilize a multicultural approach to immigrant incorporation. In their pure form, antidiscrimination approaches transform the structures of society and allow full participation of members without requiring them to adjust to specific norms.

Summary

Targeted, mainstream, and universal policies all have the potential to amplify and/or mitigate stigma. These types of policies may address aspects of the migrant experience that do not directly relate to stigma or discrimination but may inadvertently affect all stages of the stigma processes. For instance, increasing access to jobs can lead to greater financial independence and reduce stereotypes (e.g., that migrants rely on the state for benefits and services). Antidiscrimination laws, by contrast, focus specifically on the ultimate stage of stigma: discrimination.

Policy Making and Implementation

The actual practice of policy making is complex. Policies do not exist in a vacuum but are part of a larger context and political discourse surrounding their passage and implementation. Typically, policies are a mix of frameworks and types to meet the different political trade-offs that need to be made. Policies occur at multiple levels that might be aligned with or contradict each other.

Finally, heterogeneity in the implementation of policies will ultimately determine their actual impact.

Importantly, the absence of policies (i.e., "policies of inaction") can reinforce stigmatization and discrimination toward a group by actively choosing not to offer policies to address their needs or to redress the harms they experience (Link and Hatzenbuehler 2016). This lack of action could be intentional (e.g., not passing a proposed policy) or unintentional (e.g., not being concerned about the experiences of the group to propose any policies that would benefit them).

Policy Context and Political Discourse

Universal and mainstreaming policies, which are intended to benefit a specific group but offer rights to everyone, vary in whether their text explicitly mentions the target group. The political discourse surrounding the drafting and passage of such policies, however, might make the target group known. For example, a few states in the United States have passed laws that permit all state residents to obtain driver's licenses, which are specifically intended to benefit undocumented migrants (as those with documented status are already eligible for driver's licenses). While this was not stated explicitly in the proposed policies, public debate around these policies focused almost exclusively on undocumented migrants. Similarly, the political debate for policies on "deprived neighborhoods" often focuses on the concentration of migrants in these neighborhoods. In theory, policy approaches that do not label the target population should be able to mitigate stigma. In reality, however, these policies cannot be separated from the political discourse that surrounds them, which might still include labeling even if the final policy does not. Further, these debates are often rooted in the narratives of equality that already exist (mentioned above). Thus, it proves difficult to disentangle the ideological and material aspects of the policy when considering the potential stigmatizing consequences (discussed below). Whether stigma fades once the political debate is forgotten over time or whether stigma persists if the targeted group is labeled in the policy remains a question for future study.

Policy Mix and Trade-Offs

To understand the complexity of policy effects, one must bear in mind that policy regimes are not simply assimilationist, integrationist, or multicultural, and the subsequent policies are not simply universal, mainstream, or targeted. Often referred to as a "mixed bag" (de Haas et al. 2015:4) or a policy mix (Schultz et al. 2021), policies are shaped by diverse political interests influenced by economic stakeholders, democratic decision-making processes, and constitutional norms (Boswell and Geddes 2011; Hampshire 2013). Sometimes different policy dimensions might even be contradictory and reflect different policy models. Ruhs (2013) argues that there might be a trade-off between an openness expressed toward migrants and the rights they obtain once they are in the country. For example, in rich countries, where there is a negative relationship with certain migrant groups, programs that are more open to let in migrant workers also extend fewer rights to them. The policy decisions taken in such cases might be related to cost and benefit calculations: an increasing number of low-skilled workers could lead to greater welfare costs.

At the same time, some policy dimensions are viewed as more important than others. For instance, some people might care more about border controls, whereas others might be more interested in the integration of migrants. Competing interests create the basis for trade-offs in policy regulations. In a study by Helbling et al. (unpublished), preferences about policies that govern migration flows were found to be conditional on policies that govern entrance criteria and rights eligibility. Respondents in the study who oppose migration, in general, were willing to compromise and allow more migration, if entrance criteria became more selective. Others who support migration were willing to compromise and accept less migration if rights become more generous.

Demand for specific policies often arises as a reaction to specific events. In 2015, for example, in response to mass sexual assaults on women in Cologne, Germany during public festivities on New Year's Eve, there were calls for more restrictive migration policies. Calls for more expansive migration policies or greater protections from stigma and discrimination often accompany public protests and social movements that demand fair treatment for migrants.

Competition across Levels

Different jurisdictional levels (e.g., federal vs. regional) have their own policies. This creates the potential for conflicts across levels: one level may follow more restrictive policies while another may be more inclusive toward migrants. Further, policies at higher levels often need to be implemented at lower levels, creating additional opportunities for conflict, from refusal to selective implementation of a policy. When specific stigma processes are activated, this may also differ across levels. Finally, at each level, policy awareness may also differ. For example, an individual might be aware of more proximal local laws that shape everyday experiences and interactions or of larger federal or regional laws that take precedence over local ones and bear greater importance, even if they are more distal.

Policy levels are commonly organized around the macro, meso, and micro levels. Currently, there is limited literature that links multiple levels simultaneously to understand how the totality of policies across levels might amplify and/or mitigate stigma processes (for a rare exception, see Lattanner et al. 2021). A true multilevel approach would include, for example, macro-level policies, such as legal frameworks that regulate discrimination or policies that structure group-based rights as well as micro-level policies both in terms of actual execution of legal frameworks and situation-specific policies in schools or at workplaces.

International governing bodies are situated at the top macro level. Although many different actors are involved in agenda setting as well as the conceptualization, definition, and implementation of policies regarding stigma and discrimination, supranational institutions assume an important role. The agenda on antidiscrimination in Europe, for instance, has been strongly influenced and even piloted by the frameworks set by the United Nations Committee for the Elimination of Racial Discrimination (CERD),[3] the Council of Europe's European Commission against Racism and Intolerance (ECRI),[4] and more directly by the European Directives on Equality in 2000.[5] International treaties are not strictly speaking binding instruments, but CERD is exerting a soft power on state members through two mechanisms. First, members are obligated to report on the state of racism in the country every four years. Second, CERD strongly recommends that more data is collected, broken down by ethnicity and race or proxies that would give a reliable account of the disadvantages faced by minority groups. The European Directives have a direct influence on the adoption of antidiscrimination laws in European Union countries and the definition of legal and policy frameworks on racism and ethnic and racial discrimination. The transposition of these directives into national laws has not only contributed to change the legal framework, but also to create awareness among policymakers and to disseminate concepts, terminologies, and toolkits related to antidiscrimination in European Union countries, where debate about racism and discrimination was rare if not inexistent (Banton 1996; Geddes and Guiraudon 2004; Keane and Waughray 2017).

However, macro-level policies, like antidiscrimination laws or the distribution of specific rights to groups of people, may be necessary but insufficient to cause major changes in discriminatory outcomes. At the most micro level, it may be more effective to consider and target resources aimed at micro policies or the operationalization of general frameworks (Sabbagh 2011). Examples could include simple changes such as blinded job applications, external grading of pupils and students, or protocols to steer distribution of lab access at universities. Such policies have several potential advantages. First, they are more easily implemented as such policies rarely encounter major political pushback. Second, they can hinder both unintended and intended discrimination and increase barriers for intentional discriminatory behavior, while not targeting or

---

3 See "Committee on the Elimination of Racial Discrimination" at https://www.ohchr.org/en/treaty-bodies/cerd (accessed July 28, 2022).

4 See "European Commission against Racism and Intolerance" at https://www.coe.int/en/web/european-commission-against-racism-and-intolerance (accessed July 28, 2022).

5 European Directive "implementing the principle of equal treatment between persons irrespective of racial or ethnic origin," a.k.a, Racial Equality Directive 2000/43/EC and Employment Equality Framework Directive 2000/78/EC.

stigmatizing individuals for unintentional behavior. Third, they are effective at the micro level and can have positive impact, even after short periods of time. Fourth, micro policies can influence other areas, mindsets, and behaviors that contribute to larger societal changes over time. These possibilities warrant empirical investigation.

Policy Implementation

Even when a policy does exist, whether and how it is implemented (i.e., both lack of implementation and selective implementation) can amplify and/or mitigate stigma. For example, in Germany policy stipulates that undocumented migrants can obtain a certificate for health insurance from a government office so they can access health care. Nonetheless, many migrants do not take advantage of this opportunity because they fear repercussions of having to disclose their undocumented status to state officials (Mylius 2016). The existence of the policy suggests an intentional effort to decrease stigma toward migrants; however, in actuality this is not realized. Consider further examples: Following the legalization of same-sex marriage by the U.S. Supreme Court in 2015 (*Obergefell v. Hodges*, 135 S. Ct. 2584), several county clerks refused to grant marriage licenses to same-sex couples (NBC News 2022). Uneven implementation of the policy undermined its ability to reduce stigma in some geographic regions within the United States. In Denmark, there is a highly restrictive policy which stipulates that the religious curriculum in schools should only focus on Christianity. As written, this policy would amplify stigma for students from other faiths, many of whom are likely to be migrants. However, because many teachers have chosen not to implement this policy, the harmful effects of this proposed curriculum have been mitigated.

Together, these examples illustrate the role of "street-level bureaucrats" (e.g., government officials, teachers, health-care workers) who put policies into practice. They are the ones who are directly in contact with members of the community (Lipsky 2010). These individuals can be influenced by a range of factors, ranging from their awareness and interpretation of the policy to their own personal preferences and biases. Similar to the "street-level bureaucrats," civil society institutions that represent migrants' interests, or other social networks in which migrants are embedded, may also contribute to the interpretation (or misinterpretation) of policies. Inaccurate information about policies can impact their broad implementation as well as the ability for migrants to access the intended benefits and services, even when implemented fully.

Finally, in addition to official implementation of policies, there is the perceived threat of implementation. In the U.S. context, the threat of detention and deportation has been shown to deter access to health and social services to which migrants are entitled (Fleming et al. 2019); this was also seen in the German example discussed above. Additionally, there could be backlash from institutions or individuals who are not part of the implementation process. Fear of backlash can impact implementation; even when implementation occurs, subsequent backlash could also deter access to the benefits and services enumerated in the policies.

Although policy implementation is an important pathway that could help explain the heterogeneous impact of policies on stigma, there are major challenges in measuring these concepts. This constitutes an important area for future research. Implementation science applied to policy implementation provides an emerging framework that might be particularly useful for advancing future research on this topic (e.g., Purtle et al. 2022).

Assessing Policy Consequences and Impact of Structural Stigma

All policies can have dual consequences: the potential to amplify and/or mitigate stigma for both migrants and nonmigrants. To assess policy consequences, a major challenge relates to the lack of relevant categories in routine data collection. In the United States and Great Britain, the majority of datasets do not measure migration background although they do measure racial and ethnic categories. In the European Union, the majority of datasets do not measure racial and ethnic categories but do measure migration background (Voyer and Lund 2020). Thus, determining whether and how policies affect different groups is often not possible. Further, assessing policy consequences will require developing better methods for enumerating and measuring the different stigma processes (e.g., Link et al. 2004). Below we consider both the limited existing evidence and some potential strategies for assessing these consequences from these dual perspectives.

For Migrants

Research on structural stigma—defined as "societal-level conditions, cultural norms, and institutional policies and practices" (Hatzenbuehler and Link 2014:2)—provides a framework for understanding the consequences of policies that impact migrants (see Hatzenbuehler, this volume). The concept of structural stigma was developed to consider how stigma may be embedded in social institutions, including in laws and policies (e.g., Corrigan et al. 2004). Research demonstrates that policies can impact stigma, intentionally and unintentionally, in at least three ways: by amplifying or mitigating stigma, as well as through inaction caused by the absence of policies or the selective implementation of them (Link and Hatzenbuehler 2016).

There is growing evidence that structural forms of stigma, as measured via laws and policies, adversely shape the lives of the stigmatized, including individuals with mental illness and lesbian, gay, bisexual, and transgender (LGBT) populations (see Hatzenbuehler, this volume, 2016, 2017a). For instance, quasi-experimental studies have shown that rates of psychological distress increased significantly among sexual minority individuals living in U.S. states that implemented laws denying services to same-sex couples; rates, however, did not increase among sexual minorities living in states where these laws were not implemented (Raifman et al. 2018a). Conversely, health outcomes improve when laws and policies expand rights and opportunities for stigmatized groups (e.g., Hatzenbuehler et al. 2012; Krieger et al. 2013). Although there is less research on how policies amplify and/or mitigate stigma processes specifically, there is a growing literature on the impacts of policies on migrant health outcomes (Perreira and Pedroza 2019). Recent studies have shown linkages between restrictive migration policies and adverse health outcomes among migrant groups, or those perceived to be migrants (e.g., Frost 2020; Samari et al. 2020), and between more inclusive migration policies and improved outcomes among migrant groups (e.g., Young et al. 2019).

Resource and Psychosocial Pathways

Research indicates at least two pathways for how policies shape outcomes among the stigmatized, including resource and psychosocial pathways. Regarding the former, policies can influence access to economic, social, and political resources across multiple settings (e.g., employment, education, health care). For instance, in the United States, there are 1,138 statutory provisions in which marital status is a factor in receiving federal benefits, rights, and privileges (USGAO 2004), and state governments confer even more benefits (Herek 2006). The financial advantages conferred through marriage range from tax laws and employee benefits to health insurance, pension plans, and death benefits (e.g., expenses of wills and properties). When same-sex couples were denied the opportunity to marry, the dollar value of the estate tax disadvantage between same-sex and heterosexual couples was estimated to be more than $3.3 million over the life course (Steinberger 2009). For migrants, it has been proposed that immigration policy and citizenship status not only restrict access to these resources but also restrict political and civic participation (e.g., voting, running for office), which constrains their ability to change the very laws and policies that impact them in the first place (Misra et al. 2021). There is a large literature documenting associations between economic adversity and the development of health problems (e.g., Nandi et al. 2004), indicating that the financial insecurity engendered by policies can compromise health for stigmatized groups.

These examples demonstrate how laws and policies can affect health outside individuals' awareness of the policy because policies shape (and reflect) the social structure in which individuals are embedded. However, research indicates that laws and policies also influence health via appraisal pathways; that is, via subjective awareness and experience (Figure 8.1). Studies have identified several psychosocial mechanisms linking structural stigma (measured via laws and policies) and health, including identity concealment (e.g., Lattanner et al.

2021), social isolation (e.g., Pachankis et al. 2021), self-stigma (e.g., Berg et al. 2013), perceived discrimination (e.g., Frost 2020), thwarted belongingness (e.g., Lattanner and Hatzenbuehler 2022), and stress (e.g., Flores et al. 2018). In other words, in environments with policies that promulgate and reinforce stigma, stigmatized individuals are more likely to conceal their identities, to be socially isolated, to internalize negative attitudes about their group, to perceive greater discrimination (for groups that are unable to conceal their identities), to feel less social belonging, and to experience greater stress. This research suggests that many individuals are, in fact, aware of structural stigma and appraise these environments as threatening to their sense of safety (Diamond and Alley 2022; Lattanner et al. 2021), which in turn contributes to negative health effects. For migrants, both their awareness of the general political climate (e.g., Morey 2018) and enforcement (or perceived threat of enforcement) of specific migration policies, such as detention and deportation, contribute to negative psychological impacts for those directly and indirectly impacted by this enforcement (e.g., Nichols et al. 2018; Von Werthern et al. 2018).

Hatzenbuehler (this volume) provides several recommendations for future research directions related to the consequences of policies for migrants. In addition, we highlight additional empirical questions that warrant further study:

- It is clear from the evidence reviewed above that policies which impact migrants can directly and indirectly activate stigma processes for migrants. Research is needed to identify which specific policies activate which stigma processes, including labeling group differences, attaching them to stereotypes, separating groups ("us" vs. "them"), status loss, and discrimination (Link and Phelan 2001). For instance, policies that provide specific protections (i.e., targeted policies) likely label group differences, but do they also confer stereotypes and lead to status loss and discrimination? Is it possible for policies to activate some stigma processes but not others?
- How do we assess whether a policy leads to stigmatizing consequences? We generated three possibilities: (a) analyze the narrative of the policy, (b) assess the disparate impact of the policy on migrants (vs. nonmigrants), and (c) test whether the policy initiates specific stigma processes (described above). Are there other ways to evaluate this issue?
- How do we identify the right time horizon, knowing that most studies measure impacts over a very short period, whereas most policies are intended to change things over the span of multiple years? Are short-term stigmatizing effects an acceptable trade-off if longer-term benefits are achieved?
- Policy are often mixed in regard to their treatment of migrants: some policies restrict rights whereas others expand them. What overall impact does this have on migrants? How do we differentiate the stigmatization that occurs as a result of the political discourse surrounding

issues relevant to migrants from the stigmatization that results from the policy itself? Studies have begun to examine this question (e.g., Bohman 2011; Flores et al. 2018), but more research is needed.

- Most of the research reviewed above focused on pathways at the macro and micro level. What meso-level mechanisms explain the consequences of policies that amplify and/or mitigate stigma? How might the effects of policies cascade through the social networks of migrants? How might policies at the macro level affect policies and practices among institutions at the meso level (e.g., schools, workplaces)?

For Nonmigrants

Policies intended to benefit migrants and mitigate stigmatization might have positive or negative impacts on the majority or mainstream society (whom we have, for simplicity, termed "nonmigrants"), which is primarily responsible for enacting stigma toward migrants in the first place. However, limited studies have focused on how policies intended to benefit migrants intentionally or unintentionally affect nonmigrants. Often, stigmatizing policies and practices serve a function for the nonstigmatized population and the loss of that function is likely to have negative consequences (Phelan et al. 2008). Further, some individual members of the nonstigmatized population might feel that anything designed to advantage migrants *must* disadvantage them. In other words, increasing the rights or resources of migrants might also increase negative attitudes toward them. In light of this, most of the available evidence on how policies impact nonmigrants have focused on negative changes in attitudes, including experiences of threat, backlash, and polarization.

Material and Cultural Threat

A major reason why policies that are intended to benefit migrants might have a negative effect on nonmigrants is due to the real or perceived threat to material or cultural resources (Stephan et al. 1998). The threat to material resources includes perceptions that migrants have lower socioeconomic status, compete for jobs, or drain resources. The threat to cultural resources includes perceptions of undesired changes to a cultural way of life or overall social cohesion. Some evidence suggests that cultural threats matter more than economic ones (Hainmueller and Hopkins 2014). Further, since it is hard to be aware of structures such as policies, it can be easier to project negative views and behaviors onto the people who are implicated by the policies (e.g., migrants) rather than the policies themselves (e.g., policies which place migrants in subordinate positions in societies) leading to stigma at interpersonal levels.

In particular, competition for resources could be perceived as a zero-sum game (Piotrowski et al. 2019). However, illustrative experiments compared policies that were zero-sum versus non-zero-sum situations. In their study,

Helbing et al. (unpublished) analyzed meals served in canteens: whether halal dishes replaced an existing meat dish (zero-sum) or were added as another option (non-zero-sum). They also looked at the effects of replacing a religious holiday (zero-sum) versus adding another one (non-zero-sum). They found that people who identified with the political left responded well to the non-zero-sum options but those who identified with the political right did not, lending support that stigmatization of migrants is not solely due to competition for resources but likely other factors such as cultural threat.

Opinion Backlash and Polarization Processes

Multiple studies have shown that attitudes toward migrants are shaped by integration and citizenship policies. All concur that integration policies have a direct influence on individual attitudes toward migrants and that nonmigrants generally align with these policies. While integration policies are broadly about the treatment of migrants within a country, a key dimension is citizenship policies that enumerate the criteria by which migrants might become citizens of the country in which they reside. Weldon's (2006) study reports that countries with individualistic civic regimes are more tolerant than collectivistic ethnic regimes. Ariely (2012) suggests that individuals in countries with a jus soli regime (i.e., birthright citizenship) express less xenophobic attitudes than individuals in countries with a jus sanguinis regime (i.e., citizenship determined by parents' nationality). Schlueter et al. (2013) find that more liberal citizenship regimes are related to lower levels of perceived migrant threat. Finally, Wright (2011) argues that more migrant-inclusive definitions of the national community are found in countries with a jus soli regime.

These studies adopt a socialization perspective, look at the average policy effects on the population, and assume a consensus among nonmigrants, at least implicitly. A shortcoming of this approach is that it does not leave room for disagreement over these policies, which may have a polarizing effect. Instead of assuming consensus, some studies show that the general public holds conflicting views and often disagrees with the liberal policies implemented by political elites. The notion that policy decisions which are disliked or threaten the status quo could cause a negative reaction that adversely affects the group profiting from the policy is known as "opinion backlash" (Bishin et al. 2016). Backlash reactions have been documented to affect several minority groups, including ethnic or racial groups (Bratton 2002; Preuhs 2007), women (Zagarri 2007), and sexual minorities (Fejes 2008). In the United States, for example, there has been a backlash against policies in support of multiculturalism and affirmative action over time (Lawrence 1998). Similarly, Traunmüller and Helbling (2022) show that permissive policy decisions lead to a polarization in attitudes toward Muslim migrants. Citizens who agreed with decisions to let Muslim migrants hold public rallies and demonstrations (aimed at increasing recognition of their interests) became more sympathetic to their cause, whereas those who favored restrictive decisions were more critical toward Muslim migrants.

The policy feedback literature also helps us understand these polarization processes (Mettler and Soss 2004; Pierson 1993). According to this approach, policies affect politics: Policies shape citizens' attitudes and behavior by allocating resources and creating incentives, on one hand, and providing information and normative content on the other. Such policies primarily affect groups that are directly affected by these policies, but they can also influence the majority population. In their investigations into how antidiscrimination policies influence citizens' support for the democratic system and its institutions, Ziller and Helbling (2019) show that antidiscrimination measures and knowledge about rights to equal treatment foster perceptions of government responsiveness. This, in turn, increases political support not only among target groups but also among citizens who are not directly affected by these laws but advocate egalitarianism.

The experience of threat, backlash, and polarization is often measured in the short term. Thus, it remains to be determined whether these policies ultimately lead to a positive change over the longer term, and whether short-term negative reactions are unavoidable in the interim.

Feedback Processes from Stigma to Policy Change

Experiences of stigma and discrimination may propel multiple actors into action and feed back into the political process, as they advocate for new policies. One interpretation might be that people are socialized at the political level, where they adopt norms and values; another is that policies reflect the deeply held norms and values of a society. Both are likely true. While policies shape how people view migrants, there are opportunities for migrant and nonmigrant views to feed back into those policies. In addition, specific catalyzing events might activate policy feedback processes. To date, there is limited research on how stigma processes generated by policies could directly feed back into responses for migrants and nonmigrants around policy change or resistance (e.g., maintenance of status quo). Figure 8.2 illustrates potential pathways for stigma experiences to feed back into policy and inform change.

From Migrants

The top half of the heuristic model in Figure 8.2 describes the migrant perspective. Typically, migrants who experience a loss of resources due to stigmatization are financially compromised. This makes them less powerful because it takes resources to enter the political process. The right to vote allows for advocacy through official channels but is often not afforded to most migrants. This, too, inhibits their ability to participate in the political process.

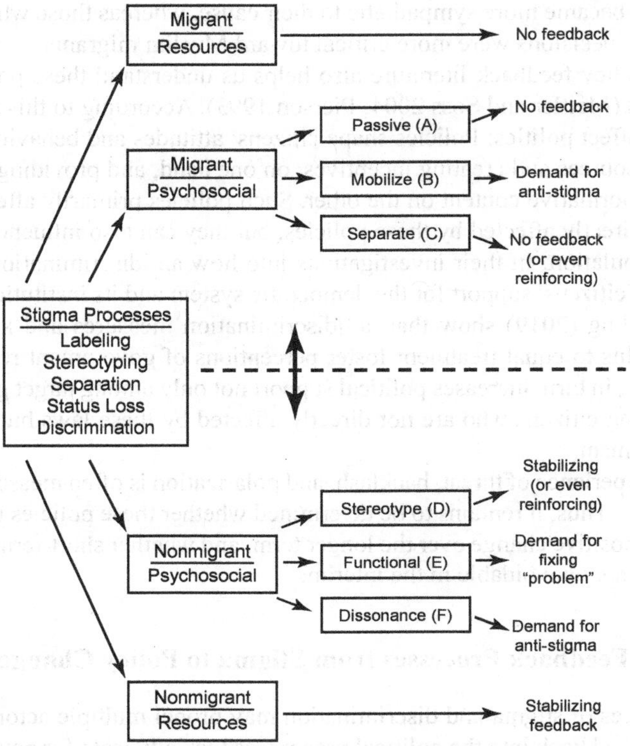

Figure 8.2 Feedback processes from stigma experiences to policy change for migration. These stigma experiences can inform a potential feedback loop back to social policies, providing another opportunity to amplify or mitigate stigma for both migrants and nonmigrants. These include resource pathways (e.g., economic, political) and multiple potential psychosocial pathways, which have the potential to mobilize for change, maintain the status quo, or reinforce beliefs to actively resist change.

Stigmatization influences the psychosocial aspects of migrants and may motivate a range of responses (Hirschman 1970). First, it may make migrants become *passive* (Figure 8.2, A) and inhibit their actions to influence policy—as if loyalty can only be demonstrated if they do not question their circumstances. One indicator could be that many migrants do not participate in the political activities even when they do have access to act, such as voting in local elections or campaigning for supportive candidates. This results in a complete lack of feedback.

Second, migrants may *mobilize* (Figure 8.2, B) to express their opposition to unfair treatment. This is the "voice" channel that demands better treatment (i.e., anti-stigma). Social movements can be used to pressure the state to change when it otherwise would not. This is often not just about access to resources, but also access to the opportunities to be allowed into the decision-making processes that govern the access to resources. The possibilities to form groups and associations are often guaranteed by constitutions and the opportunities for being heard in political systems vary. However, everything else being equal, mobilization and organization increases influence in the policy feedback loop.

Third, migrants may *separate* themselves from or exit mainstream society (Figure 8.2, C). This could occur in multiple ways, from a separation into subcultures (e.g., living in ethnic enclaves) to leaving the country altogether. When migrants leave the country, they relinquish all hope in to influence policy. Separating into subcultures runs the risk of being interpreted as deviant behavior. Not only could this reinforce negative stereotypes held by the majority population, it may reinforce stigmatizing policies and practices. All of these feedback processes can occur simultaneously, which means their effects will also interact with each other.

From Nonmigrants

Stigmatization of migrants also influences nonmigrants, as illustrated in the bottom half of Figure 8.2. In terms of resources, the existing privileges of nonmigrants are protected (e.g., in the labor market, in housing, and in voting). Everything else being equal, this should simply reproduce and reinforce existing stigmatizing policies and practices toward migrants.

However, the stigmatization of migrants influences psychosocial outcomes for nonmigrants in diverse ways. First, nonmigrants may endorse stigmatizing *stereotypes* and moral deservingness heuristics (Figure 8.2, D). A long line of research demonstrates the importance of negative stereotypes in reproducing policies toward deviant groups (Chavez 2008; Fiske 2011; Gilens 2009; Larsen 2013; Petersen and Aarøe 2013), where little is done to alter stigmatizing policies and practices. Second, nonmigrants may start to have *functional concerns* for the operation of their society (Figure 8.2, E), especially if they perceive stigmatized migrants, including through mobilization, to be materially and/or culturally threatening (as described earlier). This could feed back to the system through the demand that politicians "fix the problem," either by increasing stigmatizing policies, decreasing anti-stigmatizing policies, or some other pragmatic policy solution. Third, nonmigrants may experience *dissonance* between the creed of equality and the stigmatization that is taking place (Figure 8.2, F). This is especially common among those on the political left. The psychological need to live in a just world is well documented (Bénabou and Tirole 2006; Lerner 1980), yet the dissonance created might feed back in the form of blaming migrants (e.g., reduce their sense of dissonance by justifying the treatment of migrants). Alternatively, the dissonance might create the demand to destigmatize policies and practices to align with their views. If this demand is strong, it might face counter mobilization, which could lead to backlash and polarization (described earlier).

In this model, the best chance for feedback to demand destigmatizing policies and practices occurs when stigmatized migrants mobilize and nonmigrants experience dissonance. This would be a moment of progressive opportunity. The best case for feedback that reproduces or reinforces stigmatizing policies and practices occurs when stigmatized migrants separate or exit and nonmigrants base their policy demands on existing stereotypes, combined with moral deservingness. Although not fully realized in this model, these mechanisms are likely to be contingent on the institutions and opportunity structures that can offer agency and influence to various groups. Thus, these mechanisms may affect change or continuity on different timescales. Further, most policies are only designed for incremental change to promote equality within existing constraints, although occasionally policies can introduce dynamics that lead to more significant change over time.

Envisioning Changes to Policy Making and Policies to Reduce Stigma

Strategies to Improve Policy

Research, policy, and practice interact to set and implement policies (Figure 8.3). As discussed above, the decision to improve policy often comes in response to specific events or experiences. However, proactive strategies can also be used to advance specific goals. In terms of strategies to improve policies, the following points require consideration (Votruba et al. 2020):

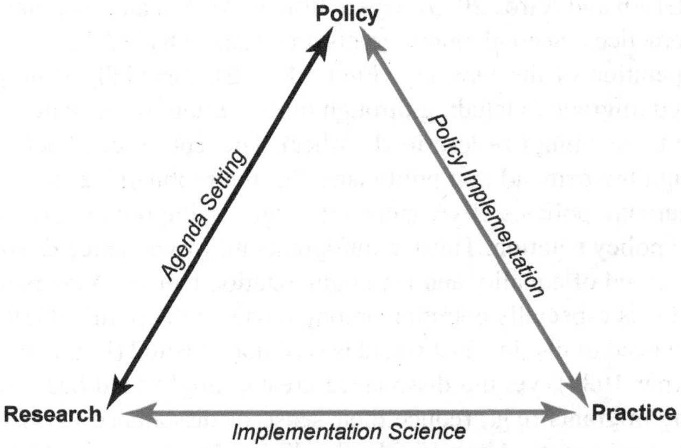

Figure 8.3 Simplified evidence-policy-practice model, showing the relationships that impact the development and evaluation of strategies designed to inform the broader social context (i.e., societal attitudes) and social policies that enable stigma processes. Adapted from Votruba et al. (2020) (https://creativecommons.org/licenses/by/4.0/).

1. Agenda setting: bringing the topic of stigma and migration onto agendas of policy makers.
2. Defining the goals of the policies you want to introduce or change.
3. Defining the outcomes or criteria you will use to evaluate the policies.
4. Developing strategies to improve policies.

First, *agenda setting* refers to bringing certain topics onto the political agenda. To achieve this, it is helpful to understand the opaque system of policy making as well as to build the capacity to communicate research findings and to have access to key people. In addition, it is important to align the topic with other policy priorities (e.g., social cohesion or poverty) and to build coalitions of stakeholders and trustful relationships with key individuals. This may be initiated by the state (if they care about change already), by migrants (and nonmigrants) mobilizing for change, or by external pressures (e.g., EU, UN).

Second, the *goal* to be achieved by the policy change must be clarified. If the issue concerns the quantity of migration, extreme goals could be the shutdown of any migration versus the complete dismantling of all borders, not to mention more measured, intermediate solutions. If the issue concerns the degree of change, options range from finetuning a functional system, incremental improvements, or radical change. In terms of the time horizon, one could think of short-term changes, possibly related to election cycles, or long-term cultural change, possibly extending over several generations. In defining goals, it is important to consider who sets the goals: members of the resident country (i.e., the elites vs. the general population), migrants who reside in the country, or both together.

Third, what *indicators* can be used to measure the success of policy change? Since any change may exhibit mixed effects on different levels (e.g., structural or individual, short or long term, local or national), it makes sense to collect multiple outcome measures over time. Further, policy implementation should be measured as to whether policies are followed under real-world conditions in different places by different actors at different times. Finally, a well-intentioned policy, even if formally implemented, may not work in practice if it creates side effects or if other barriers prevent migrants or other minorities from accessing a source of support. For stigma, some potential indicators include perceived discrimination, psychological distress or well-being, physical and mental health, civic rights (e.g., voting), human rights, level of integration (e.g., access to labor market, access to education), and reduction in income inequality.

Finally, there are a range of *strategies* to achieve policy change that can be used alone or in combination. Different stakeholders can form social movements to achieve policy change (see Okamoto and Adem, this volume). As with mental illness stigma (Rüsch 2023), protest, education and contact have the potential to improve public attitudes and acceptance of pro-migrant policies. Particular focus needs to be placed on domains that "matter most" for migrants, such as access to the labor market or voting rights. Strategies may differ depending on the level they need to address (local, regional, national, international). Any strategy may want to use (social) media to reach its audience. Finally, strategies should consider the degree to which they want to risk creating a backlash or polarization of public opinion.

Given the limited knowledge of this process, research has a vital role to play to both inform and evaluate how policy making and policies can be used to reduce stigma. Research can provide information on the differential aspects of policy narratives and policy types on stigma and can inform the development and evaluation of a range of strategies. Further, researchers can translate this work, which will assist the agenda setting process for policy makers.

Specific Considerations for Stigma Due to Migration-Generated Diversity

There may always be people who harbor stigma toward migrants, and any effort to reduce stigma faces the risk of creating backlash or further polarization. While stigma may not be possible to eradicate, it exists on a spectrum and concrete efforts can achieve significant reductions. Even if short-term negative attitudes are unavoidable, it is important to consider the impacts over longer time periods to assess meaningful change. It is also helpful to remember that policies of inaction or a lack of implementation of helpful policies may do just as much to contribute to stigma (Link and Hatzenbuehler 2016).

Since migrant experiences are so contextually dependent on individual nations (and vary for different migrant groups within countries), we offer guiding principles rather than specific strategies. For all migrants, limited or conditional citizenship and differential access to rights, resources, and opportunities constitutes a primary barrier in all nations that sets migrants apart. To dismantle this barrier, multiple approaches are needed across multiple levels and with multiple actors to implement both top-down (policies) and bottom-up (social movements to push for policy change) approaches. The state and policymakers play a particular role in reaching both migrants and nonmigrants through both resource and psychosocial pathways. However, care must be taken in institutions such as education, employment, and health care to avoid amplifying stigma. Civil society and community organizations that represent migrant or related interests often mediate relationships between the state and migrants, including the interpretation of policies. Finally, it is integral to consider the role of migrants and increase their agency to advocate for their own rights.

While discrimination is the most consequential behavioral outcome of the stigma process, and some existing policy approaches do specifically address antidiscrimination, the stigma framework offers opportunities to consider interventions for other aspects of the stigma process. Understanding that policies can both amplify and mitigate *specific* stigma processes (e.g., labeling, stereotyping, separation, status loss, discrimination; Link & Phelan, 2001), and that these processes can interact across multiple levels and multiple types of policies, offers more specificity when considering proactive strategies to generate anti-stigma policies and practices. Moreover, a broader view of stigma processes offers opportunities to consider not only the ultimate consequences (i.e., discrimination) of stigma processes but also other stages along the way (i.e., negative anti-migrant stereotypes and status loss). Of course, changing or replacing attitudes is extremely challenging and there is limited existing evidence of effective strategies. Understanding stigma as a fundamental cause of inequity (Hatzenbuehler et al. 2013) illuminates its reproducibility; in other words, if stigma is reduced in one domain, it often manifests in another domain.

Conclusions

Any policy that intentionally or unintentionally impacts migrants has the potential to generate, amplify, and/or mitigate stigma. In a utopian world, where borders are not considered fixed or necessary and there are few to no restrictions on who is considered a part of society, the distinction between migrant and nonmigrant could cease to exist. Until then, the social category of "migrant" remains necessary, even as it starts the labeling process, to track the impact of stigma. Further, stigma processes are sometimes so deeply embedded in existing systems and structures that they go undetected. Understanding that stigma often has a functional role helps identify where it exists and why it can be hard to change. When policies fail to reduce stigma, it may be because they do not adequately address the function that stigma is serving in that context. Thus, structural stigma offers a useful framework (a) to assess how policies that impact migrants contribute to stigma and (b) to enumerate key areas for future research and intervention to successfully reduce stigma toward migrants. In addition, stigma at the structural level can perpetuate stigma at other levels, so assessing these interactions is also needed. Given the lack of empirical evidence at almost every stage, theoretical concepts require testing with multiple methods and approaches to triangulate findings, including the development and evaluation of strategies to improve policies at local, regional, national, and international levels. Such strategies need to consider how the political discourse, perception of policies, and (selective) implementation of policies (or lack thereof) can impact stigma, which will inform policy feedback loops and strategic policy making to make intentional changes. A major challenge is to identify the appropriate methods, data sources, and outcomes, given limited prior efforts to measure how policies impact stigma and, more broadly, how beneficial policies can have beneficial outcomes (and on what time horizon). Because of the unique histories and contexts of each nation, strategies that work will likely vary for different migrant groups in each country. The frameworks, processes, and consequences enumerated in this chapter can inform possible approaches across contexts.

9

Structural Stigma and Health

How U.S. Policies Mitigate and Amplify Stigma

Mark L. Hatzenbuehler

Abstract

Research from across the social sciences has provided essential insights into how stigma operates to disadvantage those who are targeted by it. This research has, however, focused primarily on the perceptions of stigmatized individuals and on micro-level interactions. Over the past decade, a new line of stigma research has highlighted the adverse consequences of structural forms of stigma for members of stigmatized groups. This chapter reviews emerging evidence from cross-sectional, longitudinal, and quasi-experimental studies and demonstrates that one dimension of structural stigma—social policies—can amplify stigma processes, thereby heightening health risks. Furthermore, research shows that policy efforts that seek to mitigate structural stigma can have salubrious health effects. Strategies are discussed that researchers have used to address causal inferences regarding the relationship between social policies and health among stigmatized groups: identifying mechanisms; triangulating evidence across diverse methods, outcomes, and groups; conducting falsification tests; controlling for potential confounders; and evaluating plausible alternative explanations. Finally, ideas for future research are offered to strengthen and extend this work.

Structural Stigma and Health: How U.S. Policies Mitigate and Amplify Stigma

Stigma—defined as the co-occurrence of labeling, stereotyping, status loss, and discrimination in a context (e.g., same-sex marriage) in which power is exercised (Link and Phelan 2001)—has been a central topic of inquiry for nearly six decades across several social science disciplines, including psychology, sociology, economics, and anthropology. Most of this research has focused on the ways in which stigmatized individuals perceive and react to stigma as well as on the interactional processes that occur between the stigmatized and nonstigmatized. Although this work has significantly advanced our understanding of how stigma operates to produce disadvantage, it has been criticized by numerous scholars for overlooking broader structural processes that promulgate and reinforce stigma (e.g., Link and Phelan 2001). Over the last decade, researchers have responded to this critique by conducting theoretical and empirical research on the role of structural stigma—defined as "societal-level conditions, cultural norms, and institutional policies that constrain the opportunities, resources, and well-being of the stigmatized" (Hatzenbuehler and Link 2014:2)—in shaping the lives of the stigmatized.

In this chapter, I selectively review the relatively new field of research on structural stigma by addressing four topics. First, I define structural stigma and consider one way in which it has been operationalized in the literature; namely, via social policies that restrict the opportunities of, or yield adverse consequences for, stigmatized individuals. Second, I review research evidence which demonstrates that social policies can amplify stigma processes and heighten health risks. I also discuss research evidence which indicates that policy efforts that seek to mitigate structural stigma can have salubrious health effects. Third, I describe several strategies that research groups have used to establish strong causal inferences regarding associations between structural stigma and health. Finally, I outline future directions to advance this emerging literature.

Definitions and Measures of Structural Stigma

It is well established that stigma is a multilevel construct that exists at individual, interpersonal, and structural levels (Link and Phelan 2001). *Individual forms of stigma* refer to the cognitive, affective, and behavioral processes in which individuals engage in response to stigma, such as expectations of rejection, self-stigma (i.e., the internalization of negative societal views about your group), and concealment. In contrast, *interpersonal forms of stigma* describe interactions that occur between the stigmatized and the nonstigmatized, including interpersonal discrimination.

Researchers have recently expanded the stigma construct beyond the individual and interpersonal levels to consider broader macro-social forms of stigma—termed *structural stigma.* Link and Phelan's influential conceptualization of stigma was among the first to distinguish between individual and structural levels of stigma and to highlight that the concept of structural stigma "sensitizes us to the fact that all manner of disadvantage can result outside of a model in which one person does something bad to another" (Link and Phelan 2001:382). Following their initial use of this term, researchers began to delineate specific components underlying structural stigma. Corrigan et al. (2004), for instance, posited that structural stigma includes institutional policies that either intentionally restrict the opportunities of, or yield unintended consequences for, stigmatized individuals. One prominent example is Jim Crow laws, which maintained White privilege in Southern states from Reconstruction to the early 1960s. More recent examples of policies that promulgate stigma include constitutional amendments that banned same-sex marriage, allowing special scrutiny of people "suspected" of being undocumented, and punitive policy responses to maternal substance use during pregnancy.

Building on the work of Corrigan et al. (2004), Link and Hatzenbuehler (2016) posited that there are at least three ways in which social policies may be related to stigma processes. First, policy can invigorate stigma and produce harm. In this conceptualization, those in power use policy efforts to achieve their aims of keeping stigmatized people "in, down, or away" (Phelan et al. 2008). Second, policies can seek to mitigate stigma, thereby reducing harm. In this conceptualization, policies respond to stigmatizing conditions by reversing patterns of structural stigma or addressing stigma expressed at the interpersonal level. In these first two instances, policies are hypothesized to create, exacerbate, diminish, or mitigate stigma-related harms, thereby shaping health outcomes among the stigmatized. Additionally, Link and Hatzenbuehler (2016) argued that it is necessary to consider a third form of policy action; namely, no action at all. As they noted, "a core feature of stigma is a discounting—a mattering less—that allows and even fosters policy inattention toward the concerns of stigmatized groups" (Link and Hatzenbuehler 2016:653). Examples of policy inaction include when the circumstances of stigmatized groups are ignored or when policies are enacted but are implemented selectively or not at all, as in the case of the Americans with Disabilities Act (National Council on Disability 2007). In this conceptualization, policy inaction is a policy regime unto itself.

Research Evidence on the Health Consequences of Structural Stigma

Despite the foundational conceptualizations of structural stigma and recent attempts to operationalize this construct, there has been a dearth of empirical research linking specific measures of structural stigma to individual-level health outcomes among members of stigmatized groups. This under-representation of structural stigma (relative to individual or interpersonal forms) has been called "a dramatic shortcoming" in the literature, given that the processes involved "are likely major contributors to unequal outcomes" (Link et al. 2004:515–516). Over the last decade, however, there have been several exciting advancements in the empirical literature on the health consequences of structural stigma. A comprehensive review of this literature is beyond the scope of this chapter (for reviews, see Hatzenbuehler 2016, 2017a, b). Here, illustrative examples of this research, with potential applicability to migration research, will be described. Evidence is presented across a range of health outcomes (e.g., psychiatric morbidity, adverse birth outcomes), social groups (e.g., African Americans, immigrants, sexual minorities), and methodological approaches (e.g., observational and quasi-experimental designs). This section is divided into two types of social policies discussed by Link and Hatzenbuehler (2016) in relation to stigma processes: policies that amplify versus policies that mitigate stigmatization.

Social Policies That Amplify Stigma Processes

Several studies have examined whether social policies that amplify stigma are associated with negative health outcomes among members of stigmatized groups. These studies have largely used two methods: (a) cross-sectional, observational designs, which examine correlations between social policies and health; and (b) quasi-experimental designs, which examine whether changes in social policies are associated with changes in health outcomes.

In an early example of studies that employed a cross-sectional approach, Hatzenbuehler et al. (2009a) coded all 50 states in the United States for the presence or absence of hate crime statutes and employment nondiscrimination policies that included sexual orientation as a protected class. They linked this data on state-level policies to individual-level data on mental health and sexual orientation from the National Epidemiologic Survey on Alcohol and Related Conditions (NESARC), a nationally representative health survey of U.S. adults. The results indicated that sexual orientation disparities in psychiatric morbidity were significantly elevated in states without policy protections. For instance, lesbian, gay, and bisexual (LGB) adults who lived in states with no protective policies were nearly 2.5 times more likely to have dysthymia (a mood disorder), nearly 3.5 times more likely to have generalized anxiety disorder, and nearly five times more likely to have two or more co-occurring disorders than were heterosexuals in those same states, controlling for individual-level risk factors for psychiatric disorder prevalence (Hatzenbuehler et al. 2009a).

Another set of cross-sectional studies focused on the health consequences of social policies related to immigration, which have proliferated over the past several years in the United States. In one study (Hatzenbuehler et al. 2017b), researchers created a multisectoral policy climate index that included 14 immigration and ethnicity-specific policies across different domains, such as immigration (e.g., access to drivers' licenses for undocumented immigrants), language (e.g., English as the official state language), and agricultural worker protections (e.g., eligibility of agricultural workers for workers' compensation). This policy climate index at the state level was then linked to individual-level mental health outcomes among Latinx respondents from 31 states in the 2012 Behavioral Risk Factor Surveillance System, a population-based health survey of noninstitutionalized individuals aged 18 years or older. Latinx respondents in states with less supportive immigration policies reported greater psychological distress than those living in states with more supportive policies; this relationship was not observed for non-Latinx participants (Hatzenbuehler et al. 2017b). These results remained robust after controlling for sociodemographic characteristics, as well as for state-level confounders, including percent Latinx in the state and attitudes toward immigration and immigration policies held by residents of each state. Further, sensitivity analyses indicated that the results were specific to immigration policies. Specifically, there were no associations between psychological distress among Latinx participants and three plausible alternative factors: two indicators of political climate (percentage of the vote for Romney vs. Obama during the 2012 presidential election and the party affiliation of the governor in 2012) and state-level residential segregation between Latinos and non-Latinos (Hatzenbuehler et al. 2017b). This work suggests that a broad set of policies across multiple sectors (including transportation, education, labor, health, and social services) appear to be consequential for the mental health of Latinx populations in the United States.

Complementing these observational studies are quasi-experimental designs. Because it is not ethical to assign individuals randomly to conditions of structural stigma (i.e., to states with or without protective policies), researchers cannot conduct randomized experiments to study the health effects of structural stigma. However, it is possible to take advantage of naturally occurring changes in structural stigma (e.g., following a change in social policies targeting a specific stigmatized group) to conduct quasi-experiments, in which researchers examine whether health changes after the passage of a social policy. Because these policies represent exogenous events, quasi-experimental designs that leverage changes in social policies effectively minimize threats to validity of self-selection into the exposure status (i.e., structural stigma). Although quasi-experiments are not new, they have only recently been used to study the health consequences of structural stigma. This is due, in part, to the difficulty of conducting these studies, given that such designs require data from before and after changes in structural stigma (e.g., social policies), which are typically outside the control of researchers.

Despite these methodological challenges, a handful of studies have utilized this approach. In one study (Hatzenbuehler et al. 2010), researchers took advantage of the fact that in between two waves of data collection in the NESARC (described above), several states passed constitutional amendments banning same-sex marriage. NESARC respondents were first interviewed in 2001 and then were reinterviewed in 2005, following the passage of the same-sex marriage bans. This provided a quasi-experiment that enabled researchers to examine changes in the prevalence of psychiatric disorders among LGB and heterosexual respondents who had been assessed both before and after the bans were passed. LGB adults who lived in states that passed same-sex marriage bans experienced a 37% increase in mood disorders, a 42% increase in alcohol use disorders, and a 248% increase in generalized anxiety disorders between the two waves. In contrast, LGB respondents in states without these bans did not experience a significant increase in psychiatric disorders during the study period. Moreover, the mental health of heterosexuals in states that passed the bans was largely unchanged between the two waves, documenting result specificity (Hatzenbuehler et al. 2010).

Policies that amplify stigma processes may not only influence health, but also the utilization of health care. Senate Bill (SB) 1070 in Arizona contained numerous restrictive policies related to immigrants, including the requirement that police officers verify the immigration status of any individual they suspect to be undocumented during a lawful stop. In a quasi-experiment (Toomey et al. 2014), researchers evaluated whether utilization of preventive health care differed before and after the enactment of SB 1070, using data from an ongoing longitudinal study of the health and development of Mexican-origin adolescent mothers and their infants, who were interviewed before and after the enactment of SB 1070. Participants reported that they were less likely to take their baby to the doctor after SB 1070 was implemented. Further, younger adolescents were less likely than older adolescents to use preventive health care themselves following the law's enactment (Toomey et al. 2014), indicating that immigration policies may shape utilization of health-care services among groups targeted by these policies.

Whereas these two studies (Hatzenbuehler et al. 2010; Toomey et al. 2014) used a longitudinal panel design, other quasi-experimental studies have used repeated cross-sectional datasets to explore how changes in social policies influence the health of stigmatized populations exposed to structural stigma. In one example of this work, Raifman et al. (2018b) used a difference-in-difference analysis, an econometrics approach, to compare changes in mental distress among LGB and heterosexual respondents in three states that implemented laws denying public accommodations services (i.e., any place that is open to the public where commerce is carried out) to same-sex couples in 2015. The authors then compared this with changes in mental distress among LGB and heterosexual respondents in six geographically nearby control states with similar demographics but without these laws. Data on mental health (psychological distress) and sexual orientation came from the 2014–2016 Behavioral Risk Factor Surveillance System. The researchers first showed that in the three years leading up to the policy implementation (2012–2014), there were no differences in time trends in psychological distress between states that passed these laws denying services to same-sex couples versus control states. This evidence for "parallel trends" in difference-in-difference designs is necessary to ensure that any observed changes after the policy implementation are not due to preexisting differences between these two groups of states.

Having established these parallel trends before policy implementation, Raifman et al. then examined whether there was evidence for changes in the percentage of adults experiencing psychological distress in same-sex denial versus control states, stratified by sexual orientation identity. LGB individuals living in states with the same-sex denial law experienced a significant increase in psychological distress following the implementation of the laws, which was equivalent to a 46% relative increase in sexual-minority adults experiencing mental distress in these states (Raifman et al. 2018b). In contrast, none of the other three comparison groups (i.e., LGB individuals living in states without the same-sex denial laws, and heterosexuals living in states with and without the laws) experienced a change in psychological distress during the study period. This study used state fixed effects, which not only controlled for baseline differences in rates of mental distress across states, but also for time invariant characteristics (e.g., political climate) that could have affected both the passage of the law and the prevalence of mental distress.

A third type of quasi-experimental design utilizes a comparative interrupted time series analysis, which enables researchers to capitalize on many years of data before the policy implementation to determine whether the policy "interrupted" the general trends in a health outcome that were apparent pre-policy implementation. One research group (Samari et al. 2020) employed this approach to examine the health consequences of the 2017 travel ban on individuals from Muslim-majority countries. Using the 2009–2018 National Center for Health Statistics period linked infant birth–death data, the researchers compared the monthly odds of preterm births to women from travel ban countries (Iran, Iraq, Libya, Somalia, Sudan, Syria, and Yemen) after the January 2017 ban to the number expected, had the ban not been implemented. A 6.8% increase in the odds of delivering a preterm birth was observed among women from travel ban countries between September 2017 and August 2018 (Samari et al. 2020).

Social Policies That Mitigate Stigma Processes

Having reviewed evidence which suggests that implementing policies that amplify stigma processes exerts negative health consequences for stigmatized populations, we now look at whether abolishing structural forms of stigma through social policies improve the health of the stigmatized. Researchers have tested this hypothesis using a variety of methods, including quasi-experiments, longitudinal studies, and divergent mobility patterns. Here, I describe illustrative examples of each of these types of studies.

One quasi-experimental study that explored this question was conducted by Hatzenbuehler et al. (2012) in Massachusetts, which became the first state to legalize same-sex marriage in 2003. They obtained data from previously collected medical records from a community-based health clinic in Massachusetts to examine the effect of the law on health-care use and costs among sexual-minority men. There was a 15% reduction in mental and medical health-care utilization and costs among these men in the 12 months following the legalization of same-sex marriage, compared to the 12 months before (Hatzenbuehler et al. 2012). To determine whether these reductions in health-care use and costs were driven, in part, by improvements in health, the researchers examined the

ICD-9 diagnostic codes that were charged by the providers following each visit. Results indicated substantial reductions in several stress-related disorders, including a 14% reduction in depression and an 18% reduction in hypertension, among sexual-minority men in the 12 months after the legalization of same-sex marriage compared to the 12 months before (Hatzenbuehler et al. 2012), providing preliminary evidence for a stress pathway linking structural stigma and health.

In another innovative quasi-experimental study, Krieger et al. (2013) examined associations between the abolition of Jim Crow laws (via the 1964 Civil Rights Act) and birth cohort trends in infant death rates among Blacks and Whites. In the four years prior to the abolition of the Jim Crow laws, the Black infant death rate was 1.19 times higher in Jim Crow states than in non-Jim Crow states; in contrast, ten years later, the rate ratio shrank to 1, indicating that the infant death rate among Blacks was statistically indistinguishable between those living in states that had previously enacted Jim Crow laws and those living in states that had not enacted these laws. There was no temporal change in the magnitude of the effect of the abolition of Jim Crow laws by birth cohort for White infants, documenting the specificity of these findings to Black infants (Krieger et al. 2013). These findings provide compelling evidence that the elimination of a structural form of racism through a social policy translated into downstream beneficial health consequences for Black mothers and their children.

Quasi-experimental designs cannot rule out the possibility that some other factor that occurred contemporaneously with the change in a social policy is driving the results. However, the plausibility of these alternative factors can be evaluated by examining whether they occurred during the same time period and, if so, whether they could have contributed to the results. To determine whether other factors unrelated to the same-sex marriage law contributed to their results, Hatzenbuehler et al. (2012) examined data from the Centers for Medicare & Medicaid Services to determine trends in health-care costs during the study period (2002–2004). These data revealed that health-care costs in the general population of Massachusetts' residents actually *increased* during the study period. This pattern was in the opposite direction of those observed in the study's sample of sexual-minority men, suggesting that external factors within the Massachusetts health-care environment were unlikely to have influenced the results.

Another approach researchers have employed is to use longitudinal studies that examine whether health disparities are reduced after declines in structural stigma at a population level, as reflected through changes in social policies. In one example of this approach, researchers used a population-based dataset in Sweden that has assessed sexual orientation and mental health every five years since 2005 (i.e., 2005, 2010, 2015). Over this ten-year period in Sweden, there were marked declines in structural forms of stigma, including changes in laws and policies that provided protections to sexual minorities, as well as declines in prejudicial attitudes toward homosexuality. These declines in structural stigma were associated with reductions in the magnitude of the sexual orientation disparity in mental health. In 2005, gay men and lesbian women were nearly three times more likely to meet criteria for elevated psychological distress compared to heterosexual men and women; however, in 2015 the sexual orientation disparity in elevated psychological distress for gay men and lesbian women was eliminated (Hatzenbuehler et al. 2018). This finding suggests that sexual orientation disparities in mental health are responsive to changes in the social context and, in particular, to declines in structural stigma, as reflected through changes in social policies related to sexual orientation.

A third approach is to study stigmatized individuals who move to a different structural stigma context. This approach allows researchers to examine whether changes in exposure to diverse environments, in terms of structural stigma, are related to health. Examining whether this change in the structural stigma context is associated with health requires a novel data structure that includes

- a large sample of stigmatized individuals who have moved,
- linkage to objective indicators of structural stigma (e.g., social policies) in countries of origin and in receiving countries, and
- data on length of exposure to the receiving country and on health.

Until recently, the lack of such data has precluded researchers from leveraging mobility patterns to examine life-course variations in structural stigma exposure as a predictor of health.

Pachankis et al. (2021) used EMIS-2017/2018, a novel dataset compiled from the European Men-Who-Have-Sex-With-Men Internet Survey (n = 123,428 participants). These data were linked to an objective indicator of structural stigma related to sexual orientation, including 15 laws and policies as well as aggregated social attitudes, in respondents' countries of origin (N = 178 countries) and in their receiving countries (N = 48 countries). Among the 11,831 respondents who had moved from higher- to lower-structural stigma countries, longer exposure to the lower-structural stigma environments of their receiving countries was associated with a significantly lower risk of depression and suicidality, controlling for individual- and country-level covariates. Specifically, country-of-origin structural stigma was associated with depression and suicidality only for sexual-minority men who had recently moved (within 0–4 years) from higher- to lower-structural stigma countries. In contrast, there was no significant association between country-of-origin structural stigma and depression or suicidality among those men who had lived in their lower-structural stigma receiving country for five years or more, and who thus had longer exposure to lower levels of structural stigma (Pachankis et al. 2021).

Causal Inference

Researchers have used several different approaches to achieve the strongest causal inference possible regarding the health impact of structural stigma. As is evident from the discussion above, the field has incorporated a multi-measure, multi-method, multi-group, and multi-outcome approach to the study of structural stigma (as operationalized via social policies) and health. The use of multiple measures, methods, groups, and outcomes is an established approach to assessing validity; when convergence is demonstrated, this increases confidence that the results are not confounded by particular methods, measures, groups, or outcomes.

Another approach has been to examine whether structural stigma exerts health effects only among the stigmatized group, and not among the nonstigmatized comparison group. To the extent that structural stigma has specific effects on specific groups, confidence in a causal effect is enhanced, because such a finding is consistent with the theoretical predictions made by stigma theories (Link 1987). In addition, when relationships between structural stigma and health are observed only among members of the stigmatized group, this increases the likelihood that this result is due to structural stigma itself rather than to factors that may be associated with it (e.g., economic conditions). Studies have generally documented this kind of specificity; for instance, state-to-state variations in policies banning same-sex marriage (Hatzenbuehler et al. 2010) and in policies denying services to same-sex couples (Raifman et al. 2018b) did not negatively impact the mental health of heterosexuals. In addition to documenting specificity to the stigmatized group, researchers have also documented specificity to theoretically informed outcomes through conducting falsification tests. In falsification tests, researchers examine whether structural stigma is associated with outcomes that it should not theoretically influence, such as fruit juice consumption (Raifman et al. 2017). The lack of association between structural stigma and these alternative outcomes provides further support that structural stigma–health relationship is not biased due to omitted variables.

The identification of plausible mechanisms through which structural stigma affects health is another crucial step toward understanding causal relations. Indeed, if no evidence for mechanisms linking structural stigma and health is ascertained, the plausibility of confounding by other, unmeasured contextual characteristics is greater. Thus far, researchers have identified several mechanisms that underlie the relationship between structural stigma and health. These include identity concealment (e.g., Lattanner et al. 2021), social isolation (e.g., Pachankis et al. 2021), self-stigma (e.g., Evans-Lacko et al. 2012), perceived discrimination (Frost 2020), and stress (e.g., Flores et al. 2018).

A final approach for improving causal inferences comes through the direct assessment of alternative explanations for the relationship between structural stigma and health. For instance, it is possible that stigmatized individuals with better health move away from policy regimes and attitudinal contexts that disadvantage them, leaving unhealthy respondents behind. If this were to occur, differential selection by health status could contribute to the observed association between structural stigma and health. Studies have begun to address this possibility and as yet have not found robust evidence for this selection hypothesis (e.g., Hatzenbuehler et al. 2017a; Pachankis et al. 2021).

Future Research Directions

Despite recent developments in the study of structural stigma and health, the field is still in its relative infancy. To aid further development, I discuss a few of the most important directions for future research, particularly as they relate to social policies.

First, the predominant approach thus far has been to code the content of social policies (whether at the country, state, or municipal level) to determine the presence of structural stigma in institutions. The main advantage of this approach is that it relies on objective data sources to code the policies. However, a key limitation is that content analyses often do not capture other factors that are relevant to social policies, including implementation and inaction (Link and Hatzenbuehler 2016). The lack of research on these factors likely means that the existing research base underestimates the full range of ways in which social policies shape the health and well-being of the stigmatized. The development of measures that capture policy implementation as well as policy inaction will offer an important corrective to this general trend.

Second, existing research has typically focused on social policies at a single level of analysis, including European countries (e.g., Pachankis et al. 2021) or U.S. states (Hatzenbuehler et al. 2010; Hatzenbuehler et al. 2012; Raifman et al. 2018b). While this approach is appropriate for some research questions, analysis of policies at a single level of analysis can obscure heterogeneity at other levels. For instance, municipal-level policies that seek to lessen stigma against immigrants (e.g., so-called sanctuary cities) may exist within states that have more restrictive social policies related to immigration. The presence of divergent policy regimes raises the question of whether and how policies at different geographic levels interact to create risk for, or protection against, adverse health outcomes. Recent research suggests that the incorporation of structural stigma across multiple levels, including state and city, may, in fact, yield new insights into behavioral and psychosocial outcomes among the stigmatized (e.g., Lattanner et al. 2021).

Third, most research has tended to focus on social policies that either amplify or mitigate stigma processes as they relate to a single stigmatized identity, condition, or status (e.g., sexual orientation, gender identity, race, or immigration). While that approach can begin to illuminate how structural stigma operates to create risk for adverse health outcomes, it overlooks the fact that individuals have many social identities, some of which may be subject to stigmatization within a particular social context. In fact, one large study found that individuals reported, on average, six stigmatized identities, conditions, or statuses, suggesting that intersectionality may represent the norm, rather than the exception (Pachankis et al. 2018). Recent studies have begun to incorporate intersectional approaches in structural stigma research. For instance, a study by Pachankis et al. (2017a) created policy (and attitudinal) measures of structural stigma related both to sexual orientation and to immigration, and they linked these measures to a dataset of HIV outcomes among migrant men who have sex with men (MSM) across 38 European countries. The results indicated that these two forms of structural stigma interacted, such that the association between anti-gay structural stigma and HIV risk was significantly stronger for MSM migrants who lived in anti-immigrant receiving countries compared to those who lived in immigrant-supportive countries (Pachankis et al. 2017a). More intersectional research like this is needed to understand how social policies related to multiple social identities interrelate to shape health outcomes among stigmatized populations.

Fourth, while studies have begun to identify numerous mechanisms through which structural stigma shapes health outcomes (e.g., Frost 2020; Lattanner et al. 2021; Pachankis et al. 2021), comparatively less attention has been paid to characteristics of individuals, their interactions, and their broader social contexts that moderate the structural stigma–health association, either to potentiate or to buffer risk against adverse health outcomes. One notable exception is a study by Everett et al. (2016), who examined whether race/ethnicity and socioeconomic status moderated the relationship between the passage of a civil union law and health outcomes in an ongoing, longitudinal study of sexual-minority women. Intriguingly, they found that the benefits of the civil union law in terms of reductions in stigma consciousness, perceived discrimination, depressive symptoms, and adverse drinking consequences were concentrated largely among racial/ethnic minority women and women with lower levels of education (Everett et al. 2016). Although these findings suggest that social policies that mitigate stigma may confer stronger benefits for those most at risk for poor health, this hypothesis warrants replication in future studies.

Finally, the focus of this chapter has been on one indicator of structural stigma in the form of social policies, which represents one of the primary ways in which the field has operationalized structural stigma to date. However, researchers have also explored other measurement approaches for capturing structural stigma, including aggregated measures of explicit and implicit attitudes (e.g., Leitner et al. 2016), Google searches of racial epithets (e.g., Chae et al. 2015), Twitter-expressed negative racial sentiment (e.g., Nguyen et al. 2021), and media campaign ads run during voter referenda on the rights of stigmatized groups, such as same-sex marriage (Flores et al. 2018). Still other research groups have created multicomponent measures of structural stigma, recognizing that many dimensions of structural stigma are correlated (e.g., Lattanner et al. 2021).

The relationships among these different indicators of structural stigma are only beginning to be explored. For instance, Ofosu et al. (2019) used an interrupted time series analysis with 12 years of data and over a million responses to examine whether legalization of same-sex marriage by the U.S. Supreme Court in 2015 was associated with changes in attitudes toward sexual minorities. Whereas implicit and explicit bias toward sexual minorities were already decreasing before legalization of same-sex marriage, this decrease doubled in magnitude following the Supreme Court decision, suggesting that litigation may not only reflect, but also positively shape, public attitudes toward marginalized groups. This association was moderated, however, by whether states had previously legalized same-sex marriage locally. For states that did not legalize same-sex marriage locally before the Supreme Court decision, anti-gay bias (both implicit and explicit attitudes) increased after the decision, suggesting a reactive or backlash effect to this litigation in geographic areas where social institutions had not signaled local acceptance of same-sex marriage (Ofosu et al. 2019). That study suggests that research evaluating the interplay of different indicators of structural stigma may offer new ways of understanding the production of health inequalities that result from structural stigma.

Conclusion

Although stigma research has typically focused on individual and interpersonal processes (Link and Phelan 2001), recent work indicates that structural stigma is an important, but heretofore largely underrecognized, determinant of population health inequalities (Hatzenbuehler 2016, 2017a, b). In this chapter, I reviewed evidence from a range of methods, measures, stigmatized groups, and health outcomes demonstrating that structural stigma, in the form of social policies, is associated with the health of members of stigmatized groups. Further, this research shows that policies exacerbate stigma (thereby shaping poor health) as well as mitigate stigma (thus contributing to improved health). The consistency of this evidence and the multiple attempts to establish strong inferences suggest that these relationships are robust and are not spurious. Despite the important advancements in this literature, much remains to be understood about how social policies influence the health of stigmatized populations. Greater attention should be paid to several areas, including the creation of measures of policy implementation and inaction, the examination of policy enactment across multiple levels simultaneously, the consideration of issues of intersectionality, and the identification of moderators of the association between policies and health. Moreover, social policies are but one component of structural stigma. More research is needed into the interrelationships of social policies and other dimensions of structural stigma, such as social attitudes and institutional practices. Attending to these important questions will further expand our understanding of the manifold ways in which structural stigma operates to affect the distribution of life chances among the stigmatized, which will ultimately inform efforts to reduce stigma-induced harms.

10

Processes and Pathways of Stigmatization and Destigmatization over Time

Paolo Velásquez, Maureen A. Eger, Heide Castañeda,
Christian S. Czymara, Elisabeth Ivarsflaten,
Rahsaan Maxwell, Dina Okamoto, and Rima Wilkes

Abstract

This chapter advances a theoretical framework to understand within- and between-country variation in the level of stigmatization experienced by immigrant groups and their descendants over time. Since processes of stigmatization and destigmatization may unfold over generations, it is imperative for research to adopt a longer time horizon to identify the factors that lead to the emergence, persistence, and/or dissipation of stigma. Expanding the time frame of analysis to decades (or even centuries) requires an explicit focus on the experiences of groups rather than individuals. Based on the observation that the labeling of some groups as "migrants" does not always follow from actual histories of immigration, this framework treats "migrant" as a social category. To guide future empirical research, this chapter introduces two analytical models. The first identifies the factors and processes responsible for stigmatization or destigmatization over time. The second presents five ideal-typical pathways that immigrants and their descendants may experience in relation to stigma: non-emergence, increase, reinforcement, reduction, and status reversal.

Introduction

This chapter synthesizes a week of intense conversations among scholars from two broadly defined fields: stigma and migration. Our goal was to examine and scrutinize the processes of stigmatization and destigmatization in the context of immigration-generated diversity, with a particular focus on the emergence, persistence, and dissipation of stigma *over time*. Inherent in conceptualizations of stigma is the notion that a group's experience with stigma may change over time. The length of this time horizon is never made explicit, but in practice, empirical studies on stigma processes tend to focus on variation in experiences within individuals' lifespan. In this chapter, we argue that a significantly longer view is merited when applying a stigma framework to the phenomenon of immigration and resulting ethnic and racial diversity.

There are a number of reasons why this is necessary. First, the label of "migrant" is not only applied to immigrants who reside in a country different from the country where they were born but may also be applied to individuals who are native-born with no personal history of immigration. For example, children of immigrants are sometimes labeled as "second-generation migrants" and grandchildren as "third-generation migrants." Sometimes people with a specific race or ethnicity are labeled as having a "migrant background" despite having never immigrated. In this way, stigma is transmitted through generations.

Second, while immigrants are, by definition, individuals who reside outside their country of birth, they are also members of ethnic and racial groups, which to varying extents characterize destination countries and their existing social hierarchies. The status of these groups within these societies may fluctuate over decades and centuries, and this has implications for the level of stigma immigrants from different ethnic and racial groups face at any given point in time.

Third, there is little evidence that, on average, peoples' attitudes toward immigrants fundamentally change over time (Kustov et al. 2021), even if they move to an urban center where people have more cosmopolitan attitudes (Maxwell 2019). Instead, research shows that adults' attitudes toward immigrants and immigration are more strongly linked to immigrant presence during one's formative adolescent years than the contemporary demographic context in adulthood (Eger et al. 2022). This implies that neither native-born reactions to immigration nor the level of stigma a migrant group experiences is likely to change dramatically without cohort replacement (i.e., due to demographic processes, the replacement of older generations by new generations who happen to hold different attitudes) (e.g., Gorodzeisky 2021). Even then, research shows that cohort replacement is not a guarantee of less prejudice (Forman and Lewis 2015).

Fourth, as discussed elsewhere in this volume (e.g., Hatzenbuehler, this volume), unequal power relations are necessary for both the emergence and persistence of stigma (Link and Phelan 2001) and social policies (or their absence) that may create or amplify stigma (Link and Hatzenbuehler 2016). In democratic countries, native-born citizens hold the majority of political power, making immigrants especially vulnerable to structural barriers and institutional effects that persist over long periods of time. In the context of immigration, policies determine not only who may immigrate to a country but also immigrants' and their descendants' economic, social, and political rights (Givens and Luedtke 2005; Helbling et al. 2017). Thus, the stigmatization of individuals and groups labeled as "migrants" is a deeply embedded form of social exclusion. For this reason, we argue that an extended time horizon is necessary to understand if and how stigmatization and destigmatization occurs. Focusing on a short period of time provides only snapshot of the experiences of a stigmatized group—a strategy that risks ignoring the key factors that lead to the emergence, persistence, and/or dissipation of stigma and account for the different experiences of ethnic and racial minority groups over time.

In this chapter we develop a theoretical framework to advance the goal of explaining between- and within-country variation in levels of stigma experienced by immigrants and their descendants over time. Our focus is on variation in the status of immigrant, ethnic, and racial minority *groups* over long periods of time (e.g., decades and centuries) rather than on individuals' experiences at a specific point in time or even over the duration of a life course (e.g., Earnshaw et al. 2022). A key feature of our approach is that we treat "migrant" as a social category, recognizing that people need not have a personal history of international immigration to be labeled a migrant. Indeed, some immigrants escape the label altogether, by being referred to as "expats" (Kunz 2016), while some native-born are labeled "second- or third-generation migrants."

Our framework includes two analytical models. The first identifies the factors and processes responsible for stigmatization or destigmatization over time. The model begins with immigration to a destination country, where existing social hierarchies trigger labeling processes, determining whether an immigrant group is branded as "migrant" or not. Over time, societal domains, exogenous events, and feedback loops affect the extent to which immigrants and their descendants are subject to separation, stereotyping, status loss, discrimination, and the reinforcement of the "migrant" label.

Our second analytical model identifies five analytical pathways or ideal types that identify the different possible trajectories of groups in relation to stigma: non-emergence, increase, reinforcement, reduction, and status reversal. We also identify when and why we expect the speed of change to be faster or slower. We argue that the absence of stigma, whether due to stigma avoidance or reduction, is conceptually most similar to inclusion not integration. Some groups may be well integrated into society (e.g., high levels of participation in the labor market and knowledge of the language) but still face stigma whereas other groups are not stigmatized regardless of levels of economic and cultural integration. Thus, we do not equate the absence of stigma with immigrants' efforts to "fit in" but instead with the extent to which immigrants and their descendants are accepted and treated as full members of society.

Throughout the chapter, we offer historical or contemporary examples consistent with these five pathways. Most of these examples come from European and North and South American countries, which reflects our expertise. However, the histories of these countries are inextricably linked to colonialism and imperialism, making our discussion to some degree global in scope. Nevertheless, we aim to maintain a high level of abstraction so that this framework can be applied in a variety of future empirical research. We conclude by identifying challenges and possibilities for future empirical research, which will be important for testing and refining the ideas presented here.

Migration Stigma

Stigma is the co-occurrence of labeling, stereotyping, separation, status loss, and discrimination (Link and Phelan 2001). Applied to the phenomenon of immigration, migration stigma is the co-occurrence of these phenomena in relation to a racial or ethnic group with a history of international migration. The labeling of specific groups as migrants, the first step in stigmatization that initiates the entire process, does not always follow from a contemporary history of immigration. That is, some groups of immigrants, who reside in a country where they were not born, are never regarded as "migrants" while others who were born and raised in a particular country but whose ancestors immigrated are considered "migrants." This label is the first constitutive component of stigmatization, which has implications for stereotyping, separation, status loss, and discrimination. Thus, we contend that without this label, by definition, a group is not stigmatized.

Figure 10.1 depicts a heuristic model of our framework. While we recognize that reasons for immigration stem from both push and pull factors (Lee 1966) as well as feedback loops (O'Brien and Eger 2021), to illustrate immigration as the process of moving to a new country, we depict it as a phenomenon that begins outside of a destination country. When immigrants, motivated by personal reasons or living conditions in the origin country outside of their control, arrive at a destination country (represented by the large box), existing social hierarchies determine whether or not they are labeled "migrants." Over time, immigrants and their descendants interact with and are affected by various domains or arenas (e.g., institutions, media, education, policies, politics, social movements) that may reinforce, reduce, activate, or increase stigma.

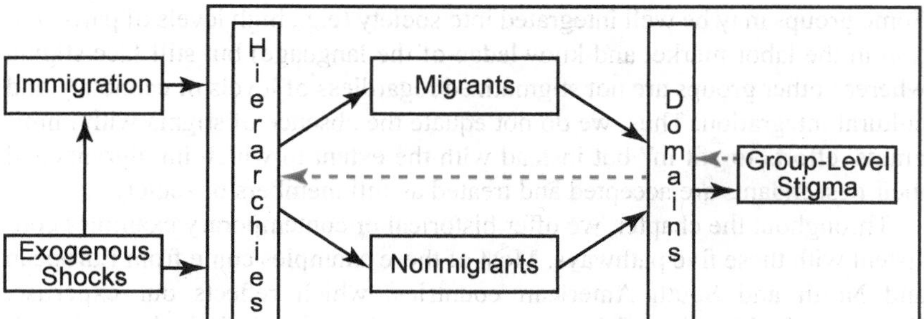

Figure 10.1 Model of stigmatization and destigmatization processes over time. Dashed lines represent possible feedback loops between group-level stigma and domains as well as between domains and hierarchies.

Additionally, other exogenous events such as wars and pandemics may contribute to migration flows and may impact the destination country in a way that is consequential to the level of stigma some immigrants and their descendants face. Exogenous shocks may even impact hierarchies and which groups are labeled migrants without necessarily increasing migratory flows. We discuss each of these elements in greater detail below.

Hierarchies

Why are some groups labeled migrants while others are not? A key component of stigma is that it requires power to stigmatize (Link and Phelan 2001). Thus, those who are in positions of power in a destination country, whether political, social or economic, have the power to stigmatize immigrants. We argue that this process depends on the existing social hierarchies (Sidanius and Pratto 1999:32) in a destination country as well as the global social order, of which origin and destination countries are a part. The most visible and arguably consequential hierarchy an immigrant group faces in a new country is race and ethnicity (e.g., Lentin 2008). Although existing racial and ethnic hierarchies are country specific, they are also embedded in and reflect a global structure shaped by the legacy of colonialism, which spanned hundreds of years in nearly all regions of the world (Go 2018). Consequently, Western Europeans and their descendants tend to sit atop their countries' ethnic and racial hierarchies even where the majority of the native-born population is non-European (e.g., Latin America; see Telles 2014). The label migrant is rarely applied to these immigrant groups (Fechter and Walsh 2010). Where Western Europeans constitute a majority, other Western Europeans (and descendants of Europeans from settler colonies) also tend to avoid the label migrant and are called expatriates or expats instead (Kunz 2020). Typically, members of these groups are included as full members of society when their knowledge of the history, culture, and/or language of the destination country is limited.

Class hierarchies, which are associated with race and ethnicity, also help determine which groups are labeled as migrants (e.g., Castañeda 2015; Fechter and Walsh 2010). As mentioned, immigrant groups from Western European countries (or from countries where a significant proportion of the population is descended from Western Europeans) are least likely to be labeled as migrants. Because these countries are also high-income countries (also related to colonialism), immigrants from these countries may not only avoid the label of migrant but may also enjoy a high status in the destination country (Kunz 2016). Due to their relatively high status in these hierarchies, they arguably face less discrimination in the labor market and have better opportunities for educational attainment and economic mobility, which reinforces their high status. Immigrant groups from lower income countries are more likely to be labeled "migrant" (Saxenian 2000). Although wealthy immigrants from non-Western or lower income countries may face fewer barriers to economic integration than their less economically well-off counterparts, economic integration neither ensures protection from stigma nor guarantees full inclusion in society (e.g., Maghbouleh 2017; Yeoh and Willis 2005).

The standing of an immigrant group's country of origin in the international world order also influences which groups are stigmatized in a destination country (e.g., Kustov 2019). This status is fundamentally connected to both ethnic and racial hierarchies and economic hierarchies and may change as a consequence of conflicts and shifting alliances between countries in the international arena. For instance, immigrants from more powerful countries may benefit from their country's higher status in a destination country whereas immigrants from less powerful countries, who may have similar individual characteristics as those from more powerful countries, see their status devalued in the destination country due to their national origin (Kunz 2016; Leonard 2010). For example, within Europe, European Union (EU) immigrants are often distinguished from non-EU immigrants regardless of immigrants' human capital. Thus, as the boundaries of the EU have changed over time, so have possibilities for stigma. War and political conflict may also affect the standing of countries and emigrants from those geographies. An egregious example of stigmatization was the incarceration and isolation of Japanese immigrants and Americans of Japanese descent during World War II. Further, shifting military and geopolitical alliances may also influence levels of stigma experienced by groups. For instance, since 2021, the level of stigma experienced by Russian and Ukrainian immigrants has likely shifted and in different directions. Descendants of these immigrant groups potentially face more or less stigma due to the contemporary status of their parents' or grandparents' country of origin. Indeed, hierarchies within and between countries intersect in order to produce various levels of group-level stigma, which may fluctuate over time.

Domains

Over time, immigrants and their descendants, who are either labeled as migrants or not, interact with and are affected by different destination country domains or arenas that can either reinforce, reduce, or increase stigma. In this section, we provide an overview of a number of domains that implicate either top-down or bottom-up processes of stigmatization and destigmatization (but note that this is far from an exhaustive list). The former are institutions and social policies, politics, media, and education. The latter are social movements and intergroup contact.

Institutions/Policies

Institutions in destination countries not only determine who may immigrate (Helbling et al. 2020; Schultz et al. 2021) but also play an important role in the experiences of immigrants after arrival. Social policies that impact the lives of immigrants once in a destination country are often referred to as "integration policies." Despite this moniker, not all policies are designed to facilitate immigrants' full participation in economic, political, or social life, comparable to that enjoyed by native-born. Instead, some policies are designed to limit immigrants' access to particular institutions, such as health care, public education, housing, or the labor market.

Theoretically, these policies may reflect attitudes toward immigrants, as native-born hold considerably more political power. However, policies also create a normative environment that may influence native-born attitudes toward immigrants (Green and Staerklé 2013; Guimond et al. 2013). Although the causal order is unclear, research shows that policies' levels of inclusivity or exclusivity are correlated with public attitudes toward immigrants (Eger and Bohman 2016; Heizmann 2016). Further, the positive relationship between native-born individuals' everyday contact with immigrants and their threat perceptions is stronger in countries with more inclusive social policies (Green et al. 2020). Research also demonstrates that these policy environments are related to outcomes for immigrants, such as health (Juárez et al. 2019) and life satisfaction (Heizmann and Böhnke 2019).

The Migrant Policy Integration Index (MIPEX 2020) tracks and measures policies associated with immigrant integration. By 2019, MIPEX included data from 56 countries across six continents and eight policy dimensions: labor market mobility, family reunion, education, health, political participation, permanent residence, access to nationality, and antidiscrimination. The index scores policy dimensions and countries on a scale of 0–100, based on the level of inclusivity of the policies. Figure 10.2 depicts the average overall score across various groupings of countries. The y-axis shows the quantitative score as well as the qualitative description of the inclusivity of the policies: critically unfavorable (0–20), slightly unfavorable (21–40), halfway favorable (41–59), slightly favorable (60–79), favorable (80–100). The bars in the top panel (a) represent the average score for groups of countries between 2010 and 2019. The average score across the full sample of countries (MIPEX56) is halfway favorable. At the low end, the European Union 13 (EU13), which includes the Eastern European countries which joined the EU after 2004, have on average policies that border what could be described as exclusive. At the high end, the average scores of traditional immigrant destination countries of Australia, Canada, the United States, and New Zealand are slightly favorable in regard to inclusivity. A noteworthy aspect of these scores is how little variation exists in the short time frame of a single decade. The bottom panel (b) in Figure 10.2 illustrates what these policies imply for basic rights, equal opportunities, and a secure future in the destination-country group in 2019. What stands out is that, on average, immigrants do not have the same access to opportunities and resources such as health care and education. Further, policies that help ensure immigrants a "secure future" (e.g., family reunification, permanent residence, and citizenship) are most exclusive in the EU15 countries of Western Europe.

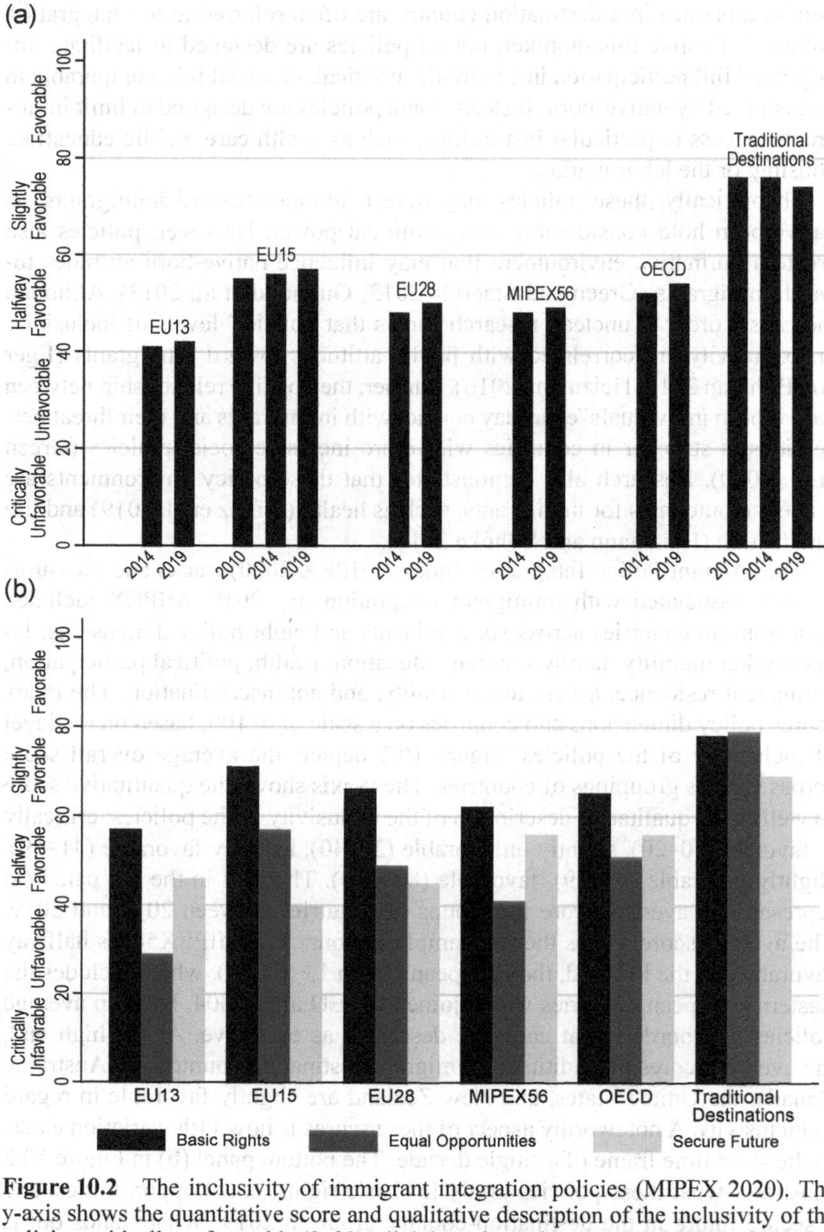

Figure 10.2 The inclusivity of immigrant integration policies (MIPEX 2020). The y-axis shows the quantitative score and qualitative description of the inclusivity of the policies: critically unfavorable (0–20), slightly unfavorable (21–40), halfway favorable (41–59), slightly favorable (60–79), favorable (80–100). The bars represent (a) the average overall score across various groupings of countries between 2010 and 2019; and (b) what these policy configurations imply for basic rights, equal opportunities, and a secure future in the destination-country group in 2019.

Politics

Another domain that affects the level of stigmatization experienced by immigrants and their descendants is the political arena. Political backlash to immigration is not a new phenomenon; it emerges even in contexts where immigration is economically beneficial (Tabellini 2020). However, contemporary anti-immigrant parties have made significant electoral gains in recent decades. These parties, often referred to as the radical right or far right, actively label, stereotype, and promote or, at the very least, do not object to discrimination against immigrants and certain ethnic and racial minorities. According to these parties, immigration poses cultural, economic, and political threats to contemporary nation-states (Eger and Valdez 2015, 2019). Their aim is to stop immigration and, in some cases, to deport immigrants and their descendants (Zaslove 2004). Especially in European countries, these parties often target Muslims (Betz 2013).

Mobilizing anti-immigrant sentiment is fundamental to the success of these parties (Arzheimer 2018; Ivarsflaten 2008), and recent decades have seen significant increases in popular support for parties such as France's National Rally, the Freedom Party of Austria, Jobbik in Hungary, the True Finns, and the Sweden Democrats, to name a few. Moreover, in countries like Spain and Germany, where such politics had remained relatively fringe in the post-World War II era, new parties have established themselves as political contenders : In Spain, Vox, and in Germany, the AfD. On the other side of the Atlantic, Donald Trump launched his political career by stigmatizing immigrants from Latin America and continued, as president, to stigmatize other racial and ethnic groups which he claimed came from "shithole countries" (Dawsey 2018). The success of these parties and politicians may, as a consequence, increase stigma. For example, Trump's hostile rhetoric shaped public attitudes toward immigrants (Flores 2018) and affected the day-to-day experiences of targeted groups (Hobbs and Lajevardi 2019). The success of radical right parties and politicians may also shape the positions of mainstream parties (Abou-Chadi and Krause 2020). The exclusionary rhetoric of mainstream political elites is correlated with more negative views of Muslim immigrants among native-born (Czymara 2020b) as well as attitudes toward immigration more generally (Bohman 2011; Schmidt-Catran and Czymara 2023). Further, feedback processes may reinforce social hierarchies within countries and internationally, perpetuating stigma over time.

Media

Mass media plays an important role in informing the general public on immigration related issues and developments (Eberl et al. 2018). Research indicates that newspapers often link immigration to negative frames such as crime and disease (Esses et al. 2013; Harris and Gruenewald 2020) and describe immigration with metaphors such as flooding (Castañeda and Holmes, this volume; Abascal et al. 2021; El Refaie 2001; Gabrielatos and Baker 2008; Grigorieff et al. 2020). In this way, mass media can contribute to the stigmatization of immigrants. However, experimental evidence suggests that providing factual information counters hostility toward immigrants (Abascal et al. 2021; Grigorieff et al. 2020). This is because, as Lutz and Bitschnau (2022) argue, misperceptions about immigration are ubiquitous in many societies.

Education

Educational institutions are one source of stability and change in stigmatization of migrants. They are intrinsically connected to other domains, but mainly to the state and politics. Schools act as microcosms of their societies at large, where they may function as conferrers of the "official" or dominant values of a given society (Selznick and Steinberg 1979). For instance, Phelan et al. (1995) suggest that the core values of the United States involve tolerance, individualism and equality of respect and opportunity (but not of outcome), and individual initiative. This implies that the role of schools in relation to stigma will partially depend on the core values or "creed" of a given country. This does not mean, however, that stigma against immigrants is absent in countries with such values. For example, the United States also has a long history of nativism and stigmatization of immigrants, including in educational settings as evidenced by episodic controversies over what aspects of American history and literature to include in and exclude from the curriculum.

Within schools and the educational system, the processes of stigmatization and destigmatization are dynamic and involve the interaction of different actors at various levels. At the micro level, intergroup contact has been found to help reduce prejudice (Bohman and Miklikowska 2021; Tropp et al. 2022), as have discussions about political and societal issues with peers (Bohman et al. 2019; Miklikowska et al. 2022) and curricula that addresses racism and xenophobia (Hjerm et al. 2018b). At the macro level, where the state sets the overall educational standards and curricula, what is taught varies on topics related to immigration, racism, and diversity. Indeed, educational institutions cannot be separated from the political milieu in which they are situated, and the content of education or what *can* be taught in educational institutions is influenced by the country's "creed" or democratic tradition. For example, education has been shown to have a stronger positive effect on attitudes toward immigrants and ethnic minorities in countries with a longer history of democracy (Coenders and Scheepers 2003). However, there is considerable variation within regime types, and the political climate of a destination country also influences to what extent education may reduce or reinforce stigma toward immigrants.

Social Movements

Social movements are an arena where immigrants can diffuse or counter stigmatization. Immigrant groups can collectively engage in efforts to express grievances or make claims through organized efforts directed at institutions or political elites (Bloemraad and Voss 2020; Ebert and Okamoto 2015; Voss and Bloemraad 2011). Such efforts can vary depending on a group or movement's particular goals, which can include improving the status of minority groups, influencing policy, or demanding independence. Social movements are not simply a response to the nation-state; they are also shaped by transnational ties as well as international norms and movements, which can provide narratives, elite support, and resources to encourage the state to address historical inequalities and implement state policies as well as to gain recognition or acceptance for stigmatized groups.

The immigrant population in a given country is often heterogeneous, as people come in from a variety of origin countries. This can pose a challenge to mobilization on the basis of immigrant status alone. For example, to address stark inequalities among Asian-origin immigrant groups in the United States, activists, students, and community members in the 1960s—most of whom were of Chinese, Japanese, and Filipino descent—built the pan-ethnic Asian American movement (Okamoto 2014). Despite their national origin, language, cultural, and religious differences, activists emphasized their shared histories and experiences as cheap laborers and unassimilable foreigners without access to citizenship, property, and civil rights, and even entry into the United States. Their efforts mobilized large-scale social movements aimed at dismantling structures of class, gender, and racial oppression (Okamoto and Adem, this volume; Mora and Okamoto 2020a; Okamoto 2003).

Both the political rights and legal status of immigrants add challenges to pro-immigration social movements. Noncitizen immigrants rarely have the right to vote or stand for office, which fundamentally limits their political voice in democracies (Bloemraad and Voss 2020). Thus, pro-immigrant movements must inspire citizens to support movement goals, including the extension of rights to immigrant populations. Research indicates that the success of particular frames varies (Voss et al. 2020) and that the struggle for recognition and inclusion by immigrants and their descendants depends largely on a destination country's notions of what it means to be a "good immigrant" (Hackl 2022). Still, research also shows that pro-immigrant social movement activity can shift public opinion (Branton et al. 2015), opening up opportunities for rights and inclusion.

Immigration

Immigration itself does not necessarily drive attitudes toward it; instead, perceptions of the size of immigrant out-groups are often more closely associated with anti-immigrant sentiment (Pottie-Sherman and Wilkes 2017). Nevertheless, new immigration has the potential to sharpen ethnic boundaries, making the label "migrant" for a particular group stickier. Long-term immigrant replenishment is the process of ongoing immigration from one country to another (see Jiménez 2008). For example, Mexican immigration to the United States has been commonplace for at least a century, increasing rapidly after 1965. As of 2019, approximately 24% of all immigrants in the United States were born in Mexico (Gonzalez-Barrera 2021), making it the largest immigrant group. Migration flows from Mexico to the United States have been constant due to their close geographic proximity, historic ties, and previous national borders. Continual Mexican immigration contributes to a rigidity in ethnic boundaries which has since disappeared for European immigrants and their descendants who no longer experience immigrant replenishment (Jiménez 2008).

Instead of bolstering ethnic boundaries, new immigration from a different origin country or region could instead reduce stigma among older immigrant groups in the destination country. This happens by contrasting the already settled immigrant groups and their descendants with the newly arrived ones, who are often perceived as more different. For example, research shows that Germans, Dutch, Swedes, and Danes prefer to grant citizenship to non-EU immigrant groups that are perceived as more culturally similar to them (i.e., non-Muslim) (Hedegaard and Larsen 2022). Similar findings come from a study of Americans, who tend to prefer immigration from neighboring Mexico as opposed to Iraq (Hainmueller and Hopkins 2015). Taken together, these results suggest that patterns of immigration and perceived cultural similarity vis-à-vis a group perceived as more culturally dissimilar may contribute to destigmatization and stigmatization processes over time. Because our focus is on explaining stigmatization and destigmatization, Figure 10.1 intentionally depicts immigration as a phenomenon that originates outside of a destination country. However, there is also likely a feedback effect connecting levels of stigmatization within a destination country to future immigration flows.

Exogenous and "Big" Events

Exogenous events (e.g., a war, natural disaster, extreme weather related to climate change or terrorism) increase possibilities not only for increased immigration but also the stigmatization or destigmatization of particular immigrant, racial, and ethnic groups. However, an increase in immigration is not necessary to increase the stigmatization of specific groups of immigrants and their descendants. For example, the events of September 11, 2001, set in motion the stigmatization of individuals with a Middle Eastern background throughout Western countries, not just in the United States. Similarly, the COVID-19 pandemic affected Asian-born immigrants and their descendants (e.g., Wu et al. 2021).

So-called big events—something "that touches deep sentiments, that seems to raise fundamental questions about relations, and that awakens strong feelings of identification with one's racial group" (Blumer 1958:6)—are another source of change in processes of stigmatization and destigmatization. When these events occur, the abstract identity of a specific out-group, in this case the relevant group labeled as migrants, is collectively reassessed, and people with greater power, prestige, and authority play larger roles in this process. Exogeneous and big events impact the portrayal of specific immigrant groups in media narratives and political rhetoric and may influence other destination country's domains such as domestic and foreign policies, which may in turn reinforce or change the level of stigma a group faces (e.g., Maghbouleh 2017; O'Brien and Eger 2021; Wu et al. 2021). For example, there are clear differences in the ways in which refugees fleeing the wars in the Middle East in 2015–2016 were perceived (Czymara and Schmidt-Catran 2017; Holmes and Castañeda 2016) and therefore treated (Frey 2020) compared to those who have fled Ukraine since 2014 (Roman et al. 2021).

Five Analytical Pathways of Stigmatization and Destigmatization

To summarize, when immigrants arrive at a destination country, existing social hierarchies determine whether or not they are labeled as "migrants." This sorting process, which culminates in the label of "migrant" or the absence of it, sets the stage for experiences across various domains in a country, which have implications for the extent to which groups are subject to separation, stereotyping, status loss, and discrimination. Stigma experiences may generate feedback effects, influencing, for example, politics and media narratives, policies including ones governing immigration, and, subsequently, social hierarchies within countries and internationally.

Migration stigma, therefore, should be understood to be on a continuous scale varying in magnitude and susceptible to change over time. The absence of group-level stigma would mean the absence of the label "migrant," stereotyping, status loss, and discrimination—put simply: full inclusion. We emphasize that inclusion does not necessarily depend on immigrants' economic or cultural integration. For example, some immigrant groups and their descendants may be relatively economically successful yet still face discrimination, whereas other groups that are not culturally integrated (e.g., lack of language skills) may not face any stigma.

In Figure 10.3, we identify the five ideal-typical pathways that immigrants and their descendants may experience over time. These pathways reflect the *theoretically possible experiences* of groups and should not be mistaken as groups themselves. This means that any given group may experience more than one pathway over time. Further, we emphasize that these pathways are not linear, as the status of groups may fluctuate. Relatedly, our conception of time is social, or "qualitative and not purely quantitative" (Sorokin and Merton 1937:623). For example, the period of arrival in a new country differs

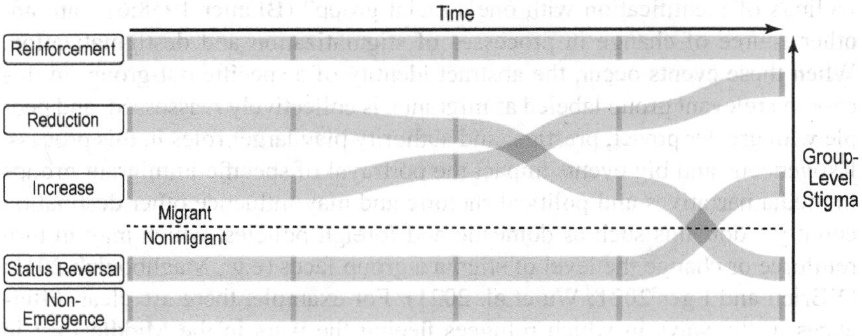

Figure 10.3 Five analytical pathways over time. Non-emergence: due to existing hierarchies, an immigrant group and their descendants are not labeled "migrants" and therefore are not stigmatized. Status reversal: an immigrant group is not initially stigmatized, but due to an exogenous shock or big event, the group is labeled as "migrants" and experiences stigmatization. Increase: an immigrant group and their descendants are labeled as "migrants," and, due to a combination of factors, the level of stigma experienced by members of the group increases over time. Reduction: Due to a combination of factors, an immigrant group and their descendants labeled "migrants" experience less stigma over time, culminating in full inclusion by the native-born majority. Reinforcement: an immigrant group and their descendants are labeled "migrants," and the level of stigma experienced by members of the group persists over time because of a combination of factors.

for groups and, due to within-country variation in domains over time, changes in the experiences of immigrants and their descendants differ between historical periods. Thus, we refrain from using specific time intervals (e.g., 10, 50, or 100 years).

The top three pathways reflect different experiences of stigma for groups labeled "migrant" that may increase, decrease, or remain stable over time. These three pathways should not necessarily be understood as a rank order of stigma. The pathway at the top, reinforcement, need not be the highest level of stigma in a society but could instead be associated with a lower level that remains stable over time. For instance, some immigrant groups might experience an increase in stigma, or even a reduction, and still encounter more stigma than another group whose stigma is reinforced across various domains throughout the same time period. The pathway at the very bottom, non-emergence, is the absence of stigma. Just above non-emergence is the fifth and arguably rarest pathway: status reversal. We discuss each ideal-typical pathway in greater detail below.

Non-Emergence

Some immigrant groups in a destination country are never stigmatized as migrants. While these groups may be seen as different, this distinction does not develop into the label "migrant," thereby precipitating negative stereotyping, separation, status loss and discrimination (i.e., the other constitutive components of stigma; see Link and Phelan 2001). As a consequence, stigma does not impede members of these groups from participating fully in civic and economic life. One possible reason for the absence of migration stigma is power. It takes power to stigmatize and if an immigrant group arrives with economic and symbolic power (such as educational credentials or wealth), then it is theoretically less likely that this group will be labeled as "migrants" and face further stigma. Another possible explanation for the absence of stigma has to do with the status of an origin country in the international arena (i.e., holding a particular passport). If immigrants come to a high-income and/or democratic country from another high-income and/or democratic country, they are arguably less susceptible to negative stereotyping and othering. A third reason implicates global racial and ethnic hierarchies, legacies of imperialism and colonialism. Immigrant groups with specific phenotypes and/or national-origin cultures may also benefit from positive stereotypes that advantage them, for example in the labor market, even compared to some native-born. However, it is worth mentioning that some immigrant groups are heterogeneous in regard to race and religion. Thus, individuals from a particular immigrant group may escape being labeled "migrant" and further stigmatization when nationality is salient but not in circumstances when race or religion is salient.

Reinforcement

Due to existing hierarchies, some immigrant groups are stigmatized on arrival. While stigma may dissipate over time (see below), experiences across societal domains and feedback processes may reinforce the label of "migrant," meaning that some immigrant groups and their descendants experience stigmatization over long periods of time. For example, for centuries, Roma have experienced marginalization, pervasive stereotyping, everyday discrimination, and institutional exclusion in European countries (e.g., Creţan et al. 2022). Multilevel stigmatization and powerful feedback effects over centuries have certainly contributed to persistent and extreme inequality. However, recent research indicates that even wealthy Roma face vehement stigmatization and that "the long-term group stigmatization of Roma" works to reinforce the "dominant perception of Roma as inferior, regardless of their individual or family characteristics, or their housing and economic circumstances" (Creţan and Powell 2018:425).

Specific domains, such as the media, contribute to the stereotyping of groups (e.g., criminals, aggressive, lazy, etc.) and therefore the reinforcement of stigma over time. During the 2015 "migration crisis," the European press often portrayed refugees as dangerous outsiders (Georgiou and Zaborowski 2017), a trope long used to characterize Middle Eastern men as violent (Said 1979). Newspapers in Scandinavia also played a role in reinforcing the perceived negative consequences of the arrival of refugees by focusing less on humanitarian aspects of the crisis over time (Hovden et al. 2018).

One implication of the reinforcement of stigma is that new immigrants from a "migrant" group are effectively stigmatized pre-arrival, which may be consequential for experiences of discrimination as well as identity. For instance, due to racial hierarchies in the United States, Caribbean immigrants racialized as black are susceptible to stigma based on migration and race, which may even manifest in their descendants' identities. Research shows that the children of Caribbean immigrants who identify as black Americans are more likely to perceive higher levels of discrimination and fewer opportunities than those identifying as West Indians (Waters 1994). Other research shows that black Caribbean immigrants may appeal to their ethnicity as a way to distance themselves from "blackness" which is considered to be more stigmatizing (Foner 2001).

Increase

An increase in stigma refers to heightened status loss and greater discrimination faced by immigrant groups. Immigrant groups labeled as "migrants" already satisfy one component of stigma (Link and Phelan 2001), that is, being labeled. We contend that separation, or identification of "us" and "them" follows. When this happens, the dominant cultural beliefs in a destination country may lead to stereotyping, or the association of undesirable characteristics with a specific "migrant" group. Increases in stigma stem from both experiences with a country's domains as well as exogenous or big events. Indeed, dramatic events, including increasing immigration, provide opportunities for an increase in stigma, as those in power across various domestic domains may seize the moment to create new narratives about immigrant groups, new and old.

Stereotypes may be reinforced or amplified by mass media, for example when television news on crime depicts ethnic minority perpetrators in a more threatening manner (Jacobs 2017). Such reporting is more prevalent in tabloid or commercial outlets that tend to frame immigration as related to criminality (Greussing and Boomgaarden 2017), lower security (Kovář 2020, 2022), and greater uncertainty (Gottlob and Boomgaarden 2020). Similarly, immigration news in commercial television tends to be somewhat more sensational (Jacobs et al. 2016).

Such reporting can lead to an increase in stigmatization, including discrimination and exclusion. A growing body of literature links such media reporting to public attitudes toward immigration and immigrants, demonstrating that mass media reporting can increase support for anti-immigrant parties (Boomgaarden and Vliegenthart 2007) and negatively influence attitudes toward immigration (Czymara and Dochow 2018; Meltzer et al. 2021; Schlueter and Davidov 2013; Van Klingeren et al. 2015). Moreover, media effects are target specific: minority groups that are usually depicted in a negative way in the media are also evaluated least positively by the public (Meeusen and Jacobs 2017), making them susceptible to both labor market (e.g., Åslund and Rooth 2005) and everyday discrimination (e.g., Wu et al. 2021).

Status Reversal

Status reversal is probably the rarest of analytical pathways, occurring when an immigrant group not initially stigmatized is, at a later point in time, labeled "migrant" and experiences the other components of stigma. Arguably, this would most likely occur after an exogenous shock or big event, for example a war or terrorist attack that changes public opinion and mobilizes antipathy toward a particular group. In all other ways, status reversal is similar to the analytical pathway of increasing stigma, though it could have additional negative consequences associated with the experience of status loss and new fears about the future.

Reduction

The reduction of stigma occurs when certain groups are increasingly included as full members of society and treated with dignity and respect. Thus, destigmatization refers to a process by which low-status groups gain recognition and worth (Okamoto and Adem, this volume). Immigration scholars have typically focused on the ways in which immigrants integrate socioeconomically into a destination country's society, and therefore rely on indicators such as income, education, and occupational status. But even if immigrants are integrating into society based on these measures, such that they are achieving parity with native-born, this does not necessarily mean that immigrants as a group are not stigmatized. Some immigrant groups outperform natives socioeconomically, yet still face stereotyping, prejudice, and discrimination, suggesting that destigmatization means gaining a type of "cultural membership" (Kymlicka 1995) that goes beyond, for example, labor market integration.

One way in which the reduction of stigma is possible is through the development of pro-immigration attitudes among the native-born and ethnic majority population. As discussed above, mass media can play a key role in how immigrants are perceived and therefore treated by native-born and ethnic majorities. Prior research suggests that positive media framing can lead to more positive attitudes: exposure to positive content about immigrants in the news is associated with more openness toward immigration (Meltzer et al. 2021) and decreases the importance that natives assign to immigration as a problem (Van Klingeren et al. 2015). Further, immigrants and their descendants may play an active role in shifting attitudes by mobilizing for recognition, respect, and rights (Bloemraad and Voss 2020; Okamoto 2003, 2014).

For groups labeled as "migrants," processes of destigmatization are typically long. This is, in part, due to the attitudes and beliefs of native-born and ethnic majorities, which can be resistant to change. Research suggests that immigration attitudes, like many other social and political attitudes, are formed during the so-called impressionable years and not necessarily related to conditions in adulthood (e.g., Eger et al. 2022). Increasingly, the scholarly consensus is that immigration attitudes are sticky and resistant to change across the life course (Kustov et al. 2021). While there is evidence that adults may become more positive or negative toward immigrants in response to dramatic events (e.g., Hangartner et al. 2019), events that make immigration salient may also amplify preexisting attitudes, making political behavior consistent with either pro- or anti-immigration attitudes more likely (Eger and Olzak 2023). Taken together, attitudinal research implies that native-born and ethnic majority contributions to destigmatization is a lengthy process that unfolds over generations.

From immigrants' point of view, reduction in stigma can also be seen through the lens of resiliency, or the capacity to respond positively despite challenges to well-being. This represents a strengths-based approach to understanding the experience of groups facing stigma as opposed to the more common focus on deficits and negative consequences for stigmatized groups. Resiliency is frequently thought of as an individual-level characteristic that is developed to increase one's ability to cope or persist in the face of adversity; thus, a criticism of an emphasis on resiliency is that it takes the focus off structural obstacles and natives' treatment of immigrants and attributes immigrants' experiences entirely to their own efforts. Still, thinking about resiliency as a group-level trait can be useful for understanding processes that can combat stigma, such as the development of social capital and other strengths.

Shifting the focus from the consequences of stigma to processes that overcome stigma allows us to reconsider what the absence of stigma, and thus the absence of the label "migrant," may entail. We have already argued that full destigmatization means inclusion, which goes beyond integration. One may also think of destigmatization as increasing the capacity of immigrants and their families to flourish. Willen et al. (2021) understand flourishing as an active, dynamic pursuit that is deeply informed both by people's sociopolitical position and by the environments in which they live, which includes the presence or absence of stigma. In developing new strategies to promote the flourishing of immigrants and their descendants, we might envision new discourses and systems that value dignity and well-being.

Speeds of Change

We identified two speeds at which change in stigma is possible: incremental and rapid. An incremental or slow change in stigma is mostly related to destigmatization, largely due to stigma being deeply embedded in institutions that are slow to change by design, making large-scale reform a rather lengthy process. Instead, institutions tend to evolve at the margins through political contestation and social change (Conran and Thelen 2016). As stigmatized immigrant groups fight for their rights and for full membership in society, institutions may not immediately respond to efforts for full inclusion. There is a tug of war between the stratum in positions of power and immigrant groups who often do not wield the necessary power or resources in order to sway public opinion or how their group is viewed. Arguably, for immigrant groups to shed stigma, some degree of integration is necessary. That process, of course, is moderated by existing social hierarchies, making some groups' paths easier and others' more challenging. For groups lower in the hierarchy, more evidence of integration is likely required as proof of worthiness for full inclusion. Thus, processes of destigmatization may unfold over generations, and even though certain immigrant groups are eventually considered fully integrated into a society, they can still experience some degree of stigma.

A rapid change in stigma is likely to be associated with an increase rather than a decrease due to the slow nature of destigmatization. These rapid changes in the reconfiguration of the abstract group identity are more likely a result from sudden events which accelerate social change (e.g., Wu et al. 2021). These catalyst events can be analytically distinguished into two categories, although they work in tandem. We can classify them as endogenous or occurring within the destination country's more dynamic domains (politics and media) (Flores 2018; Hobbs and Lajevardi 2019), or as exogenous, which occur outside a country's borders such as environmental disasters due to climate change, economic crises, and violent political conflicts resulting in a migration influx (e.g., Czymara and Schmidt-Catran 2017).

A rapid change in destigmatization is rare but theoretically may occur when a dramatic event puts a group in an entirely different light or another immigrant group and their descendants experience a surge in stigma, changing how the former group is perceived and treated. It is also theoretically possible for groups to experience an incremental increase in stigma. For example, a specific immigrant group and its descendants could face greater stigmatization due to "constant replenishment" of immigrants or increased immigration from the same country or region (e.g., Jiménez 2008).

Challenges and Future Directions for Studying Stigmatization and Destigmatization over Time

How can we study stigma processes over time? One way is to use panel survey data to measure the experiences of both the stigmatized and stigmatizers over time. For example, the Norwegian Citizen Panel (NCP) is a research purpose online panel recruited randomly from the Norwegian Population Registry and owned by the University of Bergen. This panel has enabled longitudinal and survey experimental research since 2013 resulting in a number of important publications and new insights into questions relevant to the study of immigration-generated diversity. For instance, several studies have used this data to examine attitudinal consequences of a refugee influx from people fleeing wars in Syria, Afghanistan, and Iraq in 2015/2016. Since the NCP traces attitudes over time, the panel contained a baseline measure prior to this event, which is essential for identifying and estimating causal effects. Since data collection has continued long after the event, the panel also contributes to studies of the duration of effects. One study using this data identified a causal effect in exclusionary direction of the influx of refugees to Norway in 2015 on both measures of attitudes to the social rights of refugees and general evaluation of immigration. The exclusionary response lasted for a considerable period of time but reverted to baseline after 1.5–2 years (Nordø and Ivarsflaten 2022). Another study found that attaining more education had a small but statistically significant effect on more positive attitudes toward immigrants and that individuals with a university education did not react as strongly to this migration crisis as those with lower levels of education (Velásquez and Eger 2022).

Collecting longitudinal survey data is expensive and requires research funding with a long time horizon and/or an investment in research infrastructure by universities. It is difficult to foresee when an event that has the potential to change attitudes will occur. It also remains to be seen if any platforms for collection of survey data can be maintained for long enough to register changes in underlying norms, attitudes, and values that scholarship suggests happen more gradually. Nevertheless, there is great potential for using such platforms to study attitudinal change in the wake of, for example, a change in law or social policy. For the study of stigma in the context of immigration-generated diversity, it is important to note that currently there is a gap in research infrastructures in Europe that makes reliable, representative survey-based studies of people without a migrant background much easier to conduct than survey-based studies of people with migrant backgrounds or ethnic and racial minorities. However, a good example of the latter is the Children of Immigrants Longitudinal Survey in Four European Countries (CILS4EU) which includes both ethnic majority and ethnic minority participants, but oversamples immigrants and the children of immigrants. Recent analyses of these data shed light on differences in the experiences the ethnic majority and immigrants and their descendants, such as life satisfaction (Henkens et al. 2022), mental health (Mood et al. 2017), and political participation (Dollmann 2021).

Scholars have also recently started to examine social media (e.g., Koytak and Celik 2022), textbooks (e.g., Kotowski 2013; Louie and Wilkes 2018), and other kinds of documentary data to understand the discourse and narratives used to describe and portray immigrants and immigration, key contributors to the stigmatization process. Using computational methods, including topic modeling and sentiment analysis, to examine decades or even centuries of data can help us to further understand when and how immigrants are stigmatized in public documents and by political officials (e.g., Card et al. 2022). Such methods are far less expensive than longitudinal panel data, but of course answer different questions related to processes of stigmatization. Data sources must be harmonized over time, which could be a challenge.

Conclusion

We have argued that adopting a longer time horizon means we can better explain the experiences of immigrants and their descendants. This analytical strategy also means that we can better understand stigma, specifically processes of stigmatization and destigmatization that unfold over generations. We also contend that expanding the time period of analysis to include the experiences of groups, rather than individuals, over many decades and even centuries allows us to consider more explicitly intergroup processes in the medium and longer term. This approach does not negate the experiences of individuals (within groups) and individual-level processes in the shorter term. Rather we argue that individuals' experiences at any one point are shaped by levels of stigma faced by immigrant groups and their descendants, and that group-level stigma may change over time.

This chapter makes at least two original contributions. We identified five ideal-type pathways that immigrants and their descendants may experience over time. In doing so, we provide a general immigration–stigma theoretical framework to guide future research that seeks to explain the presence or absence of stigma and why levels of migrant stigma experienced by specific immigrant groups and their descendants vary within and between countries over time. We have also theorized that the status of groups is due to various factors, including the different hierarchies that exist in destination countries and internationally, exogenous events that catalyze strong reactions to migration, endogenous domains that reinforce or reduce the stigmatization of certain migrant groups, and the status in the international arena of sending countries vis-à-vis the destination countries. We believe this framework contributes to both the fields of migration and stigma, while bridging a gap between the two.

First, in migration research, the concept of stigma tends to be used or used superficially to identify a group facing interpersonal prejudice and discrimination that impedes integration, an important concept in sociological and political science scholarship related to immigration. Applying a stigma framework to international migration makes clear that immigrant integration is orthogonal to the concept of stigma. Some immigrant groups and/or their descendants may be integrated economically (labor market), socioculturally (participation in social and cultural life), and politically (civic participation and citizenship) but still stigmatized as "migrants" and set apart as outsiders. Other immigrant groups may not be well integrated on one or more of those dimensions but not stigmatized as such. Based on this observation, we have argued that the absence of stigma is conceptually closer to *inclusion* rather than integration. In practice, full inclusion likely requires both an appreciation of diversity

(Hjerm et al. 2019) and recognition/acceptance that that immigrants and their descendants contribute to a shared national identity (Ivarsflaten and Sniderman 2022:4). This is a much different metric than integration, and this distinction requires scholarly attention going forward.

Research on stigma also has implications for how scholars of migration see the role of prejudice and discrimination in society. Scholars of stigma contend that "keeping people down, keeping people in and keeping people away" (i.e., exploitation and domination, norm enforcement and disease avoidance) serve psychological, societal, and biological functions (Phelan et al. 2008:365). An implication of the notion that stigma is functional (Pachankis and Wang, this volume) is that migration stigma is a durable societal-level feature, though who counts as a "migrant" and which groups are stigmatized may change over time.

Second, it is for this reason that we believe the field of stigma research should also benefit from applying our analytical framework to the study of stigma in the context of immigration-generated diversity. Previous research on stigma has focused mainly on experiences within the life course, examining the implications of stigma on, for example, mental illness, stress, and life chances. Adopting a longer-term perspective that focuses on the experiences of groups has the potential to clarify the causes of stigmatization and destigmatization processes and their consequences for the status of groups. Indeed, by taking a longer view, we are better suited to identify the specific causes underlying the different trajectories of immigrant groups—and therefore the experience of individuals within those groups—over time. In addition, the notion of stigma as functional may become even more apparent if the same immigrant groups diverge in their experiences with stigma in different regions or destination countries. Such a finding would suggest that it is not about the characteristics of specific immigrant groups per se, but the role/function they play in the destination country. Insights gleaned from future research of this type could change our theoretical understanding of stigma and its application to other stigmatized groups (e.g., long-term changes in attitudes toward people with mental illness) beyond international immigrants.

While we see clear benefits of adopting our framework, we acknowledge that empirical research is needed to test and further refine our propositions. We also note that in advancing our analytical framework, we have mostly relied on scholarship on the North American and European contexts. In addition to investigating migration stigma within countries over time, the fields of immigration and stigma scholarship would benefit from comparing how these processes operate in all parts of the world. Research that makes use of global variation in immigration, hierarchies, domains, exogeneous events and their interaction should provide a fuller understanding of stigma in the context of immigration-generated diversity.

11

Immigrants and Processes of Destigmatization

Dina Okamoto and Muna Adem

Abstract

Immigration-related diversity in the contemporary era poses a challenge for democratic societies, as immigrants continue to face stigmatization, which includes processes such as stereotyping, devaluation, exclusion, and discrimination. This chapter reviews the social conditions that contribute to processes of destigmatization among immigrants in the United States and Europe. Throughout the chapter, reference is made to "immigrants"—a complex term that includes, but is not limited to, economic migrants, refugees, citizens, legal permanent residents, and the undocumented who vary by national origin, language, religion, ethnicity, and race. Destigmatization processes are analyzed within European and U.S. contexts at three levels: structural (in terms of policies), institutional (the role of political elites, media, and social movements), and individual (as it relates to intergroup contact). The chapter concludes with a discussion of open areas for future research.

Defining Destigmatization

Immigrants, along with racial minorities and the poor, experience exclusion and discrimination; these groups also are not often associated with social worth nor do they experience full cultural membership. Lamont (2018) refers to these disparities as recognition gaps. Some groups are viewed as more deserving than others, and the unequal devaluation of groups has broad implications for the distribution of social and material resources. Destigmatization, defined as the social process by which low-status groups gain recognition and worth (Lamont 2018), provides an approach to address such inequalities. This process can also shape public understandings of stigmatized groups and expand policies and practices that may currently underserve or exclude such populations.

Scholars suggest that destigmatization involves *changing cultural constructions of groups*, or the content and value associated with a group (e.g., Clair et al. 2016). Once a group has been established as undeserving and low status, it is often difficult to change this view in the larger society, as there are also material foundations and histories associated with this status. Scholars have found that changing cultural constructions of groups is a complex process that involves a number of different social actors such as experts, social movement activists, media, and policymakers, who can draw on existing ideologies and historical contexts to establish new narratives and understandings about disparaged groups (Lamont 2018). Such efforts aim to change beliefs and attitudes among majority populations, often by dismantling stereotypes, disrupting negative associations, and drawing similarities between the in-group and out-group (Link and Phelan 2001). As an example, Clair et al. (2016) detailed the ways in which scientific experts, activists, advocacy organizations, and lawyers were able to shift the cultural construction of people living with HIV/AIDS, from that of immorality and fear to "people just like us."

Beyond stigma associated with medical conditions or disease, research has also focused on changing cultural constructions of ethno-racial minorities and the working class. This research has explored how advocates, social movements, and experts have drawn upon cultural repertories related to boundaries of national citizenship and created new narratives to shift the cultural notions, images, and ideas about who immigrants are and what their value is in the larger society. We detail some of this work, but first address a large and extensive literature on assimilation that documents *the shifting* and *transformation of group boundaries*, which can potentially contribute to destigmatization processes.

Assimilation, Integration, and Immigrants in Host Societies

Research on immigrants in the United States and Europe has documented how ethnic, racial, and religious differences remain salient, such that "bright" boundaries—which are unambiguous about who belongs within and outside of them—operate to distinguish immigrants from host-society members. Alba (2005) explains that the immigrant–nonimmigrant boundary is largely constructed by the majority group within the host society and shaped by the different histories of immigrant and majority groups, as well as how certain domains such as language, citizenship, and race are institutionalized in host societies. Thus, when group boundaries are "bright" and clearly distinguish immigrants from majority groups on the basis of access to citizenship, for example, this affects equal access to opportunities and life chances for immigrants and their children. It is when the distinctions between immigrants and the majority group in host-society populations decline (i.e., when group boundaries become "blurry") that immigrants become more integrated or assimilated into the host society (Alba and Nee 2003; Drouhot and Nee 2019).

Numerous studies in the United States and Europe have examined the ways in which immigrants have become more similar to host-society populations by measuring economic, political, and social outcomes such as educational and linguistic attainment, occupational status, voting, and intermarriage. Scholars in the United States, mostly sociologists and economists, have developed full panel data sets that link immigrant parents to their children by leveraging historical U.S. census data. These data allow scholars to track generations over time and investigate processes of economic assimilation (see Abramitzky et al. 2012; Catron 2019). Other studies use contemporary census data to analyze patterns of social and residential assimilation over time (see Qian and Lichter 2007). In Europe, scholars often use country specific register data from Norway or Denmark (Hermansen 2016) or cross-national survey data from Sweden, Germany, the Netherlands, and England (e.g., the Children of Immigrants Longitudinal Study in Four European Countries, CILS4EU) to examine adaptation processes of first- and second-generation immigrants across various social domains (see Kalter et al. 2019).

Fewer studies focus on the extent to which immigrants gain status and value outside of these social and economic measures. Yet studies that compare gaps in measures of educational attainment, for instance, over time between immigrants and host-society members can provide insights into the destigmatization process. Such studies answer the question of how group boundaries have shifted, such that immigrants are no longer outsiders on particular social and economic dimensions, which provides the foundation for destigmatization. More generally, research in the United States and Europe suggest that immigrants are assimilating over generations in terms of socioeconomic outcomes (see Drouhot and Nee 2019). Some scholars, however, challenge these results, finding evidence of downward assimilation, delayed incorporation, or blocked acculturation of the second generation (Wimmer and Soehl 2014). Still others find mixed results depending on the immigrant group and national context (see Drouhot 2021 on Muslim immigrants in France; for a review, see Heath et al. 2008). Other studies further suggest that if immigrants do too well, they are considered a threat and group boundaries are redrawn once again (Jiménez and Horowitz 2013).

Domains of Destigmatization

Research has traditionally focused on the broader "contexts of reception" that immigrants face in a host society: governmental policies, labor markets, and other key social institutions that affect how immigrants become incorporated into society (Portes and Rumbaut 2001; Portes and Zhou 1993). We argue that destigmatization depends on these contexts of reception inasmuch as they relate to immigrant integration. We note, however, that a host of institutional domains aid or inhibit whether and to what extent immigrants are viewed as deserving and valued citizens. Such domains include, but are not limited to, laws and policies; politics and media; social movements and advocacy organizations; and individual interactions.

Laws and Policies

Laws and policies related to antidiscrimination, citizenship, and immigration, as well as access to key institutions such as the welfare state are important because they designate who is protected and worthy, and who is included in the polity. Such policies extend symbolic and material access, and establish norms about inclusion or exclusion, which can, in turn, shape immigrant integration as well as host populations' views of immigrants. In this way, laws and policies can directly and indirectly affect the destigmatization process.

A key line of research examines the effects of integration and multiculturalism policies on host-society attitudes toward immigrants in Europe. Integration policies aim to ensure that immigrants receive the same rights and access to institutions (e.g., education, labor market, health care) as host society members, while multiculturalism policies recognize immigrants' cultural identities within public schools and create programs to provide various benefits and support for immigrants (Banting and Kymlicka 2013). Studies have found that more tolerant multicultural and integration policies are related to positive attitudes and less threat toward immigrants, as well as greater levels of trust among the broader population (Tatarko and Jurcik 2021; Wright and Bloemraad 2012). Studies have linked the Migration Integration Policy Index (MIPEX) to survey data, such as the European Social Survey (ESS), using cross-national comparison designs, while others have used longitudinal data to analyze within-country variations (Hooghe and de Vroome 2015; Schlueter et al. 2020; Wright et al. 2017). It is plausible that majority groups who already hold positive attitudes toward immigrants are more likely to support integration and multicultural policies in the first place, but longitudinal data help to address the issue of reverse causality. The positive effects of multicultural and integration policies are not, however, uniform across all studies. Furthermore, some scholars argue that multiculturalism has actually discouraged the integration of immigrants, creating separate and parallel societies, and recent studies question some of the established findings linking, for example, multicultural or integration policies to a decrease in anti-immigration attitudes (see Bartram and Jarochova 2022). It is unclear whether the mixed results are due to variations in measurement of policies, analytical approach, or research design.

In the United States, research has focused on understanding how state policies related to racial classification and citizenship shape the integration processes of immigrants. From a historical view, scholars argue that because European immigrants who arrived in the United States in the early 1900s were classified as White by the state, they were able to integrate smoothly into U.S. society, especially compared to Black Americans as well as Mexican and Asian immigrants— groups that experienced race-based exclusion within institutions as well as racial barriers to citizenship and intermarriage (Fox and Guglielmo 2012; see also López 1996; Zolberg 2006). Other scholars have pointed out the limits of whiteness and white designation by law. Catron (2019) challenges the notion that European immigrants in the early 1900s were treated as "de facto citizens" because they were classified White and finds that citizenship acquisition—not simply whiteness—was associated with greater economic benefits.

Focusing on the contemporary era, U.S. scholars have examined how anti-immigrant laws and policies shape the integration of undocumented immigrants, given that the debate about "illegality" remains one of the most salient immigration issues to date. Using case studies, surveys, and administrative data, research has examined how legal status operates as a key dimension of inequality in the United States, excluding undocumented immigrants from key institutions such as labor markets, education, and health care, and how restrictive immigration laws shape the everyday lives of immigrants (see Asad 2020; García 2019; Gonzales 2011; Menjívar 2006). Case in point, Flores (2014) found that the proposal of a local restrictive ordinance directed at undocumented immigrants in Hazelton, Pennsylvania, increased the stigmatization of the local Hispanic population. The political rhetoric surrounding the proposal not only led to a heightened sense of threat and fear among long-time residents and increased anti-immigrant activism, but it also associated Latinos with illegality and crime, complicating a smooth integration process.

Few studies in the U.S. context have examined how inclusionary policies impact the cultural constructions of immigrants, but research has documented the effects of such policies on immigrant outcomes. Gonzales (2011), for instance, finds that the introduction of the Deferred Action for Childhood Arrivals (DACA) in 2012—an executive action that provides renewable work permits and temporary relief from deportation—continues to have a significant and positive impact on educational and economic outcomes as well as overall well-being for undocumented youth in the United States Other studies find some evidence that dropout rates for undocumented students attending four-year colleges were higher after DACA, suggesting that some youth may be leaving school for full-time work (Hsin and Ortega 2018). This highlights the complexities in how inclusionary policies may not necessarily have uniform effects across groups, which has implications for destigmatization.

Political and Media Narratives

Political elites construct narratives around immigrant belonging, citizenship, and communities that can reinforce or bridge differences between immigrants and host-society populations. Studies have examined how political officials use overt and symbolic language that blames vulnerable groups for societal problems, and how this language shapes public views toward those groups (Bohman 2011). Using evidence from a survey experiment, Flores (2018), for instance, finds that Donald Trump's 2016 presidential election campaign—in which he referred to Mexican immigrants as "rapists" and "criminals"—negatively influenced public opinion toward immigrants, particularly among Republicans and individuals without college degrees. Using a cross-national dataset, Czymara (2020b) demonstrated that native Europeans' attitudes toward Muslim immigrants are more negative in countries in which political elites employ more exclusionary language, and more welcoming when elite discourse is more inclusionary. Thus, the framing and language employed by political elites can shape majority groups' attitudes and behaviors toward immigrant groups, which in turn can influence how majority groups apply value and worth to immigrants (but see Hjerm and Schnabel 2010).

The media also plays a key role in generating narratives about immigrants. Extensive research has demonstrated that media coverage of immigration increases the salience of immigration as a central issue in society and can play a vital role in shaping and reproducing anti-immigration attitudes, both in the United States and Europe (Eberl et al. 2018; Hopkins 2010). Focusing on German news coverage between 1993 to 2005, Boomgaarden and Vliegenthart (2009) found that the frequency and tone of media coverage influenced patterns of anti-immigrant prejudice. Similarly, other scholars find that a negative media environment influences immigrant stereotyping, ethnic competition, and support for anti-immigrant political parties (Damstra et al. 2021; Farris and Silber Mohamed 2018).

If news media can foster or support anti-immigrant attitudes, can it also play a role in destigmization processes? A growing body of scholarship is exploring this very question. In Switzerland, Schemer (2012) reports that frequent exposure to positive news helped to reduce the activation of negative out-group attitudes among people with low to moderate knowledge about immigrants. Van Klingeren et al. (2015) suggest that in the Netherlands, media tone affects public discourse: a positive tone in news reports reduces anti-immigration attitudes. In the United States, some studies find that visual media that include positive images of immigrants tend to have a positive effect on peoples' attitudes while negative images (e.g., emphasizing criminality or illegality) increase support of restrictive policies (Haynes et al. 2016).

Social Movements and New Narratives

Social movements remain important in the destigmatization process for immigrants because they can bring attention to issues of discrimination and exclusion, and change cultural constructions, which in turn can shift public attitudes and policies toward immigrants (for further discussion, see Misra et al., this volume). In the United States, scholars have studied the ways in which activists and advocates have historically created pan-ethnic narratives and ethno-racial categories to raise the visibility, profile, and representation of immigrant groups (Okamoto 2014; Okamoto and Mora 2014). For example, and Okamoto (2020b) demonstrate how, in the 1970s, Hispanic leaders, advocates, and community members created a new narrative, which highlighted the contributions of Hispanic soldiers in the military and to past American wars, in their attempts to change the views of Hispanics as a domestic minority rather than a foreign group in the American imagination.

In the contemporary era, advocacy organizations and immigrant rights activists in Europe and the United States have focused on improving conditions for migrants and refugees. This has been particularly the case since the European migrant crisis in 2015: native-born citizens and migrants across Europe continue to protest against deportation and advocate for social inclusion (Ataç et al. 2016). Similarly, in the United States, a key objective for immigrant rights organizations and movements has been to destigmatize attitudes toward undocumented and noncitizen immigrants in an effort to expand their membership, both legally and socially. Thus, activists and organizations have been working to reframe the deservingness of immigrants to be recognized as citizens and to gain access to state resources. Immigrant rights activists, for example, have reframed welfare debates by underscoring the government's moral obligation to protect the elderly, disabled, and veterans, regardless of citizenship status (Fujiwara 2005). Local nonprofit organizations have successfully advocated for benefits like municipal ID cards for all by highlighting how immigrants contribute to civic life, just like other residents (De Graauw 2016; Gast et al. 2021). At the national level, organizations have defined undocumented youth brought to the United States at a young age as "citizens but for papers," who have long-standing civic and educational ties to U.S. communities (Patler 2018a), with the aim of altering current immigration discourse and policy (also see Nicholls 2019). While scholars disagree regarding the extent to which social movements and advocacy can shape policies and public opinion, there is some evidence to suggest that they do matter.

Intergroup Contact

While policies and social movements can contribute to destigmatization processes, individual interactions also play a key role (see García et al., this volume). Drawing primarily from contact theory, an extensive body of research examines how intergroup contact can help to reduce prejudice, increase intergroup trust and cooperation, and hamper feelings of threat (Brown and Hewstone 2005; Pettigrew and Tropp 2006). Existing studies generally find that positive intergroup contact is associated with more positive attitudes toward immigrants, less opposition toward inclusive immigration policies, and more participation in protests promoting the interests of immigrant outgroups (Kotzur et al. 2019; McLaren 2003). For example, drawing upon survey data, Tropp et al. (2018) find that when U.S.-born groups have greater levels of contact with Mexican and Indian immigrants, the more welcoming they are toward immigrant groups, even when controlling for respondents' demographic characteristics and indicators of intergroup exposure. Cross-sectional survey data are limited in addressing the issue of causality, but experimental and longitudinal studies have demonstrated that contact effects still seem to matter. Studies, however, have also shown that preexisting intergroup attitudes contribute to perceptions of interactions with immigrants (as positive or negative), such that more prejudiced people report engaging less frequently in intergroup contact and having less positive interactions with immigrants than less prejudiced people, which has implications for contact effects (Kotzur and Wagner 2021).

As we have already noted, institutions and policies can encourage positive views of immigrants. They also can create structures of opportunity where immigrants and the native-born come together and interact, possibly leading to greater intergroup understanding and reduction of prejudice. Local residents may begin to view immigrants as part of their communities because of what newcomers bring to withering local economies or because local political parties need new members to consolidate power (Okamoto and Ebert 2016). No matter what the mechanisms are, research has shown that institutions and policies can encourage intergroup contact. Green et al. (2020) found that tolerant migrant integration policies at the country level were associated with higher levels of everyday contact and lower perceptions of symbolic threat across twenty European countries, and that higher levels of everyday contact were related to lower perceptions of migrants as threats. Indeed, institutional support can facilitate contact and its effects. Yet, the positive effect of intergroup contact on immigration attitudes, whether encouraged by institutional support or not, might not be generalizable to all groups nor across contexts. Analyzing ESS data, Ponce (2020) examined how the European public distinguishes between desirable and undesirable migrants along a racial-ethnic hierarchy. Specifically, he found that contact with immigrants—a key mechanism that can reduce xenophobia and prejudice—tempers anti-immigrant attitudes most effectively with same-race migrants and least effectively with Muslim migrants. This suggests that race and religion constitute strong social boundaries.

A growing body of research (mostly in Europe) has started to explore the *dark* side of intergroup contact, also referred to as the integration paradox; that is, how increased contact with native groups may not always be beneficial for immigrants or, at the very least, does not always produce the intended effect (Verkuyten 2016). Challenging classical integration and assimilation theories, studies find that immigrants who are more structurally integrated report higher levels of perceived discrimination, stronger ethnic identification, and lower levels of perceived acceptance (de Vroome et al. 2014; Schaeffer 2019; Tolsma et al. 2012). It remains to be seen if (and how) the integration paradox will complicate destigmatization processes for immigrant groups in Europe.

Remaining Questions and Future Directions

Our review of the literature suggests that destigmatization processes for immigrant groups occur at various levels and in different domains. Lamont (2018) suggests three important steps to improve public attitudes toward stigmatized groups: (a) provide support for laws and policies that incorporate groups, (b) provide positive constructions of groups and behaviors, and (c) improve beliefs and attitudes through institutions and informal interactions. Although these are useful and important suggestions based on extensive research, several questions remain:

Which destigmatization strategies work for the most disparaged groups? Research has shown that nation-states can implement policies directed at immigrant socioeconomic integration, and advocacy organizations and activists can generate campaigns to shift the ways in which immigrants are viewed and understood by the larger public. Often, though, destigmatization processes involve a historical component and are context specific and thus might not work in the same ways in different contexts or even in the same way for all immigrant groups. Furthermore, Muslims in Europe and undocumented immigrants in the United States continue to face significant challenges posed by discrimination and exclusion. It will be important to determine which destigmatization strategies work best for the most disparaged groups as well as for immigrant groups in general.

What type of policies matter the most? One fruitful direction of research would be to examine why some policies work to encourage cultural membership for some groups but not others, and which types of policies are most effective. Scholars have suggested that abstract or universal policies, which include all groups, improve majority-group attitudes toward immigrants because they emphasize normative messages, while policies that provide immigrants with special provisions may have the opposite effect because their implementation may threaten majority groups' access to resources. Future studies should explore how different types of policies across various national contexts can shape immigration attitudes among host-society populations, a sense of belonging among immigrants, and how this can complicate (or encourage) destigmatization processes.

What key institutions can help to destigmatize immigrants? We discussed the role of the state as well as the media and advocacy organizations in contributing to the destigmatization of immigrants. Other institutions such as schools, public services, and health-care systems can also operate to include immigrants as full members of society that are treated with dignity and care. How do these institutions, in combination with others, work to increase the status of immigrants?

How does integration relate to destigmatization? Another unresolved issue concerns the role of integration in expanding cultural membership. Bloemraad et al. (2019) observe that Western societies have witnessed an expansion of formal membership via access to citizenship. Interestingly, this trend has been accompanied by a retraction in social rights, such that over the past fifty years, immigrants and other minorities have been seen as less deserving members of the polity even as their citizenship rights are expanding. Relatedly, studies in the United States and Europe show that even when immigrants are structurally and economically integrated and have access to formal citizenship, cultural membership does not necessarily follow, particularly for non-White immigrant groups (Beaman 2017; Schachter 2016; see also Blasco et al., this volume). Are certain forms of integration more effective in generating cultural membership? For which immigrant groups is the integration-cultural membership link tighter or weaker? What role does race, legal status, or citizenship play?

What role can fact-based treatments play in destigmatization? Given the growing prominence of misinformation, another fruitful direction for research would be to examine the consequences and benefits of correcting people's beliefs about immigrants: their impacts, proportions, and characteristics. Abascal et al. (2021) examine beliefs about how immigrants impact four social domains (cultural, labor, crime, fiscal burden) and find that providing Americans with factual information about immigrants' impacts increases support for immigration, at least in the short run. Focusing on immigrants' characteristics, Grigorieff et al. (2020) find that people develop more positive attitudes toward immigrants when additional information confirms that immigrants living in the country are similar to the "deserving" immigrant they have formed in their minds. Other scholars find limited evidence of fact-based treatments pertaining to the correction of misperceptions about the size of immigrant groups (Hopkins et al. 2019). What other types of fact-based treatments are effective, and how can we extend the length of their effects? Such treatments could be an important future step to increase the perceived status and value of immigrants in the United States and Europe.

Which frames are the most effective in shifting attitudes? Scholars are beginning to unpack specific frames regarding immigrants and immigration that resonate best with the public. Using a survey experiment design, Bloemraad et al. (2016) found that a "family unity" framing moves political conservatives toward greater acceptance of legalization for undocumented immigrants and that frames related to human rights appeals resonate the least with political moderates. Additionally, European scholars find that when the framing of grievances is not aligned between nonimmigrant activists and immigrants, it is more difficult to achieve measurable changes in immigration laws and policies (Fadaee 2015). Further exploring the types of frames that resonate with the majority group will be essential to support destigmatization processes. Relatedly, as there has been a surge of more visible social movements and protests held by immigrants and ethno-racial minorities both in the United States and Europe, a critical future direction for the field is to examine the strategies that immigrants themselves are employing to respond to stigma and exclusion while attempting to promote destigmatization processes for their own group and others (for an extensive comparative study on the responses to stigma and discrimination, see Lamont et al. 2016).

Conclusion

In this chapter, we reviewed the state of the literature regarding processes of destigmatization as they relate to immigrants and racial minorities. Integrating literature from various social science fields, we examined how these processes have occurred at the structural, meso, and individual levels. Clearly, more work must be done at all levels to raise the worth and deservingness of immigrant groups, so that they will have equal access to life chances and opportunities afforded to majority groups. While there is evidence to suggest that the boundaries between immigrants and host-society populations are shifting, future work should address how the different domains link to one another and the processes through which social change can occur. Here, we discussed each domain as if they were independent of one another, but undoubtedly, they interact and, at times, can reinforce one another to create opportunities to further stigmatize or destigmatize immigrants. Economic and political elites can drive and enact laws, policies, and practices, which can set norms and reinforce social and symbolic boundaries related to immigrants. Media and political narratives can reinforce one another, and it is still unclear which narratives get picked up and why. We also know that interactions on the ground and social movements can shape agendas and push policymakers to bend to public opinion. Clearly, multiple actors play a role in the destigmatization process for immigrants, yet it remains to be seen which strategies of destigmatization work most effectively across and within national contexts, for which immigrant and refugee groups, and at what level and in which domains these interventions will fare best. A systematic focus on past case studies and generating new research from and especially beyond the United States and Europe will be a fruitful and critical way forward.

Bibliography

Note: Numbers in square brackets denote the chapter in which an entry is cited.

Abascal, M., T. J. Huang, and V. C. Tran. 2021. Intervening in Anti-Immigrant Sentiments: The Causal Effects of Factual Information on Attitudes toward Immigration. *Ann. Am. Acad. Polit. Soc. Sci.* **697**:174–191. [10, 11]

Abou-Chadi, T., and W. Krause. 2020. The Causal Effect of Radical Right Success on Mainstream Parties' Policy Positions: A Regression Discontinuity Approach. *Br. J. Polit. Sci.* **50**:829–847. [10]

Abramitzky, R., L. Boustan, and K. Eriksson. 2012. Europe's Tired, Poor, Huddled Masses: Self-Selection and Economic Outcomes in the Age of Mass Migration. *Am. Econ. Rev.* **102**:1832–1856. [11]

Abrego, L. J. 2008. Legitimacy, Social Identity, and the Mobilization of Law: The Effects of Assembly Bill 540 on Undocumented Students in California. *Law Soc. Inq.* **33**:709–734. [5]

———. 2018. Renewed Optimism and Spatial Mobility: Legal Consciousness of Latino Deferred Action for Childhood Arrivals Recipients and Their Families in Lost Angeles. *Ethnicities* **18**:192–207. [7]

Abrego, L. J., and S. M. Lakhani. 2015. Incomplete Inclusion: Legal Violence and Immigrants in Liminal Legal Statuses. *Law & Policy* **37**:265–293. [7]

Abrego, L. J., and C. Menjívar. 2011. Immigrant Latina Mothers as Targets of Legal Violence. *Int. J. Sociol. Family* **37**:9–26. [7]

Abrego, L. J., and G. Negrón-Gonzales. 2020. We Are Not Dreamers: Undocumented Scholars Theorize Undocumented Life in the United States. Durham, NC: Duke Univ. Press. [7]

Adorno, T. W., E. Frenkel-Brunswik, D. J. Levinson, and R. N. Sanford. 1950. The Authoritarian Personality. In: Studies in Prejudice Series, ed. M. Horkheimer and S. H. Flowerman, vol. 1. New York: Harper. [3, 4]

Aigner, D. J., and G. G. Cain. 1977. Statistical Theories of Discrimination in Labor Markets. *Indust. Labor Rel. Rev.* **30**:175–187. [6]

Alba, R. 2005. Bright vs. Blurred Boundaries: Second-Generation Assimilation and Exclusion in France, Germany, and the United States. *Ethn. Racial Stud.* **28**:20–49. [5, 11]

Alba, R., and N. Foner. 2015. Strangers No More: Immigration and the Challenges of Integration in North America and Western Europe. Princeton: Princeton Univ. Press. [5]

Alba, R., and V. Nee. 2003. Remaking the American Mainstream: Assimilation and Contemporary Immigration. Cambridge, MA: Harvard Univ. Press. [5, 11]

Alba, R., J. Reitz, and P. Simon. 2012. National Conceptions of Assimilation, Integration and Cohesion. In: The Changing Face of World Cities: Young Adult Children of Immigrants in Europe and the United States, ed. M. Crul and J. Mollenkopf, pp. 44–61. New York: Russell Sage Foundation. [8]

Alexander, K. M., and J. W. Shofield. 2012. Stereotype Threat, Erwartungseffekte und organisatorische Differenzierung: Schulische Leistungsbarrieren und Ansätze zu ihrer Überwindung. In: Migration und Schulischer Wandel: Leistungsbeurteilung, ed. S. Fürstenau and M. Gomolla, pp. 65–87. Wiesbaden: VS Verlag für Sozialwissenschaften. [6]

Allport, G. W. 1954. The Nature of Prejudice. Cambridge, MA: Addison-Wesley. [2–4]

Altemeyer, B. 1981. Right-Wing Authoritarianism. Winnipeg: Univ. of Manitoba Press. [4]

Althusser, L. 1971. Ideology and Ideological State Apparatuses. In: Lenin and Philosophy and Other Essays, ed. L. Althusser, pp. 85–126. New York: Monthly Rev. Press. [5]

Amengay, A., and D. Stockemer. 2019. The Radical Right in Western Europe: A Meta-Analysis of Structural Factors. *Polit. Stud. Rev.* **17**:30–40. [3]

Angermeyer, M. C., A. Holzinger, and H. Matschinger. 2010. Emotional Reactions to People with Mental Illness. *Epidemiol. Psychiatric Sci.* **19**:26–32. [2]

Angermeyer, M. C., and H. Matschinger. 1996. The Effect of Personal Experience with Mental Illness on the Attitude Towards Individuals Suffering from Mental Disorders. *Soc. Psychiatry Psychiatr. Epidemiol.* **31**:321–326. [2]

———. 2003. The Stigma of Mental Illness: Effects of Labelling on Public Attitudes Towards People with Mental Disorder. *Acta Psychiatr. Scand.* **108**:304–309. [2]

Anthias, F. 2007. Ethnic Ties: Social Capital and the Question of Mobilisability. *Sociol. Rev.* **55**:788–805. [5]

Aranda, A. M., W. S. Helms, K. D. Patterson, T. J. Roulet, and B. A. Hudson. 2023. Standing on the Shoulders of Goffman: Advancing a Relational Research Agenda on Stigma. *Business & Society* **62**:1339–1377. [5]

Ariely, G. 2012. Do Those Who Identify with Their Nation Always Dislike Immigrants? An Examination of Citizenship Policy Effects. *National. Ethn. Pol.* **18**:242–261. [8]

Armenta, B. E., R. M. Lee, S. T. Pituc, et al. 2013. Where Are You From? A Validation of the Foreigner Objectification Scale and the Psychological Correlates of Foreigner Objectification among Asian Americans and Latinos. *Cul. Div. Ethnic Min. Psychol.* **19**:131–142. [5]

Arrow, K. J. 1972. Some Mathematical Models of Race Discrimination in the Labor Market. In: Racial Discrimination in Economic Life, ed. A. H. Pascal, pp. 187–203. Lanham, MD: Lexington Books. [6]

Arzheimer, K. 2018. Explaining Electoral Support for the Radical Right. In: The Oxford Handbook of the Radical Right, ed. J. Rydgren, pp. 143–165. Oxford: Oxford Univ. Press. [10]

Asad, A. L. 2020. On the Radar: System Embeddedness and Latin American Immigrants' Perceived Risk of Deportation. *Law Soc. Rev.* **54**:133–167. [5, 11]

Åslund, O., and D. O. Rooth. 2005. Shifts in Attitudes and Labor Market Discrimination: Swedish Experiences after 9-11. *J. Pop. Econ.* **18**:603–629. [10]

Ataç, I., K. Rygiel, and M. Stierl. 2016. Introduction: The Contentious Politics of Refugee and Migrant Protests and Solidarity Movements: Remaking Citizenship from the Margins. *Citizensh. Stud.* **20**:527–544. [11]

Bade, K. J., and J. Oltmer. 2007. Deutschland. In: Enzyklopedie Migration in Europa Vom 17. Jahrhundert Bis Zur Gegenwart, ed. K. J. Bade et al., pp. 141–170. Paderborn: Ferdinand Schöningh. [6]

Banting, K., and W. Kymlicka. 2013. Is There Really a Retreat from Multiculturalism Policies? New Evidence from the Multiculturalism Policy Index. *Comp. Eur. Politics* **11**:577–598. [11]

Banton, M. 1996. International Action against Racial Discrimination. Oxford: Clarendon Press. [8]

Bargh, J. A. 1989. Conditional Automaticity: Varieties of Automatic Influence in Social Perception and Cognition. In: Unintended Thought, ed. J. S. Uleman and J. A. Bargh, pp. 3–51. New York: Guilford Press. [4]

Bartram, D., and E. Jarochova. 2022. A Longitudinal Investigation of Integration/Multiculturalism Policies and Attitudes Towards Immigrants in European Countries. *J. Ethn. Migr. Stud.* **48**:153–172. [11]

Bassett, J. F., and J. N. Connelly. 2011. Terror Management and Reactions to Undocumented Immigrants: Mortality Salience Increases Aversion to Culturally Dissimilar Others. *J. Soc. Psychol.* **151**:117–120. [4]

Beaman, J. 2017. Citizen Outsider: Children of North African Immigrants in France. Oakland: Univ. of California Press. [11]

Becker, G. S. 1971. The Economics of Discrimination, 2nd Ed. Chicago: Univ. of Chicago Press. [6]

Beicht, U., and G. Walden. 2019. Der Einfluss von Migrationshintergrund, Sozialer Herkunft und Geschlecht auf den Übergang nicht Studienberechtigter Schulabgänger/-Innen in Berufliche Ausbildung. Wissenschaftliche Diskussionspapiere No. 198. Bonn: Bundesinstitut für Berufsbildung. [6]

Bénabou, R., and J. Tirole. 2006. Belief in a Just World and Redistributive Politics. *Q. J. Econ.* **121**:699–746. [8]

Berg, R. C., M. W. Ross, P. Weatherburn, and A. J. Schmidt. 2013. Structural and Environmental Factors Are Associated with Internalised Homonegativity in Men Who Have Sex with Men: Findings from the European MSM Internet Survey (EMIS) in 38 Countries. *Soc. Sci. Med.* **78**:61–69. [8]

Betz, H.-G. 2013. Mosques, Minarets, Burqas and Other Essential Threats: The Populist Right's Campaign against Islam in Western Europe. In: Right Wing Populism in Europe: Politics and Discourse, ed. R. Wodak et al., pp. 71–88. London: Bloomsbury Acad. [10]

Bishin, B. G., T. J. Hayes, M. B. Incantalupo, and C. A. Smith. 2016. Opinion Backlash and Public Attitudes: Are Political Advances in Gay Rights Counterproductive? *Am. J. Pol. Sci.* **60**:625–648. [8]

Blalock, H. M. 1967. Toward a Theory of Minority-Group Relations. New York: Wiley. [2, 3]

Blank, R. M., M. Dabady, and C. F. Citro. 2004. Measuring Racial Discrimination: Panel on Methods for Assessing Discrimination. Washington, D.C.: National Research Council, The National Academies Press. [6]

Bloemraad, I. 2006. Becoming a Citizen in the United States and Canada: Structured Mobilization and Immigrant Political Incorporation. *Soc. Forces* **85**:667–695. [5]

Bloemraad, I., W. Kymlicka, M. Lamont, and L. S. Son Hing. 2019. Membership without Social Citizenship? Deservingness & Redistribution as Grounds for Equality. *Daedalus* **148**:73–104. [11]

Bloemraad, I., F. Silva, and K. Voss. 2016. Rights, Economics, or Family? Frame Resonance, Political Ideology, and the Immigrant Rights Movement. *Soc. Forces* **94**:1647–1674. [11]

Bloemraad, I., and K. Voss. 2020. Movement or Moment? Lessons from the Pro-Immigrant Movement in the United States and Contemporary Challenges. *J. Ethn. Migr. Stud.* **46**:683–704. [10]

Blumer, H. 1958. Race Prejudice as a Sense of Group Position. *Pac. Sociol. Rev.* **1**:3–7. [1–3, 10]

Bobo, L. D. 1983. Whites' Opposition to Busing: Symbolic Racism or Realistic Group Conflict? *J. Pers. Soc. Psychol.* **45**:1196–1210. [2, 3]

———. 1999. Prejudice as Group Position: Microfoundations of a Sociological Approach to Racism and Race Relations. *J. Soc. Issues* **55**:445–472. [2, 3]

Bobo, L. D., and M. Tuan. 2006. Prejudice in Politics: Group Position, Public Opinion, and the Wisconsin Treaty Rights Dispute. Cambridge, MA: Harvard Univ. Press. [2]

Bohman, A. 2011. Articulated Antipathies: Political Influence on Anti-Immigrant Attitudes. *Int. J. Comp. Sociol.* **52**:457–477. [3, 8, 10, 11]

Bohman, A., M. Hjerm, and M. A. Eger. 2019. Politics and Prejudice: How Political Discussion with Peers Is Related to Attitudes About Immigrants During Adolescence. *Front. Sociol.* **4**:1–11. [10]

Bohman, A., and M. Miklikowska. 2021. Does Classroom Diversity Improve Intergroup Relations? Short- and Long-Term Effects of Classroom Diversity for Cross-Ethnic Friendships and Anti-Immigrant Attitudes in Adolescence. *Group Process. Intergroup Relat.* **24**:1372–1390. [10]

Bonefeld, M., O. Dickhäuser, and K. Karst. 2020. Do Preservice Teachers' Judgments and Judgment Accuracy Depend on Students' Characteristics? The Effect of Gender and Immigration Background. *Soc. Psychol. Educ.* **23**:189–216. [6]

Boomgaarden, H. G., and R. Vliegenthart. 2007. Explaining the Rise of Anti-Immigrant Parties: The Role of News Media Content. *Elect. Stud.* **26**:404–417. [10]

———. 2009. How News Content Influences Anti-Immigration Attitudes: Germany, 1993-2005. *Eur. J. Polit. Res.* **48**:516–542. [11]

Boswell, C., and A. Geddes. 2011. Migration and Mobility in the European Union. Houndmills: Palgrave Macmillan. [8]

Bourgois, P. 1988. Conjugated Oppression: Class and Ethnicity among Guaymi and Kuna Banana Workers. *Am. Ethnol.* **15**:328–348. [7]

Bourgois, P., S. M. Holmes, K. Sue, and J. Quesada. 2017. Structural Vulnerability: Operationalizing the Concept to Address Health Disparities in Clinical Care. *Acad. Med.* **92**:299–312. [7]

Bowen, J. 2010. Can Islam Be French? Pluralism and Pragmatism in a Secularist State. Princeton: Princeton Univ. Press. [8]

Branscombe, N. R., M. T. Schmitt, and R. D. Harvey. 1999. Perceiving Pervasive Discrimination among African Americans: Implications for Group Identification and Well-Being. *J. Pers. Soc. Psychol.* **77**:135–149. [6]

Branton, R., V. Martinez-Ebers, T. E. Carey, and T. Matsubayashi. 2015. Social Protest and Policy Attitudes: The Case of the 2006 Immigrant Rallies. *Am. J. Pol. Sci.* **59**:390–402. [10]

Bratton, K. A. 2002. The Effect of Legislative Diversity on Agenda Setting: Evidence from Six State Legislatures. *Am. Politics Res.* **30**:115–142. [8]

Brown, R., and M. Hewstone. 2005. An Integrative Theory of Intergroup Contact. In: Advances in Experimental Social Psychology, ed. M. P. Zanna, pp. 255–343, vol. 37. New York: Academic Press. [11]

Bursell, M. 2014. The Multiple Burdens of Foreign-Named Men: Evidence from a Field Experiment on Gendered Ethnic Hiring Discrimination in Sweden. *Eur. Sociol. Rev.* **30**:399–409. [3]

———. 2021. Perceptions of Discrimination against Muslims: A Study of Formal Complaints against Public Institutions in Sweden. *J. Ethn. Migr. Stud.* **47**:1162–1179. [3]

Burton, C. L., K. Wang, and J. E. Pachankis. 2018. Does Getting Stigma under the Skin Make It Thinner? Emotion Regulation as a Stress-Contingent Mediator of Stigma and Mental Health. *Clin. Psychol. Sci.* **6**:590–600. [4]

Bygnes, S. 2022. Experiencing and Resisting Interwoven Social Boundaries: The Case of Highly Educated Recent Refugees in Norway. *J. Ethn. Migr. Stud.* **48**:4941–4956. [5]

Caprariello, P. A., A. J. C. Cuddy, and S. T. Fiske. 2009. Social Structure Shapes Cultural Stereotypes and Emotions: A Causal Test of the Stereotype Content Model. *Group Process. Intergroup Relat.* **12**:147–155. [4]

Card, D., S. Chang, C. Becker, et al. 2022. Computational Analysis of 140 Years of US Political Speeches Reveals More Positive but Increasingly Polarized Framing of Immigration. *PNAS* **119**: [10]

Castañeda, H. 2015. European Mobilities or Poverty Migration? Discourses on Roma in Germany. *Int. Migr.* **53**:87–99. [10]

———. 2019. Borders of Belonging: Struggle and Solidarity in Mixed-Status Immigrant Families. Stanford: Stanford Univ. Press. [5, 7]

Castañeda, H., S. M. Holmes, D. S. Madrigal, et al. 2015. Immigration as a Social Determinant of Health. *Annu. Rev. Public Health* **36**:375–392. [7]

Castles, S. 2016. Understanding Global Migration: A Social Transformation Perspective. In: An Anthology of Migration and Social Transformation, ed. A. Amelina et al., pp. 19–41, Imiscoe Research Series. Cham: Springer. [2]

Catron, P. 2019. The Citizenship Advantage: Immigrant Socioeconomic Attainment in the Age of Mass Migration. *Am. J. Sociol.* **124**:999–1042. [11]

Chae, D. H., S. Clouston, M. L. Hatzenbuehler, et al. 2015. Association between an Internet-Based Measure of Area Racism and Black Mortality. *PLOS ONE* **10**:e0122963. [9]

Chae, D. H., L. K. D., N. E. Adler, and S. L. Syme. 2010. Do Experiences of Racial Discrimination Predict Cardiovascular Disease among African American Men? The Moderating Role of Internalized Negative Racial Group Attitudes. *Soc. Sci. Med.* **71**:1182–1188. [5]

Chaudoir, S. R., V. A. Earnshaw, and S. Andel. 2013. "Discredited" versus "Discreditable": Understanding How Shared and Unique Stigma Mechanisms Affect Psychological and Physical Health Disparities. *Basic Appl. Soc. Psychol.* **35**:75–87. [4]

Chavez, L. R. 2008. The Latino Threat: Constructing Immigrants, Citizens, and the Nation. Stanford: Stanford Univ. Press. [7, 8]

———. 2017. Anchor Babies and the Challenge of Birthright Citizenship. Stanford: Stanford Univ. Press. [7]

Chen, J. 2013. Perceived Discrimination and Subjective Well-Being among Rural-to-Urban Migrants in China. *J. Soc. Soc. Welfare* **40**:131–156. [4]

Chen, X., B. Stanton, L. Kaljee, et al. 2011. Social Stigma, Social Capital Reconstruction, and Rural Migrants in Urban China: A Population Health Perspective. *Hum. Organ.* **70**:22–32. [4]

Chou, C. C., and J. A. Chronister. 2011. Social Tie Characteristics and Psychiatric Rehabilitation Outcomes among Adults with Serious Mental Illness. *Rehabil. Couns. Bull.* **55**:92–102. [4]

Clair, M., C. Daniel, and M. Lamont. 2016. Destigmatization and Health: Cultural Constructions and the Long-Term Reduction of Stigma. *Soc. Sci. Med.* **165**:223–232. [11]

Clark, K. A., S. D. Cochran, A. J. Maiolatesi, and J. E. Pachankis. 2020. Prevalence of Bullying among Youth Classified as LGBTQ Who Died by Suicide as Reported in the National Violent Death Reporting System, 2003-2017. *JAMA Pediatr.* **174**:1211–1213. [4]

Coenders, M., and P. Scheepers. 2003. The Effect of Education on Nationalism and Ethnic Exclusionism: An International Comparison. *Polit. Psychol.* **24**:313–343. [10]

Collins, P. H., and S. Bilge. 2016. Intersectionality. Cambridge: Polity Press. [2]

Combahee River Collective. 1977. A Black Feminist Statement. https://www.blackpast.org/african-american-history/combahee-river-collective-statement-1977/. (accessed Nov. 14, 2022). [7]

———. 1983. Home Girls: A Black Feminist Anthology. New York: Kitchen Table Women of Color Press. [2]

Conran, J., and K. Thelen. 2016. Institutional Change. In: The Oxford Handbook of Historical Institutionalism, ed. O. Fioretos et al., pp. 51–70. Oxford: Oxford Univ. Press. [10]

Córdova Jr., D., and R. C. Cervantes. 2010. Intergroup and Within-Group Perceived Discrimination among US-Born and Foreign-Born Latino Youth. *Hisp. J. Behav. Sci.* **32**:259–274. [7]

Cornejo, M., and J. A. Kam. 2021. Exploring the Ascribed and Avowed Identities of Deferred Action for Childhood Arrivals (DACA) Recipients in Early Adulthood. *Cul. Div. Ethnic Min. Psychol.* **27**:460–470. [7]

Corrigan, P. W. 2000. Mental Health Stigma as Social Attribution: Implications for Research Methods and Attitude Change. *Clin. Psychol. Sci. Pract.* **7**:48–67. [2]

———. 2011. Best Practices: Strategic Stigma Change (SSC): Five Principles for Social Marketing Campaigns to Reduce Stigma. *Psychiatr. Serv.* **62**:824–826. [2]

Corrigan, P. W., J. E. Larson, and N. Rüsch. 2009. Self-Stigma and the "Why Try" Effect: Impact on Life Goals and Evidence-Based Practices. *World Psychiatry* **8**:75–81. [5]

Corrigan, P. W., F. E. Markowitz, and A. C. Watson. 2004. Structural Levels of Mental Illness Stigma and Discrimination. *Schizophr. Bull.* **30**:481–491. [8, 9]

Corrigan, P. W., S. B. Morris, P. J. Michaels, J. D. Rafacz, and N. Rüsch. 2012. Challenging the Public Stigma of Mental Illness: A Meta-Analysis of Outcome Studies. *Psychiatr. Serv.* **63**:963–973. [4]

Corrigan, P. W., K. J. Powell, and P. J. Michaels. 2014. Brief Battery for Measurement of Stigmatizing Versus Affirming Attitudes About Mental Illness. *Psychiatry Res.* **215**:466–470. [2]

Corrigan, P. W., J. Rafacz, and N. Rüsch. 2011. Examining a Progressive Model of Self-Stigma and Its Impact on People with Serious Mental Illness. *Psychiatry Res.* **189**:339–343. [2]

Cottrell, C. A., and S. L. Neuberg. 2005. Different Emotional Reactions to Different Groups: A Sociofunctional Threat-Based Approach to "Prejudice". *J. Pers. Soc. Psychol.* **88**:770–789. [4]

Crandall, C. S., and D. Moriarty. 1995. Physical Illness Stigma and Social Rejection. *Br. J. Soc. Psychol.* **34**:67–83. [2, 4]

Crenshaw, K. W. 1991. Mapping the Margins: Intersectionality, Identity Politics, and Violence against Women of Color. *Stan. L. Rev.* **43**:1241–1299. [2]

———. 2017. On Intersectionality: Essential Writings. New York: The New Press. [7]

Creţan, R., P. Kupka, R. Powell, and V. Walach. 2022. Everyday Roma Stigmatization: Racialized Urban Encounters, Collective Histories and Fragmented Habitus. *Int. J. Urb. Reg. Res.* **46**:82–100. [10]

Creţan, R., and R. Powell. 2018. The Power of Group Stigmatization: Wealthy Roma, Urban Space and Strategies of Defence in Post-Socialist Romania. *Int. J. Urb. Reg. Res.* **42**:423–441. [10]

Crocker, J., B. Major, and C. Steele. 1998. Social Stigma. In: The Handbook of Social Psychology, ed. D. Gilbert et al., pp. 504–553, vol. 2. New York: Academic Press. [4, 5]

Crocker, J., K. Voelkl, M. Testa, and B. Major. 1991. Social Stigma: The Affective Consequences of Attributional Ambiguity. *J. Pers. Soc. Psychol.* **60**:218–228. [6]

Crocker, J., and C. T. Wolfe. 2001. Contingencies of Self-Worth. *Psychol. Rev.* **108**:593–623. [4]

Cuddy, A. J. C., S. T. Fiske, and P. Glick. 2007. The Bias Map: Behaviors from Intergroup Affect and Stereotypes. *J. Pers. Soc. Psychol.* **92**:631–648. [4]

Czopp, A. M. 2008. When Is a Compliment Not a Compliment? Evaluating Expressions of Positive Stereotypes. *J. Exp. Soc. Psychol.* **44**:413–420. [4]

Czymara, C. S. 2020a. Attitudes toward Refugees in Contemporary Europe: A Longitudinal Perspective on Cross-National Differences. *Soc. Forces* **99**:1306–1333. [3]

———. 2020b. Propagated Preferences? Political Elite Discourses and Europeans' Openness toward Muslim Immigrants. *Int. Migr. Rev.* **54**:1212–1237. [10, 11]

Czymara, C. S., and S. Dochow. 2018. Mass Media and Concerns about Immigration in Germany in the 21st Century: Individual-Level Evidence over 15 Years. *Eur. Sociol. Rev.* **34**:381–401. [3, 10]

Czymara, C. S., and A. W. Schmidt-Catran. 2017. Refugees Unwelcome? Changes in the Public Acceptance of Immigrants and Refugees in Germany in the Course of Europe's 'Immigration Crisis'. *Eur. Sociol. Rev.* **33**:735–751. [10]

Damstra, A., L. Jacobs, M. Boukes, and R. Vliegenthart. 2021. The Impact of Immigration News on Anti-Immigrant Party Support: Unpacking Agenda-Setting and Issue Ownership Effects over Time. *J. Elect. Public Opin. Parties* **31**:97–118. [11]

Dancygier, R., N. Egami, A. Jamal, and R. Rischke. 2022. Hate Crimes and Gender Imbalances: Fears over Mate Competition and Violence against Refugees. *Am. J. Pol. Sci.* **66**:501–515. [3]

Dawsey, J. 2018. Trump Derides Protections for Immigrants from "Shithole" Countries, January 18. *The Washington Post*. [10]

Debrosse, R., M. Destin, M. Rossignac-Milon, D. Taylor, and L. O. Rogers. 2020. Immigrant Adolescents' Roots and Dreams: Perceived Mismatches between Ethnic Identities and Aspirational Selves Predict Engagement. *Self Identity* **19**:1–15. [5]

De Genova, N. P. 2002. Migrant "Illegality" and Deportability in Everyday Life. *Annu. Rev. Anthropol.* **31**:419–447. [5]

De Genova, N. P., and N. Peutz, eds. 2010. The Deportation Regime: Sovereignty, Space, and the Freedom of Movement. Durham, NC: Duke Univ. Press. [5]

De Graauw, E. 2016. Making Immigrant Rights Real: Nonprofits and the Politics of Integration in San Francisco. Ithaca: Cornell Univ. Press. [11]

de Haas, H., K. Natter, and S. Vezzoli. 2015. Conceptualizing and Measuring Migration Policy Change. *Comp. Migr. Stud.* **3**:1–21. [8]

Derogatis, L. 1994. Scl-90—R, Brief Symptom Inventory, and Matching Clinical Rating Scales. In: The Use of Psychological Testing for Treatment Planning and Outcome Assessment, ed. M. E. Maruish, pp. 217–248. Lawrence Erlbaum. [2]

de Vroome, T., B. Martinovic, and M. Verkuyten. 2014. The Integration Paradox: Level of Education and Immigrants' Attitudes Towards Natives and the Host Society. *Cul. Div. Ethnic Min. Psychol.* **20**:166–175. [3, 11]

Diamond, L. M., and J. Alley. 2022. Rethinking Minority Stress: A Social Safety Perspective on the Health Effects of Stigma in Sexually-Diverse and Gender-Diverse Populations. *Neurosci. Biobehav. Rev.* **138**:104720. [8]

Diehl, C., and P. Fick. 2016. Ethnische Diskriminierung Im Deutschen Bildungssystem. In: Ethnische Ungleichheiten Im Bildungsverlauf: Mechanismen, Befunde, Debatten, ed. C. Diehl et al., pp. 243–286. Wiesbaden: Springer VS. [6]

Diehl, C., E. Liebau, and P. Mühlau. 2021. How Often Have You Felt Disadvantaged? Explaining Perceived Discrimination. *Köln. Z. Soziolog. Sozialpsychol.* **73**:1–24. [6]

Dilthey, W. 1927. The Understanding of Other Persons and Their Expressions of Life. In: Descriptive Psychology and Historical Understanding, ed. W. Dilthey, pp. 121–144. Dordrecht: Springer [5]

Dixon, J. C. 2006. The Ties That Bind and Those That Don't: Toward Reconciling Group Threat and Contact Theories of Prejudice. *Soc. Forces* **84**:2179–2204. [3]

Dollmann, J. 2010. Türkischstämmige Kinder Am Ersten Bildungsübergang: Primäre und Sekundäre Herkunftseffekte. Wiesbaden: VS Verlag für Sozialwissenschaften. [6]

———. 2017. Positive Choices for All? Ses- and Gender-Specific Premia of Immigrants at Educational Transitions. *Res. Soc. Stratif. Mobil.* **49**:20–31. [6]

———. 2021. The Political Integration of Immigrants: How Pre- and Postmigration Contexts Matter. *J. Int. Migr. Integr.* **23**:1091–1125. [10]

Dollmann, J., and M. Weißmann. 2020. The Story after Immigrants' Ambitious Educational Choices: Real Improvement or Back to Square One? *Eur. Sociol. Rev.* **36**:32–47. [6]

Dovidio, J. F., K. Kawakami, and S. L. Gaertner. 2000. Reducing Contemporary Prejudice: Combating Explicit and Implicit Bias at the Individual and Intergroup Level. In: Reducing Prejudice and Discrimination, ed. S. Oskamp, pp. 137–163. Hillsdale, NJ: Lawrence Erlbaum. [5]

Dovidio, J. F., L. A. Penner, S. K. Calabrese, and R. L. Pearl. 2018. Physical Health Disparities and Stigma: Race, Sexual Orientation, and Body Weight. In: The Oxford Handbook of Stigma, Discrimination, and Health, ed. B. Major et al., pp. 29–51. Oxford: Oxford Univ. Press. [4]

Downey, G., and S. I. Feldman. 1996. Implications of Rejection Sensitivity for Intimate Relationships. *J. Pers. Soc. Psychol.* **70**:1327–1343. [2]

Downing, J. M., and E. Rosenthal. 2020. Prevalence of Social Determinants of Health among Sexual Minority Women and Men in 2017. *Am. J. Prev. Med.* **59**:118–122. [4]

Drouhot, L. G. 2021. Cracks in the Melting Pot? Religiosity and Assimilation among the Diverse Muslim Population in France. *Am. J. Sociol.* **126**:795–851. [11]

Drouhot, L. G., and V. Nee. 2019. Assimilation and the Second Generation in Europe and America: Blending and Segregating Social Dynamics between Immigrants and Natives. *Annu. Rev. Sociol.* **45**:177–199. [11]

Earnshaw, V. A., and S. R. Chaudoir. 2009. From Conceptualizing to Measuring HIV Stigma: A Review of HIV Stigma Mechanism Measures. *AIDS Behav.* **13**:1160–1177. [2]

Earnshaw, V. A., R. J. Watson, L. A. Eaton, et al. 2022. Integrating Time into Stigma and Health Research. *Nat. Rev. Psychol.* **1**:236–247. [10]

Eberl, J.-M., C. E. Meltzer, T. Heidenreich, et al. 2018. The European Media Discourse on Immigration and Its Effects: A Literature Review. *Ann. Int. Commun. Assoc.* **42**:207–223. [10, 11]

Ebert, K., and D. Okamoto. 2015. Legitimating Contexts, Immigrant Power, and Exclusionary Actions. *Soc. Prob.* **62**:40–67. [10]

———. 2016. Group Boundaries, Immigrant Inclusion, and the Politics of Immigrant–Native Relations. *Am. Behav. Sci.* **60**:224–250. [10]

Eger, M. A., and A. Bohman. 2016. The Political Consequences of Contemporary Immigration. *Sociol. Compass* **10**:877–892. [10]

Eger, M. A., C. A. Larsen, and J. Mewes. 2020. Welfare Nationalism before and after the Migration Crisis. In: Welfare State Legitimacy in Times of Crisis and Austerity, ed. T. Laenen et al., pp. 177–198. Cheltenham: Edward Elgar. [1, 3]

Eger, M. A., J. Mitchell, and M. Hjerm. 2022. When I Was Growing Up: The Lasting Impact of Immigrant Presence on Native-Born American Attitudes Towards Immigrants and Immigration. *Eur. Sociol. Rev.* **38**:169–188. [3, 10]

Eger, M. A., and S. Olzak. 2023. The Polarizing Effect of Anti-Immigrant Violence on Radical Right Sympathies in Germany. *Int. Migr. Rev.* **57**:746–777. [3, 10]

Eger, M. A., and S. Valdez. 2015. Neo-Nationalism in Western Europe. *Eur. Sociol. Rev.* **31**:115–130. [10]

———. 2019. From Radical Right to Neo-Nationalist. *Eur. Polit. Sci.* **18**:379–399. [10]

El Refaie, E. 2001. Metaphors We Discriminate By: Naturalized Themes in Austrian Newspaper Articles about Asylum Seekers. *J. Sociolinguist.* **5**:352–371. [10]

Erhard, L., R. H. Heiberger, and M. Windzio. 2021. Diverse Effects of Mass Media on Concerns about Immigration: New Evidence from Germany, 2001–2016. *Eur. Sociol. Rev.* **38**:629–647. [3]

Ernest, B. 1973. The Denial of Death. New York: Simon and Schuster. [4]

Esses, V. M., S. Medianu, and A. S. Lawson. 2013. Uncertainty, Threat, and the Role of the Media in Promoting the Dehumanization of Immigrants and Refugees. *J. Soc. Issues* **69**:518–536. [10]

Evans-Lacko, S., E. Brohan, R. Mojtabai, and G. Thornicroft. 2012. Association between Public Views of Mental Illness and Self-Stigma among Individuals with Mental Illness in 14 European Countries. *Psychol. Med.* **42**:1741–1752. [9]

Everett, B. G., M. L. Hatzenbuehler, and T. L. Hughes. 2016. The Impact of Civil Union Legislation on Minority Stress, Depression, and Hazardous Drinking in a Diverse Sample of Sexual-Minority Women: A Quasi-Natural Experiment. *Soc. Sci. Med.* **169**:180–190. [9]

Fadaee, S. 2015. The Immigrant Rights Struggle, and the Paradoxes of Radical Activism in Europe. *Soc. Mov. Stud.* **14**:733–739. [11]

Fanon, F. 2003. Algeria Unveiled. In: Decolonization: Perspectives from Now and Then, ed. P. Duara, pp. 42–55. London: Routledge. [5]

Farris, E. M., and H. Silber Mohamed. 2018. Picturing Immigration: How the Media Criminalizes Immigrants. *Polit. Group. Ident.* **6**:814–824. [11]

Faulkner, J., M. Schaller, J. H. Park, and L. A. Duncan. 2004. Evolved Disease-Avoidance Mechanisms and Contemporary Xenophobic Attitudes. *Group Process. Intergroup Relat.* **7**:333–353. [4]

Fechter, A. M., and K. Walsh. 2010. Examining "Expatriate" Continuities: Postcolonial Approaches to Mobile Professionals. *J. Ethn. Migr. Stud.* **36**:1197–1210. [10]

Fejes, F. 2008. Gay Rights and Moral Panic: The Origin of America's Debate on Homosexuality. New York: Palgrave Macmillan. [8]

Feldman, D. B., and C. S. Crandall. 2007. Dimensions of Mental Illness Stigma: What about Mental Illness Causes Social Rejection? *J. Soc. Clin. Psychol.* **26**:137–154. [4]

Fetzer, J. S. 2000. Economic Self-Interest or Cultural Marginality? Anti-Immigration Sentiment and Nativist Political Movements in France, Germany and the USA. *J. Ethn. Migr. Stud.* **26**:5–23. [2]

Fibbi, R., H. M. Arnfinn, and S. Patrick. 2021. Migration and Discrimination. Imiscoe Short Reader. Cham: Springer. [8]

Fiorito, T. R. 2019. Beyond the Dreamers: Collective Identity and Subjectivity in the Undocumented Youth Movement. *Mobilization* **24**:345–363. [7]

Fiske, S. T. 1998. Stereotyping, Prejudice, and Discrimination. In: The Handbook of Social Psychology, ed. D. T. Gilbert et al., pp. 357–411. New York: McGraw-Hill. [6]

———. 2011. Envy up, Scorn Down: How Status Divides Us. New York: Russell Sage Foundation. [8]

Fiske, S. T., A. J. C. Cuddy, P. Glick, and J. Xu. 2002. A Model of (Often Mixed) Stereotype Content: Competence and Warmth Respectively Follow from Perceived Status and Competition. *J. Pers. Soc. Psychol.* **82**:878–902. [4]

Fiske, S. T., and S. L. Neuberg. 1990. A Continuum of Impression Formation, from Category-Based to Individuating Processes: Influences of Information and Motivation on Attention and Interpretation. In: Advances in Experimental Social Psychology, ed. M. P. Zanna, pp. 1–74, vol. 23. New York: Academic Press. [4]

Fiske, S. T., and M. A. Pavelchak. 1986. Category-Based versus Piecemeal-Based Affective Responses: Developments in Schema-Triggered Affect. In: Handbook of Motivation and Cognition: Foundations of Social Behavior, ed. R. M. Sorrentino and E. T. Higgins, pp. 167–203. New York: Guilford Press. [4]

Fleming, P. J., N. L. Novak, and W. D. Lopez. 2019. U.S. Immigration Law Enforcement Practices and Health Inequities. *Am. J. Prev. Med.* **57**:858–861. [8]

Flores, A. R., M. L. Hatzenbuehler, and G. J. Gates. 2018. Identifying Psychological Responses of Stigmatized Groups to Referendums. *PNAS* **115**:3816–3821. [8, 9]

Flores, R. D. 2014. Living in the Eye of the Storm: How Did Hazelton's Restrictive Immigration Ordinance Affect Local Interethnic Relations? *Am. Behav. Sci.* **58**:1743–1763. [11]

———. 2018. Can Elites Shape Public Attitudes toward Immigrants? Evidence from the 2016 US Presidential Election. *Soc. Forces* **96**:1649–1690. [10, 11]

Flores-González, N. 2017. Citizens but Not Americans: Race and Belonging among Latino Millennials. New York: New York Univ. Press. [7]

Foner, N., ed. 2001. New Immigrants in New York. New York: Columbia Univ. Press. [10]

Foner, N., and P. Simon. 2015. Fear, Anxiety and National Identity: Immigration and Belonging in North America and Western Europe. New York: Russell Sage Foundation. [8]

Fong, K. 2019. Concealment and Constraint: Child Protective Services Fears and Poor Mothers' Institutional Engagement. *Soc. Forces* **97**:1785–1810. [5]

Ford, R. 2011. Acceptable and Unacceptable Immigrants: How Opposition to Immigration in Britain Is Affected by Migrants' Region of Origin. *J. Ethn. Migr. Stud.* **37**:1017–1037. [3]

Forman, T. A., and A. E. Lewis. 2015. Beyond Prejudice? Young Whites' Racial Attitudes in Post–Civil Rights America, 1976 to 2000. *Am. Behav. Sci.* **59**:1394–1428. [10]

Foroutan, N., J. Karakayali, and R. Spielhaus, eds. 2018. Postmigrantische Perspektiven: Ordnungssysteme, Repräsentationen, Kritik. Frankfurt a.M., New York: Campus. [7]

Fox, C., and T. A. Guglielmo. 2012. Defining America's Racial Boundaries: Blacks, Mexicans, and European Immigrants,1890–1945. *Am. J. Sociol.* **118**:327–379. [11]

Frable, D. E., L. Platt, and S. Hoey. 1998. Concealable Stigmas and Positive Self-Perceptions: Feeling Better around Similar Others. *J. Pers. Soc. Psychol.* **74**:909–922. [4]

Fredman, S. 2011. Discrimination Law, vol. 2. Oxford: Oxford Univ. Press. [8]

Freitag, M., and N. Hofstetter. 2022. Pandemic Threat and Intergroup Relations: How Negative Emotions Associated with the Threat of Covid-19 Shape Attitudes Towards Immigrants. *J. Ethn. Migr. Stud.* **48**:1–20. [4]

Frey, A. 2020. "Cologne Changed Everything": The Effect of Threatening Events on the Frequency and Distribution of Intergroup Conflict in Germany. *Eur. Sociol. Rev.* **36**:684–699. [10]

Frost, D. M. 2020. Hostile and Harmful: Structural Stigma and Minority Stress Explain Increased Anxiety among Migrants Living in the United Kingdom after the Brexit Referendum. *J. Consult. Clin. Psychol.* **88**:75–81. [4, 8, 9]

Fujiwara, L. H. 2005. Immigrant Rights Are Human Rights: The Reframing of Immigrant Entitlement and Welfare. *Soc. Prob.* **52**:79–101. [11]

Fussell, E. 2014. Warmth of the Welcome: Attitudes toward Immigrants and Immigration Policy. *Annu. Rev. Sociol.* **40**:479–498. [2]

Gabrielatos, C., and P. Baker. 2008. Fleeing, Sneaking, Flooding: A Corpus Analysis of Discursive Constructions of Refugees and Asylum Seekers in the UK Press, 1996-2005. *J. Engl. Linguist.* **36**:5–38. [10]

Gabrielli, G., S. Longobardi, and S. Strozza. 2021. The Academic Resilience of Native and Immigrant-Origin Students in Selected European Countries. *J. Ethn. Migr. Stud.* **48**:2347–2368. [6]

Ganzeboom, H. B., P. M. De Graaf, and D. J. Treiman. 1992. A Standard International Socio-Economic Index of Occupational Status. *Soc. Sci. Res.* **21**:1–56. [6]

García, A. S. 2019. Legal Passing: Navigating Undocumented Life and Local Immigration Law. Oakland: Univ. of California Press. [5, 11]

García, S. J. 2017. Racializing "Illegality": An Intersectional Approach to Understanding How Mexican-Origin Women Navigate an Anti-Immigrant Climate. *Sociol. Race Ethnicity* **4**:474–490. [5]

———. 2018. Living a Deportation Threat: Anticipatory Stressors Confronted by Undocumented Mexican Immigrant Women. *Race Soc. Prob.* **10**:221–234. [5]

Gast, M., D. Okamoto, and E. Nguyen. 2021. Making Requests: Filipino/a and Latino/a Claims-Making and Racialization. *Ethn. Racial Stud.* **44**:1211–1230. [11]

Geddes, A., and V. Guiraudon. 2004. Britain, France, and EU Anti-Discrimination Policy: The Emergence of an EU Policy Paradigm. *West Eur. Polit.* **27**:334–353. [8]

Gee, G. C., M. S. Spencer, C. J., and D. Takeuchi. 2007. A Nationwide Study of Discrimination and Chronic Health Conditions among Asian Americans. *Am. J. Public Health* **97**:1275–1282. [5]

Gentrup, S., G. Lorenz, C. Kristen, and I. Kogan. 2021. Self-Fulfilling Prophecies in the Classroom: Teacher Expectations, Teacher Feedback and Student Achievement. *Learn. Instr.* **66**:101296. [6]

Georgiou, M., and R. Zaborowski. 2017. Media Coverage of the "Refugee Crisis": A Cross-European Perspective. Brussels: Council of Europe. [10]

Geurts, N., T. Davids, and N. Spierings. 2021. The Lived Experience of an Integration Paradox: Why High-Skilled Migrants from Turkey Experience Little National Belonging in the Netherlands. *J. Ethn. Migr. Stud.* **47**:69–87. [3]

Gilens, M. 2009. Why Americans Hate Welfare: Race, Media, and the Politics of Antipoverty Policy. Chicago: Univ. of Chicago Press. [8]

Givens, T., and A. Luedtke. 2005. European Immigration Policies in Comparative Perspective: Issue Salience, Partisanship and Immigrant Rights. *Comp. Eur. Politics* **3**:1–22. [10]

Go, J. 2018. Postcolonial Possibilities for the Sociology of Race. *Sociol. Race Ethnicity* **4**:439–451. [10]

Goffman, E. 1963. Stigma: Notes on the Management of Spoiled Identity. Englewood Cliffs, NJ: Prentice-Hall. [2, 4, 5]

Goldberg, R. T. 1974. Adjustment of Children with Invisible and Visible Handicaps: Congenital Heart Disease and Facial Burns. *J. Couns. Psychol.* **21**:428–432. [4]

Gonzales, R. G. 2011. Learning to Be Illegal: Undocumented Youth and Shifting Legal Contexts in the Transition to Adulthood. *Am. Sociol. Rev.* **76**:602–619. [7, 11]

Gonzales, R. G. 2016. Lives in Limbo. Oakland: Univ. of California Press. [7]

Gonzales, R. G., C. Suárez-Orozco, and M. C. Dedios-Sanguineti. 2013. No Place to Belong: Contextualizing Concepts of Mental Health among Undocumented Immigrant Youth in the United States. *Am. Behav. Sci.* **57**:1174–1199. [7]

Gonzalez-Barrera, A. 2021. Before COVID-19, More Mexicans Came to the U.S. Than Left for Mexico for the First Time in Years, July 2, 2021. Pew Research Center. [10]

Goodall, J. 1986. Social Rejection, Exclusion, and Shunning among the Gombe Chimpanzees. *Ethol. Sociobiol.* **7**:227–236. [4]

Goodhart, D. 2017. The Road to Somewhere: The New Tribes Shaping British Politics. London: Penguin. [2]

Gorodzeisky, A. 2013. Mechanisms of Exclusion: Attitudes toward Allocation of Social Rights to Out-Group Population. *Ethn. Racial Stud.* **36**:795–817. [2]

———. 2021. The Influx of Refugees and Temporal Change in Attitudes Towards Asylum Seekers: A Cross-National Perspective. *Eur. Sociol. Rev.* **38**:648–662. [10]

Gorodzeisky, A., and I. Leykin. 2022. On the West–East Methodological Bias in Measuring International Migration. *J. Ethn. Migr. Stud.* **48**:3160–3183. [2]

Gorodzeisky, A., and M. Semyonov. 2016. Not Only Competitive Threat but Also Racial Prejudice: Sources of Anti-Immigrant Attitudes in European Societies. *Int. J. Public Opin. Res.* **28**:331–354. [3]

———. 2020. Perceptions and Misperceptions: Actual Size, Perceived Size and Opposition to Immigration in European Societies. *J. Ethn. Migr. Stud.* **46**:612–630. [3]

Gottlob, A., and H. G. Boomgaarden. 2020. The 2015 Refugee Crisis, Uncertainty and the Media: Representations of Refugees, Asylum Seekers and Immigrants in Austrian and French Media. *Communications* **45**:841–863. [10]

Green, E. G. T., and C. Staerklé. 2013. Migration and Multiculturalism. In: Oxford Handbook of Political Psychology, ed. L. Huddy et al., pp. 852–889. Oxford: Oxford Univ. Press. [10]

Green, E. G. T., E. P. Visintin, O. Sarrasin, and M. Hewstone. 2020. When Integration Policies Shape the Impact of Intergroup Contact on Threat Perceptions: A Multilevel Study across 20 European Countries. *J. Ethn. Migr. Stud.* **46**:631–648. [10, 11]

Greenberg, J., T. Pyszczynski, and S. Solomon. 1986. The Causes and Consequences of a Need for Self-Esteem: A Terror Management Theory. In: Public Self and Private Self, ed. R. F. Baumeister, pp. 189–212, Springer Series in Social Psychology. New York: Springer. [2]

Greenberg, J., S. Solomon, and T. Pyszczynski. 1997. Terror Management Theory of Self-Esteem and Cultural Worldviews: Empirical Assessments and Conceptual Refinements. In: Advances in Experimental Social Psychology, ed. M. P. Zanna, pp. 61–139, vol. 29. New York: Academic Press. [4]

Greussing, E., and H. G. Boomgaarden. 2017. Shifting the Refugee Narrative? An Automated Frame Analysis of Europe's 2015 Refugee Crisis. *J. Ethn. Migr. Stud.* **43**:1749–1774. [10]

Grigorieff, A., C. Roth, and D. Ubfal. 2020. Does Information Change Attitudes toward Immigrants? *Demography* **57**:1117–1143. [10, 11]

Guimond, S., P. De Oliveira, K. N. Lalonde, et al. 2013. Diversity Policy, Social Dominance, and Intergroup Relations: Predicting Prejudice in Changing Social and Political Contexts. *J. Pers. Soc. Psychol.* **104**:941–958. [10]

Guyll, M., K. A. Matthews, and J. T. Bromberger. 2001. Discrimination and Unfair Treatment: Relationship to Cardiovascular Reactivity among African American and European American Women. *Health Psychol.* **20**:315–325. [4]

Hackl, A. 2022. Good Immigrants, Permitted Outsiders: Conditional Inclusion and Citizenship in Comparison. *Ethn. Racial Stud.* **45**:989–1010. [10]

Hainmueller, J., and D. J. Hopkins. 2014. Public Attitudes toward Immigration. *Annu. Rev. Polit. Sci.* **17**:225–249. [8]

———. 2015. The Hidden American Immigration Consensus: A Conjoint Analysis of Attitudes toward Immigrants. *Am. J. Pol. Sci.* **59**:529–548. [10]

Hampshire, J. 2013. The Politics of Immigration: Contradictions of the Liberal State. Cambridge: Polity Press. [8]

Handulle, A., and A. Vassenden. 2021. The Art of Kindergarten Drop Off: How Young Norwegian-Somali Parents Perform Ethnicity to Avoid Reports to Child Welfare Services. *Eur. J. Soc. Work* **24**:469–480. [5]

Haney-López, I. 2018. Dog Whistle Politics: Strategic Racism, Fake Populism, and the Dividing of America. New York: Oxford Univ. Press. [5]

Hangartner, D., E. Dinas, M. Marbach, K. Matakos, and D. Xefteris. 2019. Does Exposure to the Refugee Crisis Make Natives More Hostile? *Am. Polit. Sci. Rev.* **113**:442–455. [10]

Harell, A., S. Soroka, and S. Iyengar. 2017. Locus of Control and Anti-Immigrant Sentiment in Canada, the United States, and the United Kingdom. *Polit. Psychol.* **38**:245–260. [2]

Harris, A., and A. Karimshah. 2019. Young Muslims, Stigma and the Work of Normality. *Sociology* **53**:617–633. [5]

Harris, C. T., and J. Gruenewald. 2020. News Media Trends in the Framing of Immigration and Crime, 1990–2013. *Soc. Prob.* **67**:452–470. [10]

Hatzenbuehler, M. L. 2016. Structural Stigma: Research Evidence and Implications for Psychological Science. *Am. Psychol.* **71**:742–751. [2, 4, 5, 8, 9]

———. 2017a. Advancing Research on Structural Stigma and Sexual Orientation Disparities in Mental Health among Youth. *J. Clin. Child Adolesc. Psychol.* **46**:463–475. [8, 9]

———. 2017b. Structural Stigma and Health. In: The Handbook of Stigma, Discrimination and Health, ed. B. Major et al., pp. 105–121. Oxford: Oxford Univ. Press. [9]

Hatzenbuehler, M. L., R. Bränström, and J. E. Pachankis. 2018. Societal-Level Explanations for Reductions in Sexual Orientation Mental Health Disparities: Results from a Ten-Year, Population-Based Study in Sweden. *Stigma Health* **3**:16–26. [9]

Hatzenbuehler, M. L., A. R. Flores, and G. J. Gates. 2017a. Social Attitudes Regarding Same-Sex Marriage and LGBT Health Disparities: Results from a National Probability Sample: Same-Sex Marriage and LGBT Health. *J. Soc. Issues* **73**:508–528. [9]

Hatzenbuehler, M. L., K. M. Keyes, and D. S. Hasin. 2009a. State-Level Policies and Psychiatric Morbidity in Lesbian, Gay, and Bisexual Populations. *Am. J. Public Health* **99**:2275–2281. [9]

Hatzenbuehler, M. L., and B. G. Link. 2014. Introduction to the Special Issue on Structural Stigma and Health. *Soc. Sci. Med.* **103**:01–06. [1, 8, 9]

Hatzenbuehler, M. L., K. A. McLaughlin, K. M. Keyes, and D. S. Hasin. 2010. The Impact of Institutional Discrimination on Psychiatric Disorders in Lesbian, Gay, and Bisexual Populations: A Prospective Study. *Am. J. Public Health* **100**:452–459. [9]

Hatzenbuehler, M. L., S. Nolen-Hoeksema, and J. Dovidio. 2009b. How Does Stigma "Get under the Skin"? The Mediating Role of Emotion Regulation. *Psychol. Sci.* **20**:1282–1289. [4]

Hatzenbuehler, M. L., C. O'Cleirigh, C. Grasso, et al. 2012. Effect of Same-Sex Marriage Laws on Health Care Use and Expenditures in Sexual Minority Men: A Quasi-Natural Experiment. *Am. J. Public Health* **102**:285–291. [8, 9]

Hatzenbuehler, M. L., J. C. Phelan, and B. G. Link. 2013. Stigma as a Fundamental Cause of Population Health Inequalities. *Am. J. Public Health* **103**:813–821. [4, 7, 8]

Hatzenbuehler, M. L., S. J. Prins, M. Flake, et al. 2017b. Immigration Policies and Mental Health Morbidity among Latinos: A State-Level Analysis. *Soc. Sci. Med.* **174**:169–178. [9]

Haubert, J., and E. Fussell. 2006. Explaining Pro-Immigrant Sentiment in the U.S.: Social Class, Cosmopolitanism, and Perceptions of Immigrants. *Int. Migr. Rev.* **40**:489–507. [3]

Haynes, C., J. Merolla, and S. K. Ramakrishnan. 2016. Framing Immigrants: News Coverage, Public Opinion, and Policy. New York: Russell Sage Foundation. [11]

Heath, A. F., and Y. Brinbaum. 2007. Explaining Ethnic Inequalities in Educational Attainment. *Ethnicities* **7**:291–305. [6]

Heath, A. F., E. Davidov, R. t. Ford, et al. 2020. Contested Terrain: Explaining Divergent Patterns of Public Opinion Towards Immigration Within Europe. *J. Ethn. Migr. Stud.* **46**:475–488. [2]

Heath, A. F., and L. Richards. 2019. How Do Europeans Differ in Their Attitudes to Immigration? Findings from the European Social Survey 2002/03–2016/17. OECD Social, Employment and Migration Working Papers (Issue 222). Paris: OECD Publishing. [3]

Heath, A. F., C. Rothon, and E. Kilpi. 2008. The Second Generation in Western Europe: Education, Unemployment, and Occupational Attainment. *Annu. Rev. Sociol.* **34**:211–235. [11]

Heath, A. F., S. L. Schneider, and S. Butt. 2016. Developing a Measure of Socio-Cultural Origins for the European Social Survey. Cologne: GESIS Leibniz-Institut für Sozialwissenschaften. [5]

Hebl, M. R., J. B. Foster, and L. M. Mannix. 2002. Formal and Interpersonal Discrimination: A Field Study of Bias toward Homosexual Applicants. *Pers. Soc. Psychol. Bull.* **28**:815–825. [4]

Hebl, M. R., and R. E. Kleck. 2002. Acknowledging One's Stigma in the Interview Setting: Effective Strategy or Liability? *J. Appl. Soc. Psychol.* **32**:223–249. [4]

Hebl, M. R., J. Tickle, and T. F. Heatherton. 2000. Awkward Moments in Interactions between Nonstigmatized and Stigmatized Individuals. In: The Social Psychology of Stigma, ed. T. F. Heatherton et al., pp. 275–306. New York: Guilford Press. [2]

Hedegaard, T. F., and C. A. Larsen. 2022. Who Can Become a Full Member of the Club? Results from a Conjoint Survey Experiment on Public Attitudes about the Naturalisation of Non-EU Migrants in Germany, the Netherlands, Sweden and Denmark. *Scand. Polit. Stud.* **45**:433–455. [10]

Heizmann, B. 2016. Symbolic Boundaries, Incorporation Policies, and Anti-Immigrant Attitudes: What Drives Exclusionary Policy Preferences? *Ethn. Racial Stud.* **39**:1791–1811. [10]

Heizmann, B., and P. Böhnke. 2019. Immigrant Life Satisfaction in Europe: The Role of Social and Symbolic Boundaries. *J. Ethn. Migr. Stud.* **45**:1027–1050. [10]

Helbling, M., L. Bjerre, F. Römer, and M. Zobel. 2017. Measuring Immigration Policies: The Impic Database. *Eur. Polit. Sci.* **16**:79–98. [10]

Helbling, M., S. Simon, and S. D. Schmid. 2020. Restricting Immigration to Foster Migrant Integration? A Comparative Study across 22 European Countries. *J. Ethn. Migr. Stud.* **46**:2603–2624. [10]

Heller, K. A., and C. Perleth. 2000. Kognitiver Fähigkeits-Test (Revision) Für 4.–12. Klassen (KFT 4–12+ R). Weinheim: Beltz-Testgesellschaft. [6]

Hellwig, T., and A. Sinno. 2017. Different Groups, Different Threats: Public Attitudes towards Immigrants. *J. Ethn. Migr. Stud.* **43**:339–358. [2]

Henkens, J. H. D., M. Kalmijn, and H. A. G. de Valk. 2022. Life Satisfaction Development in the Transition to Adulthood: Differences by Gender and Immigrant Background. *J. Youth Adolesc.* **51**:305–319. [10]

Hennette-Vauchez, S. 2017. Is French Laïcité Still Liberal? The Republican Project under Pressure (2004–15). *Hum. Rights Law Rev.* **17**:285–312. [8]

Herda, D. 2010. How Many Immigrants? Foreign-Born Population Innumeracy in Europe. *Public Opin. Q.* **74**:674–695. [3]

Herek, G. M. 2006. Legal Recognition of Same-Sex Relationships in the United States: A Social Science Perspective. *Am. Psychol.* **61**:607–621. [8]

Hermansen, A. S. 2016. Moving up or Falling Behind? Intergenerational Socioeconomic Transmission among Children of Immigrants in Norway. *Eur. Sociol. Rev.* **32**:675–689. [11]

Hetey, R. C., and J. L. Eberhardt. 2018. The Numbers Don't Speak for Themselves: Racial Disparities and the Persistence of Inequality in the Criminal Justice System. *Curr. Dir. Psychol. Sci.* **27**:183–187. [4]

Hirschman, A. O. 1970. Exit, Voice and Loyalty: Responses to Decline in Firms, Organizations and States. Cambridge, MA: Harvard Univ. Press. [8]

Hjerm, M. 2007. Do Numbers Really Count? Group Threat Theory Revisited. *J. Ethn. Migr. Stud.* **33**:1253–1275. [3]

———. 2009. Anti-Immigrant Attitudes and Cross-Municipal Variation in the Proportion of Immigrants. *Acta Sociol.* **52**:47–62. [3]

Hjerm, M., M. A. Eger, A. Bohman, and F. Fors Connolly. 2019. A New Approach to the Study of Tolerance: Conceptualizing and Measuring Acceptance, Respect, and Appreciation of Difference. *Soc. Indicat. Res.* **147**:897–919. [10]

Hjerm, M., M. A. Eger, and R. Danell. 2018a. Peer Attitudes and the Development of Prejudice in Adolescence. *Socius* **4**: doi: 10.1177/2378023118763187. [7]

Hjerm, M., I. Johansson Sevä, and L. Werner. 2018b. How Critical Thinking, Multicultural Education and Teacher Qualification Affect Anti-Immigrant Attitudes. *Int. Stud. Sociol. Educ.* **27**:42–59. [10]

Hjerm, M., and K. Nagayoshi. 2011. The Composition of the Minority Population as a Threat: Can Real Economic and Cultural Threats Explain Xenophobia? *Int. Sociol.* **26**:815–843. [2]

Hjerm, M., and A. Schnabel. 2010. Mobilizing Nationalist Sentiments: Which Factors Affect Nationalist Sentiments in Europe? *Soc. Sci. Res.* **39**:527–539. [11]

Hobbs, W., and N. Lajevardi. 2019. Effects of Divisive Political Campaigns on the Day-to-Day Segregation of Arab and Muslim Americans. *Am. Polit. Sci. Rev.* **113**:270–276. [10]

Hodson, G., S. M. Hogg, and C. C. MacInnis. 2009. The Role of "Dark Personalities" (Narcissism, Machiavellianism, Psychopathy), Big Five Personality Factors, and Ideology in Explaining Prejudice. *J. Res. Pers.* **43**:686–690. [4]

Holmes, S. M. 2013. Fresh Fruit, Broken Bodies Migrant Farmworkers in the United States. Oakland: Univ. of California Press. [5, 7]

Holmes, S. M., E. Castañeda, J. Geeraert, et al. 2021. Deservingness: Migration and Health in Social Context. *BMJ Glob. Health* **6 (Suppl 1)**:e005107. [5]

Holmes, S. M., and H. Castañeda. 2016. Representing the European Refugee Crisis in Germany and Beyond: Deservingness and Difference, Life and Death. *Am. Ethnol.* **43**:12–24. [7, 10]

Hooghe, M., and T. de Vroome. 2015. How Does the Majority Public React to Multiculturalist Policies? A Comparative Analysis of European Countries. *Am. Behav. Sci.* **59**:747–768. [11]

Hooks, B. 1984. Feminist Theory: From Margin to Center. Boston: South End Press. [2]

———. 1992. The Oppositional Gaze: Black Female Spectators. In: Black Looks: Race and Representation, ed. B. Hooks, pp. 115–131. New York: Routledge. [7]

Hopkins, D. J. 2010. Politicized Places: Explaining Where and When Immigrants Provoke Local Opposition. *Am. Polit. Sci. Rev.* **104**:40–60. [11]

Hopkins, D. J., J. Sides, and J. Citrin. 2019. The Muted Consequences of Correct Information about Immigration. *J. Polit.* **81**:315–320. [11]

Horton, S. B. 2016. From "Deportability" to "Denounceability:" New Forms of Labor Subordination in an Era of Governing Immigration through Crime. *Polit. Legal Anthropol. Rev.* **39**:312–326. [7]

Hovden, J. F., H. Mjelde, and J. Gripsrud. 2018. The Syrian Refugee Crisis in Scandinavian Newspapers. *Communications* **43**:325–356. [10]

Hsin, A., and F. Ortega. 2018. The Effects of Deferred Action for Childhood Arrivals on the Educational Outcomes of Undocumented Students. *Demography* **55**:1487–1506. [11]

Hunkler, C. 2014. Ethnische Ungleichheit Beim Zugang Zu Ausbildungsplätzen Im Dualen System. Wiesbaden: Springer VS. [6]

Inzlicht, M., L. McKay, and J. Aronson. 2006. Stigma as Ego Depletion: How Being the Target of Prejudice Affects Self-Control. *Psychol. Sci.* **17**:262–269. [4]

Iqbal, H. 2014. Multicultural Parenting: Preparation for Bias Socialization in British South Asian and White Families in the UK. *Int. J. Intercult. Rel.* **43**:215–226. [6]

Ivarsflaten, E. 2008. What Unites Right-Wing Populists in Western Europe? *Comp. Polit. Stud.* **41**:3–23. [10]

Ivarsflaten, E., and P. M. Sniderman. 2022. The Struggle for Inclusion: Muslim Minorities and the Democratic Ethos. Chicago: Univ. of Chicago Press. [10]

Jackman, M. R. 1994. The Velvet Glove: Paternalism and Conflict in Gender, Class, and Race Relations. Oakland: Univ. of California Press. [2]

Jackson, M. 2012. Bold Choices: How Ethnic Inequalities in Educational Attainment Are Suppressed. *Oxf. Rev. Educ.* **38**:189–208. [6]

Jacobs, L. 2017. Patterns of Criminal Threat in Television News Coverage of Ethnic Minorities in Flanders (2003–2013). *J. Ethn. Migr. Stud.* **43**:809–829. [10]

Jacobs, L., C. Meeusen, and L. D'Haenens. 2016. News Coverage and Attitudes on Immigration: Public and Commercial Television News Compared. *Eur. J. Commun.* **31**:642–660. [10]

Jasinskaja-Lahti, I., K. Liebkind, and R. Perhoniemi. 2006. Perceived Discrimination and Well-Being: A Victim Study of Different Immigrant Groups. *J. Commun. Appl. Soc. Psychol.* **16**:267–284. [4]

Jasinskaja-Lahti, I., K. Liebkind, and E. Solheim. 2009. To Identify or Not to Identify? National Disidentification as an Alternative Reaction to Perceived Ethnic Discrimination. *Appl. Psychol.* **58**:105–128. [6]

Jiménez, T. R. 2008. Mexican Immigrant Replenishment and the Continuing Significance of Ethnicity and Race. *Am. J. Sociol.* **113**:1527–1567. [10]

———. 2009. Replenished Ethnicity: Mexican Americans, Immigration, and Identity. Oakland: Univ. of California Press. [5]

Jiménez, T. R., and A. L. Horowitz. 2013. When White Is Just Alright: How Immigrants Redefine Achievement and Reconfigure the Ethnoracial Hierarchy. *Am. Sociol. Rev.* **78**:849–871. [11]

Johnson, K. 2004. The Huddled Masses Myth: Immigration and Civil Rights. Philadelphia: Temple Univ. Press. [5]

Jones, C. P. 2001. "Race," Racism, and the Practice of Epidemiology. *Am. J. Epidemiol.* **154**:299–304. [5]

Jones, E. E., A. Farina, A. Hastorf, et al. 1984. Social Stigma: The Psychology of Marked Relationships. New York: W. H. Freeman. [2, 4]

Jones, J. A. 2019. The Browning of the New South. Chicago: Univ. of Chicago Press. [5]

Jonsson, J. O., and F. Rudolphi. 2011. Weak Performance–Strong Determination: School Achievement and Educational Choice among Children of Immigrants in Sweden. *Eur. Sociol. Rev.* **27**:487–508. [6]

Joppke, C. 2007. Transformation of Immigrant Integration: Civic Integration and Antidiscrimination in the Netherlands, France, and Germany. *World Polit.* **59**:243–273. [8]

Jost, J. T., and M. R. Banaji. 1994. The Role of Stereotyping in System-Justification and the Production of False Consciousness. *Br. J. Soc. Psychol.* **33**:1–27. [4]

Jost, J. T., M. R. Banaji, and B. A. Nosek. 2004. A Decade of System Justification Theory: Accumulated Evidence of Conscious and Unconscious Bolstering of the Status Quo. *Polit. Psychol.* **25**:881–919. [4]

Jost, J. T., B. W. Pelham, O. Sheldon, and B. N. Sullivan. 2003. Social Inequality and the Reduction of Ideological Dissonance on Behalf of the System: Evidence of Enhanced System Justification among the Disadvantaged. *Eur. J. Soc. Psychol.* **33**:13–36. [4]

Juárez, S. P., H. Honkaniemi, A. C. Dunlavy, et al. 2019. Effects of Non-Health-Targeted Policies on Migrant Health: A Systematic Review and Meta-Analysis. *Lancet Glob. Health* **7**:e420–e435. [10]

Jussim, L., T. R. Cain, J. T. Crawford, K. Harber, and F. Cohen. 2009. The Unbearable Accuracy of Stereotypes. In: Handbook of Prejudice, Stereotyping, and Discrimination, ed. T. D. Nelson, pp. 199–227. London: Psychology Press. [6]

Kalter, F. 2003. Chancen, Fouls und Abseitsfallen. Wiesbaden: VS Verlag für Sozialwissenschaften. [6]

Kalter, F., and A. F. Heath. 2018. Dealing with Diverse Diversities: Defining and Comparing Minority Groups. In: Growing Up in Diverse Societies: The Integration of the Children of Immigrants in England, Germany, the Netherlands and Sweden, ed. F. Kalter et al., pp. 62–83. Oxford: Oxford Univ. Press. [5]

Kalter, F., A. F. Heath, M. Hewstone, et al. 2016. Children of Immigrants Longitudinal Survey in Four European Countries (CILS4EU): Full Version. Za5353 Data File Version 1.2.0. Cologne: GESIS Data Archive. [6]

Kalter, F., I. Kogan, and J. Dollmann. 2019. Studying Integration from Adolescence to Early Adulthood: Design, Content, and Research Potential of the CILS4EU-De Data. *Eur. Sociol. Rev.* **35**:280–297. [6, 11]

———. 2021. Children of Immigrants Longitudinal Survey in Four European Countries: (CILS4EU-De) Full Version. Za6655 Data File Version 6.0.0. Cologne: GESIS Data Archive. [6]

Kao, G., and M. Tienda. 1998. Educational Aspirations of Minority Youth. *Am. J. Educ.* **106**:349–384. [6]

Kaufmann, E., and M. J. Goodwin. 2018. The Diversity Wave: A Meta-Analysis of the Native-Born White Response to Ethnic Diversity. *Soc. Sci. Res.* **76**:120–131. [3]

Keane, D., and A. Waughray, eds. 2017. Fifty Years of the International Convention on the Elimination of Racial Discrimination: A Living Instrument. Manchester: Manchester Univ. Press. [8]

Kleinman, A. 1999. Experience and Its Moral Modes: Culture, Human Conditions, and Disorder. In: The Tanner Lectures on Human Values, ed. G. B. Peterson, pp. 357–420, vol. 20. Salt Lake City: Univ. of Utah Press. [2, 5]

———. 2006. What Really Matters: Living a Moral Life Amidst Uncertainty and Danger. New York: Oxford Univ. Press. [2, 5]

Kleinman, A., V. Das, and M. Lock, eds. 1997. Social Suffering. Berkeley: Univ. of California Press. [2, 5]

Kleinman, A., and R. Hall-Clifford. 2009. Stigma: A Social, Cultural and Moral Process. *J. Epidemiol. Commun. Health* **63**:418–419. [5]

Kline, N., and H. Castañeda. 2020. Immigration Enforcement Policies and Latinx Health: State of Knowledge. In: New and Emerging Issues in Latinx Health, ed. A. D. Martinez and S. D. Rhodes, pp. 253–269. Cham: Springer. [7]

Kogan, I. 2011. New Immigrants, Old Disadvantage Patterns? Labour Market Integration of Recent Immigrants into Germany. *Int. Migr.* **49**:91–117. [6]

Koopmans, R. 2013. Multiculturalism and Immigration: A Contested Field in Cross-National Comparison. *Annu. Rev. Sociol.* **39**:147–169. [8]

Kosterman, R., and S. Feshbach. 1989. Toward a Measure of Patriotic and Nationalistic Attitudes. *Polit. Psychol.* **10**:257–274. [3]

Kotowski, J. M. 2013. Narratives of Immigration and National Identity: Findings from a Discourse Analysis of German and U.S. Social Studies Textbooks. *Stud. Ethn. Nationalism* **13**:295–318. [10]

Kotzur, P. F., S. J. Schäfer, and U. Wagner. 2019. Meeting a Nice Asylum Seeker: Intergroup Contact Changes Stereotype Content Perceptions and Associated Emotional Prejudices and Encourages Solidarity-Based Collective Action Intentions. *Br. J. Soc. Psychol.* **58**:668–690. [11]

Kotzur, P. F., and U. Wagner. 2021. The Dynamic Relationship between Contact Opportunities, Positive and Negative Intergroup Contact, and Prejudice: A Longitudinal Investigation. *J. Pers. Soc. Psychol.* **120**:418. [11]

Kovář, J. 2020. A Security Threat or an Economic Consequence? An Analysis of the News Framing of the European Union's Refugee Crisis. *Int. Commun. Gaz.* **82**:564–587. [10]

———. 2022. Media Framing of Immigrants in Central Europe in the Period Surrounding the Refugee Crisis: Security, Negativity, and Political Sources. *Communications* **48**:5–27. [10]

Koytak, H. Z., and M. H. Celik. 2022. A Text Mining Approach to Determinants of Attitude Towards Syrian Immigration in the Turkish Twittersphere. *Soc. Sci. Comput. Rev.* **2022**:1–18. [10]

Krahn, G. L., D. K. Walker, and R. Correa-De-Araujo. 2015. Persons with Disabilities as an Unrecognized Health Disparity Population. *Am. J. Public Health* **105**:S198–S206. [4]

Krieger, N., J. T. Chen, B. Coull, P. D. Waterman, and J. Beckfield. 2013. The Unique Impact of Abolition of Jim Crow Laws on Reducing Inequities in Infant Death Rates and Implications for Choice of Comparison Groups in Analyzing Societal Determinants of Health. *Am. J. Public Health* **103**:2234–2244. [8, 9]

Kristen, C. 2006. Ethnische Diskriminierung in Der Grundschule? *Köln. Z. Soziolog. Sozialpsychol.* **58**:79–97. [6]

Kristen, C., and N. Granato. 2007. The Educational Attainment of the Second Generation in Germany: Social Origins and Ethnic Inequality. *Ethnicities* **7**:343–366. [6]

Kristen, C., D. Reimer, and I. Kogan. 2008. Higher Education Entry of Turkish Immigrant Youth in Germany. *Int. J. Comp. Sociol.* **49**:127–151. [6]

Kunz, S. 2016. Privileged Mobilities: Locating the Expatriate in Migration Scholarship. *Geogr. Compass* **10**:89–101. [10]

———. 2020. Expatriate, Migrant? The Social Life of Migration Categories and the Polyvalent Mobility of Race. *J. Ethn. Migr. Stud.* **46**:2145–2162. [10]

Kurzban, R., and M. R. Leary. 2001. Evolutionary Origins of Stigmatization: The Functions of Social Exclusion. *Psychol. Bull.* **127**:187–208. [4]

Kustov, A. 2019. Is There a Backlash against Immigration from Richer Countries? International Hierarchy and the Limits of Group Threat. *Polit. Psychol.* **40**:973–1000. [10]

———. 2022. "Bloom Where You're Planted": Explaining Public Opposition to (E) Migration. *J. Ethn. Migr. Stud.* **48**:1113–1132. [2]

Kustov, A., D. Laaker, and C. Reller. 2021. The Stability of Immigration Attitudes: Evidence and Implications. *J. Polit.* **83**:1478–1494. [10]

Kymlicka, W. 1995. Multicultural Citizenship: A Liberal Theory of Minority Rights. New York: Clarendon Press. [10]

Lamont, M. 2018. Addressing Recognition Gaps: Destigmatization and the Reduction of Inequality. *Am. Sociol. Rev.* **83**:419–444. [11]

Lamont, M., G. M. Silva, J. Welburn, et al. 2016. Getting Respect: Responding to Stigma and Discrimination in the United States, Brazil, and Israel. Princeton: Princeton Univ. Press. [8, 11]

Larsen, C. A. 2013. The Rise and Fall of Social Cohesion. The Construction and De-Construction of Social Trust in the USA, UK, Sweden and Denmark. Oxford: Oxford Univ. Press. [8]

Lattanner, M. R., J. Ford, N. Bo, et al. 2021. A Contextual Approach to the Psychological Study of Identity Concealment: Examining Direct, Interactive, and Indirect Effects of Structural Stigma on Concealment Motivation across Proximal and Distal Geographic Levels. *Psychol. Sci.* **32**:1684–1696. [8, 9]

Lattanner, M. R., and M. L. Hatzenbuehler. 2022. Thwarted Belonging Needs: A Mechanism Prospectively Linking Multiple Levels of Stigma and Interpersonal Outcomes among Sexual Minorities. *J. Soc. Issues* **79**:410–445. [8]

Lawrence, B. 1998. Race, Interests, and Beliefs About Affirmative Action: Unanswered Questions and New Directions. *Am. Behav. Sci.* **41**:985–1003. [8]

Lebowitz, M. S. 2014. Biological Conceptualizations of Mental Disorders among Affected Individuals: A Review of Correlates and Consequences. *Clin. Psychol.* **21**:67–83. [4]

Lee, E. S. 1966. A Theory of Migration. *Demography* **3**:47–57. [10]

Lee, J. 2006. Civility in the City: Blacks, Jews, and Koreans in Urban America. Cambridge, MA: Harvard Univ. Press. [5]

Lee, J., and M. Zhou. 2014. From Unassimilable to Exceptional: The Rise of Asian Americans and "Stereotype Promise". *New Diversities* **16**:1–22. [6]

———. 2015. The Asian American Achievement Paradox. New York: Russell Sage Foundation. [5]

Lee, S., and S. F. Waters. 2021. Asians and Asian Americans' Experiences of Racial Discrimination during the COVID-19 Pandemic: Impacts on Health Outcomes and the Buffering Role of Social Support. *Stigma Health* **6**:70–78. [5]

Leitner, J. B., E. Hehman, O. Ayduk, and R. Mendoza-Denton. 2016. Blacks' Death Rate Due to Circulatory Diseases Is Positively Related to Whites' Explicit Racial Bias: A Nationwide Investigation Using Project Implicit. *Psychol. Sci.* **27**:1299–1311. [9]

Lentin, A. 2008. Europe and the Silence about Race. *Eur. J. Soc. Theory* **11**:487–503. [10]

Leonard, P. 2010. Old Colonial or New Cosmopolitan? Changing White Identities in the Hong Kong Police. *Soc. Polit.* **17**:507–535. [10]

Lerner, M. J. 1980. The Belief in a Just World: A Fundamental Delusion. New York: Plenum Press. [8]

Levy, B. R., and C. E. Pilver. 2012. Residual Stigma: Psychological Distress among the Formerly Overweight. *Soc. Sci. Med.* **75**:297–299. [2]

Lewis, A., and J. B. Diamond. 2015. Despite the Best Intentions: How Racial Inequality Thrives in Good Schools. Transgressing Boundaries: Studies in Black Politics and Black Communities, C. Cohen and F. Harris, series ed. Oxford: Oxford Univ. Press. [5]

Librado, E., S. N. Librado, E. Ventura, H. Ventura, and S. M. Holmes. 2021. First Time Home. www.firsttimehomefilm.com. (accessed Nov. 15, 2022). [7]

Lin, D., X. Li, B. Wang, et al. 2011. Discrimination, Perceived Social Inequity, and Mental Health among Rural-to-Urban Migrants in China. *Community Ment. Health J.* **47**:171–180. [4]

Lindemann, K. 2020. How Labor-Market Integration Affects Perceptions of Discrimination: School-to-Apprenticeship Transitions of Youth with Migration Background in Germany. *Int. Migr. Rev.* **54**:1045–1071. [6]

Link, B. G. 1987. Understanding Labeling Effects in the Area of Mental Disorders: An Assessment of the Effects of Expectations of Rejection. *Am. Sociol. Rev.* **52**:96–112. [2, 9]

Link, B. G., and F. T. Cullen. 1986. Contact with the Mentally Ill and Perceptions of How Dangerous They Are. *J. Health Soc. Behav.* **27**:289–302. [2]

Link, B. G., F. T. Cullen, J. Frank, and J. F. Wozniak. 1987. The Social Rejection of Former Mental Patients: Understanding Why Labels Matter. *Am. J. Sociol.* **92**:1461–1500. [2]

Link, B. G., F. T. Cullen, E. Struening, P. E. Shrout, and B. P. Dohrenwend. 1989. A Modified Labeling Theory Approach to Mental Disorders: An Empirical Assessment. *Am. Sociol. Rev.* **54**:400–423. [2, 5]

Link, B. G., and M. L. Hatzenbuehler. 2016. Stigma as an Unrecognized Determinant of Population Health: Research and Policy Implications. *J. Health Polit. Pol. Law* **41**:653–673. [8–10]

Link, B. G., and J. C. Phelan. 1995. Social Conditions as Fundamental Causes of Disease. *J. Health Soc. Behav.* **Spec No**:80–94. [4]

———. 2001. Conceptualizing Stigma. *Annu. Rev. Sociol.* **27**:363–385. [1–11]

———. 2005. Fundamental Sources of Health Inequalities. In: Policy Challenges in Modern Health Care, ed. D. Mechanic et al., pp. 71–84. New Brunswick, NJ: Rutgers Univ. Press. [7]

———. 2006. Stigma and Its Public Health Implications. *Lancet* **367**:528–529. [7]

———. 2014. Stigma Power. *Soc. Sci. Med.* **103**:24–32. [2, 5]

Link, B. G., J. C. Phelan, M. Bresnahan, A. Stueve, and B. A. Pescosolido. 1999. Public Conceptions of Mental Illness: Labels, Causes, Dangerousness, and Social Distance. *Am. J. Public Health* **89**:1328–1333. [2]

Link, B. G., J. Wells, J. C. Phelan, and L. H. Yang. 2015. Understanding the Importance of "Symbolic Interaction Stigma": How Expectations About the Reactions of Others Adds to the Burden of Mental Illness Stigma. *Psychiatric Rehabil. J.* **38**:117–124. [2]

Link, B. G., L. H. Yang, J. C. Phelan, and P. Y. Collins. 2004. Measuring Mental Illness Stigma. *Schizophr. Bull.* **30**:511–541. [2, 8, 9]

Lipsky, M. 1980. Street-Level Bureaucracy: Dilemmas of the Individual in Public Services. New York: Russell Sage Foundation. [5]

———. 2010. Street-Level Bureaucracy: Dilemmas of the Individual in Public Service, 30th Anniversary Expanded Edition. New York: Russell Sage Foundation. [8]

Logan, R. I., M. A. Melo, and H. Castañeda. 2021. Familial Vulnerability: Legal Status and Mental Health within Mixed-Status Families. *Med. Anthropol.* **40**:1–14. [7]

López, I. H. 1996. White by Law: The Legal Construction of Race. New York: New York Univ. Press. [11]

Lopez, M. M., and S. M. Holmes. 2020. Raids on Immigrant Communities during the Pandemic Threaten the Country's Public Health. *Am. J. Public Health* **110**:958–959. [7]

Lorenz, G., S. Gentrup, C. Kristen, P. Stanat, and I. Kogan. 2016. Stereotype Bei Lehrkräften? Eine Untersuchung Systematisch Verzerrter Lehrererwartungen. *Köln. Z. Soziolog. Sozialpsychol.* **68**:89–111. [6]

Louie, P., and R. Wilkes. 2018. Representations of Race and Skin Tone in Medical Textbook Imagery. *Soc. Sci. Med.* **202**:38–42. [10]

Lukate, J. M. 2023. On the Precariousness of Address: What Narratives of Being Called White Can Tell Us about Researching and Re/Producing Social Categories in Research. *Br. J. Soc. Psychol.* **62**:56–70. [5]

Lutz, P., and M. Bitschnau. 2022. Misperceptions about Immigration: Reviewing Their Nature, Motivations and Determinants. *Br. J. Polit. Sci.* **53**:674–689. [10]

Macrae, C. N., A. B. Milne, and G. V. Bodenhausen. 1994. Stereotypes as Energy-Saving Devices: A Peek inside the Cognitive Toolbox. *J. Pers. Soc. Psychol.* **66**:37–47. [4]

Maghbouleh, N. 2017. The Limits of Whiteness: Iranian Americans and the Everyday Politics of Race. Stanford: Stanford Univ. Press. [10]

Major, B., W. B. Mendes, and J. F. Dovidio. 2013. Intergroup Relations and Health Disparities: A Social Psychological Perspective. *Health Psychol.* **32**:514–524. [4]

Major, B., and L. T. O'Brien. 2005. The Social Psychology of Stigma. *Annu. Rev. Psychol.* **56**:393–421. [2, 4, 6]

Mak, W. W. S., and R. Y. M. Cheung. 2008. Affiliate Stigma among Caregivers of People with Intellectual Disability or Mental Illness. *J. Appl. Res. Intellect. Disabil.* **21**:532–545. [2]

Margalit, Y., and O. Solodoch. 2022. Against the Flow: Differentiating between Public Opposition to the Immigration Stock and Flow. *Br. J. Polit. Sci.* **52**:1055–1075. [8]

Marley, C., and B. Mauki. 2018. Resilience and Protective Factors among Refugee Children Post-Migration to High-Income Countries: A Systematic Review. *Eur. J. Public Health* **29**:706–713. [6]

Massey, D. S., and N. Denton. 1993. American Apartheid. Chicago: Univ. of Chicago Press. [5]

Matejskova, T., and H. Leitner. 2011. Urban Encounters with Difference: The Contact Hypothesis and Immigrant Integration Projects in Eastern Berlin. *Soc. Cult. Geogr.* **12**:717–741. [2]

Maxwell, R. 2019. Cosmopolitan Immigration Attitudes in Large European Cities: Contextual or Compositional Effects? *Am. Polit. Sci. Rev.* **113**:456–474. [10]

Mays, V. M., S. D. Cochran, and N. W. Barnes. 2007. Race, Race-Based Discrimination, and Health Outcomes among African-Americans. *Annu. Rev. Psychol.* **58**:201–225. [5]

McGregor, H. A., J. D. Lieberman, J. Greenberg, et al. 1998. Terror Management and Aggression: Evidence That Mortality Salience Motivates Aggression against Worldview-Threatening Others. *J. Pers. Soc. Psychol.* **74**:590–605. [4]

McLaren, L. M. 2003. Anti-Immigrant Prejudice in Europe: Contact, Threat Perception, and Preferences for the Exclusion of Migrants. *Soc. Forces* **81**:909–936. [11]

Meeusen, C., and L. Jacobs. 2017. Television News Content of Minority Groups as an Intergroup Context Indicator of Differences between Target-Specific Prejudices. *Mass Commun. Soc.* **20**:213–240. [10]

Meltzer, C. E., J. M. Eberl, N. Theorin, et al. 2021. Media Effects on Policy Preferences toward Free Movement: Evidence from Five EU Member States. *J. Ethn. Migr. Stud.* **47**:3390–3408. [10]

Mendoza-Denton, R., G. Downey, V. J. Purdie, A. Davis, and J. Pietrzak. 2002. Sensitivity to Status-Based Rejection: Implications for African American Students' College Experience. *J. Pers. Soc. Psychol.* **83**:896–918. [4]

Menjívar, C. 2006. Liminal Legality: Salvadoran and Guatemalan Immigrants' Lives in the United States. American Journal of Sociology. *Am. J. Sociol.* **111**:999–1037. [11]

Mentges, H. 2020. Studium oder Berufsausbildung? Migrationsspezifische Bildungsentscheidungen von Studienberechtigten. Eine kritische Replikation und Erweiterung der Studie von Kristen et al. (2008). *Soziale Welt* **70**:403–434. [6]

Merton, R. K. 1948. The Self-Fulfilling Prophecy. *Antioch Rev.* **8**:193–210. [6]

Messing, V., and B. Ságvári. 2019. Still Divided but More Open: Mapping European Attitudes Towards Migration before and after the Migration Crisis. Flight, Migration, Integration in Europe. Budapest: Friedrich-Ebert-Stiftung. [3]

Mettler, S., and J. Soss. 2004. The Consequences of Public Policy for Democratic Citizenship: Bridging Policy Studies and Mass Politics. *Persp. Polit.* **2**:55–73. [8]

Meyer, I. H. 1995. Minority Stress and Mental Health in Gay Men. *J. Health Soc. Behav.* **36**:38–56. [2]

———. 2003. Prejudice, Social Stress, and Mental Health in Lesbian, Gay, and Bisexual Populations: Conceptual Issues and Research Evidence. *Psychol. Bull.* **129**:674–697. [4]

Miklikowska, M., R. Rekker, and A. Kudrnáč. 2022. A Little More Conversation a Little Less Prejudice: The Role of Classroom Political Discussions for Youth's Attitudes toward Immigrants. *Polit. Commun.* **39**:405–427. [10]

Miller, C. T., and C. R. Kaiser. 2001. A Theoretical Perspective on Coping with Stigma. *J. Soc. Issues* **57**:73–92. [2]

Min, P. G. 1996. Caught in the Middle: Korean Communities in New York and Los Angeles. Berkeley: Univ. of California Press. [5]

MIPEX. 2020. Migrant Integration Policy Index. https://mipex.eu/. (accessed Dec. 5, 2022). [10]

Misra, S., S. C. Kwon, A. F. Abraído-Lanza, et al. 2021. Structural Racism and Immigrant Health in the United States. *Health Educ. Behav.* **48**:332–341. [8]

Modood, T. 2007. Multiculturalism: A Civic Idea. Cambridge: Polity Press. [8]

Mood, C., J. O. Jonsson, and S. B. Låftman. 2017. The Mental Health Advantage of Immigrant-Background Youth: The Role of Family Factors. *J. Marriage Fam.* **79**:419–436. [10]

Mora, G. C., and D. G. Okamoto. 2020a. Boundary Articulation and Emergent Identities: Asian and Hispanic Panethnicity in Comparison 1970-1980. *Soc. Prob.* **67**:56–76. [10]

———. 2020b. Postcolonialism, Racial Political Fields, and Panethnicity: A Comparison of Early "Asian American" and "Hispanic" Movements. *Sociol. Race Ethnicity* **6**:450–467. [11]

Morey, B. N. 2018. Mechanisms by Which Anti-Immigrant Stigma Exacerbates Racial/Ethnic Health Disparities. *Am. J. Public Health* **108**:460–463. [5, 8]

Morone, J. A. 1997. Enemies of the People: The Moral Dimension to Public Health. *J. Health Polit. Pol. Law* **22**:993–1020. [7]

Motti-Stefanidi, F. 2014. Immigrant Youth Adaptation in the Greek School Context: A Risk and Resilience Developmental Perspective. *Child Dev. Perspect.* **8**:180–185. [6]

Mylius, M. 2016. Die Medizinische Versorgung von Menschen Ohne Papiere in Deutschland: Studien Zur Praxis in Gesundheitsämtern und Krankenhäusern. Bielefeld: transcript. [8]

Nandi, A., S. Galea, M. Tracy, et al. 2004. Job Loss, Unemployment, Work Stress, Job Satisfaction, and the Persistence of Posttraumatic Stress Disorder One Year after the September 11 Attacks. *J. Occup. Environ. Med.* **46**:1057–1064. [8]

National Council on Disability. 2007. Implementation of the Americans with Disabilities Act: Challenges, Best Practices, and New Opportunities for Success. Washington, D.C.: National Council on Disability. [9]

NBC News. 2022. Judge Rules against Kentucky Clerk Who Denied Same-Sex Marriage Licenses. March 21, 2022. https://www.nbcnews.com/nbc-out/out-news/judge-rules-kentucky-clerk-denied-sex-marriage-licenses-rcna20858. (accessed Dec. 6, 2022). [8]

Neuberg, S. L., and S. T. Fiske. 1987. Motivational Influences on Impression Formation: Outcome Dependency, Accuracy-Driven Attention, and Individuating Processes. *J. Pers. Soc. Psychol.* **53**:431–444. [4]

Neuberg, S. L., D. T. Kenrick, and M. Schaller. 2011. Human Threat Management Systems: Self-Protection and Disease Avoidance. *Neurosci. Biobehav. Rev.* **35**:1042–1051. [4]

Newman, K. 2002. No Shame: The View from the Left Bank. *Am. J. Sociol.* **107**:1577–1599. [4]

Nguyen, T. T., D. Huang, E. K. Michaels, et al. 2021. Evaluating Associations between Area-Level Twitter-Expressed Negative Racial Sentiment, Hate Crimes, and Residents' Racial Prejudice in the United States. *SSM Population Health* **13**:100750. [9]

Nicholls, W. J. 2019. The Immigrant Rights Movement: The Battle over National Citizenship. Stanford: Stanford Univ. Press. [11]

Nichols, V. C., A. M. W. Lebrón, and F. I. Pedraza. 2018. Policing Us Sick: The Health of Latinos in an Era of Heightened Deportations and Racialized Policing. *Polit. Sci. Polit.* **51**:293–297. [8]

Nordø, Å. D., and E. Ivarsflaten. 2022. The Scope of Exclusionary Public Response to the European Refugee Crisis. *Eur. J. Polit. Res.* **61**:420–439. [10]

Nosek, B. A., M. R. Banaji, and A. G. Greenwald. 2002. Harvesting Implicit Group Attitudes and Beliefs from a Demonstration Web Site. *Group Dyn.* **6**:101–115. [4]

O'Brien, M. L., and M. A. Eger. 2021. Suppression, Spikes, and Stigma: How Covid-19 Will Shape International Migration and Hostilities toward It. *Int. Migr. Rev.* 55:640–659. [10]

Ofosu, E. K., M. K. Chambers, J. M. Chen, and E. Hehman. 2019. Same-Sex Marriage Legalization Associated with Reduced Implicit and Explicit Antigay Bias. *PNAS* **116**:8846–8851. [9]

Ogbu, J. U. 2003. Black American Students in an Affluent Suburb: A Study of Academic Disengagement. Mahwah, NJ: Lawrence Erlbaum. [6]

Okamoto, D. G. 2003. Toward a Theory of Panethnicity: Explaining Asian American Collective Action. *Am. Sociol. Rev.* **68**:811–842. [10]

———. 2014. Redefining Race: Asian American Panethnicity and Shifting Ethnic Boundaries. New York: Russell Sage Foundation. [10, 11]

Okamoto, D. G., and K. Ebert. 2016. Group Boundaries, Immigrant Inclusion, and the Politics of Immigrant–Native Relations. *Am. Behav. Sci.* **60**:224–250. [11]

Okamoto, D. G., and G. C. Mora. 2014. Panethnicity. *Annu. Rev. Sociol.* **40**:219–239. [11]

Olczyk, M., J. Seuring, G. Will, and S. Zinn. 2016. Migranten und Ihre Nachkommen Im Deutschen Bildungssystem. Ein Aktueller Überblick. In: Ethnische Ungleichheiten Im Bildungsverlauf Mechanismen, Befunde, Debatten, ed. C. Diehl et al., pp. 33–70. Wiesbaden: Springer VS. [6]

Olzak, S. 1992. The Dynamics of Ethnic Competition and Conflict. Stanford: Stanford Univ. Press. [3]

Owens, J., and S. M. Lynch. 2012. Black and Hispanic Immigrants' Resilience against Negative Ability Racial Stereotypes at Selective Colleges and Universities in the United States. *Sociol. Educ.* **85**:303–325. [6]

Pachankis, J. E. 2007. The Psychological Implications of Concealing a Stigma: A Cognitive-Affective-Behavioral Model. *Psychol. Bull.* **133**:328–345. [2]

Pachankis, J. E., M. R. Goldfried, and M. E. Ramrattan. 2008. Extension of the Rejection Sensitivity Construct to the Interpersonal Functioning of Gay Men. *J. Consult. Clin. Psychol.* **76**:306–317. [4]

Pachankis, J. E., M. L. Hatzenbuehler, R. C. Berg, et al. 2017a. Anti-LGBT and Anti-Immigrant Structural Stigma: An Intersectional Analysis of Sexual Minority Men's HIV Risk When Migrating to or within Europe. *J. Acquir. Immune Defic. Syndr.* **76**:356–366. [9]

Pachankis, J. E., M. L. Hatzenbuehler, R. Bränström, et al. 2021. Structural Stigma and Sexual Minority Men's Depression and Suicidality: A Multilevel Examination of Mechanisms and Mobility across 48 Countries. *J. Abnorm. Psychol.* **130**:713–726. [4, 8, 9]

Pachankis, J. E., M. L. Hatzenbuehler, M. Mirandola, et al. 2017b. The Geography of Sexual Orientation: Structural Stigma and Sexual Attraction, Behavior, and Identity among Men Who Have Sex with Men across 38 European Countries. *Arch. Sex. Behav.* **46**:1491–1502. [4]

Pachankis, J. E., M. L. Hatzenbuehler, K. Wang, et al. 2018. The Burden of Stigma on Health and Well-Being: A Taxonomy of Concealment, Course, Disruptiveness, Aesthetics, Origin, and Peril across 93 Stigmas. *Pers. Soc. Psychol. Bull.* **44**:451–474. [2, 4, 9]

Pachankis, J. E., H. J. Rendina, A. Restar, et al. 2015. A Minority Stress–Emotion Regulation Model of Sexual Compulsivity among Highly Sexually Active Gay and Bisexual Men. *Health Psychol.* **34**:829–840. [4]

Pareek, M., M. N. Bangash, N. Pareek, et al. 2020. Ethnicity and COVID-19: An Urgent Public Health Research Priority. *Lancet* **395**:1421–1422. [4]

Pascoe, E. A., and L. Smart Richman. 2009. Perceived Discrimination and Health: A Meta-Analytic Review. *Psychol. Bull.* **135**:531–554. [4]

Patler, C. 2018a. Citizens but for Papers: Undocumented Youth Organizations, Anti-Deportation Campaigns, and the Reframing of Citizenship. *Soc. Prob.* **65**:96–115. [11]

———. 2018b. To Reveal or Conceal: How Diverse Undocumented Youth Navigate Legal Status Disclosure. *Sociol. Persp.* **61**:857–873. [5]

Perreira, K. M., and J. M. Pedroza. 2019. Policies of Exclusion: Implications for the Health of Immigrants and Their Children. *Annu. Rev. Public Health* **40**:147–166. [8]

Peter, L.-J., S. Schindler, C. Sander, et al. 2021. Continuum Beliefs and Mental Illness Stigma: A Systematic Review and Meta-Analysis of Correlation and Intervention Studies. *Psychol. Med.* **51**:716–726. [2]

Petersen, M. B., and L. Aarøe. 2013. Politics in the Mind's Eye: Imagination as a Link between Social and Political Cognition. *Am. Polit. Sci. Rev.* **107**:275–293. [8]

Pettigrew, T. F. 1998. Intergroup Contact Theory. *Annu. Rev. Psychol.* **49**:65–85. [2]

Pettigrew, T. F., and R. W. Meertens. 1995. Subtle and Blatant Prejudice in Western Europe. *Eur. J. Soc. Psychol.* **25**:57–75. [2]

Pettigrew, T. F., and L. R. Tropp. 2006. A Meta-Analytic Test of Intergroup Contact Theory. *J. Pers. Soc. Psychol.* **90**:751. [11]

Phelan, J. C. 2005. Geneticization of Deviant Behavior and Consequences for Stigma: The Case of Mental Illness. *J. Health Soc. Behav.* **46**:307–322. [4]

Phelan, J. C., B. G. Link, and J. F. Dovidio. 2008. Stigma and Prejudice: One Animal or Two? *Soc. Sci. Med.* **67**:358–367. [2–4, 7–10]

Phelan, J. C., B. G. Link, A. Stueve, and R. E. Moore. 1995. Education, Social Liberalism, and Economic Conservatism: Attitudes toward Homeless People. *Am. Sociol. Rev.* **60**:126–140. [10]

Phelps, E. S. 1972. The Statistical Theory of Racism and Sexism. *Am. Econ. Rev.* **62**:659–661. [6]

Phinney, J. S., T. Madden, and L. J. Santos. 1998. Psychological Variables as Predictors of Perceived Ethnic Discrimination among Minority and Immigrant Adolescents. *J. Appl. Soc. Psychol.* **28**:937–953. [6]

Pierson, P. 1993. When Effect Becomes Cause: Policy Feedback and Political Change. *World Polit.* **45**:595–628. [8]

Pinel, E. C. 1999. Stigma Consciousness: The Psychological Legacy of Social Stereotypes. *J. Pers. Soc. Psychol.* **76**:114–128. [2, 5]

Piotrowski, J., J. Różycka-Tran, T. Baran, and M. Żemojtel-Piotrowska. 2019. Zero-Sum Thinking as Mediator of the Relationship of National Attitudes with (Un) Willingness to Host Refugees in Own Country. *Int. J. Psychol.* **54**:722–730. [8]

Pistotnik, S., and D. A. Brown. 2018. Race in the Balkans: The Case of Erased Residents of Slovenia. *Interventions* **20**:832–852. [2]

Ponce, A. 2020. Affective Solidarities or Group Boundaries? Muslims' Place in America's Racial and Religious Order. *Ethn. Racial Stud.* **43**:2785–2806. [11]

Portes, A., and R. G. Rumbaut. 2001. Legacies: The Story of the Immigrant Second Generation. Berkely: Univ. of California Press. [5, 11]

———. 2014. Immigrant America: A Portrait, 4th Edition, Updated, and Expanded. Berkeley: Univ. of California Press. [5]

Portes, A., and M. Zhou. 1993. The New Second Generation: Segmented Assimilation and Its Variants. *Ann. Am. Acad. Polit. Soc. Sci.* **530**:74–96. [5, 11]

Pottie-Sherman, Y., and R. Wilkes. 2017. Does Size Really Matter? On the Relationship between Immigrant Group Size and Anti-Immigrant Prejudice. *Int. Migr. Rev.* **51**:218–250. [3, 10]

Pratsinakis, M. 2014. Resistance and Compliance in Immigrant–Native Figurations: Albanian and Soviet Greek Immigrants and Their Interaction with Greek Society. *J. Ethn. Migr. Stud.* **40**:1295–1313. [2]

Preuhs, R. R. 2007. Descriptive Representation as a Mechanism to Mitigate Policy Backlash: Latino Incorporation and Welfare Policy in the American States. *Polit. Res. Q.* **60**:277–292. [8]

Priebe, S., S. Watzke, L. Hansson, and T. Burns. 2008. Objective Social Outcomes Index (SIX): A Method to Summarise Objective Indicators of Social Outcomes in Mental Health Care. *Acta Psychiatr. Scand.* **118**:57–63. [2]

Purtle, J., K. L. Nelson, L. Gebrekristos, F. Lê-Scherban, and S. E. Gollust. 2022. Partisan Differences in the Effects of Economic Evidence and Local Data on Legislator Engagement with Dissemination Materials about Behavioral Health: A Dissemination Trial. *Implement. Sci.* **17**:1–15. [8]

Qian, Z., and D. T. Lichter. 2007. Social Boundaries and Marital Assimilation: Interpreting Trends in Racial and Ethnic Intermarriage. *Am. Sociol. Rev.* **72**:68–94. [11]

Quesada, J., L. K. Hart, and P. Bourgois. 2011. Structural Vulnerability and Health: Latino Migrant Laborers in the United States. *Med. Anthropol.* **30**:339–362. [7]

Quillian, L. 1995. Prejudice as a Response to Perceived Group Threat: Population Composition and Anti-Immigrant and Racial Prejudice in Europe. *Am. Sociol. Rev.* **60**:586–611. [2, 3]

———. 2006. New Approaches to Understanding Racial Prejudice and Discrimination. *Annu. Rev. Sociol.* **32**:299–328. [3]

Raifman, J., E. Moscoe, S. B. Austin, M. L. Hatzenbuehler, and S. Galea. 2018a. Association of State Laws Permitting Denial of Services to Same-Sex Couples with Mental Distress in Sexual Minority Adults: A Difference-in-Difference-in-Differences Analysis. *JAMA Psychiatry* **75**:671–677. [8]

———. 2018b. Association of State Laws Permitting Denial of Services to Same-Sex Couples with Mental Distress in Sexual Minority Adults: A Difference-in-Difference-in-Differences Analysis. *JAMA Psychiatry* **75**:671. [9]

Raifman, J., E. Moscoe, S. B. Austin, and M. McConnell. 2017. Difference-in-Differences Analysis of the Association between State Same-Sex Marriage Policies and Adolescent Suicide Attempts. *JAMA Pediatr.* **171**:350. [9]

Raijman, R., and M. Semyonov. 2004. Perceived Threat and Exclusionary Attitudes Towards Foreign Workers in Israel. *Ethn. Racial Stud.* **27**:780–799. [2]

Raleigh, E., and G. Kao. 2010. Do Immigrant Minority Parents Have More Consistent College Aspirations for Their Children? *Soc. Sci. Q.* **91**:1083–1102. [6]

Rendina, H. J., K. E. Gamarel, J. E. Pachankis, et al. 2017. Extending the Minority Stress Model to Incorporate HIV-Positive Gay and Bisexual Men's Experiences: A Longitudinal Examination of Mental Health and Sexual Risk Behavior. *Ann. Behav. Med.* **51**:147–158. [4]

Ritsher, J. B., P. G. Otilingam, and M. Grajales. 2003. Internalized Stigma of Mental Illness: Psychometric Properties of a New Measure. *Psychiatry Res.* **121**:31–49. [2]

Rivera-Salgado, G., and L. Rabadan. 2020. Asociaciones de Immigantes, Reproduccion Cultural y Agencia Entre Inmigrantes Mexicanos Indígenas en Estados Unidos. **48**:161–186. [7]

Roccas, S., G. Horenczyk, and S. H. Schwartz. 2000. Acculturation Discrepancies and Well-Being: The Moderating Role of Conformity. *Eur. J. Soc. Psychol.* **30**:323–334. [4]

Roman, N., A. Young, and S. C. Perkins. 2021. Displaced and Invisible: Ukrainian Refugee Crisis Coverage in the US, UK, Ukrainian, and Russian Newspapers. *Negot. Confl. Manag. Res.* **14**:153–169. [10]

Römhild, R. 2017. Beyond the Bounds of the Ethnic: For Postmigrant Cultural and Social Research. *J. Aesthet. Cult.* **9**:69–75. [8]

———. 2018. Global Heimat: (Post)Migrant Productions of Transnational Space. *Anthropol. J. Eur. Cult.* **27**:27–29. [7]

———. 2021. Postmigrant Europe: Discoveries Beyond Ethnic, National and Colonial Boundaries. In: Postmigration: Art, Culture, and Politics in Contemporary Europe, ed. A. M. Gaonkar et al., pp. 45–55. Bielefeld: Transcript. [7]

Rosenblatt, A., J. Greenberg, S. Solomon, T. Pyszczynski, and D. Lyon. 1989. Evidence for Terror Management Theory: I. The Effects of Mortality Salience on Reactions to Those Who Violate or Uphold Cultural Values. *J. Pers. Soc. Psychol.* **57**:681–690. [4]

Ruhs, M. 2013. The Price of Rights. Regulating International Labor Migration. Princeton: Princeton Univ. Press. [7, 8]

Rüsch, N. 2023. The Stigma of Mental Illness: Strategies against Social Exclusion and Discrimination. Oxford: Elsevier. [8]

Sabbagh, D. 2011. Affirmative Action: The U.S. Experience in Comparative Perspective. *Daedalus* **140**:109–120. [8]

Said, E. W. 1979. Orientalism. UK: Vintage/Penguin Random House. [10]

Saine, M. E., T. M. Moore, J. E. Szymczak, et al. 2020. Validation of a Modified Berger HIV Stigma Scale for Use among Patients with Hepatitis C Virus (HCV) Infection. *PLOS ONE* **15**:e0228471. [2]

Salikutluk, Z. 2016. Why Do Immigrant Students Aim High? Explaining the Aspiration: Achievement Paradox of Immigrants in Germany. *Eur. Sociol. Rev.* **32**:581–592. [6]

Samari, G., R. Catalano, H. E. Alcalá, and A. Gemmill. 2020. The Muslim Ban and Preterm Birth: Analysis of US Vital Statistics Data from 2009 to 2018. *Soc. Sci. Med.* **265**:113544. [8, 9]

Samuels, E. A., L. Orr, E. B. White, et al. 2021. Health Care Utilization before and after the "Muslim Ban" Executive Order among People Born in Muslim-Majority Countries and Living in the US. *JAMA Netw. Open* **4**:e2118216. [4]

Sandín Esteban, M., and A. Sánchez-Martí. 2014. Beyond Compulsory Schooling: Resilience and Academic Success of Immigrant Youth. *Procedia* **132**:19–24. [6]

Sarrasin, O., E. G. T. Green, C. Bolzman, E. P. Visintin, and E. Politi. 2018. Competition- and Identity-Based Roots of Anti-Immigration Prejudice among Individuals with and without an Immigrant Background. *Int. Rev. Soc. Psychol.* **31**:1–12. [2]

Savage, M. 2015. Social Class in the 21st Century. London: Pelican. [2]

Saxenian, A. 2000. Networks of Immigrant Entrepreneurs. In: The Silicon Valley Edge, ed. C. M. Lee et al., pp. 248–268. Stanford: Stanford Univ. Press. [10]

Schachter, A. 2016. From "Different" to "Similar" an Experimental Approach to Understanding Assimilation. *Am. Sociol. Rev.* **81**:981–1013. [11]

Schaeffer, M. 2019. Social Mobility and Perceived Discrimination: Adding an Intergenerational Perspective. *Eur. Sociol. Rev.* **35**:65–80. [11]

Schalk-Soekar, S. R. G., F. J. R. van de Vijver, and M. Hoogsteder. 2004. Attitudes toward Multiculturalism of Immigrants and Majority Members in the Netherlands. *Int. J. Intercult. Rel.* **28**:533–550. [3]

Schaller, M., and S. L. Neuberg. 2012. Danger, Disease, and the Nature of Prejudices. In: Advances in Experimental Social Psychology, ed. J. M. Olson and M. P. Zanna, pp. 1–54, vol. 46. New York: Academic Press. [4]

Schaller, M., and J. H. Park. 2011. The Behavioral Immune System (and Why It Matters). *Curr. Dir. Psychol. Sci.* **20**:99–103. [4]

Scheepers, P., M. Gijsberts, and M. Coenders. 2002. Ethnic Exclusionism in European Countries. Public Opposition to Civil Rights for Legal Migrants as a Response to Perceived Ethnic Threat. *Eur. Sociol. Rev.* **18**:17–34. [2]

Schemer, C. 2012. The Influence of News Media on Stereotypic Attitudes toward Immigrants in a Political Campaign. *J. Commun.* **62**:739–757. [11]

Scheve, K. F., and M. J. Slaughter. 2001. Labor Market Competition and Individual Preferences over Immigration Policy. *Rev. Econ. Stat.* **83**:133–145. [2, 3]

Schlueter, E., and E. Davidov. 2013. Contextual Sources of Perceived Group Threat: Negative Immigration-Related News Reports, Immigrant Group Size and Their Interaction, Spain 1996-2007. *Eur. Sociol. Rev.* **29**:179–191. [10]

Schlueter, E., A. Masso, and E. Davidov. 2020. What Factors Explain Anti-Muslim Prejudice? *J. Ethn. Migr. Stud.* **46**:649–664. [11]

Schlueter, E., B. Meuleman, and E. Davidov. 2013. Immigrant Integration Policies and Perceived Group Threat: A Multilevel Study of 27 Western and Eastern European Countries. *Soc. Sci. Res.* **42**:670–682. [8]

Schmidt-Catran, A. W., and C. S. Czymara. 2023. Political Elite Discourses Polarize Attitudes toward Immigration Along Ideological Lines. A Comparative Longitudinal Analysis of Europe in the Twenty-First Century. *J. Ethn. Migr. Stud.* 49:85–109. [10]

Schmitt, M. T., N. R. Branscombe, T. Postmes, and A. Garcia. 2014. The Consequences of Perceived Discrimination for Psychological Well-Being: A Meta-Analytic Review. *Psychol. Bull.* **140**:921–948. [4, 6]

Schneider, S. L. 2008. Anti-Immigrant Attitudes in Europe: Outgroup Size and Perceived Ethnic Threat. *Eur. Sociol. Rev.* **24**:53–67. [3]

Scholten, P. 2020. Mainstreaming Versus Alienation: A Complexity Approach to the Governance of Migration and Diversity. London: Palgrave Macmillan. [8]

Schomerus, G., C. Sander, S. Schindler, E. Baumann, and M. C. Angermeyer. 2022. Public Attitudes Towards Protecting the Human Rights of People with Mental Illness: A Scoping Review and Data from a Population Trend Study in Germany. *Int. Rev. Psychiatry* **35**:167–179. [2]

Schuchart, C., and M. Rürup. 2017. Alternative Wege Zur Studienberechtigung und Die Weitere Bildungs- und Berufskarriere: Können Durch Die Öffnung Des Gegliederten Schulsystems Ungleichheiten Reduziert Werden? In: Bildungsgerechtigkeit. Festschrift Für Hartmut Ditton Zum 60. Geburtstag, ed. F. van Tubergen, pp. 249–267. Wiesbaden: Springer VS. [6]

Schultz, C., P. Lutz, and S. Simon. 2021. Explaining the Immigration Policy Mix: The Relative Openness Towards Asylum and Labour Migration. *Eur. J. Polit. Res.* **60**:763–784. [8, 10]

Schuster, L., and N. Majidi. 2015. Deportation Stigma and Re-Migration. *J. Ethn. Migr. Stud.* **41**:635–652. [5]

Seif, H. 2016. We Define Ourselves: 1.5-Generation Undocumented Immigrant Activist Identities and Insurgent Discourse. *N. Am. Dialogue* **19**:23–35. [7]

Selznick, G. J., and S. Steinberg. 1979. The Tenacity of Prejudice: Anti-Semitism in Contemporary America. Westport, CT: Greenwood Press. [10]

Semyonov, M., R. Raijman, and A. Gorodzeisky. 2006. The Rise of Anti-Foreigner Sentiment in European Societies, 1988-2000. *Am. Sociol. Rev.* **71**:426–449. [2]

Sheller, M., and J. Urry. 2006. The New Mobilities Paradigm. *Environ. Plann. A* **38**:207–226. [2]

Sherif, M. 1967. Group Conflict and Co-Operation: Their Social Psychology. London: Psychology Press. [2]

Sherif, M., and C. W. Sherif. 1953. Groups in Harmony and Tension: An Integration of Studies of Intergroup Relations. New York: Harper. [3]

Shih, M., N. Ambady, J. A. Richeson, K. Fujita, and H. M. Gray. 2002. Stereotype Performance Boosts: The Impact of Self-Relevance and the Manner of Stereotype Activation. *J. Pers. Soc. Psychol.* **83**:638–647. [4]

Sibley, C. G., and J. Duckitt. 2008. Personality and Prejudice: A Meta-Analysis and Theoretical Review. *Pers. Soc. Psychol. Rev.* **12**:248–279. [4]

Sidanius, J., and F. Pratto. 1999. Social Dominance: An Intergroup Theory of Social Hierarchy and Oppression. New York: Cambridge Univ. Press. [4, 6, 10]

Sides, J., and J. Citrin. 2007. European Opinion About Immigration: The Role of Identities, Interests and Information. *Br. J. Polit. Sci.* **37**:477–504. [2]

Simon, P. 2017. The Failure of the Importation of Ethno-Racial Statistics in Europe: Debates and Controversies. *Ethn. Racial Stud.* **40**:2326–2332. [8]

Skrobanek, J. 2009. Perceived Discrimination, Ethnic Identity and the (Re-) Ethnicisation of Youth with a Turkish Ethnic Background in Germany. *J. Ethn. Migr. Stud.* **35**:535–554. [6]

Smart, L., and D. M. Wegner. 1999. Covering up What Can't Be Seen: Concealable Stigma and Mental Control. *J. Pers. Soc. Psychol.* **77**:474–486. [4]

Smith, S. A., and H. Castañeda. 2021. Nonimmigrant Others: Belonging, Precarity and Imperial Citizenship for Chuukese Migrants in Guam. *Polit. Legal Anthropol. Rev.* **44**:138–155. [7]

Solomon, S., J. Greenberg, and T. Pyszczynski. 1991. A Terror Management Theory of Social Behavior: The Psychological Functions of Self-Esteem and Cultural Worldviews. In: Advances in Experimental Social Psychology, ed. M. P. Zanna, pp. 93–159, vol. 24. New York: Academic Press. [2–4]

———. 2000. Pride and Prejudice: Fear of Death and Social Behavior. *Curr. Dir. Psychol. Sci.* **9**:200–204. [4]

Sorokin, P. A., and R. K. Merton. 1937. Social Time: A Methodological and Functional Analysis. *Am. J. Sociol.* **42**:615–689. [10]

Sprietsma, M. 2013. Discrimination in Grading: Experimental Evidence from Primary School Teachers. *Emp. Econ.* **45**:523–538. [5, 6]

Spruyt, B., and M. Elchardus. 2012. Are Anti-Muslim Feelings More Widespread Than Antiforeigner Feelings? Evidence from Two Split-Sample Experiments. *Ethnicities* **12**:800–820. [3]

Steele, C. M. 1997. A Threat in the Air: How Stereotypes Shape Intellectual Identity and Performance. *Am. Psychol.* **52**:613–629. [3, 4]

Steele, C. M., and J. Aronson. 1995. Stereotype Threat and the Intellectual Test Performance of African Americans. *J. Pers. Soc. Psychol.* **69**:797–811. [6]

Steele, C. M., S. J. Spencer, and J. Aronson. 2002. Contending with Group Image: The Psychology of Stereotype and Social Identity Threat. In: Advances in Experimental Social Psychology, ed. M. P. Zanna, pp. 379–440, vol. 34. New York: Academic Press. [4]

Steinberger, M. D. 2009. Federal Estate Tax Disadvantages for Same-Sex Couples. Los Angeles: The Williams Institute, UCLA. [8]

Steinmann, J. P. 2019. The Paradox of Integration: Why Do Higher Educated New Immigrants Perceive More Discrimination in Germany? *J. Ethn. Migr. Stud.* **45**:1377–1400. [3]

Stephan, W. G., and C. W. Stephan. 2000. An Integrated Threat Theory of Prejudice. In: Reducing Prejudice and Discrimination, ed. S. Oskamp, pp. 23–45, The Claremont Symposium on Applied Social Psychology. Mahwah, NJ: Lawrence Erlbaum. [2, 6]

Stephan, W. G., O. Ybarra, C. M. Martinez, J. Schwarzwald, and M. Tur-Kaspa. 1998. Prejudice toward Immigrants to Spain and Israel: An Integrated Threat Theory Analysis. *J. Cross Cult. Psychol.* **29**:559–576. [8]

Stephan, W. G., O. Ybarra, and K. R. Morrison. 2009. Intergroup Threat Theory. In: Handbook of Prejudice, Stereotyping, and Discrimination, ed. T. D. Nelson, pp. 43–59. London: Psychology Press. [6]

Strabac, Z. 2011. It Is the Eyes and Not the Size That Matter. *Eur. Soc.* **13**:559–582. [3]

Stutterheim, S. E., A. E. Bos, J. B. Pryor, et al. 2011. Psychological and Social Correlates of HIV Status Disclosure: The Significance of Stigma Visibility. *AIDS Educ. Prev.* **23**:382–392. [4]

Suárez-Orozco, C. 2000. Identities under Siege: Immigration Stress and Social Mirroring among the Children of Immigrants. In: Cultures under Siege: Collective Violence and Trauma, ed. A. C. G. M. Robben and M. M. Suárez-Orozco, pp. 194–226. Cambridge: Cambridge Univ. Press. [5, 7]

Sutin, A. R., Y. Stephan, M. Luchetti, et al. 2016. The Five-Factor Model of Personality and Physical Inactivity: A Meta-Analysis of 16 Samples. *J. Res. Pers.* **63**:22–28. [6]

Tabellini, M. 2020. Gifts of the Immigrants, Woes of the Natives: Lessons from the Age of Mass Migration. *Rev. Econ. Stud.* **87**:454–486. [10]

Tajfel, H. 1982. Social Psychology of Intergroup Relations. *Annu. Rev. Psychol.* **33**:1–39. [6]

Tajfel, H., and J. C. Turner. 1979. An Integrative Theory of Intergroup Conflict. In: The Social Psychology of Intergroup Relations, ed. W. G. Austin and S. Worchel, pp. 33–47. Monterey, CA: Brooks/Cole. [2]

———. 1986. The Social Identity Theory of Intergroup Behavior. In: Psychology of Intergroup Relation, ed. S. Worchel and W. G. Austin, pp. 7–24. Chicago: Nelson Hall. [6]

Tatarko, A., and T. Jurcik. 2021. Migrant Integration Policies, Perceived Group Threat and Generalized Trust: A Case of European Countries. *J. Int. Migr. Integr.* **22**:705–727. [11]

Taylor, D. M., S. C. Wright, F. M. Moghaddam, and R. N. Lalonde. 1990. The Personal/Group Discrimination Discrepancy: Perceiving My Group, but Not Myself, to Be a Target for Discrimination. *Pers. Soc. Psychol. Bull.* **16**:254–262. [6]

Telles, E. E. 2014. Race in Another America: The Significance of Skin Color in Brazil. Princeton: Princeton Univ. Press. [10]

Teney, C., P. Devleeshouwer, and L. Hanquinet. 2013. Educational Aspirations among Ethnic Minority Youth in Brussels: Does the Perception of Ethnic Discrimination in the Labour Market Matter? A Mixed-Method Approach. *Ethnicities* **13**:584–606. [6]

Terriquez, V. 2015. Intersectional Mobilization, Social Movement Spillover, and Queer Youth Leadership in the Immigrant Rights Movement. *Soc. Prob.* **62**:343–362. [5]

Thoits, P. A. 2011. Resisting the Stigma of Mental Illness. *Soc. Psychol. Q.* **74**:6–28. [2]

———. 2016. "I'm Not Mentally Ill": Identity Deflection as a Form of Stigma Resistance. *J. Health Soc. Behav.* **57**:135–151. [2]

Thoits, P. A., and B. G. Link. 2016. Stigma Resistance and Well-Being among People in Treatment for Psychosis. *Soc. Mental Health* **6**:1–20. [2]

Tjaden, J. D. 2017. Migrant Background and Access to Vocational Education in Germany: Self-Selection, Discrimination, or Both? *Z. fur Soziol.* **46**:107–123. [6]

Tjaden, J. D., and C. Hunkler. 2017. The Optimism Trap: Migrants' Educational Choices in Stratified Education Systems. *Soc. Sci. Res.* **67**:213–228. [6]

Tolsma, J., M. Lubbers, and M. Gijsberts. 2012. Education and Cultural Integration among Ethnic Minorities and Natives in the Netherlands: A Test of the Integration Paradox. *J. Ethn. Migr. Stud.* **38**:793–813. [3, 11]

Toomey, R. B., A. J. Umaña-Taylor, D. R. Williams, et al. 2014. Impact of Arizona's SB 1070 Immigration Law on Utilization of Health Care and Public Assistance among Mexican-Origin Adolescent Mothers and Their Mother Figures. *Am. J. Public Health* **104**:S28–S34. [9]

Tough, H., J. Siegrist, and C. Fekete. 2017. Social Relationships, Mental Health and Wellbeing in Physical Disability: A Systematic Review. *BMC Public Health* **17**:414–414. [4]

Townsend, S. S., B. Major, C. E. Gangi, and W. Berry Mendes. 2011. From "in the Air" to "under the Skin": Cortisol Responses to Social Identity Threat. *Pers. Soc. Psychol. Bull.* **37**:151–164. [4]

Traunmüller, R., and M. Helbling. 2022. Backlash to Policy Decisions. How Citizens React to the Permission and Banning of Immigrants' Right to Demonstrate. *Political Sci. Res. Methods* **10**:279–297. [8]

Trawalter, S., J. A. Richeson, and J. N. Shelton. 2009. Predicting Behavior during Interracial Interactions: A Stress and Coping Approach. *Pers. Soc. Psychol. Rev.* **13**:243–268. [4]

Tropp, L. R., D. G. Okamoto, H. B. Marrow, and M. Jones-Correa. 2018. How Contact Experiences Shape Welcoming: Perspectives from U.S.-Born and Immigrant Groups. *Soc. Psychol. Q.* **81**:23–47. [11]

Tropp, L. R., F. White, C. L. Rucinski, and C. Tredoux. 2022. Intergroup Contact and Prejudice Reduction: Prospects and Challenges in Changing Youth Attitudes. *Rev. Gen. Psychol.* **26**:342–360. [10]

Tyler, I., and T. Slater. 2018. Rethinking the Sociology of Stigma. *Sociol. Rev.* **66**:721–743. [5]

Uhlhaas, P. J., and S. J. Wood, eds. 2019. Youth Mental Health: A Paradigm for Prevention and Early Intervention. Strüngmann Forum Reports, vol. 28. J. R. Lupp, series ed. Cambridge, MA: MIT Press. [Preface]

Urry, J. 2007. Mobilities. Cambridge: Polity Press. [2]

U.S. Citizenship and Immigration Services. 2022. Deferred Action for Childhood Arrivals. Federal Register 86, no. 185. A Proposed Rule by the Homeland Security Department. [5]

USGAO. 2004. Defense of Marriage Act: Update to Prior Report. GAO-04-353R Defense of Marriage Act. [8]

Valentín-Cortés, M., Q. Benavides, R. Bryce, et al. 2020. Application of the Minority Stress Theory: Understanding the Mental Health of Undocumented Latinx Immigrants. *Am. J. Commun. Psychol.* **66**:325–336. [5]

Valenzuela, A. 1999. Subtractive Schooling: US-Mexican Youth and the Politics of Caring, vol. 20. SUNY Series, the Social Context of Education. Albany: SUNY Press. [5]

van Doorn, M., P. Scheepers, and J. Dagevos. 2013. Explaining the Integration Paradox among Small Immigrant Groups in the Netherlands. *J. Int. Migr. Integr.* **14**:381–400. [3]

Van Klingeren, M., H. G. Boomgaarden, R. Vliegenthart, and C. H. De Vreese. 2015. Real World Is Not Enough: The Media as an Additional Source of Negative Attitudes toward Immigration, Comparing Denmark and the Netherlands. *Eur. Sociol. Rev.* **31**:268–283. [3, 10, 11]

van Maaren, F. M., and A. van de Rijt. 2020. No Integration Paradox among Adolescents. *J. Ethn. Migr. Stud.* **46**:1756–1772. [3]

Vaquera, E., H. Castañeda, and E. Aranda. 2021. Legal and Ethnoracial Consciousness: Perceptions of Immigrant Media Narratives among the Latino Undocumented 1.5 Generation. *Am. Behav. Sci.* **66**:1606–1626. [7]

Velásquez, P., and M. A. Eger. 2022. Does Higher Education Have Liberalizing or Inoculating Effects? A Panel Study of Anti-Immigrant Sentiment before, during, and after the European Migration Crisis. *Eur. Sociol. Rev.* **38**:605–628. [2, 3, 10]

Verkuyten, M. 2016. The Integration Paradox: Empiric Evidence from the Netherlands. *Am. Behav. Sci.* **60**:583–596. [3, 11]

Von Werthern, M., K. Robjant, Z. Chui, et al. 2018. The Impact of Immigration Detention on Mental Health: A Systematic Review. *BMC Psychiatry* **18**:382. [8]

Voss, K., and I. Bloemraad, eds. 2011. Rallying for Immigrant Rights: The Fight for Inclusion in 21st Century America. Oakland: Univ. of California Press. [10]

Voss, K., F. Silva, and I. Bloemraad. 2020. The Limits of Rights: Claims-Making on Behalf of Immigrants. *J. Ethn. Migr. Stud.* **46**:791–819. [10]

Votruba, N., J. Grant, and G. Thornicroft. 2020. The EVITA Framework for Evidence-Based Mental Health Policy Agenda Setting in Low- and Middle-Income Countries. *Health Policy Plan.* **35**:424–439. [8]

Voyer, A., and A. Lund. 2020. Importing American Racial Reasoning to Social Science Research in Sweden. *Sociologisk forskning* **57**:337–362. [8]

Wang, K., C. L. Burton, and J. E. Pachankis. 2018. Depression and Substance Use: Towards the Development of an Emotion Regulation Model of Stigma Coping. *Subst. Use Misuse* **53**:859–866. [4]

Wang, K., A. Silverman, J. D. Gwinn, and J. F. Dovidio. 2015. Independent or Ungrateful? Consequences of Confronting Patronizing Help for People with Disabilities. *Group Process. Intergroup Relat.* **18**:489–503. [4]

Wanjala, S. W., E. K. Too, S. Luchters, and A. Abubakar. 2021. Psychometric Properties of the Berger HIV Stigma Scale: A Systematic Review. *Int. J. Environ. Res. Public Health* **18**:13074. [2]

Waters, M. C. 1994. Ethnic and Racial Identities of Secondgeneration Black Immigrants in New York City. *Int. Migr. Rev.* **28**:795–820. [10]

Weiner, B. 1995. Judgments of Responsibility: A Foundation for a Theory of Social Conduct. New York: Guilford Press. [2]

Weiner, B., R. P. Perry, and J. Magnusson. 1988. An Attributional Analysis of Reactions to Stigmas. *J. Pers. Soc. Psychol.* **55**:738–748. [4]

Weise, D. R., T. Arciszewski, J. F. Verlhiac, T. Pyszczynski, and J. Greenberg. 2012. Terror Management and Attitudes toward Immigrants. *Eur. Psychol.* **17**:63–72. [4]

Weiß, R. H. 2006. Grundintelligenztest Skala 2 (CFT 20). . Göttingen: Hogrefe Verlag. [6]

Weißmann, M., J. Dollmann, and I. Kogan. 2023. Direct Links and Detours: Educational and School-to-Work Pathways of Majority and Ethnic Minority Youth in Germany. In: Migrant Youth at the Crossroads after Leaving School: Migrant Resilience, ed. E. Smyth and M. Darmody. London: Routledge, in press. [6]

Weldon, S. A. 2006. The Institutional Context of Tolerance for Ethnic Minorities: A Comparative, Multilevel Analysis of Western Europe. *Am. J. Pol. Sci.* **50**:331–349. [8]

Wenz, S. E. 2020. Discrimination in Education: Methodology, Theory, and Empirics of Teachers' Stereotypes, Prejudice, and Discriminatory Behavior. Gesis Scientific Series 26. Cologne: GESIS Leibniz Institute for the Social Sciences. [6]

Wicht, A. 2016. Occupational Aspirations and Ethnic School Segregation: Social Contagion Effects among Native German and Immigrant Youths. *J. Ethn. Migr. Stud.* **42**:1825–1845. [6]

Willen, S. S. 2007. Toward a Critical Phenomenology of "Illegality": State Power, Criminalization, and Abjectivity among Undocumented Migrant Workers in Tel Aviv, Israel. *Int. Migr.* **45**:8–38. [7]

Willen, S. S., N. Selim, E. Mendenhall, et al. 2021. Flourishing: Migration and Health in Social Context. *BMJ Glob. Health* **6**:1–6. [10]

Williams, D. R., and C. Collins. 2001. Racial Residential Segregation: A Fundamental Cause of Racial Disparities in Health. *Public Health Rep.* **116**:404–416. [4]

Williams, D. R., Y. Yu, J. S. Jackson, and N. B. Anderson. 1997. Racial Differences in Physical and Mental Health: Socio-Economic Status, Stress and Discrimination. *J. Health Psychol.* **2**:335–351. [2]

Williams, R. M. 1988. Racial Attitudes and Behaviors. In: Surveying Social Life: Papers in Honor of Hubert H. Hyman, ed. H. O'Gorman, pp. 331–352. Middletown, CT: Wesleyan Univ. Press. [2]

Wimmer, A., and T. Soehl. 2014. Blocked Acculturation: Cultural Heterodoxy among Europe's Immigrants. *Am. J. Sociol.* **120**:146–186. [11]

Wright, M. 2011. Policy Regimes and Normative Conceptions of Nationalism in Mass Public Opinion. *Comp. Polit. Stud.* **44**:598–624. [8]

Wright, M., and I. Bloemraad. 2012. Is There a Trade-Off between Multiculturalism and Socio-Political Integration? Policy Regimes and Immigrant Incorporation in Comparative Perspective. *Persp. Polit.* **10**:77–95. [11]

Wright, M., R. Johnston, J. Citrin, and S. Soroka. 2017. Multiculturalism and Muslim Accommodation: Policy and Predisposition across Three Political Contexts. *Comp. Polit. Stud.* **50**:102–132. [11]

Wu, C., Y. Qian, and R. Wilkes. 2021. Anti-Asian Discrimination and the Asian-White Mental Health Gap during COVID-19. *Ethn. Racial Stud.* **44**:819–835. [10]

Yang, L. H., F. Chen, K. J. Sia, et al. 2014. What Matters Most: A Cultural Mechanism Moderating Structural Vulnerability and Moral Experience of Mental Illness Stigma. *Soc. Sci. Med.* **103**:84–93. [1, 2, 5]

Yang, L. H., A. Kleinman, B. G. Link, et al. 2007. Culture and Stigma: Adding Moral Experience to Stigma Theory. *Soc. Sci. Med.* **64**:1524–1535. [1, 2, 5]

Yeoh, B. S. A., and K. D. Willis. 2005. "Singapore Unlimited"? Transnational Elites and Negotiations of Social Identity in the Regionalization Process. *Asian Pac. Migr. J.* **14**:71–95. [10]

Yoshino, K. 2006. Covering: The Hidden Assault on Our Civil Rights. New York: Random House. [2]

Young, M. E. D. T., G. Leon-Perez, C. R. Wells, and S. P. Wallace. 2019. Inclusive State Immigrant Policies and Health Insurance among Latino, Asian/Pacific Islander, Black, and White Noncitizens in the United States. *Ethn. Health* **24**:960–972. [8]

Zagarri, R. 2007. Revolutionary Backlash: Women and Politics in the Early American Republic. Philadelphia: Univ. of Pennsylvania Press. [8]

Zaslove, A. 2004. Closing the Door? The Ideology and Impact of Radical Right Populism on Immigration Policy in Austria and Italy. *J. Polit. Ideol.* **9**:99–118. [10]

Zhou, M. 1997. Segmented Assimilation: Issues, Controversies, and Recent Research on the New Second Generation. *Int. Migr. Rev.* **31**:825–858. [5]

Zhou, M.. 2004. Are Asian Americans Becoming "White"? *Contexts* **3**:29–37. [2]

Zhou, M., and X. Li. 2003. Ethnic Language Schools and the Development of Supplementary Education in the Immigrant Chinese Community in the United States. *New Dir. Youth Dev.* **100**:57–73. [5]

Ziller, C., and M. Helbling. 2019. Antidiscrimination Laws, Policy Knowledge, and Political Support. *Br. J. Polit. Sci.* **49**:1027–1044. [8]

Zinn, H. 1968. Disobedience and Democracy: Nine Fallacies on Law and Order. New York: Vintage. [4]

Zolberg, A. R. 2006. A Nation by Design: Immigration Policy in the Fashioning of America. Cambridge, MA: Harvard Univ. Press/Russell Sage Foundation. [11]

Subject Index

Strüngmann Forum Report Series*

Exploring and Exploiting Genetic Risk for Psychiatric Disorders
Edited by Joshua A. Gordon and Elisabeth Binder
DOI: https://doi.org/10.7551/mitpress/15380.001.0001
ISBN electronic: 9780262377423

Intrusive Thinking: From Molecules to Free Will
Edited by Peter W. Kalivas and Martin P. Paulus
ISBN: 9780262542371

Deliberate Ignorance: Choosing Not to Know
edited by Ralph Hertwig and Christoph Engel
ISBN 9780262045599

Youth Mental Health: A Paradigm for Prevention and Early Intervention
Edited by Peter J. Uhlhaas and Stephen J. Wood
ISBN: 9780262043977

The Neocortex
Edited by Wolf Singer, Terrence J. Sejnowski and Pasko Rakic
ISBN: 9780262043243

Interactive Task Learning: Humans, Robots, and Agents Acquiring New Tasks through Natural Interactions
Edited by Kevin A. Gluck and John E. Laird
ISBN: 9780262038829

Agrobiodiversity: Integrating Knowledge for a Sustainable Future
Edited by Karl S. Zimmerer and Stef de Haan
ISBN: 9780262038683

Rethinking Environmentalism: Linking Justice, Sustainability, and Diversity
Edited by Sharachchandra Lele, Eduardo S. Brondizio, John Byrne, Georgina M. Mace and Joan Martinez-Alier
ISBN: 9780262038966

Emergent Brain Dynamics: Prebirth to Adolescence
Edited by April A. Benasich and Urs Ribary
ISBN: 9780262038638

The Cultural Nature of Attachment: Contextualizing Relationships and Development
Edited by Heidi Keller and Kim A. Bard
ISBN (Hardcover): 9780262036900 ISBN (ebook): 9780262342865
Winner of the Ursula Gielen Global Psychology Book Award

Investors and Exploiters in Ecology and Economics: Principles and Applications
edited by Luc-Alain Giraldeau, Philipp Heeb and Michael Kosfeld
ISBN (Hardcover): 9780262036122 ISBN (eBook): 9780262339797

---

* Available at https://mitpress.mit.edu/books/series/strungmann-forum-reports

Computational Psychiatry: New Perspectives on Mental Illness
edited by A. David Redish and Joshua A. Gordon
ISBN: 9780262035422

Complexity and Evolution: Toward a New Synthesis for Economics
edited by David S. Wilson and Alan Kirman
ISBN: 9780262035385

The Pragmatic Turn: Toward Action-Oriented Views in Cognitive Science
edited by Andreas K. Engel, Karl J. Friston and Danica Kragic
ISBN: 9780262034326

Translational Neuroscience: Toward New Therapies
edited by Karoly Nikolich and Steven E. Hyman
ISBN: 9780262029865

Trace Metals and Infectious Diseases
edited by Jerome O. Nriagu and Eric P. Skaar
ISBN 9780262029193

Pathways to Peace: The Transformative Power of Children and Families
edited by James F. Leckman, Catherine Panter-Brick and Rima Salah,
ISBN 9780262027984

Rethinking Global Land Use in an Urban Era
edited by Karen C. Seto and Anette Reenberg
ISBN 9780262026901

Schizophrenia: Evolution and Synthesis
edited by Steven M. Silverstein, Bita Moghaddam and Til Wykes,
ISBN 9780262019620

Cultural Evolution: Society, Technology, Language, and Religion
edited by Peter J. Richerson and Morten H. Christiansen,
ISBN 9780262019750

Language, Music, and the Brain: A Mysterious Relationship
edited by Michael A. Arbib
ISBN 9780262019620

Evolution and the Mechanisms of Decision Making
edited by Peter Hammerstein and Jeffrey R. Stevens
ISBN 9780262018081

Cognitive Search: Evolution, Algorithms, and the Brain
edited by Peter M. Todd, Thomas T. Hills and Trevor W. Robbins,
ISBN 9780262018098

Animal Thinking: Contemporary Issues in Comparative Cognition
edited by Randolf Menzel and Julia Fischer
ISBN 9780262016636

Disease Eradication in the 21st Century: Implications for Global Health
edited by Stephen L. Cochi and Walter R. Dowdle
ISBN 9780262016735

Better Doctors, Better Patients, Better Decisions: Envisioning Health Care 2020
edited by Gerd Gigerenzer and J. A. Muir Gray
ISBN 9780262016032

Dynamic Coordination in the Brain: From Neurons to Mind
edited by Christoph von der Malsburg, William A. Phillips and Wolf Singer,
ISBN 9780262014717

Linkages of Sustainability
edited by Thomas E. Graedel and Ester van der Voet
ISBN 9780262013581

Biological Foundations and Origin of Syntax
edited by Derek Bickerton and Eörs Szathmáry
ISBN 9780262013567

Clouds in the Perturbed Climate System: Their Relationship to Energy Balance, Atmospheric Dynamics, and Precipitation
edited by Jost Heintzenberg and Robert J. Charlson
ISBN 9780262012874
Winner of the Atmospheric Science Librarians International Choice Award

Better Than Conscious? Decision Making, the Human Mind, and Implications For Institutions
edited by Christoph Engel and Wolf Singer
ISBN 978-0-262-19580-5